GERAR

CRUCIAL COMMUNICATION SKILLS

FOR EVERYDAY

5 BOOKS in 1

PUBLIC SPEAKING PRINCIPLES,
SIMPLE SMALL TALK,
ALPHA ASSERTIVENESS,
CONFLICT RESOLUTION TECHNIQUES
AND BOLD BODY LANGUAGE

FREE GIFT

This book includes a bonus booklet. Download may be for a limited time only. All information on how you can secure your gift right now can be found at the end of this book.

CONTENTS

PUBLIC SPEAKING

PRINCIPLES

The Success Guide for Beginners for Efficient Communication and Presentation Skills:

How to Rapidly Lose Fear and Excite Your Audience as a Confident Speaker, Without Anxiety

---

Gerard Shaw

Table of Contents

INTRODUCTION

No one is born a naturally gifted public speaker. I wish I could say that I was phenomenal the first time I spoke in front of an audience but that would be a lie. It took several failures for me to learn how to master public speaking. It's only now, after more than a decade of practicing and teaching public speaking, that I've come to have answers for those who want to take on their own career. Questions always range in topic but most of them have dealt with the fear that comes with public speaking. I began to realize that there are so many people starting out where I did, and so many of them want to learn how to overcome their fears before they step out onto the stage.

I want you to learn from what I've gone through before you begin your own journey. The concepts in this book are ones that I've applied to my own career, and they've allowed me, and those I've mentored, success in their own public speaking goals. I know there'll be a time when you run into the same moments I did in my early career and, where I failed miserably, I *know* you'll prosper.

In this book, I'll go over empowering solutions, along with detailed guidelines on how you can overcome your crippling fears. You'll gain the knowledge to help you develop and transform yourself into a confident and inspiring speaker. These are practical strategies for crafting winning speeches and being able to properly articulate your core message. I know these strategies will work for you because they've worked for me over my lengthy and, in the beginning, sometimes difficult, career.

You picked up this book, which means there's a fire inside you that's pushing you forward and wanting you to become the kind of presenter that leaves an audience in awe. Seeing that you have an interest in public speaking, there's a good chance that you're already engaged in giving speeches and presentations, maybe for professional, academic, civic, or social reasons. Whatever your reasons, I can only imagine the weight placed on you when you speak. Perhaps these engagements will lead to a new career path or a promotion; regardless of the reasons, it's clear that you want to enhance your skills.

When I was younger the thought of speaking in front of others made me cringe with fear. Having to stand in front of a class and introduce myself was enough to put me on edge. I had to forge a long and tedious path to become the successful public speaker I am now. I don't want you to have to tread that long, tedious path that I suffered through. Throughout this arduous journey, I've learned these concepts I'm about to share. It was only after my own success that I began offering my knowledge to clients. I've seen incredible changes in numerous public speakers. Once they adopted the techniques, strategies, and methods in this book, new speakers always returned with an overwhelming amount of appreciation for the confidence I helped them learn and the ways their public speaking career improved. Because of my coaching, I've seen people go from not even being able to step onto a stage, to wowing a crowd of hundreds while talking about what they love most; it didn't matter if the audience was at a university lecture, socially telling their own stories, or advocating changes that they felt needed to be made in the world.

You, too, can become a successful public speaker, overcome your fears, and forge your own path to success. The journey begins with knowledge:

- We will go over fear and the many ways it can cripple your ability to captivate an audience.
- You'll learn how to defeat your anxiety by using proven, science-backed techniques.
- You'll be given techniques on how to build a speech, find your message, and deliver it with confidence!

All the concepts in this book have come from years of experience in training world-class speakers, managing to perfect them over the years. You can now use them to build your own public speaking career. You'll be receiving all of this now!

Early experiences might mean there's a chance you may have even considered giving up public speaking. By choosing this book you've proven that giving up isn't the solution. You know enough time has been wasted giving into your negative feedback loops. Beginning now, you no longer need to give those loops the power they *don't* deserve. Once you start acting on this book's sure-fire strategies, you'll notice the changes in yourself right away! I have no doubt that you'll see just how your life can change now that you've taken the first step forward.

This book bundle comes with a FREE booklet on masterminding a winning routine to improve calmness and your level of confidence daily. Head to the bottom of this book bundle for instructions on how you can secure your copy today.

CHAPTER ONE

Modern Predators Can't Eat You

Let's face it - fear is essential for our biological self-preservation. Our ancestors needed fear to survive. It was a necessary sensation that played a huge part in our past; in fact, you and I probably wouldn't be here today had our ancestors fearlessly chosen to stand around and get eaten by saber-toothed tigers instead of running away. So, fear has a purpose and an important one at that! That being said - it doesn't have a place in our current society. The things we fear now just don't hold the same meaning as predatory felines did in the past. We live very comfortable lives and most of our present-day fears are mental phantoms we allow to threaten our present-day bliss.

Therefore, fear shouldn't determine our mindset, and we should endure anxious moments. We can't ignore fear, per se, just let it run its course. Among the many emotions we harbor, fear is the succubus - it invades our subconscious muttering to itself about the end of the world and stealing our confidence. It's paranoid and overpowers every other emotion while it's present. It constantly searches for danger even when we're no longer running away from predators or hunting with spears to avoid predatory hunger. Those types of adrenaline-pumping terrors stem from our ancestry - and that kind of fear is a dated emotion. Our subconscious has no clue that, most of the time, we're *not* in mortal danger, just giving a speech before strangers. This is why fear holds you back - it's always trying to get the upper hand. Fear stymies growth and, like a demon, it enjoys keeping you in a bubble of suspicion. Send fear to the back of your mind and let it come out when you need it - not when you're only feeling nervous about public speaking. Fear doesn't belong there. *You* belong here, standing next to your confidence and pride. So, leave fear behind the curtains muttering to itself about all the things that won't come to be.

The Psychology of Fear

Primitive, irrational fear comes from the beginning of evolution. But, now, look around you. Is anything chasing you? Let's face it - unless you're in the middle of a dangerous situation with this book on your tablet or in paper form, somehow being able to read - you understand that fear is antiquated emotion. There's no doubt that it keeps us alive and safe, but it's a hindrance to our everyday lives.

So, what is the *psychology* behind fear? Naturally, it's all in the mind, like a weed in a garden patch. Once planted in your thoughts, fear grows at the expense of your confidence. Real or psychological fear triggers a chemical reaction in every part of your body. Once your thoughts start to perceive a threat, your body goes into protective mode; that's when the physical reactions hit - sweating, shaking, and an increased heart rate. Everyone recognizes these warning signs and has felt it show up, and it expands. When anxiety hits, sometimes your stomach churns and an impending feeling of dread fills your whole body. Psychologists call this primal response the *flight or fight conflict;* in public speaking the emotion doesn't care if you have an audience to impress or an important message to communicate.

Trauma can leave marks on people's psychologies. These traumas can stem from early childhood experiences, but they can sometimes be from recent stage fright experiences that left an emotional imprint. Public speaking is a traumatic occasion for most people. Maybe you've had a bad situation in the past, where you misspoke the wrong word or fumbled on stage. Let me tell you this now: you're not alone. Many people have done those same things. Don't consider it as an emotional scar - consider it a stepping stone making up a learning curve. Keep in mind that there are more people out there who've made a mistake during a presentation than people who've given perfect presentations.

So, we've established that your fear takes place in memories, and if you let those overwhelm your current situation, you're going to run into the same issues repeatedly. It becomes a mental negative feedback loop, which rewires your brain to seek out familiar, and therefore comfortable, failure. Irrational fear will inhibit your way of living should you give into it too often.

I know firsthand what kind of toll bad memories can take on future endeavors. Once, when I was speaking in front of a group, I made a joke that didn't land well. When outlining my presentation, I remember being proud of myself for coming up with this witticism. I was in the middle of my presentation and, well, the joke came up right on cue. My audience was in a boardroom, and I had everyone's attention on me. I popped the joke, smiled, and waited for their response. In complete and utter silence. No one laughed. Not even a snicker. Now, silence can be a good thing in a presentation, but when humor fails, even veteran public speakers feel the tension.

So, what did I do? I could have beaten myself up over the failed presentation for weeks, if not months, and I wanted to. I still remember how it left me feeling like I was going to be sick right there at the head of that table. I stammered. My face turned red. I could feel my heart racing. Did that bad joke haunt me for a while? Yeah. I'd be lying if I said it didn't. But I didn't let it stop me.

It took some time before I could look at myself in the mirror and figure out why I was so upset with myself. It was then that I knew I had to accept the situation. It was hard to say to myself that I'd screwed up; however, admitting I had a humor skill problem was the first step for improvement. Later, I confronted what about this failure bothered me so much and why I was so nervous to give that presentation again, which I faced the following week. I started that presentation so proud of myself, but embarrassment and my reaction to the deadpanned crowd equaled a fright reaction. In reflection, I told myself that if I could have continued with my presentation as though nothing had happened, I wouldn't have felt so awful about it. *That* was my truth and *that* was at the heart of my fear. I was scared to have that reaction next week. I was embarrassed about how my hands shook and the fact that I'd sweat through my light blue shirt throughout the presentation. I had to get to the core of my fear to prepare for the end of the presentation. So, once I knew that fear is just fear and had no lasting consequences, I let go and decided to make some changes. I wore black at the next presentation and eliminated the joke. The next time I presented I stepped out in front of the crowd and had no issues. I found out that I had nothing to worry about and walked away feeling a sense of pride

That was me overcoming the situation by not giving in to my fear. Instead of giving in, I accepted it, figured out what it was, and made some necessary changes. Those feelings have come up again from time to time and those memories aren't gone, but I just don't give in to them. There are times you'll say things out of turn that causes *you* to sweat profusely. Just try not to pay that feeling of defeat too much mind. The people sitting there listening to your voice are genuinely interested in the information that you have to offer. They want you to succeed in filling their time meaningfully. Work with them, reject fear.

I know that this is a difficult subject for a lot of people. Emotional and physical insecurities manifest themselves in the same dry-mouthed, quivering knees responses. Know that you're not the only one feeling overwhelmed by public speaking can be reassuring. Confidence, like fear, is a complex emotion. When you understand that you choose how you react to fear, I know you'll learn how to look at the saber-toothed tiger in the eyes and refuse to let it dominate you. The first step is to acknowledge the tiger in the room.

Acknowledging and Accepting Fear

You now understand that fear of public speaking is psychological, and that you're not alone. So, let's get into how you can overcome it! Anyone can defeat their fear so long as they have the confidence to approach it and work on it. After all, people who fear public speaking often have psychologically negative feedback loops. In preparing to step in front of a crowd, the groundwork of overcoming fear starts with acceptance and acknowledgment, which are two practices that improve will improve your overall life satisfaction.

You'll need to be aware of your emotions at first, but deny them as a tool for self-improvement. Begin by keeping track of your emotions - maybe keep a journal for just a couple of days to find out how often emotions impact decision making. You'll have to be honest with yourself about how and what you feel as they show up. It has to become a habit, so you should practice emotional awareness throughout the day.

When it comes to fear, you'll need to remember to practice acceptance anytime that impending sense of doom sweeps over you. This is the opposite of ignoring it. For example, when you start to feel fear, allow it to happen, be aware of the sensations, objectively as possible watch how it unfolds at the moment, then conservatively consider your alternative responses after the fact. This latter part of the process will probably not happen during the event but is a positive personal feedback technique.

Avoiding negative emotions may seem like a survival strategy. There's nothing pleasant about feeling overwhelmed. We often just want the feeling to go away, and it's not the kind of thing you want sticking around, making you feel uncomfortable. And negative emotions - sadness, hopelessness, loneliness -- have stressed our bodies and reduce our otherwise positive energy. Unlike joy and public speaking successes, negative, fear-causing emotions tend to stick around longer, even though we want them to pass quickly.

So, what's the first response we naturally have? We ignore it. It's an instinctual response that, if we simply disregard its presence, it will go away on its own. Unfortunately, it never really does go away on its own. These emotions linger until there's nothing for our bodies to do other than expel them, usually inconveniently. For example, when you're sad and you push it aside day after day, there'll come a time when you just burst out in tears. This is because you avoid the emotions. They end up having an adverse effect on your body and then erupt so that you experience it at heightened levels after any given time. Suppression makes negative emotions worse. Think of your psychological body like a volcano - at some point, negative emotions are gonna blow! When you sense this starting to happen, I want you to do something unfathomable - *accept it*. Yes, you read that right. Bring it on, hold it close like a long-lost relative. Hug the feeling like a planned response and then let it go.

For those of you who might be in denial, you might ask, "Why *should* you accept it?"

It's been scientifically proven that emotional avoidance is chaotic to your physical and mental wellbeing. Avoiding a situation due to fear quickly becomes a trap because it's an easily accessible state of comfort that you grow accustomed to. When you ignore fear, you fake happiness by avoiding situations and people that trigger you. By avoiding the very things that brought you fear in the past. You'll soon find yourself staying in and staying away from moments that could turn out to be fulfilling. Such rationalized comfort is like the runner who turns to junk food after a stone bruise sets him down for a couple of days -- getting overweight is easier than standing up and risking an encounter with a stray rock. You'll become more fearful of the memory of the stone bruise than the actual pain and the junk food will seem more comfortable than you can bear to give up. All because you avoid your fear.

Then there's the old, awful friend that we've all dealt with at one point or another - anxiety. When you're avoiding your fears, there's a raw sense of anticipation that comes along with it. You start to dread having to deal with it. Anxiety breeds itself. In fact, no, anxiety feeds on itself. The best way to deal with fear is to accept it, including the physical and mental signs that accompany it. When fear gets magnified into a big, bad monster that you avoid, the chihuahua becomes harder to face. No one wants to experience monsters, but protect your ankles and there's no reason to let a tiny canine intimidate you. Move forward.

Facing Down Your Fear

You can't avoid fear. Accepting it and letting it go is the first step to wowing your audience. Once you've done that, there's only one thing to do next - face the fear and do it anyway. It's not a secret that public speaking can be daunting. In fact, surveys have shown that public speaking is ranked higher than death when it comes to our worst fears. Think about that. *Death.* The majority of people would rather die than speak in front of a crowd. This might come as a shock, or maybe you can relate to that feeling of dread. Regardless, if you've picked up this book, it means that you're ready to take it on full-force.

Here's the good news! Knowing your fear will actually calm your mind. Psychologists know that their phobic patients must face their fears to be cured. The same ideas help public speakers. Studies have proved that after you've faced a fear, you'll be overcome with an adrenaline-induced sense of well-being that sweeps throughout the body. Intense nervousness disappears, and, in the aftermath of euphoric success, you'll feel a sense of calm as cortisol hormone levels drop. This is why so many people take risks for a living - it's a natural high. When considering the risks of first responders or military professionals, public speaking seems pretty tame. But, since many people would rather risk death instead of speaking in public, you place yourself above fear and in hero status when you constantly put yourself in the way of your stage fright. You might be thinking, *why would I need to do that? I'm not a risk-taker. I don't live off adrenaline.* Well, science says you need to poke your fears until they no longer control you.

If you face your fears repeatedly, your mind will no longer see it as a threat.

Mentally beat up that bad boy stage fright over and over. *It will no longer be a threat.* The entire chemistry of your brain will change with this new acceptance and you'll no longer have the intense physical and emotional symptoms towards the thing you fear. I have no doubt that during this process you'll want to avoid the very thing you're terrified of but this is all about not giving in. Confront stage fright in little steps, indulge the shiver of your anxiety but feel it pass; you'll be able to train your body to feel anticipation for the rush of defeating your fear so it will no longer control you.

Most of Our Fears are Absurd

Sounds pretty rough, doesn't it? Well, it's not meant to make you think as though your fears aren't valid - that's not what I'm getting at. What this means is that your fears aren't based in reality. I would say the majority of them aren't. Falling from that building?

Yeah, that's definitely something to be afraid of. But standing in front of that crowd? Not so much.

What goes through your mind when you become fearful?

Worst-case scenarios! Now, these worst-case scenarios are just that - scenarios. They don't exist. They show up imagined and, like some kind of movie, show you all the worst things that could happen. It then gets replayed over and over again. The issue here? These moments that you're seeing are all created in your mind. There's a good chance that they will never come to fruition. If you continue believing that these scenarios are real then you're giving in to the feeling of dread that comes along with them.

This can also be considered as another form of avoidance. You're avoiding the thing that gives you anxiety and making it an even bigger problem - subconsciously it gives you excuses to not end up actually stepping up and facing it.

So, I want you to go over all your fears when it comes to public speaking. I want you to see them, accept them and acknowledge them, and then let them go. If you need to say it out loud, say it! But I want you to tell yourself, "These situations do not exist, and none of them will happen." If you can start to convince yourself using these sentences that you are safe, and that everything is made up in your mind, you're one step closer to overcoming your negative thought patterns. Your mind will then see these imagined scenes for what they are - your self-defeating imagination.

You'll start to feel good when you begin confronting your fears. There's a balance to build confidence by doing things you never thought possible - this is why some people live their lives as risk-takers. I want you to feel that pride that comes with being able to control how you react to your fears, and I know it's only a matter of time!

The NBA Star Turned Interview Comedian - Profile - Klay Thompson

If you're not an avid fan of the NBA, you may not know who Klay Thompson is. He's a five-time NBA All-Star and a three-time NBA champion. You'd think it would be easy for him to report on the sport he loves most, especially when discussing it in interviews. Unfortunately, Klay has had several instances of messing up while in front of the camera. These have made him a favorite among fans but, at the time, for all the wrong reasons.

One of the most notorious was when he gave a, now infamous, interview after a winning game. Not only did Klay get tongue-tied, but he barely made sense. It went viral over Twitter and had many people laughing - pretty much at his expense.

So, what did Klay do? He didn't stop! He kept giving interviews, no matter what the occasion. He even showed up on local news segments to hone his interviewing skills. As a competitor, he knew that he had to practice to get better. Want to know the best part? He started incorporating humor. He eventually became a sort of comedian and soon became the funny man of NBA interviews.

He never let that moment, or a few of the others where he'd been embarrassed, bring him down. He overcame the Internet and journalists alike. You can now find compilations of his interviews where he's unabashedly himself and doesn't care about what people have to say about him.

CHAPTER TWO

Your Audience Expects A Fearless Speaker

I want you to think of someone you recognize as a hero fearless. Who are they? Why do you consider them *fearless*? I want you to consider what about them persuades you to believe that they have no fear. When I think of fearless, I think of people who've made a difference - Gandhi, Malala Yousafzai, or Martin Luther King Jr. These are all household heroes who have not only spoken to sympathetic and adversarial crowds but advanced our society's moral consciousness. Did they speak fearlessly? Absolutely. Do I expect you, as an emerging public speaker, to start a revolution? Maybe. In a sense. I want you to revolutionize *your* life and give speeches and presentations about your passions. You and I want your voice to be heard because you have something to say. There's no doubt that whatever you're passionate about, there's an entire group of people who are passionate about the very same thing.

I know you'll be able to carry a room, while also becoming the best version of yourself. I want you to excel as I know you can - even in a stressful situation. You can forge your way ahead, becoming fearless despite the obstacles that you'll face along the way. This is all about building the confidence to be yourself and not look back on your fears. It's always easy to think of fear as though it's an emotion that's just *there*. It often sits in the background like a child, kicking its legs when it wants attention. It can feel impossible to eliminate and, in some ways, it is. However, fear is only as noticeable as you allow it to be. You can still feel the emotions, acknowledge, and accept them, as mentioned previously, but it no longer needs to control you.

It probably sounds ridiculous. Become fearless? Who am I to tell you that? Well, I used to get so nervous before stepping out in front of a crowd that I'd feel sick. It was like being filled with the opposite of butterflies - my stomach would churn and I'd become dizzy. These are just some of the symptoms I'd have to deal with once I was about to step out in front of a crowd. It was difficult to look anyone in the eyes because I was so used to looking down. When I used to pass people in hallways I'd be hunched over with my eyes to the floor. This was my natural state - and I had to change it the more I spoke about the things I was passionate about. I didn't realize at the time, but I was stuck in a constant state of fear. I'd always think of the ways people would judge me. I figured if I disappeared, they wouldn't have anything to judge. When I presented to an audience, though, I had no choice but to be noticed.

There was something I learned, though - after public speaking, I felt grateful for the fear I had before the event. There was always that sense of pride and relief that came afterward. It was bliss! But that bliss wouldn't have been possible if I didn't confront and overcome my anxiety and go forward with my passion. I want you to feel that too. Prepare to practice the steps in the next chapter by being able to recognize the effects fear has had on your day-to-day. By knowing the effects, you can then learn to tame your saber-toothed tiger and train it to roar on command.

The Effects of Fear

While we've all experienced the neurological impact of fear, recognizing the underlying issues causing fear can help us fight fear's symptoms. Even experienced public speakers dealing with situational issues from time to time. Understanding the way our mind and body respond to fear will explain those bouts where you've had no control over your body or your thoughts. You must first know your enemy to defeat it.

Fear Paralyzes Thought

As a child, did you ever feel as though you were being watched by some malevolent ghost so you ended up freezing in place? Or have you awakened from a nightmare paralyzed in bed? It was like all your limbs were stuck in the same position and running wasn't even an option. What you experienced is what it means when people say, *"paralyzed with fear."*

Let me tell you this - it's common. So common that most people the world over had it happen to them. It doesn't matter if you're scared of the dark or public speaking. This issue is one that has neurological origins from a *very* young age. Your ability to even hold memories in your mind wasn't developed yet. So, you ask, why haven't I outgrown this fear Well, it's a reflex. A naturally occurring reflex.

Fear Paralysis Reflex is a withdrawal reflex and it starts as early as the womb. Yes, you were a fetus when this first appeared in the instinctually primitive part of your developing brain. Symptoms of FPR include difficulty breathing, feelings of being overwhelmed, isolation, withdrawal from touch, and many others. In the womb, you'd end up reacting to stressful situations by withdrawing and freezing, a kind of teamwork response with your mother's body and both of you instinctively keeping you safe. The bad news? The learned responses to stress can stay on later in life, continuing the reflexive freezing even when no real threat exists.

Remember, public speaking is not a real threat. For you, the public speaker, the good news is that primitive functions can be trained like that wild predator in a cage. Your mind is the master of the beast.

Have you ever seen a movie where the lead character is about to go up on stage, finally makes it there and then stands in complete shock while looking at the audience? Well, that's based on real life. It's a representation of FPR. It happens just as it does in the movies - your body reacts with FPR and you end up losing your thoughts just as your body shuts down physically clenching uncontrollably. Now that you know about FPR, know that, like anything, it can be overcome.

Fear Stifles Expression

Open body language combats FPR. It's all about showing that you have confidence, especially if you're nervous. Nothing portrays confidence quite as well as a strong physical presence. Humans subconsciously take in other people's body language every day. Our ongoing habits of reading body language is why sometimes remote communications - as in writing or texting - can result in misunderstandings. It's all because there's no body language to add to the meanings of the words we read. In public speaking, most people can correctly interpret a smile or embracing hand gestures or stepping forward as symbols of confidence. However, when fear shows up, you'll lose the ability to control your body's message, which can be a detriment to you while you're in the middle of a public speaking engagement.

It can take a lot of effort to maintain eye contact when you're nervous. After all, when FPR adrenaline rushes through your body, all you want to do is run and hideaway. If you don't maintain eye contact it might look as though you're trying to avoid your audience. You should always remember that the audience invested their time and effort to gather to hear your message. If they feel you want to avoid them, instead of empathizing with your anxiety, they might see your message as not worth their attention, which is the opposite of what you want to portray.

Body language can be so meaningful and can encourage respect and engagement from your audience. So, be sure to encourage them with meaningful, spontaneous body movements and hand gestures, as these will direct everyone's eyes to where you want them to look, all while helping you express your presentation effectively. For example, persuasive speakers often build intensity with just a step back from the podium before fostering motivation by opening their arms wide.

This is more about your body language and what it displays to your audience. Giving in to your nervousness will only cause your body to naturally start to close in on itself, as though you're trying to hide in plain sight. It shows in your body language as dropped shoulders, a lowered head, and crossed arms - which shows to your audience you're uncomfortable. They'll subconsciously translate what they see into doubts about your message. Your expression, whether through body language or facial gesture, can be the difference between a bad or a good presentation or speech. You can't avoid emitting non-verbal cues, so if fear stifles your ability to express and makes your body naturally close off, a distracted audience may not hear the significant words you prepared for them.

Fear Disrupts Connection

You want to connect to your audience. Let me fix that last statement. You *need* to connect to your audience to have a successful speech or presentation. I'm sure you know that, and I'm sure that you're looking for that fire that will help you light the audience aflame - all while using only your words. This is the connection that can only be made when you're feeling confident and present. The issue here is that fear will impact your ability to do this.

Not only is fear breaking down your entire body with the physical sensations, but your mind gets set to mute. This is why you might forget your words or lose your train of thought when you're nervous. Nothing really connects when fear takes the wheel. FPR is a factor but so are the neurological sensors in your mind. When fear takes over, it becomes difficult for us to read cues, both verbal and non-verbal. You'll have a harder time reading your audience.

It doesn't matter if you're just talking to a small boardroom of co-workers or doing a TED talk, I'm sure that connecting with your audience is of the utmost importance. Allowing fear to take the wheel when you're trying to navigate is asking for trouble.

Fear Affects Your Mental Health

Your mental health is incredibly important when it comes to public speaking. After all, you want to be in the best state to present. Being on high alert consistently will impact your health in negative ways and, in turn, disrupt your presentations. You can't expect to motivate a crowd if you're suffering from fear and anxiety just from being around them. It's not easy to dig yourself out of a mental health issue but you should seek ways to better it.

Beyond just the visual aspect of what fear does to your body language, it can affect your presentation further than what meets the eye. When you're practicing for your speech, you often go over certain sentences and information repeatedly.

Fear interrupts your memory by debilitating the ability to form long-term memories. This is one of the reasons why you have difficulty remembering certain words, phrases, facts, or punchlines. Studies found that anxiety impairs memories, thereby affecting work and personal relationships - not inhibiting the power of public speaking.

To Fully Express Yourself, Be Fearless

Expressiveness isn't just about emphasizing words, statements, or punchlines, or behaving over the top. You've met expressive individuals; you know how they affect people – everyone in the room pays attention. They have something about them that brings people in because there's always something to respond to. Typically, they generate different vocal tones, increase pauses, and mesmerize with a multitude of gestures and facial expressions. Being expressive isn't just about divulging all your life stories to your audience, or how naturally engaging the topic might be. It's about the way you present yourself. I understand that there's a fear that you might come off as too emotional or unprofessional, but that's not always the case - especially if you're expressive in the right ways.

Expression, in the way I describe it here, is more about being articulate, that what you're saying is tied to your own emotions. People interpret this kind of sincerity as authentic; we get into authenticity in a later chapter. When you're expressive, your voice conveys meaning regarding your subject. You will always appear as more charismatic and passionate because your voice and body support your words.

There's no denying it - being expressive is one of the best ways to captivate your audience. By using fluid motions, mixed with the meaningful gestures and the inviting way you use your voice, you can engage an audience's attention throughout. Turning loose your fear lets you exude fearlessness, allows you to overcome stiffness, removes barriers between you and your audience, lets you connect. When you're being yourself, you'll find that you feel a natural state on stage.

Of course, you already know that being yourself isn't always simple. One great way of sharing yourself can be to put yourself into the presentation - literally! Feel free to share stories from your own life, or tell everyone how you feel about the product or the situation at hand. You'll notice once you start doing this, it can become a more relaxing process because it's like you're sharing with friends. Remember the audience wants you to fill their time with meaning; getting to know you may be the important connection they seek before they accept your message.

From Fired to Hired - Profile - Oprah Winfrey

Now I know what you must be thinking: *how could Oprah Winfrey fail?* Her name is world-renowned and she's considered a one-woman success story. She owns an empire completely built on her name. Oprah Winfrey is the incredible talk show host who became an author, an Oscar-nominated actress, and a TV mogul who owns her own channel and produces TV shows seen all around the world. She is known for her incredible voice and being able to interview even the most difficult of people. So, how is it that this amazing woman ever failed?

Well, Oprah was young once and, before she was the woman she is now, she was fired from her job as a news reporter WJZ-TV in Baltimore. Yes, that's right. *Oprah Winfrey* was fired. It was a difficult time for the talk show host, who had only just started her career.

"It shook me to my very core," she reminisced years later.

Oprah was told she was "unfit for TV." If she'd listened to her previous boss, she would never have had the life she has built for herself. She overcame her fear and went back on television anyway. She relocated and became the voice for a failing talk show called *People Are Talking*. Oprah would go on to become the ambitious, successful woman we all know her as today.

CHAPTER THREE

Bravery in Modern Jungles

Now that you have an idea of what fear can do to you, let's get into how to gain confidence while public speaking! These are the core concepts that will help you build yourself up so that no amount of fear will take you down. I've seen clients implement these over the years and see success in all their speaking engagements. It takes a lot of practice and control, but there's no doubt in my mind that you can achieve those same results! You *can* overcome your stage fright and learn how to take control when you step onto that stage. It all starts with building yourself up first.

Practical Steps to Get Rid of Fear and Stage Fright

Fear and stage fright go hand in hand, as one can't exist without the other. Stage fright is defined as *nervousness before or during an appearance before an audience*. It's a debilitating feeling that happens not only in your mind but in your body. It appears and causes you to lose faith and confidence in yourself faster than any other emotion

Stage fright can be frustrating to have to deal with day after day. Especially if you want to succeed in certain areas. After all, stage fright can cause you to fail an assignment or lose out on a promotion. It's like its number one priority is to hold you back! You should never feel embarrassed if you suffer from it. As I mentioned previously, surveys have proved that most people suffer from it. Everyone experiences fear in one form or another – this just happens to be one of yours.

There's more to it than that, though. First, we must start with fear, as it tends to be the number one enemy to those having to face an audience. You need to begin by understanding where your fear stems from so that you don't experience stage fright again. Once you find the deterrent that speaks most to you, you can then begin working on how to ease it.

I want you to be able to implement these steps into your own life, as they'll set you up for success while trying to conquer your stage fright and anxiety. If you complete all these exercises, I know that you'll feel intrinsically better. You owe it to yourself to try them and find which ones work best for you.

Each of these will no doubt take some work. You'll have to practice them constantly for them to make a long-term impact. You'll need to remind yourself when you're speaking in public, when you're at work, or even when you're out with friends. You'll also need to make time for yourself as you practice each of these steps so that you can start to hone in on them.

Silence Your Inner Critic

When we hear a voice in the back of our mind, it's not always an intuitive voice pushing you forward. This, unfortunately, is the voice you hear when you've made a mistake, or feel as though you're about to embarrass yourself. Your inner critic often appears out of nowhere, even when you're just minding your own business. It keeps you up while you lie awake in bed trying to sleep. Your inner critic stops you from achieving your potential and it keeps you in your comfort zone.

There's no doubt that there are times when we need to listen, like before cheating on that test or yelling at the person we love. These are instances where we need to take a moment to hear where we've lost ourselves. However, these situations are far and few between - your inner critic does more damage in your everyday life than it does good.

Throughout our lives, it becomes second nature to fight ourselves over our shortcomings. Even if there are no external critics, your inner child hears, "*You're not good enough*, *no one likes you* or *you're wasting your time.*" Sabotaging thoughts like these do not reflect your true reality! We created these deceptions about ourselves, and they nag until we come to believe them like excuses for doing nothing to improve ourselves.

I'm here to tell you to silence that voice. That voice emerging from your apprehension closet is not you. Your inner critic is doing you no good by traipsing around in your mind telling you terrible lies about yourself. That cranky critic only hinders you from growing. If you examine it, you'll remember that such negativism is often born of difficult childhood memories or unhappy encounters with negative people. Letting that negative vocal loop play will sabotage not only the moments before an important event but your future happiness because failure will get to be a habit.

One way you can silence your inner critic is by daily practicing self-affirmations. Instead of hitting auto replay on the negative loops in your past, record new scripts beginning with *I'm getting better at this every day*. By changing the monologue, you strangle negativity. Watch for the pity voice when it appears and alter it into a powerful voice that better suits your needs.

As mentioned previously, like fear, your inner critic must be acknowledged. Hear what it has to say and then make a conscious effort to let it go. If you relinquish emotions attached to that voice, you'll soon forget that it exists at all. Your inner critic will come up again, but when it does, you won't worry about it - strictly because it's not necessary anymore. You'll hear it and then release it without feeling a thing.

If you find that your inner voice is overwhelming, you can always write down what it says. Some people keep journals or use the notes app on their phones - you can decide what works for you. Write down what it says, even though it might be painful. Looking at your doubts written down, you might even believe them. Don't give in, though. Once you see those words written out, it'll expose their irrationality. Respond by writing next to it the truth. For example, if you write, "No one wants to hear me," you can then edit that script with, "I have something important to say and people enjoy listening to me."

Overcome negativity. Practice positivity. Reading positive affirmations, you write down will start to form until you begin believing them. Let those optimistic words become the new voice in your head. Repeat them to yourself until they become law. This is one instance where some old adages - like *fake it till you make it* and *practice makes perfect* - really hold true.

Visualization

You may have never heard of visualization, but I'm sure you've practiced it before without even knowing. If you've ever imagined yourself walking onto a stage and accepting an award, or dreaming about driving a specific car, then you've implemented visualization into your own life. This is a core concept that you can use to ease your anxiety before a big speech or presentation. Not only will it help you face obstacles, but it will help you imagine how to proceed with nerve-wracking situations because it'll feel like you've already accomplished them.

Why would you use visualization? Well, the science backs it up! Studies have proven that when you're visualizing, the brain can't tell if what you're experiencing is real or not. Whenever you imagine a situation vividly, the chemistry in your brain will change to compliment what you're seeing. For example - if you're imagining winning a trophy, the muscles in your arms will start to fire as you imagine yourself raising the trophy because your mind thinks it's really happening.

As you now know, fear can often stem from the anxiety of imagining something bad will happen before the situation becomes reality. Instead of allowing that situation, such as a toast or a presentation, remain unknown, visualize yourself doing it. Your visualization will have you feeling as though you've already succeeded - all because, technically, you have!

Let's get into how you can practice visualizing right away. First off, best-used visualization happens when you're alone in a space where you know you'll be relaxed. Choose an area of your house where silence is your only audience. For truly relaxed approach to visualization, lie down in bed or sit in a comfortable chair. Breathe deeply three times and close your eyes. See your speaking venue. Imagine the friendly faces you find in the audience and imagine your wealth of knowledge you prepared for this occasion.

Now, when you start imagining how you want the situation to go, focus on the small things so that the scene becomes more vivid. Imagine how warm the room is, what your hands are doing, how loud your voice is. It's these small details that will make it more realistic for you. Think warm, happy thoughts about your opportunity here. This is your performance. Really *feel* the emotions you know you'll have after giving an outstanding presentation. You can also give in and *feel* the excitement of capturing the audience with your speech. You know your message is worthwhile; now imagine other people agreeing.

Once you've finished your visualization, allow yourself to breathe slowly and come back to the room. Relax and feel those positive emotions flowing through you. That sensation inside your chest is confident pride. This is a good thing! Keep that feeling and bring it with you to your public speaking engagement.

As a novice speaker, practice visualization at least three times a week, if not more. Rehearsal is always a confidence booster. Practicing positive anticipation will also keep away those negative moments that we tend to picture if we haven't retrained our emotions to be strongly supportive. You'll be thinking of how amazing they'll be.

Be in the Moment

Being mindful is not mystical. I'm definitely not going to tell you to stand up on stage and chant in front of the audience in a lotus pose. This is about being in the moment and feeling as though you're in the right place, with the right people, your audience. Being in the moment is key to giving a great presentation.

Until you practice and master the technique, there's no doubt that, even if you've heard the phrase, you may find it hard to describe what *being in the moment* entails and why it's so important. It's something so many people talk about but we all struggle with staying in that moment. So, I can already hear you asking me, "What do you mean in the moment? I'm in the moment right now, idiot." Yeah, no. You might think you're in the moment, but that's just it – you're thinking. If you focus so much on the little details, you miss the big picture. Being in the moment is more about seeing everything but filtering out any distractions interfering with your message.

I will describe it this way – have you ever been in a flow? I'm not talking about a river where you're bobbing up and down. Flow is when you enjoy doing something so much that you lose yourself in the process and time flies by. When you're in flow, you're in the moment, as well. There's usually a sense of calm involved. It's all about taking a moment to relax your thoughts!

What's one of the first things that you wanted the presentation to be before you've even started? Over with. Yeah, that's probably not the first thing that came to your mind, but I know it shows up right before the presentation starts and your heart jumps off the starting blocks ahead of your words. I can remember back to when I was younger and in school. There was always that dread when I knew it would be my turn to present in front of the class. My hands shook. My backbone turned to jelly. I watched the last presenter wrap up and dreaded standing up to walk forward. I wanted my speech finished, over and done within moments if not sooner. Then, my moment passed because I was never really there; I was too busy trying to skip to the finish anxiously to the end of the presentation.

You may have found yourself in a similar situation. Your dread denied you the pleasure of your preparation. Speakers just going through the presentation motions suck the life from the opportunity and what the audience sees and hears quickly becomes dull. If we're so anxious to be quick on our speech, the audience knows and they want it over with too. So, the best way to keep yourself in the moment is to take a step back and assess what it is you're saying. You may be stuck with a speech topic you're not too excited about, but there must be something dynamic you can do with the message to make it come alive. Once you start making it interesting for yourself, you'll find that others want to listen even more.

Great speakers often pause before they launch their message. They are finding the moment by taking a few deep breaths while the audience adjusts to the change in personnel. Inside themselves, those great speakers find a quiet mental space. Scanning the audience for benevolent listeners, they breathe in through the mouth and exhale past the nostrils, relax their shoulders and then calmly take charge of their opportunity. Practice this as many times as you need until you feel your heartbeat easing.

Fake It 'Till You Make It

Fake it till you make it. It's a sentence I'm sure you've heard before, but it can have a lasting impact on your confidence. Just like editing a written speech shapes the message into a tighter, more meaningful format, most often making your body act confident ensures that you're in a powerful position that can affect the outcome of your presentation.

Any superhero has a pose so perfect it becomes an icon in people's minds. Hours of mirror experiments must be part of that pose phenomenon, right? Consider this: in her now-famous TED talk, Amy Cuddy, a Harvard Business social psychologist, shared the effects of how powerful poses can change body chemistry. She developed a study where her subjects did various stances. In one, subjects struck power stances where they placed their hands on their hips and raised their heads high. In the adverse experiment, subjects practiced lowering their heads and allowing their shoulders to slump. Her study discovered that physiologically those who practiced power poses experienced heightened testosterone and lower cortisol, a hormone present during intrusive stress. Cuddy's experiments proved that positive behaviors created chemically enhanced confidence in her subjects. Confidence allowed her subjects to demonstrate dominance that leads to more confidence. All this confidence just from striking a superhero pose.

Based on Cuddy's proof, when you feel nervous before stepping out into that boardroom or onto that stage, practice a powerful pose. Stand tall with your head held high, place your hands on your hips, and open up your chest. You can also choose to lift your hands high as though you've just won a race. These are poses that cause the testosterone in the body to rise, which sends a signal to your brain that you're feeling confident. It's a naturally occurring phenomenon that happens with the body and will help you ease some of the interfering natural tension.

As long as you're faking power, allow yourself to feel as though you've already become a successful public speaker. Tell yourself a manta day after day that helps you feel this way. For example, say sincerely, "Everyone applauds me when I walk onstage." It's a simple visualization, but it's just one way to feel as though you've already made your mark in the public speaking world. After a time, you'll gain the confidence to stand out there and feel as though you do have something important to say to the audience, and you won't fear their gazes. Become that person even if you don't feel like it. In just a few moments you'll find that your body aligns with that stance and you'll unconsciously become the very person you're pretending to be. With practice, you can be that person, and it's only a matter of moments until you are.

Don't be Afraid to Learn

We already know that you're not born a master at public speaking. Sure, you might have been outgoing as a child - this doesn't mean you were meant to move crowds. It typically means you were cute and liked to bust a move at weddings. No one wakes up at the age of three and decides to be a master public speaker. A veterinarian, sure. A firefighter? Yeah, that sounds about right. The kind of person that can stand in front of a crowd and wow them with voice, intellect, and a powerful vocabulary? Not really. This is the beautiful thing about public speaking, though - you can learn as you go. It's meant to be a learned skill that evolves upward the more you practice.

Public speaking is an ancient art, but learning to be effective now involves learning new, rapidly changing strategies. No matter the circumstance, you should always be learning. With society changing and adapting, be certain you are meeting the world on its terms. Even when you think that you're done learning a new skill, there's always something new that comes around. When it comes to public speaking, there's a huge amount of diversity with the technology involved with presentations. To continue honing your skills allows you to have success in your future endeavors. You should always learn new advantages – that's the only way to become a professional.

Professionals adapt and never let fear step in. Often, when we're faced with something new and challenging, it's easy to procrastinate. It's hard to stand up, raise your hand and say, "Yeah. I want to make mistakes!" The issue, too, is that you will make mistakes, exposing your imperfections but making you try harder. If you're already trying as hard as you can, adaptations can certainly push you to the brink of your comfort zone, and that's why fear can reappear – the FRP monster knows that you're nervous. You must push past it and evolve your skills anyway.

Practice public speaking more so the better you'll become. Remember, there's no real threat to getting nervous. There are no real tigers. Give yourself some space to feel those nerves, and accept them, tame them. You will learn to master public speaking and that's all part of the fun! Learning new skills fortifies our mental health and sense of well-being. So have fun with it. Practice until your voice hurts. Do those powerful poses. Envision yourself speaking to hundreds of people and inspiring a crowd. If you do all these things, you'll discover that you were already that person that you were looking to become - you just need to hone those skills. It's as Bruce Lee once said, "Knowing is not enough. We must apply. Willing is not enough. We must do."

Believe in Yourself

It's a phrase we've all heard - *believe in yourself*. Ever since you were little, people have said it. It's on posters, in movies, and books. It's an overused phrase that, at this point, doesn't seem to hold much meaning anymore except to those people, professionals, who practice the exercise. Unlike the athlete whose body parts can wear out, the constant practice of self-belief only gets stronger. Find a believer at peace with who he or she is and watch the audience respond to that confidence. You can be the same kind of dynamic speaker.

Comparison Depletes Confidence

Let's say, hypothetically, you have a speaking engagement at a convention. At risk is that you, with your message and a particular set of speaking skills, may have to follow a dynamic public speaking superhero. If the crowd responses told you they loved the last guy, you may start to beat yourself up before you get to the podium, fearing you won't be as good. Remember, it's too late to compare your notes and your visual aids to his, and so what if his punchlines always got laughs? Self-doubt is what happens when we compare ourselves to others. Never trick yourself into believing that someone is better than you because *you* think they are. They might be just a little more skilled, and you use that; You're unique, and your presentation is deserving of being heard. Your voice matters. No one can take that away from you, except you. Set aside comparing yourself, focus on your own work, and stand up there knowing that you have something new to say.

Attitude of Gratitude

When you begin to practice gratitude in your life, you'll begin to notice subtle changes in your day-to-day attitude. It starts small, but gradually grows the more you practice. You're probably wondering what being grateful has to do with your ability to believe in yourself. I know that they seem like separate subjects, but they're really not. Being able to show gratitude for the small things in your life will begin to lift you from a place of self-pity. Not only will it help you develop a positive attitude, but you'll discover that there's more to you than just the negative aspects. This is crucial to building joy in your life.

You can choose to write down several various things you're grateful for in the morning and get started with your day. You can also choose to do it right before your next public speaking engagement. If you feel your nerves getting the best of you, you can always choose to start a mental list of things you're grateful for. These can range from the venue that you've booked, your job, or even the outfit you're wearing. You'll find that not only will it help you relax, but you'll go into it believing that you deserve to be there – all because you were grateful.

The Celebrity Who Fumbled, Only to Rise Again - Profile - Steve Harvey

He's charming, funny, and the host of his TV talk show. He's a household name who has authored books and spoken to crowds for most of his career. However, there was one mistake made one evening that was heard all around the world. When Steve Harvey took on the role to host Miss Universe in 2015, he wasn't expecting to make a catastrophic mistake. When announcing the Miss Universe winner, he accidentally announced the wrong contestant's name. Impromptu and on live television, Harvey owned up to his mistake, apologized and announced the corrected winner's name, recanting the previous 15 seconds of mistake before an international audience.

The next few weeks would be the hardest of Steve Harvey's career. Tabloids the world over screamed Harvey's mistake in large black letters. In the weeks following, Harvey found himself the laughing stock of news channels and comedians, his gaff resurrected repeatedly on the cover of magazines for the whole world to see. Even his innocent family wasn't spared, receiving death threats because of Harvey's unintentional mistake on stage. Of course, that put Harvey in a position he'd never felt before.

Owning up to his part in the mistaken announcement, Harvey took steps the very year to capitalize on his mistake and thereby caused another uproar. Instead of fading away into humiliation, Harvey hosted the Miss Universe pageant the very next year and made jokes about his difficult situation. He took all of his fear, bottled it, set it aside 12 months, and stepped back out onto the stage. Courageously Harvey told jokes on himself throughout a flawless pageant. One of the jokes was a skit with the former Miss Universe delivering a pair of reading glasses to the stage before his big announcement. Good humor, grade under fire, and professional strength let Harvey manage to put the whole spectacle behind him, and all because he stepped back out onto that very stage that he'd first made his big, nearly career sinking mistake.

CHAPTER FOUR

Building Communication Skills

You can't become a renowned public speaker without being able to communicate with your audience. Knowing how to adapt, connect and thrill your audience will lead you to be the best presenter you can be.

Communication is About Connection

I want you to think of a close friend of yours. What is it that makes you friends? Is it the things you do together? Maybe you both may like the same bands? Let me answer this for you, as I'm sure you're already thinking the same thing - heck, no! What makes us care about people, things, and situations is *not* the thing itself, but often the connection we have to it. Yes, you might hear a certain song and enjoy it. Often, though, it's about feeling connected to that song at the moment. Something about that song moves you. That's what makes a great public speaker. If you can connect to your audience and I mean, really *connect* with them, then you're looking at presenting successfully.

But how can you connect to complete strangers? It's not like you're going to go out for a drink with them after your meeting and talk about that TV show that you both happen to watch. No, that would be a definite connection but it wouldn't be because of your presentation. You want to be able to connect with them from the stage - which is even harder to do.

How to Adapt to an Audience

Okay. You've had those days where you want to crawl into a hole because of something you said or did. This could be saying a bad joke in front of a group of friends or giving a customer the wrong amount of change. Regardless, guess what? We've all been there! Especially with bad presentations. Whether it was in your childhood, or even now, it's likely you've been forced to sit through a presentation that makes you want to fall asleep or jump out of your seat and run for the door from boredom. There are a few reasons why those other presentations were so bad. They could have been too over-the-top on trying to sell you something; maybe the person giving the presentation had no charisma, or maybe the presentation was half an hour longer than it should be. It doesn't really matter. You sat there wishing you had your time back.

As public speakers, we certainly want to avoid punishing our audience as we were once punished. Fortunately, those punishing presentations are rare; most often, when they happen, the real cause is because the speaker failed to adapt the presentation to the audience. Speaking skills can be a real reason for memorable bad jobs. For instance, when you were younger maybe one of your classmates mumbled every other word, talking way longer than they needed, or didn't make the topic interesting by throwing in some passion and knowledge. What's the defining feature here? Well, it's the lack of entertainment for a younger crowd. A group of young students won't want to sit still for that long listening to someone without a proper voice! Of course, it was awful.

But, you, the seeker of oratorical skills, aren't that mumbling, bumbling, scared presenter. Still, keep this in mind: *Public speaking isn't about you. It's about the audience.* Now, repeat that rule a few times until it sticks - because it's vital to a great speech or presentation.

Meet Them Before

For the sake of the audience, and the eventual respect they give your message, do these adaptations; by the way, these professional connection skills work in everyday life and relationships as well. First, know who your audience is. No matter what type of public speaking you're doing, you need to know as much as you can about your demographic. This means you want to know them. This is the only way your speech or presentation will meet their needs and keep them captivated. No one expects you to stalk social media profiles, just be a student of people When possible, background research the group you're presenting to; find out why they associate with each other. If circumstances are more intimate and the opportunity exists, introduce yourself at the door. This way, if you're unsure of what kind of audience you have, eye contact and a few words of greeting can help gauge the audience's general backgrounds and ages as they step inside.

Speak Their Language

The way you speak should be guided by whom you're speaking to. For instance, the way you speak to your boss will be very different from the way you speak to friends at the pub. In public speaking, the background of the audience can dictate the language, tone, and word choices. Retired professors will need to hear you be different from the way you'd speak to a group of high school construction trades students. If you can figure out your demographics, you'll find your voice while speaking to them. You can then manage your tone, what you say, and how you say it. This way you can fine-tune your presentation to perfection. It helps you define what kind of words you're going to use. If you're not sure about your demographic before you go into your presentation, make broad statements but set up a few key points to adapt. Part of this can be done using an audience engagement survey. Get the audience participating in your presentation by asking non-threatening rhetorical questions they can raise a hand toward indicating their preferences of answers. Asking audiences to participate in paper surveys after the show can collect data you can use to adapt to future presentations. The big idea is to get audience connections without being intrusive. The side benefit is that collecting information gets the audience thinking about what you're presenting.

Find Out More

Usually, you're scheduled to speak at a specific venue. If you're unsure about the area and the typical demographic, you can always ask the organizer about audiences that show up. You can find out what they typically respond to, and get to know the type of people that frequent the venue. If it's a professional meeting with another agency or a client, you can always ask the manager what you can expect. You can always familiarize yourself with them beforehand so that you're better prepared. The point is – never be afraid to ask. This can only help you in the long run.

Get to Know Them

You can't make a connection with some people without formally knowing them first. There are a multitude of ways that you can go about this. You can just get to know them after and during the presentation so that you can know what kind of demographic is interested in your topic. Feel free to ask questions to the audience, create a survey, or introduce yourself if some people are waiting for you afterward. It makes all the difference, and it helps you acclimate in front of them better. You can also choose an option that works best with your presentation and whichever one you feel more comfortable with. It also makes the presentation feel more personal for them because they now have a personal stake in your subject so they'll be more receptive while you're speaking.

They Want You to Succeed

The crowd may be seen as the enemy when it comes to public speaking, and it can feel overwhelming when stepping out onto the stage. I'm sure you remember the stereotypical advice that comes with the crowd – imagine them naked. Well, let's *not* actually do that. Yes, public speaking can be terrifying. It's like walking up to a guillotine. There's always the assumption that we're going to be judged the minute that we walk out with all those eyes on us. Any mistakes will be remembered forever. Fortunately, that's not always the case.

You'd be surprised to know that your audience isn't always against you. Some want to be entertained, while others are there to learn. They don't want you to mess up in front of them – it's the opposite. They want to see you succeed. This is the opposite of what we normally learn from movies and books. Usually, the main character is belittled in front of a crowd a la Stephen King's Carrie. Real-life doesn't happen that way, though.

I want you to think about when you were a part of that audience. When you see the speaker mess up, you don't automatically jeer them. This isn't stand-up comedy where you can heckle the comedian to make them notice you. No, this is on a completely different level. The typical reaction to someone losing their train of thought in front of a crowd doesn't want to berate them. It's the opposite – you feel bad for them. You want them to just stumble through and continue from where they left off. There's a feeling that washes over the whole crowd when this happens.

So, to adapt to your audience, you always need to remember that they want to see you win. They're there to be entertained. They're not thinking of how you're going to fail in front of them and how great that will be. I'd go as far as to say they're supporting you. Don't go in assuming you're heading to a death sentence. It's anything but that. You're going out there to win.

Verbal Communication

What involves verbal communication? Well, it's essentially comprised of your words and voice. When using both with fluidity, you'll find that you're like a conductor orchestrating a symphony, and word choices and voice tone make up half the battle when winning over your audience. Physically if your voice takes up fifty percent of your communication, that could very well be enough to hook listeners, even if your other fifty percent (body language) isn't up to par.

When I mention voice and words, I'm not talking about the gist of your presentation or speech. That is a completely different topic. When I cover the physical half of verbal communication, I'm talking about your tone, the speed of your words and the loudness of your voice. Each of these is crucial to public speaking whether a microphone is available or not. For example, if your voice is too low and doesn't project well enough, there's a good chance that some people may not hear you. Also, poor articulation, pronunciation clarity, can leave audiences confused and wondering why they bothered trying to listen at all. Therefore, actual verbal skills matter - not only will these skills be inclusive of everyone, but a distinctive speaking voice can also keep everyone's attention.

Pausing

Pause. And go. Pause. And go. Just by reading those words, your mind automatically pauses and hangs on. When you're speaking to an audience, the same thing happens. You can pause for effect when you're speaking to keep your audience on the edge of their seats. There are a few different pauses you can use to get the best results. Most of these pauses can be used in anything - a presentation, a speech, or even just while in a meeting. However, be sure to use them minimally and keep the pauses short. An intentional pause for effect held too long becomes an awkward pause, the last thing you'd want. Make sure pauses remain shorter than 4-5 seconds long. Any longer and the audience's brains could move to new distractions. Be sure you know your motivation why you pause:

- *Reflective pause* - This is when you use a pause to get the audience to reflect on what you just said. To accomplish this, you ask the audience to reflect on the topic at hand. You can say something like, "Now, we'll take a minute to think about how this will affect you."
- *Dramatic pause* - this pause is used when you're looking to add effect to what you've been saying. Usually, this pause is used to get the audience to hold

their breath, and tighten tensions right before a punchline or a dramatic declaration.

- *Topic pause* - this pause provides transitions between topics. Don't drag out this pause too long if when you only want your audience to understand that you're shifting the focus from one area to another.
- *Visual pause* - are you about to bring up a new visual aide shortly after speaking on a different topic? No matter whether it's the number of sales accrued in graph form or a picture of something related to your core message, you can always pause in between visual displays. This allows your audience to take in the information before you start speaking about it right away.

Have you ever been to a theatre and just when the scary villain is about to pop out, everyone falls silent, waiting for the moment? That's what happens when you use pauses effectively. Be sure to incorporate them to establish tension in the room.

Slowing It Down

Your topic is important to you, no matter whether it's a professional topic or an informational topic. Emphasize your topic and lead your audience without them realizing, and all by slowing down the way you're speaking and by articulating your words. Slowing down also exercises power over your nerves and demonstrates that you have authority on the subject at hand.

Altering vocal pace is pleasant for listeners, and gives them time to reflect on the topic at hand.

Never rush through your words at such a pace that the tone of your voice heightens with strain. Audiences interpret fast words with something unimportant, commercial, or trivial that can easily be skimmed over. You exemplify for your audience which information is most significant, which statements are most credible and what parts of the presentation are most appreciable - all by slowing down.

Emphasis

You can get a whole new sentence just by emphasizing certain words. It helps to add variety and can clarify your core message to more people. See these examples:

- The *future* is in our hands.
- The future is in *our* hands.

So, emphasize your presentation's key topics. Emphasis will be particularly important in your concluding remarks; there you'll want to summarize, motivate, or make your audience think. You can get two very different results by changing your tone towards a particular word, so be sure to practice which one you're looking to focus on.

Tone

Voice tone conveys emotions so you want those emotions clearly understood. Like an actor, you must practice different pitches, timbres, and vocal force to match your message. For instance, if you want to convey sadness about something, you can lower your tone to a deeper pitch, add a quiver in your vocal cords, and execute a stage whisper. If you're looking to get everyone riled up by your subject, you can crescendo the tone of your voice while resonating from your chest and projecting to the back rows of the venue. In general, especially when speaking informatively, remember to keep your overall pitch pleasing to listen to. When practicing, modern technology lets most people record their voices so they hear how audiences perceive their speech strategies. You can do the same if you're unsure if you're hitting the right tone.

Non-Verbal Communication

Our subconscious automatically picks up on body language. In fact, there are also those who have been able to read body language for a living. That's because each person, no matter who they are, has body language that's subjective of how we're feeling and what we're doing. This is incredibly important, especially when you have people watching you. That's why you should always keep in mind that your body should be telling a story, alongside your words and the way you speak them.

It's all about being in control of your body. So even if you might be freaking out internally, you can make it so that your body is saying something completely different! There are small areas you can focus on to maximize the effects of your body language on your audience.

Hands

All right, let's get down to the obvious part - your hands. You want to speak with your hands. Studies have found that the most popular TED talk speakers used about 465 hand gestures, nearly double the amount of those who weren't nearly as popular. So, integrate those hands! You may find that those who speak with their hands can be a little distracting, which is understandable, as they're often right in front of you and speaking one on one. Here's the great part though - you want to keep people's eyes on you.

Not only do hand movements allow you to convey your message better, but hands can be a great way to attract your audience's attention to particular details they may not have noticed. For example, during a wedding speech, usually, the person conducting the toast keeps their glass in their hand, ready at any moment. This gives everyone in the room anticipation for when they will, in turn, raise their glasses to toast to the couple. This is a social example of where audiences understand body language and gestures.

When rehearsing your presentation, consciously incorporate enough hand movements to keep any audience's eyes towards the board for your presentation or toward your face when you want to express something important. Use your hand gestures to emphasize your words, and you'll find that public speaking will feel even more natural to you.

Eyes

Maintain eye contact is probably the most important advice given to anyone interested in mastering public speaking. Eye contact may also be the most difficult tactic for shy speakers to learn. Confidence emanates from direct eye contact, so new speakers should find friendly eyes in a quick audience scan and speak to those. The impact of establishing that one-on-one contact will spread across the adjacent listeners, keeping their attention. Also, your eyes, when used correctly, can bring in those of the audience who may not be paying attention back to your message. After all, if you're staring at the floor the whole time, you'll find that your audience will quickly become bored.

Eyes communicate people's intentions, as eyes can sometimes be the most expressive part of our face. When we make eye contact, we automatically assume the person we're speaking to has confidence equal to our own; this holds true whether you participate as a speaker or listener. You should keep eye contact in mind, even if you're speaking to a large audience. Scan over them, and take in their expressions. Acknowledging them can be a great way to keep their attention.

As with much of our nonverbal communications, experienced speakers make eye contact subconsciously. Among our intimate communicators, we seldom plan our eye messages. Such as when you're angry with someone, you might squint your eyes at them. When you see someone upset like that, you don't even need to see their body expression - all you need is to see their eyes. Therefore, as the speaker, you want to maintain eye contact properly. Keep your eyes soft and open so the audience feels you haven't judged them or are antagonistic toward them. Who needs a room full of antagonized listeners?

Posture

Look in the mirror and stand as you typically do. This is your average posture, and although it might be comfortable for you - it's not typically the posture you need to have while public speaking. When you're standing in front of a crowd it's best to use your *public speaking posture.*

Ideally, a good speaker leads with the chest raised so the back's straight. You want to stand with a slight lean toward the audience as though the people in the room are pulling at your heart. Demonstrating an open, accepting posture is to not be as stiff! You want to utilize your whole body to communicate with your audience, so practice your posture before you step out on stage. This posture often leads with authority and confidence - perfect for public speaking.

Energy

Honing in on an energetic presence doesn't mean that you have to do backflips before your presentation or entertain the crowd like a popstar. No, this simply means that you'll want to keep a light tone to your voice and move around. If you move during your presentation, even a little bit, you'll catch the eyes of anyone who may not have been paying attention.

When you're more energetic, people will naturally see you as being warm and approachable making their connection to you, and your message, easier. Having great energy is like looking at the crowd and yelling, "LISTEN TO ME!" without actually yelling it aloud.

There are some proven ways you can get yourself energized before a presentation.

Some people, like the public speaker great Tony Robbins, exercise before they head out on stage. I'm not telling you to run a marathon, but you could always do some jumping jacks before the presentation to get your heart racing - in a different way than nerves will give you. Robbins prefers to jump on a jogger's trampoline while inhaling and exhaling quickly to get his blood rushing. Even doing a few push-ups will give you a little adrenaline kick and take your mind off the crowd before you start.

If you're having trouble keeping up energy during your presentation, re-engage the audience by telling a story that matters to you. Anything anecdote that evokes emotion in you will help you bring up the drama in the room and add depth to your voice. Walking back and forth in front of the audience from time to time, which will bring eyes to focus on you again.

Just remember, be aware of your energy as you present. Everyone in the room can pick up on your energy, and it'll need to be invigorating to keep them interested.

Communication! Who Is It Good For?

The easy answer: communication is for *them* - your audience. It's for those who have given you their time and are waiting on your every word. If you want to become a master of public speaking, you first need to know that communication is a vital asset to have on hand. It's easy to say that it's all about body language and your tone, but this is so much more than that. Being able to have people know your name because of the presentations you give, to have a reputation as being able to communicate clearly, can make or break your career.

Communication is used to change people's minds, influence them, motivate them, and build relationships. It can easily cross language barriers and cultures. Developing your communication skills is vital to leading a fulfilled life, and should never be overlooked - even if you're honing in on it just to master public speaking. It's so much more than that! After all, so many people use communication to mend their relationships and to relay information.

You should always remember that communication is a two-way process. This is why your ability to communicate effectively is so important. I mentioned listening earlier in this chapter. Well, communication is a two-way street. You must be able to listen to your audience, even when they don't use words, and in this way, it becomes a shared experience between you and everyone in the room. When you're towards the end of your presentation, and audience feedback is part of the plan, really listening to their questions or concerns, and being able to reply properly can end the time spent together on a great note. It's an always-evolving process between you both and should be treated that way.

The Singer Who Rose Above Her Fear with A Little Help - Profile - Adele

It probably comes as a shock to learn the incredible songstress suffers from stage fright. This, of course, is the kind of woman who has sung in front of numerous audiences, including at awards shows. She's certainly one of the most popular singers in the world, so you'd think she'd be accustomed to audiences cheering her name. However, Adele has been very open about her stage fright and anxiety.

There was one incident where the singer bolted out of a fire escape rather than face a crowd. Another time she admitted to projectile puking on someone before heading out on stage. Still, despite pre-show jitters, Adele performs. But what helped her?

You'd be surprised. The singer has admitted that another singer gave her a hedge against stage fright. It was someone who she idolized before becoming famous herself. As the story goes, when Adele was about to meet Beyoncé for the first time, the shy performer almost had a panic attack. However, when Adele came face to face with Beyoncé, the mega-star gushed to Adele, "You're amazing! When I listen to you, I feel like I'm listening to God."

Sometimes it's the kind words of those we value that can give us the confidence to step out in front of everyone and give our best. If you're afflicted with stage fright, present to someone you trust and get a home team opinion - you might just find that a few kind words can help you when you're feeling anxious.

CHAPTER FIVE

Crafting Amazing Speeches

It doesn't matter if you're the greatest speaker in the world. If you don't have a topic that's well researched and written, your progress will have been for nothing. A mediocre speech, no matter how well recited and spoken, will not move the crowd. It won't be remembered. I'd go as far as to say it'll just leave them feeling empty.

You need to walk out onto that stage knowing that you've done everything you can to prepare yourself. You should go into it knowing that you'll keep your audience captivated - which I know you can! There are multiple techniques you can use to ensure that the people that you're speaking to will hang onto every word and start to care about what you're presenting.

Pillars of a Speech

Building a speech is a difficult process, and you want to go about it the right way. That's why I'm going to start with what you should keep in mind first. You can consider these pillars of a speech, as they deal with the public and will help you solidify what kind of speech you are wanting to create in order to get your core message across more clearly. I know that once you begin applying either, or all, of these principles, you'll soon see a difference in the way your audience listens.

Persuasion

We usually think of persuasion as a bad thing. I would go so far as to say it almost sounds like a manipulative word. Persuasion has a bad rep, and shouldn't be considered as sinister as all that. When you're trying to persuade someone, after all, it is the attempt to influence someone to decide on something. You use it to change people's minds and, when it comes to speeches, it's usually backed up by facts.

You can scour the internet for one, but there are very few speeches that include even the slightest hint of persuasion. It's used more often than we think – whether it's to persuade our boss for a raise or trying to get our significant other to get along with our mother. The great thing about persuasion is that it's fluid and doesn't take just one shape. It can be molded to better your argument, whatever it might be, and it's usually not as crass as manipulation, which often uses planning and tactics to force someone to change their minds.

If you want to be persuasive, you're going to have to give everyone a reason to change their views. You can use several techniques – emotional responses, logic, or even appealing to a personal reason from your past. You want to know both sides of the argument so that you can best contrast them. This way you can present them with the argument and have them consider your stance based on the reasons you've given. It will help your cause to know both sides - that way, if anyone disagrees with you, you'll have counterpoints if you have a question segment at the end of your presentation.

Entertainment

I'm sure you want your speech to be entertaining no matter what, and I'm sure it will be! This is more for those speeches that are based primarily on entertainment. These are also to help you understand how to have your speech be, effectively, a little less boring. If you find your subject is eye-watering and tiresome, you might want to spruce it up with some entertainment.

An entertaining speech is often used to wow your audience and get their attention, while also delivering your core message. When you're focusing on entertainment, the way you speak will be different than when you're offering an informative or persuasive speech. For instance, think about the last entertaining speech you heard. Usually, we dredge up memories of toasts at weddings, or when someone is being given an award. It's not all just about the humor, either. It's about using your voice in a way that excites the audience.

Many people think that entertaining speeches can just be done on the fly. Add a little humor, maybe some funny hand gestures and stories and everyone will laugh. Well, that's not how it works.

When people do this, their speeches can falter and the audience is left sitting in awkward silence. You want to put as much preparation into an entertaining speech as much as you do any other.

You want to be more open with your body language and use a lighter language. Be sure to keep things light by changing up the tone of your voice (which we get into later). You can apply small parts of entertainment in the most serious of speeches for a little liveliness, as well. You don't have to feel burdened to be entertaining – no one's expecting you to bust out a guitar and start singing Wonderwall. You just must keep in mind that entertainment can move crowds emotionally with drama, and that's something everyone loves.

Informing

Informative speeches are usually meant for topics that are a little more hard-hitting or for those who lecture focused on specific subjects. These types of speeches are all about the facts and must convey those facts to the audience so that they're easily understood. Essentially, you're informing your audience.

There's an obvious issue with informational speeches - they're dry. It's a substantial amount of information that needs to be conveyed in a short amount of time. It really doesn't leave a lot of space for anything but the facts. It's easy to find your audience falling asleep, despite your passion for the subject. If you find it is really tedious information, you'll need to add a bit of entertainment to shock your audience away again. It's always recommended to incorporate stories, or maybe even personalize the information so that the audience can relate to the subject more easily.

The informative speech can be overwhelming, as you need to be highly organized to get all the facts crammed in. Use your citations wisely and add visual aids and clues while your present. You want to get all the information into your allotted time, and visuals can be a key to cramming a lot of information into a short time without overwhelming the audience. You can always add a quick story from your own life in there, and you should be well within your time, so long as you organize everything and practice beforehand.

It's always important to keep even dull subject matter interesting. What you have to say matters! So, for the best informative speeches, always mix in a little of either entertainment or persuasion. This is one of the speech pillars that need help from the others because, although important, it can grow dull quickly.

Well-Defined Message

Your speech is your message - so make sure it's well defined. The way you craft your speech is integral to the way it's taken by the audience and considered important to them. Consider yourself as the initiator of a conversation, and you want them to get in on it. You make it easy enough for them to understand, while also being able to connect with it and you'll not only hold their attention, but you'll have them intrigued.

So, how do you define a message? It depends entirely on what you're trying to convey but it's an overarching theme that can be used for any kind of public speaking engagement you may have. There are a few questions you can use to help you define your message.

- Who is your audience?
- What do you want them to learn?
- How can you make what you're saying integral to them, while also staying true to the keynotes?
- How many people will be there?
- What is the time limit?

Consider all these things while determining your message. You need to make your message as clear as possible, and these questions will help you figure out your key points. You want all your points to be subsets of your defining message - which is why it's so important to develop one in the first place.

You can choose to open your presentation with your message, or you can choose to deliver it after a number of points, making it clear to the crowd just what they're in for. Now, knowing which to choose will be based on what your message is, of course. You also want to be comfortable with the placement. Definitely don't choose something that will make you unsure! If you choose to open with your message too quickly and get lost along the way, you might lose your audience - so keep it straightforward and be smart about the placement.

The Ultimate Beginning

The first few moments are the most important! Studies have found that a first impression lasts only seven seconds - so the time you spend in the beginning is crucial to winning your audience. There are multiple ways you can begin a presentation or a speech - whichever you choose should, as mentioned before, be one you're comfortable with. It should be known that each one will have a different effect on your audience and knowing this effect will leave a lasting impression for the rest of your presentation.

Storytelling

Public speaking is an art form, and using your words to create or refer to a personal story can be a great way to connect with the crowd. There is a rule to this, though - don't, and I repeat, don't interrupt your speech or presentation with your story. Don't start your presentation and then stop just to tell the story. You want it to be streamlined into it so that it weaves seamlessly, as this way it won't distract everyone from your main message. The story option is an effective opener as, since infanthood, we've been thrilled when we hear the beginnings of a story - so make sure it's an entertaining one!

Example: "I was like you once, just a teenager. I spent my days skipping school and hanging out with bad people. Drugs were rampant with this group, and it led me to do some awful things."

Ask Away

First, if you open with a question, you want to give a statement or a what-if scenario. Not only will this get the crowd thinking but it'll get their attention. This is a strong opener because it gets everyone involved from the moment you start.

Example: "It's said that only ten percent of the people in our world find the key to happiness. It takes a lot of key steps to finding your own happiness. Are you willing to put in the work so that you, too, can achieve a level of bliss that spills into every facet of your life?"

Make A Statement

Nothing gets a person's attention like a statement that pertains to them. If you're looking to get people hooked on every word, you can choose to make a statement that relates to each person in the room. The statement doesn't need to be negative - but it should pertain to your core message and fit in with the research you've made. Be sure to mention whichever source you've chosen, if there is research involved. You don't want everyone in the room thinking that you're making things up.

Example: "Global warming is not slowing. In fact, it affects all of us. It's been discovered that we've had our 16th warmest year in NASA's 134-year temperature study."

Be Thankful

This is a great way to start, as you're showing humility and gratitude. If you're speaking to a venue, you must thank those who've organized it for you, as well as thanking the audience for attending. You actually end up making everyone in the room feel important and excited for the presentation to come.

Example: "To start, I'd like to thank everyone for coming today. It's important to me that you've all arrived, and thank you to the coordinators for making this happen. Can we get a round of applause for everyone who helped put this together today?"

Be Complementary

It might come across as sucking up, but it helps everyone see you as someone willing to listen and observe everyone in the room. By complimenting them, you're making your message more about them than yourself - and it makes a fantastic first impression.

Example: "So, to start, I'd like to say that it's been a pleasure working with you throughout the years. I know that this presentation applies to all of us, especially since I've been able to get to know all of you well during our work hours."

Using Imagination

Imagination is endless - use it to your advantage! This brings everyone into a cohesive feeling where they can visualize a situation together. Not only will it give you some respite before jumping into your presentation, but it'll help you connect with everyone in the room.

Example: "Imagine you're standing in front of your boss, and you've just been told you've had a raise. Feel that feeling, and now open your eyes. Success is what we make it."

Your Speech Outline

This part will be intensive, but I know you can handle it! After all, once you've mastered your body language and tone, your words are your next vital key to delivering a perfect presentation. Your speech outline will make it so that you're organized and understand your key points. This will be what you'll need to memorize to the best of your abilities before you go up in front of the crowd. I know from personal experience that having an unorganized outline can lead to an increasingly difficult presentation.

There are multiple parts to an outline, and each should be dependent on the other. You want to transition them properly so that you're not repeating information. Each key point serves its own purpose and has its place. Listed below are some guidelines to follow so that you can ensure that your outline is perfect for your public speaking event.

Introduce Yourself

You need to start with a bang - so be sure to use at least one of the concepts listed in this chapter. I want your audience to be wowed the moment you step out onto that stage or into that boardroom. No matter where you are, you should start with a strong intro so that everyone is automatically listening. Feel free to use some of the introductions offered in this chapter and adapt them to your own presentation.

The introduction has a number of key parts that you want to follow. These are listed in order as they are the first parts. Some are optional, but others are key to beginning your speech. Each one that's considered optional will be stated. Follow them in order and you're sure to come up with a perfect introduction.

Grab Their Attention

The first sentence you utter sets the tone for the rest of the presentation. It's vital to how the rest of it will unfold, so be sure that the first thing you say will impact your audience. It's been proven that you have less than twenty seconds to make a first impression. It can't be changed after that, so be sure to use an opening sentence that reflects your core message, but also grabs their attention.

Establish Credibility

If you're speaking to an unfamiliar crowd, give them a reason to listen to you. Tell them why you're the person to speak to them on the subject. Giving them some background, either about your knowledge on the subject or through a story of your personal life, you can have them believe the words you're saying.

Core Message

This is where you introduce the message of your entire speech. You want to let them know why they're there. This is great if you're speaking publicly about a specific topic, especially an opinion. If you're giving a presentation to your work colleagues, this is where you'd tell them the main focus of your research, whether it's the new product or changing a policy in the departments. You want to have a core message and a good introduction to it. This will be what you build your key points on.

Preview of Presentation

This step is optional and can help you if you have a longer presentation. It can also set the stage so that everyone knows what they can expect from you throughout the time allotted. Here you would place a short slide or offer a quick overview of what they can expect. This is especially useful if you have a longer presentation on an intensive subject that has a variable of points.

Part Two - Key Points and Subpoints

Your part two comes directly after your introduction, so make sure you transition smoothly between your beginning into your key points. After you've given your central idea and message, you can then get to the key points or the reasons as to why your core message is what it is. You want to have primarily one point per slide, and then subpoints that help you prove them. These will lend credibility to your message, so be sure the main portion of part two should be your subpoints. These will help you to maintain a focus on your message.

Now, you can use as many key points as you need - just be sure to back up your information with proper research and citations! If you're applying any statistics or information from a survey, be sure to mention where you got it from. You don't have to put this information in the slideshow or presentation itself, you just need to say it.

Part Three - Argue for Your Message

It's all about the contrast! If you're trying to convince the crowd of your point, be sure to use contrasting arguments and refuting them. You want to do this before the last part of your presentation so that they leave on the note that your core message is correct. Applying these too early in the presentation might cause the audience to forget, especially if you have a lot of information that you need to relay to the crowd.

When you use contrasting points in your presentation, you'll find that it captures the attention of your audience. It surprises them and makes them consider the subject matter – particularly because when you're contrasting something, it adds a sense of drama. The more you sustain their attention, the more they'll remember your core message. Using contrasting points also adds facts to your words by placing them next to differing ideas. It helps everyone in the crowd understand your point of view a little more if you can offer examples.

There are three parts to a contrasting argument – first is your core message, which should be the first thing you discuss. You want to talk about all the implications of why they need to take your message into account. The second part is analyzing the outcome, and why the current method doesn't work. You then finish with the positives about your message and how it can change things.

Example:

Step 1 - *Taxes need to be raised on the rich. It will help us develop better communities and bring about better housing and necessities for our areas.*

Step 2 - *Without taxing the rich, they'll only get what? Richer. This is how things are now – they have a number of assets that they don't need.*

Step 3 - *So, when we look at taxing the rich, you'll see that we can put that money into different areas, such as schools and transportation. If we do this sooner, we can see changes made quicker.*

I want it to be known that that's just an example. I'm contrasting two points, while also making you consider my message. I give you reasons and then elaborate on them. Of course, your presentation won't be so minimal, but you get the idea. It makes you wonder what more could be said, and if it's a possibility. That's the beauty of contrasting ideas.

Part Four - Say It Again for the People in the Back

Part four is directly before your conclusion, which should be a separate part altogether. You can use this part to summarize your key points and core message. This is a basic formula for a speech or presentation but is always effective. You can always choose to change things slightly, especially if you're looking to create a unique presentation.

In this last part, be sure to capture the attention of the audience. This is towards the conclusion, and you want them to leave your presentation understanding everything they've just heard. So, if you are summarizing a heavy amount of information, try to really narrow it down to the most important points and keep it minimal so that it's easier to understand. You should consider your summary more like an explanation.

Conclusion - Say Your Last Words

I want you to think about some of your favorite movies. What was it about them that really grabbed your attention? Why do you love them? For some people, it's the way the movie ends. When a truly great movie reaches its climax, everyone in the audience is moved to silence. I want you to be able to finish your presentations and speeches with such a feeling. There are ways to have your last words to be just as memorable as the first.

Besides, there might be times when your message gets lost in the ruckus in the middle of the speech. Maybe you accidentally lost your way? No need to worry. You can end it on the right note and have your core message be the last thing people leave the room with.

Challenge Them

Were you looking to stir action into the crowd? If you were, we all know that there's nothing like a challenge to get them to feel that they, too, need to act. It's a sort of call to action. If you start your conclusion with your main message and then tell them what they can do to change the outcome or even their own lives.

Compare

If you're given a speech about something that needs to be changed, then a great way to end it is to compare the thing you're against. You'll possibly have already done this in part three. However, if you're looking to convince them to change their minds, it's a great way to remind them. This will have the audience question the validity of the opposition. For example, you can say, "we either destroy the Earth with global warming, or we build a future for our children." Not only are you reinforcing your message, but you're leaving the audience on a note of the change.

Storytime

Do you want to have them speak about your presentation as they leave? End it with humor. Nothing sets up a crowd to leave with smiles on their faces like ending with a joke. You can always choose a joke that has aspects of your core message embedded into it, or one that repeats a key point that you'll have made earlier. If you do choose this conclusion, be sure to use the joke on a friend or two to determine whether it's actually funny. The last thing you want to do is end with silence and crickets in the room.

Thank you, Thank you

I'm sure you already know where I'm going with this! You want to make it clear to everyone in the room that you've finished.

This is a casual, but humble way to end your presentation. You simply thank the audience for listening and attending - this is a simple but effective way to finish. It's been done many times but it never really gets old because people always feel appreciative of someone recognizing their time spent to hear your message.

Visual Stimuli

Have you given your closing statement? Well, this would be a great time to impact the audience. To do this, you can always use an image that makes the crowd think. So, choose an image that refers to your message and that makes your crowd sit for a minute or two before leaving and gives them think.

The Business Mogul Who Overcame His Fear - Profile - Warren Buffett

There's a good chance you've heard the man's name. After all, he's one of the richest men in the world. He's likely attended more meetings and presentations than we will in our entire lives, seeing as he's the CEO of Berkshire Hathaway and an investor. There's no doubt people pitch to him everyday. As a businessman, though, he's had to pitch or present to others. Unfortunately, in his early career, Warren Buffet was terrified of public speaking.

The business mogul is open about his early stage fright, and how it impacted his career. It could be said that if he didn't overcome his fears, he may not have become the man we've all heard of today. So, how did he do it?

You may be surprised he followed steps similar to what I've laid out in this book you're reading now. He's even admitted to taking a public speaking course, only to drop out because he was too nervous! There's no doubt he had many obstacles to overcome, and he did it one step at a time.

The billionaire signed up for a public speaking course and, after graduating, began to speak as a lecturer at a local college. He started by exposing himself to possibilities where he'd need to rely on his public speaking. He also began to practice alone, trying to get into the mindset that he could stand in front of that crowd without ruining his lecture.

Although he didn't realize it, Warren Buffett faced his fears and did it anyway. It's likely because of this that he's become the fearless business magnate he is today. There's no way to tell, of course, but he's certainly come a long way since being that young man who was too terrified to even stand before a crowd.

CHAPTER SIX

Designing a Stellar Presentation

You should use the outline from the previous chapter to focus on the first part of your presentation. This part, however, is going to be all about how to make a presentation. This includes what tools you can use, data visualizations and finding the words to emphasize your message to the audience. I have no doubt that your presentation, after using some of the options in this chapter, will wow the people in the room.

Tools to Use

Having the right presentation starts with having the right program to create your slideshow. There's one popular presentation creator that most companies use - Microsoft PowerPoint. It's synonymous with presentations but it's not your only option. I've listed below several different slide presentation programs that might just suit what you need! Beyond that, I've included only programs that can be downloaded for free.

Google Slides

Using this online option is effective when you need to work on your presentation from anywhere. You won't need a USB or a particular computer, either. You can work on it on any device because your file will be kept on your Google account. This option is also great when you're working with a group, as anyone in the group will be able to adjust your presentation as you go along. You can allow access to the document to certain people.

Keynote

Are you an Apple fan? If you are, then Keynote should become your preferred program. This is because this program is best used with iCloud, iOS, and Mac devices. Like many of the ones listed here, this is an easy program to adapt to. It comes with a variety of different options, such as using it on multiple devices, special effects for your presentation and unique themes that you can customize. One of the downsides is that this program is only available on Apple devices.

Photostage Slideshow Software

You'll find this program to be one of the easiest to use. It allows for the seamless creation of professional slideshows and also has a variety of editing options. Like most slideshow applications, you can include pictures, transitions, and music. You can also turn the slideshow into a DVD, if necessary, or upload it to YouTube for easy streaming from anywhere.

Movavi Slideshow Maker

This is an easy program, and it allows you to create personalized slideshows with a variety of different options. The real winning point to this program is the premade slideshow templates and library of free background music, filters, and special effects. This is the program you'd want to use if you're looking to create a presentation that has more customization options. It's the best program for a more unique slideshow.

Building Your Slideshow

What makes a good slideshow into an outstanding slideshow? I want you to think of a few things you notice immediately when you're looking at a presentation. Is it its appeal visually? Is it the words that are chosen? Maybe how the information is displayed? Let me tell you one thing - it's everything combined. To create a slideshow that not only shows your information correctly but also is aesthetically pleasing isn't as easy as it may sound. You don't just click a few buttons on the screen and suddenly have it all figured out.

There are certain steps you can take to create a slideshow worthy of your subject, while also being aesthetic. You can avoid the kind of presentation that people tend to look away from by using these steps, which gives you a guideline to go by. Feel free to adapt it - just know that you should keep each step and not throw any that aren't optional away.

Outline

It goes without saying, but you should always outline your presentation before you start creating it in the program. After all, you need to know what you're going to say. No matter how much information you put into each slide, if you're just winging it, chances are it'll come out as messy and unprofessional. To do an outline, just write down the information you want to appear on each slide and divide it up between the subject matter. You'll have already created an outline for the entirety of your presentation, so you can use that as a basis and then place the information in order into the slideshow.

Here is just one example of an outline for a slideshow presentation:

1. Introduction
2. Core Message
3. Proposition (or Summary)
4. Why They Should Consider the Proposition (Key Points)
5. More Reasons to Consider (Examples of Key Points)
6. Conclusion
7. Thanks/Questions

This is just a basic presentation. Each one doesn't include just one slide, as there might be multiple key points or reasons to consider with your topic, especially if it's a comparison statement.

It doesn't matter how many you need to use - just make sure the information is clear and concise on each slide.

Tone

You'll need to set the tone depending on what type of presentation you're doing. Now, if you're going for a professional tone, for example, you won't want to go with a snowman theme (obviously). You'll also want to use jargon related to your field of work, whatever it might be. If your presentation is humorous, you'll want to set your slideshow up so that it has lighter colors so that everyone knows what to expect right away. You shouldn't be too wary of not using a specific tone that's a variation of what you typically see. This is your slideshow, so feel free to make it unique, while also staying in the realm of what tone you're setting. Professional meetings can be informal, so don't worry and make the experience enjoyable for everyone - even if the information might be a little dry.

Utilize Your Key Points

Your main points should be the focus of your talk. Not only will they help you remember specific aspects of your subject, but they'll help you with timing your information properly so that you don't veer off. You should always make a list of your key points that revolve around your core message. You should have cues embedded in your presentation so that you can jog your memory in case you lose your way or forget a specific thing. When considering your main points, you should classify them properly – whether you're doing a professional presentation or a speaking engagement. Titling them is important, as you can make them serious or humorous.

Don't forget to back them up with sub-points. We'll get into that later, but you want each point to be clarified with proper information. You can then use this data to substantiate your core message and prove your point, no matter what it is.

Your Visuals Speak for You

There are certain colors that the eyes naturally gravitate to, but it's not just about placing these colors wherever. When you're building a slideshow for your presentation, you always want to follow simple rules to have it capture everyone's attention. After all, we may not always judge a book by a cover, but that's only for books. The way your presentation appears will have your audience's eyes, so make sure they have something nice to look at.

Visual Style

You can always use a template, but that looks kind of lazy - especially if someone recognizes it! God forbid that happen. So, instead, you should build your own theme so that you can choose your own style and colors. One thing you don't want to do is have many different styles throughout your presentation. This is likely to get everyone's attention, and not for good reasons. It'll be a distraction if anything else. You want your slides to be streamlined and to follow a certain style that you've chosen. So, keep it consistent throughout the whole slideshow. This includes any textboxes or charts you might use - keep the color scheme the same throughout.

Leave Some Space

No one likes clutter. Whether it's on your desk or in your home, it's a jumbled mess that doesn't appeal to the eye. Make sure you keep your slides clutter-free! Less is always more when it comes to your presentation. You should use your words, rather than adding all the words you're going to say to your slides. You want the others in the room to be listening rather than reading the entire time, otherwise, you could have just emailed it to them.

Colors Are A Crowds' Best Friend

Say hello to one of the main setups for your slideshow. If you use colors properly, you'll discover that the style will truly come together. If you work for a company, there may be specific colors you can use - so use them wisely! If you're just looking to present an original idea, be sure to choose colors that go together well and contrast the other. Try to avoid colors that look too similar to each other, like indigo and navy. You want there to be a flow to your slideshow. For example, blue and white and contrasting colors that feed off each other well and still appeal to the eye.

When choosing your font color, you want to stick to something dark that will make it so that everyone can read them. Don't use bright colors! If you use a light color on a dark background, such as yellow on black, it might look unprofessional. If you are dead-set on using a light color on a dark background, only make your font white. If the font is narrow stroked, make the face bold so the image is clearly legible. Also, avoid using too many words on a single slide, the audience can't read that fast and listen and watch you. Stay away from the red font, as it will appear as though everything is written wrong. Red is the typical color for marking mistakes, so everyone will subconsciously apply it to your presentation.

If you're unsure of how many colors you should use, it's always best to stick to a smaller amount. So, try to only have about two or three to start - you can always change it if you feel like it looks a little bland. Choose two opposing colors, such as white and black, and then a secondary color to add some definition.

Charts and Diagrams

Charts are an easy way to get information across without having to say out the numbers or list them, which can be an eyesore. Be mindful of how you use color, and make the information in the charts clear enough so everyone can understand it just from seeing it. Only add charts that are important to the subject at hand - you don't want to overwhelm them with data. It's also best if you don't add too many numbers or text alongside your chart, as it can be cluttered. You can always say the details of the chart, too, instead of adding an abundant amount of numbers in the slide.

Charts to consider and they're best uses:

- Column chart - this chart is best used when you're comparing multiple subjects. You might choose to add in a few different dates, products, or options for your work. The information you add in is up to you, but using this chart will help you easily relay the information so that everyone can see the differences.

- Scatter chart - use this one if you're comparing numbers, usually meant for sales or consensus. If you have innumerable subjects, this one's your best bet. It's usually used for comparing locations, or dates and for the many different subjects you may have.
- Stacked column charts - this one's best for composition. Use a maximum of four composition items so that the chart doesn't appear too big in the slideshow.

Animation and Transitions

Be careful when using animations and transitions! You don't want your slideshow to look unprofessional which can happen - especially if you're adding a ridiculous amount of animation in each slide. You want to use animations to add style to your slideshow and add to the content involved. Make sure that it's not distracting, but rather appeals to the eye and blends into the slideshow effortlessly. If you're doing a company presentation, take it easy and make the transitions slow. One of the best ways to incorporate animation is to reveal your sub-points that relate to your key points or to go from one subject to another while transitioning slides.

Finding the Words

We've all had to sit through a bad presentation. Let me ask you this: what do you think constitutes a bad presentation? It's often all in the words we use. This doesn't include just when we're speaking, but it's also based on what we're looking at. Usually, these are also presentations that are longer than they need to be and aren't visually stimulating.

Your audience, whether they know it or not, are picky about the text that appears in your slideshow. Typically, they'll respond best to presentations that offer visuals and minimal text. They tend to be more engaged with these types of slideshow presentations. Not only do you not bombard them with a ridiculous amount of information, but you also leave some out, which is great for getting them to ask questions.

You wouldn't want your audience reading a book, so know that it can be overwhelming to them when they're confronted with a wall of text. It's like trying to read a thesis – no one wants to do that. It will often confuse everyone because they expect to *hear* the information rather than read it. Therefore, you should only include the necessary information. Leave yourself space to explain each part of your key points.

This is why you'll want to focus on your core message. Make sure that each slide communicates your message by adding information to its key points (this is also why outlining your slideshow is vital to the success of your presentation). Once you focus on your message, it'll be easier to get across with fewer words.

So, bring on the edits! You'll want to get rid of any excess information. Finish your slides and then, with a stern eye, edit the crap out of them. If there's information in there that doesn't need to be seen, just delete it. You can always say the information rather than having it on the slide. You want to go for a minimalistic look – think in bullet points, then elaborate yourself and add informational graphs so that they can understand if there are numbers involved.

I know how difficult it can be to cut the information down, especially when you're passionate about the subject, but you shouldn't keep any extra wording that doesn't add to your presentation. Let your passion show with what you say, rather than what you show on the screen. This also keeps you from repeating anything, as you'll have the points to keep you in check. When you go overboard with the wording in your presentation, you may unknowingly repeat yourself a few times, which will only make it seem as though you didn't spend enough time on it.

Wrapping It Up

First off, you want to put it all together far before the date when you'll present. This will help you be better prepared and give you enough time to practice. The better rehearsed you are, the more natural the presentation will be.

You want your core message to be important to you and you want to find reasons to be passionate about it. You can always feign interest but you'll lose your audiences that way. They'll pick up that you're not that interested regardless of how enthusiastic you might pretend to be. So, make sure that you've chosen things that you enjoy and then everyone that you're presenting to will enjoy it as well. This goes for your titles, your slides, and your visuals. If everything comes together so that you're pleased, that'll reflect onto the audience.

Build on your central theme, and make sure your presentation encompasses that. I'm sure there'll be nerves beforehand – it happens to even the best of us. But if your presentation is ready, all the information is put together properly, and you've given yourself time to rehearse, there's a good chance you'll soar.

How A Golf Great Overcame His Stutter - Profile - Tiger Woods

Tiger Woods is a household name, and he's a living golf legend. He also had a stutter he had to get through to become the person he is today. He credits his competitiveness in every aspect of his life as something that has helped him overcome his difficulty in forming words. There have been interviews where his stutter returns.

But how did he do it? The answer will probably surprise you. Not only was it his enduring ability to work through it, but it was also being able to speak to his dog. He would practice speaking to his dog until the good boy would fall asleep.

"I finally learned how to do that, without stuttering all over myself," he said, without so much as a pause.

Stuttering stems from childhood and can be difficult to overcome. There are speech therapies and schools that help students defeat their way of talking. Sometimes, though, it takes a little practice and a best friend to help you deal with your fear of speaking in front of others - no matter what the reason.

CHAPTER SEVEN

Successfully Attract Your Audience

There's something different about public speakers. Somehow, they're able to stand in front of a crowd, speak to them, and move them to action. If you want to master public speaking, there's more to it than just being able to entertain. You have to be able to motivate them, too, and have them *really* listen to you. Your audience will appreciate you for it, and being able to do so will allow you to create a network of people that can help you build a strong career later down the line. By speaking with that magnetism that brings people in, you'll likely end up booking extra speaking engagements through word of mouth.

This is all about being a magnet and drawing people into what you're saying with your voice, your words, and your body language. It's a trifecta that, when brought together, can change the way you hold yourself on stage. It also changes the way people react to you, no matter what subject you're speaking on. Once you understand that each gesture and each word will have a different effect, you can then work on your presence. This is where you do the work on the inside so that it can radiate from you - which I know it can!

Lead the Way

I want you to think of someone you know that has a commanding presence. Now, this can be a celebrity or someone you know - it doesn't matter. Try to think of what it is that brings you in when they speak or when they enter a room. Do your eyes follow them? Do you hang onto every word they say? This can be considered the *je ne sais quoi* factor. You'd think that they were born with it, but it's often something that's built through life experiences and natural leadership skills. Want to know the best part? You can learn how to harness this so that you can develop your own *je ne sais quoi* factor every time you enter a room and present.

All About Interest

Sure, you can learn to speak and woo a crowd. That's fine. Do you know what isn't? Not listening to feedback or when someone else is speaking. The best way to gain other people's respect is to not only be interesting but to also be interested in what they say.

I used to have a bad habit of scanning the room out of nervousness when someone was speaking to me. My eyes would jump from person to person, as though I was waiting for a new opportunity for a new conversation, even if that wasn't the case. How do you think that made the person speaking feel? I can only imagine they felt pretty awful and wanted to finish that conversation as quickly as possible.

I've since learned to make eye contact and *really* listen to what people have to say. This includes when you're the center of attention and onstage. If someone has a question or wants to give some feedback, take a moment to let them speak and finish their sentences. Don't interrupt them - just listen. If you show that you're interested, they'll be interested too.

Strength - Not the Muscle Kind

Do you know your strengths? If you don't, you definitely should! After all, each public speaker is distinct and will have a flare in varying ways. I want you to figure out what your strengths are so you can play to them and enhance your public speaking abilities. It's not always about how you can just talk to a crowd - it can be so many other things! Do people think your funny? Are you great at telling stories? Do you have a calming presence with new people? These are just some of the things you can consider before you write down your strengths. Look over them and think of ways you can apply these strengths and enhance your presentation.

Use Your Experiences

Instead of using sentences like, "you might understand", or "if this happened to you once". That won't get your audience fully involved with your presentation. Instead, use the experiences you've had in your own life as examples. Sure, this can be a little intimidating. I have no doubt that you'll feel naked at first, and that's okay. But here's a fun fact - everyone will relate to you. Want to know why? We're all human. We may not have the exact same life experiences, but most of us have shared emotions relating to your own life stories. There's a part of us in each of them and, in that way, we're all similar. So, use your stories, and you'll see that a spark will show up within the crowd as they start to see themselves while you speak your truth.

Don't Fear Silence

Whenever we watch a movie, you'll notice that the entire audience is silent. We get frustrated if someone starts talking in the middle of an important scene. If your speaking and the crowd remains silent, don't get overexcited or nervous. This is often a good sign.

As a speaker, you'll run into these situations often. The room might be so quiet that you can hear a pencil drop or someone coughing in the back. I want you to embrace the silence. You might even want to pause and let the silence seep into the room, creating a type of surmounting tension before you begin speaking again. If you show that you have a grasp of the silence, you'll find that you come across as more confident. Normally nervous speakers try to laugh their way out of the stillness of a crowd or try to fill it with their voice. Do the opposite and you'll gain the respect of the people in the room without them even knowing.

Be Authentic

One thing you might notice about the many ways to emphasize leadership skills while presenting is all about listening, donning your strengths like armor, and speaking from experience. What's the one thing they all have in common? Authenticity. Let that sink in. *You* are worthy of being authentic in front of a crowd. You are enough and I know that people will want to hear what you have to say. Sometimes, though, it's all about the way we say it. This is why I know the concepts in this book will help you reveal your true self and make you feel at ease while public speaking. Often, it's all about being truthful to who we are. Maybe it's why we fear being in front of a crowd - we're essentially alone. Let me tell you this: it's not always a bad thing.

When you think of the famous speeches ever written, it wasn't always about the words, as moving as they may be. What we remember is usually how it was said. It was the way Martin Luther King, Jr. said, "I have a dream," that brought people to bring their hands together and clap. The way he spoke was true to his authentic self. When we see something that bores us, it's not always because the person speaking is nervous – sometimes it's because they hate what they're doing. They're just going with the motions. They don't want to be there, so you don't want to be there. If you find yourself being one of those people, try to find something about the subject matter you're covering (especially if it's for a job) and get passionate about it. When you're authentic about your excitement, other people will sense that off you and start to feel it, too.

This is an important leadership quality because authenticity makes people want to be around you. When you start to be authentic and speak your mind in a way that really tries to come from a place of understanding, it's hard to question what you've said. I've been in the industry for over a decade – this is one of those attributes that lie at the core of most public speakers whose names you can list off the top of your head. I know how difficult it is to get to that place, though. Sometimes, in fact, it can feel impossible. I'm going to tell you why it isn't, and why your authentic self matters!

Finding Your Authentic Voice

I know there's the fear of seeming as though you're just speaking from a sheet. We've all seen those presentations with cue cards, where the presenter shuffles it around in their hands, searching for the next thing to say. These don't communicate to your audience that you're there to wow them – this is why authenticity is such an asset. You certainly don't want to lose your credibility in the eyes of those who've come to see you present.

Why do you connect to your core message? Really consider it. Why is it important to you? You might just be presenting a product to a client, or doing a wedding toast, but it doesn't matter. You've been given the task to speak to a crowd. You need to make a connection to the statement you're trying to make and apply it yourself. In essence, it's not always about what you're speaking publicly about. It's how it relates to you. After all, if you relate it to yourself, you can also relate it to the audience. When you consider it this way your words then become your truth.

But how do you determine this? You must know who you are. This doesn't just mean your life story - it's deeper than that. Where do you see yourself in the world? When you can start answering this kind of question, you can find your identity. You can then connect unique things to your passions, what you don't like or even how it pertains to your everyday routine.

You don't want to lie or be inconsistent. People can tell when you're lying. It's like when you walk out of a change room, look to the salesperson, and ask them if it looks good. When they reply with a lie, you can tell - you don't end up buying the product. It's the exact same concept as standing in front of a crowd and being inauthentic. They can tell. So, incorporate yourself into the presentation. You'll be surprised by the reaction you get.

Practicing Authenticity

There's no doubt that practicing before a speaking engagement is crucial to being able to deliver a good speech. However, you don't want to sound overly rehearsed. One of the ways you can avoid this is by forcing yourself to do gestures that you're uncomfortable with. You do want to maintain eye contact with your audience – but *don't* creep them out! You don't want to have a staring contest with the person in the front row all because you're trying to watch your body language. *Do* be aware of what your body is doing, but don't be too forceful – everyone in the room will be able to tell if you are.

You're probably wondering, *how do I become authentic, then*? Sure, body language was already mentioned in this book. It's a subtle way of communicating with your audience, and its importance to your presentation can't be overstated. If you want to create an authentic feel to your presentation or your speech, you'll want to practice while considering the audience. If you practice your gestures too much, they might come off as robotic.

There are some rules you can use to help you rehearse to perfection, while also maintaining your authenticity. You want to listen, be excited about what you're talking about and always be facing the audience with an open stance. If you can do these, there's a better chance of you succeeding. You can use these three rules to rehearse and practice gestures. Feel free to use a mirror if you're unsure.

Variety Show

Okay, so you have a boring topic. You've read the book up until this point and you're staring at the pages, thinking, "what if I need to sell a vacuum cleaner to a multimillionaire?" Well, that doesn't sound very fun - especially if it's not your vacuum cleaner. I'm sure doing a presentation on suction isn't the greatest way to go about your day, but you need to get it done. And I know you can do it! This is where you bring in variety, and spice up your presentation so that both you and everyone in the room don't fall asleep.

Add Some Sparks

You have a boring topic - it doesn't mean it gives you a pass at being a boring speaker! You might be nearly crying from a breakdown because you hate what you have to present, but it's all about using a different angle to make it more entertaining. So, stop staring at a blank screen and boring presentation. We're about to fix it.

You can think of it from a strategic point of view - what angle do I take to make this interesting? Many people approach topics that aren't that interesting from different angles, to find one that suits their needs in an entertaining way.

Disrupt It

I'm definitely not talking about jumping up and down while suddenly juggling. Obviously. We usually think of disruptions as bad things, but it can actually draw attention back if the crowd has begun to lose interest. It's essentially about surprising everyone in the room. This will not only have their eyes on you but they'll keep them there.

This works best if you have a boring and flat presentation, as disrupting it will regain the crowd's attention. It's all about breaking up the flow of your words with entertainment. At one point in the presentation, you can stop and surprise the audience with something new – whether it's a survey, a graphic, a quote, or even a video.

You want to make sure it's relevant to the topic. Once you see that the material, which might be dry, has taken its course, you can do an impromptu questionnaire. This will bring them back to your presentation and get them involved. Remember, you want it to flow. Make your disruption necessary to continue with your topic.

Relatability

A great way to get your audience involved is to check social media trends. You can give your subject relevance by relating it to something happening in the world at that very moment. Check out popular trends happening in the world and adapt a part of your presentation to it. You can even allow a debate to get started where you compare your subject to something relevant happening right now. Not only will this get people's attention, but it'll get them riled up, too. Just be sure to use something that relates to the content in some way. I also recommend being careful of what you choose, as you don't want to get the crowd riled up because you've done something offensive.

Metaphorically Speaking

If you have a dry subject that might be hard to understand, you can always use metaphors during your presentation to make it more interesting and to get everyone thinking. When you use a metaphor, you're asking a rhetorical question that the audience can answer in their heads. The idea isn't to give them the answer - have them do that for themselves. So, you can ask them, what is it like? Or, if you were to compare it to these things, which would it be, to you? You allow them to elaborate on the subject on their own, which gives them the independence they need to figure out your subject for themselves, rather than being forced to know it offhand.

Have the Answers

One thing you'll notice about people that naturally attract people to them is that they're never afraid to say what's on their minds. When you're standing on stage, this might be a difficult thing to do, as you've rehearsed for hours, if not days.

If you've chosen to end your speech or presentation with a Q and A, you might find that you'll hit a snag in the road when people start coming up with questions you weren't prepared for. I'm sure you've come across someone who comes up with a one-worded answer whenever you speak to them. Whenever this happens, you can't help but think to yourself that there's not much substance there. So, when you've decided to end with questions, make a list of answers that you can use.

When you choose your answers, make sure they have depth and personality. Research until you can't research anymore, or add some anecdotes from your own life if you're unsure. Offering a true and authentic response will help others see you as more personally available to them. It's an amazing tool to utilize, as it's highly overlooked. Most people don't expect such thoughtful answers. You can not only leave on a good note, but you'll make an impression on them right before they leave the venue or board room.

Magnetism Comes from Within

I can only imagine that you'll feel like a fraud at first, as though you're faking your way through becoming a more magnetic person, as though you're trying to manipulate your way into getting people to like you. This is how it starts but soon you'll notice shifts in your own attitude and personality.

Your magnetism comes from within. This is the *je ne sais quoi* factor. It's not about what's on the outside because, as attractive as you might be, you need to work on the inside. If you're the most attractive person in the world but you don't have amiable qualities on the inside, you'll find that people will walk away just as quickly as they walked in. Magnetism is being your authentic self, being considerate for others, choosing your words and possessing self-control. These are not only incredible leadership qualities but they're qualities the world needs more of.

It'll lead you to the right kind of magnetism that'll outside even the worst of presentations. This isn't to say that you can just wing it on stage, but your ability to connect to a crowd will be amplified. I know that it'll take some practice, but I have no doubt that you'll be able to be your true self and allow others to see the wonderful aspects that make you who you are.

The Actor Who Stepped Up Despite His Fears - Profile - Harrison Ford

You know him as Han Solo and Indiana Jones. This incredible actor has been famous for over 30 years so you'd think he'd get used to speaking in front of strangers. His job is to literally perform in front of dozens of people - action scenes included. So how does someone like him suffer from a fear of public speaking?

Despite his incredible career on screen, Harrison Ford has admitted that public speaking fills him with "terror and anxiety". It was when he went to receive the Life Achievement Award of the American Film Institute, Harrison admitted having issues giving his speech.

He spoke to journalists saying that, "the greatest fear in my life is public speaking." What did he do then? He still went up. Despite his fears, Harrison walked up onto that stage, gave a speech, and accepted his award. The only thing you can do is just go up there and do it, despite the nerves and anxiety.

It also doesn't help if you're accepting an award – that makes it a little bit nicer afterward.

CHAPTER EIGHT

Avoiding Self-Sabotages

There's one great thing about mistakes - you learn from them! But what if you already knew what mistakes you shouldn't make? Then, you can avoid them. This isn't like avoiding fear - this is about being prepared. To be prepared, you need to know what not to do and what not to include in your presentations. I want you to succeed with each public speaking engagement you have, especially by avoiding the mistakes I, and many others, have made before.

About the Audience

If you're not talking to an audience, you're talking to an empty room. Keep this in mind when you're presenting. Your audience makes it so that you're a public speaker. Without them, you won't have anyone to relay your information to. These mistakes will make it so that you upset or lose your audience - be sure to keep them out of your presentation. I want you to gain an audience as you go, so avoid the mistakes that can cause angst while you're public speaking.

Information Overload

I can remember when I first started public speaking. I wanted the crowd to know just how much I knew about gaining confidence. I was standing there with the glare of the lights in my face and the silence of the crowd in front of me and I went ten minutes over the time when I was supposed to finish. I had seven key points broken down into three subsections each. I told them about body language and voice and cited all the studies - there were lots of charts involved. Can you guess what happened? Some of them left, and I even saw two of them falling asleep. I learned from that moment that, although I was prepared, I had let my core message down.

When you spend too much time on the information and not enough on the message, you end up losing your audience. You want to say everything concisely - keep it simple. You'll always hold their attention if you make your points and move on. I can think of a few teachers who went on and on about certain subjects and eventually we'd all start passing notes to each other because we weren't paying attention. This is the kind of thing that happens when you're droning on.

Unless it's relevant, keep it minimal. Your pie charts only show off how much you studied for the subject at hand. Too many and you'll just overwhelm everyone with needless information. Their time is just as valuable as yours, so maintain that integrity and tell them what they need to know, not everything they don't.

Don't Assume Anything

Well, we all know how looked down upon stereotyping is. To say it's an awful thing to do would be an understatement. So, please, *don't* assume anything about your audience. Have a certain political stance? Favorite color? Are you trying to figure out if they're all rich? Don't. Just do the opposite of Nike - *don't* do it. Assuming anything like this about your audience can make it so that your presentation becomes obsolete.

If you walk into a room and just assume that everyone is a fan of Nickelback, you're going to have a bad day. There are ways to figure out these things about your audience - starting your presentation or speech by blasting *Look at This Photograph* for the entirety of the song is probably not your best move, no matter how much you might like the song.

Ignorance Is Not Bliss

Are you passionate about your subject? If you answered yes, then this applies to you. I know that sometimes we can get swept away with our subject and go on for hours. We want everyone to know just how great it is! Like everything in life, though – there's a catch. You might forget that your audience exists. That, and they may not know the subject at hand, so it's up to you to explain it to them. Going on rants about it won't help them and they'll easily become bored.

You should always let your audience know what they're in for before you begin. This allows them to understand it better. Taking questions at the end of the presentation is also a good idea, as you can always give them the information they're looking for if you've not touched on it. You want them to be able to focus on the presentation at hand without getting lost. So, don't ignore them! Be sure to always keep them in mind as you go along while explaining things openly.

Overselling

So, you have a presentation that's more of a sales meeting. Okay, I can roll with that. Do you know what the biggest mistake is when trying to sell a product in a meeting? It's right in the title. Overselling. We all know that a salesman is either super charismatic or that dingy person in cartoons trying to sell broken products. I don't believe either of these to be true in real life - they're just stereotypes.

That being said, it can be easy for people to pick up on these kinds of first impressions due to those stereotypes. Nothing will turn a customer off more from buying or investing your product like overselling. I know this sounds basic, but I'm sure you're wondering to yourself how not to oversell. Well, there are a few things you can do.

Use open-ended questions. For example, instead of saying, "What do you mean your company can't afford this product?" You should ask, "What kind of price would you pay for so-and-so abilities?" Don't try to cut your customer off by appearing disgruntled if they can't afford a product, or are questioning the amount. Try to reason with them why the amount is worth it, instead of forcing them to buy.

This goes hand in hand with empathy. Be sure to be empathetic while presenting. You want to find points where you can understand why they're interested in the product. Depending on the product, they might have a need that only your product can offer. You can always talk about personal experiences with them, and ask them questions as to why they feel their current products aren't doing the best job.

Overselling is dangerous when it comes to sales, but by being genuine in your understanding and being open to questions that your audience might have, you'll find that you'll naturally have a more charismatic presentation.

Offensive Is Not Effective

It's a new world out there. Humor is not what it was years ago, as the internet has made it so that we're changing. Our society has become more aware of edgy humor, and it's certainly not as commonplace as it was. At the same time, humor is also objective, and not everyone laughs at the same jokes. That's okay. Sometimes it's based on our own lives or how we grew up. This doesn't mean that there should be any offensive material in a presentation. Those jokes that were okay are no longer representations of language that we should use. You need to be more concerned about how your humor might affect your audience, and take into account all walks of life. Crass humor is no longer appreciated - it's just offensive.

When used properly, humor is a fantastic way to immerse your audience and ensure that they laugh and enjoy themselves. There's a fine line with humor, though. There are times when it can be overboard. Some humor in presentations is an excellent tool to relax your audience, build rapport and enhance your presentation. However, bad jokes will always be bad jokes. And someone laughing at their own bad jokes is even more uncomfortable to watch. Know your audience and always avoid jokes about politics or religion or anything sexist or racist.

Instead look for humorous stories in your own life to share, especially when the joke is on you; self-deprecating humor can be very funny and endearing. When people are relaxed, they take in information more effectively so making them smile and laugh can be very useful during your presentation; just leave out the bad jokes and controversial material.

Avoid the Ego

I believe that pride is a virtue - if you've managed to get to the point where you are now, I see no reason as to why you should be proud of yourself. That being said, ego and pride share a very slimline and most of it is limited to when we are surrounded by others.

When you're speaking to a crowd it can be easy to get a little cocky, especially if you're a professional on your subject. You know all the latest up-to-date information because you've researched the subject for months, if not years. You may have even dedicated your life to it. So why wouldn't people need to listen to you? You have the information, and you're basically giving it away.

This view can give you an abundance of confidence, which people will appreciate. You'll need to watch your tone when you deliver the information, though. When you allow ego to take hold of your attitude and your actions, you'll end up with a crowd that no longer feels happy to be there. They'll feel like they're being lectured to. You'll lose the connection with them because they'll feel as though their opinions or thoughts don't matter. It'll seem as though your mind is occupied by your own grandeur, rather than stimulating your audience.

This also goes if you have a difficult person in the audience. Don't give in to their moods and don't reflect the mood back onto them. If you have someone asking you inane questions, just try to answer them as best you can until they pass. Don't allow them to prevent you from continuing your presentation. The audience will deeply respect it.

About the Presentation

There's no doubt that we have routines that we do when we're presenting. After all, it's always easier to do something we've always done rather than change it. Sometimes, though, these mistakes we're making can be debilitating to our presentation. We might not even know we're messing up at the moment! No one tells us - so we continue to make the same mistakes, all while being blissfully unaware. Don't worry if you find yourself making these common mistakes and just try to work them out as you go along. Once you know that they're present, you can then begin to rule them out.

Using Fillers

You might think that fillers are just information dumps, but it's actually based on the words you're using while presenting. So, what do I mean by fillers? Um, you know, I mean, it's really hard to say. Did you notice something about that sentence? Those are the fillers I'm referring to. They're the words we use as backups when we have nothing of note to say, or if we've forgotten a part of our presentation. Unfortunately, these words make the audience question how professional you are. Try to avoid these words when you feel them on the tip of your tongue. If you do feel them coming up, you can always add a pause between your sentences to fill the momentary space - just be sure you don't pause for too long!

Is That A Question?

Have you ever heard someone speak in a way that makes it sound as though everything their saying sounds like a question? Well, this is a natural thing that can happen when we're trying to get someone's attention. It's gone about all the wrong way, though. You need to have reflection after each question, and if everything you're saying sounds like one, it gives off the wrong impression to the audience. So, keep them to a minimum and use them only for impact.

The Funny Guy

Okay, humor is great. I love humor as much as the next person, as it can help entertain your audience. There's nothing like getting everyone in the room to laugh at once - it's an amazing feeling! It can also help if you're talking about a serious subject that can cause negativity in the room. It's a wonderful tool to utilize that sets everyone at ease.

So, what's wrong with a little humor? Nothing. This applies only if you're using too much humor. You must remember that public speaking is different than being a comedian. You're not up there to crack jokes constantly as though you're at a comedy club. This is about delivering a speech or a presentation that wows the audience. You'll want to keep your humor to lighten the mood, otherwise, your audience may not take you seriously and your presentation will be wholly misremembered.

Practice, Practice, Practice

You might notice that most public speakers don't mess up. I know that in the beginning, I never truly prepared. Where did that leave me? Adlibbing. No one adlibs unless they've walked into the room unprepared. To get the best results for your presentation, practice as much as you need to. Some people need to practice a dozen times, others even more. Once you practice enough that you feel comfortable, you're ready to step out on that stage. I will say, though, once you start to get better at public speaking, you'll feel the need to leave out the practicing. Don't do it! Always practice, or you might just find yourself speechless in front of a crowd that's hanging onto every word.

Timing Is Everything

So, you've practiced. Did you make a small mistake to not check something while you were practicing? I know I did at the beginning of my career. There's a trick to public speaking that is integral to your engagement - the time! Time yourself during every practice. You shouldn't be halfway through the allotted time and only have two more slides to go. You should be prepared and fill in the time (if you have any extra while practicing) with information that the audience should know, not just fillers that will leave them bored.

If you know that there will be audience participation, then leave some time for that. Give yourself about a third of your presentation to questions, should they be something the presentation needs. Otherwise, leave only a few minutes towards the end for audience participation and leave it at that. Then, once all the questions have been asked, use your closing line. You want to make sure that you don't walk off the stage as soon as the last person asks the question. Always have a closing line available to let everyone in the room know that you've finished. You don't want them wasting their time seeing if you'll come back.

Houston, We Have Technical Issues

We've all been there. One minute you're getting set up for your presentation, but when you turn to look at your slideshow, the projector isn't working and the screen is black. Technical difficulties are frustrating and make it awkward for starting a presentation. You can't always stop technical issues from showing up, as it might not be your fault – could be the venue, the internet connection, or even the lighting. Some things will be out of your hands. There are ways that you can avoid some of these issues, though.

If you've never presented at the location before, show up early so that you can set everything up. If you can't show up early, be sure to ask some questions about previous speakers and any technical issues they've encountered before. This way you can look up these issues and be well-versed in fixing them if you can. You can always practice with connecting your computer to different outputs and displays or bring a friend along who knows computers well.

As long as you take charge when these situations do happen, instead of standing there dumbfounded, you won't lose your appeal to the audience. Yes, it'll be frustrating. Yes, you can't always control it, but you can control how you react and what you do in the time that you're waiting for the situation to be fixed.

Liar, Liar

I understand that, if you have something that you desperately need to sell, you might become desperate. You don't want to do this transgression because, if you get figured out, you'll not only lose your audience, but you might lose a whole lot more. You never, ever want to lie about your facts. Always use proper sources.

Don't up the numbers of your sales and don't fabricate important details. These changes, which might seem minute to you, might be a big red flag to someone who really knows the subject at hand. It doesn't matter if you're standing in front of your class or a client, you need to have your facts straight. You should already know the information off the top of your head, and where you got the information. Wikipedia isn't always the resource you think it is.

Prepare yourself in case people do question your research or your numbers. Tell them exactly where they came from. This will be easy if you've prepared properly. So, don't lie. The only one you'll be lying to in the end is you, and it'll only make you feel uneasy when the presentation's finished.

Let Go of Mistakes

There will be times when you can't control what happens - whether it's a technological error (which happens more often than we'd like) or a missing slide during a presentation that you hadn't noticed. It's harsh to say, but there's a high chance that you'll make mistakes regardless of how careful you are. You need to anticipate them because they'll happen more often than not. It's all about constant improvement and learning from your mistakes.

No matter what, you'll grow from your mistakes, just as I did in my early career. To reach your goals you'll always need to plan ahead. The mistakes you make do not define who you are because mistakes are inevitable, and all you can do is prepare yourself for those mistakes the next time around. You'll have to be able to let that go and learn how to do better the next time.

They don't automatically make you any less of a great public speaker - even if it's the kind of mistake that you end up being upset afterward. If anything, they're an opportunity to grow and adapt to your work. So, don't make the mistake of believing that you're a failure just because you messed up. Brush it off, learn from it and take another step forward - that's the secret to growth and success.

Overcoming Fear - Profile - You

I want you to envision yourself standing in front of a crowd of hundreds. You walk out on stage, and the crowd applauds as you step out and stand in front of them. You smile at the audience. The light is blinding from where you're standing, and you can barely make out the faces of everyone in the audience. Despite this, you can tell that the theatre is full.

You can feel your heart racing in your chest but you accept it and bring the microphone to your mouth. You breathe out slowly before you introduce yourself. There are no mistakes and there are no fumbles. It's just you and the audience, and they're hanging onto every word.

This is your story and I know you can make it happen. I want you to visualize whatever it is you see yourself doing and practice it as you go. Write down your goals, celebrate your accomplishments, and revel in the fact that you're making a difference in not only your life but in the lives of others.

Now you just have to get to work.

FINAL WORDS

Public speaking is a life-changing career, as it teaches you discipline, confidence, and pride. It can be a platform to share your ideas and move others to act on what you believe to be important. When I tell people how my life changed once I began public speaking, many didn't believe me. It was through hard work and years of learning that I was able to show how my life has changed. There are days when even I look around in awe. I've been fortunate enough to have seen this same transformation in so many people - from CEOs to philanthropists.

I know that the concepts in this book will lead you down a path that, at this moment in time, might be difficult to fathom. You'll find yourself performing better at work with each meeting or that you're no longer scared to shake that man at the pub's hand. Maybe you're no longer nervous to give that toast at your best friend's wedding. Whatever the case may be, I know that you can overcome it so long as you follow the principles I've laid out for you.

Being a part of your breakthrough gives me the motivation to continue speaking and helping others. I can only hope that you'll grow to accomplish incredible things, and I'm so grateful to you for allowing me to play a part in that. I've only set up the ways you can do this but you'll have to set it in motion.

This is the part where you take the reins and get to work. I recommend re-reading whichever part speaks most to you, and use this book to your advantage as you excel in your own public speaking career. All it takes is one step and your journey has just begun.

REFERENCES

"7 Things You Need to Know About Fear." Psychology Today, Sussex Publishers, www.psychologytoday.com/us/blog/smashing-the-brainblocks/201511/7-things-you-need-know-about-fear.

"Acknowledging Your Fear and Finding Your Way Forward -." The Center for Transformational Presence, 12 Feb. 2019, www.transformationalpresence.org/alan-seale-blog/acknowledging-your-fear-and-finding-your-way-forward/

Beqiri, Gini. "Best Practices for Designing Presentation Slides." VirtualSpeech, VirtualSpeech, 20 Sept. 2018, www.virtualspeech.com/blog/designing-presentation-slides.

Boundless. "Boundless Communications." Lumen, www.courses.lumenlearning.com/boundless-communications/chapter/steps-of-preparing-a-speech/.

Chapter 5: Adapting to Your Audience, www.cengage.com/resource_uploads/static_resources/0534637272/16296/PSEA_Summary_c05_rc.htm.

"Chris Guillebeau." It's Not About Overcoming Your Fears; It's About Acknowledging and Moving On : The Art of Non-Conformity, www.chrisguillebeau.com/acknowledging-and-moving-on/

"Fear." Psychology Today, Sussex Publishers, www.psychologytoday.com/us/basics/fear.

"Fear of Public Speaking: How Can I Overcome It?" Mayo Clinic, Mayo Foundation for Medical Education and Research, 17 May 2017, www.mayoclinic.org/diseases-conditions/specific-phobias/expert-answers/fear-ofpublic-speaking/faq-20058416.

Fearn, Nicholas. "Best Presentation Software of 2020: Slides for Speeches and Talks." TechRadar, TechRadar Pro, www.techradar.com/best/best-presentation-software.

Grayson, Lee. "Setting the Tone of a Speech." Small Business - Chron.com, Chron.com, 21 Nov. 2017, www.smallbusiness.chron.com/setting-tone-speech-41439.html.

Hart, Bridgett. "4 Strategies to Overcome Fear Paralysis." Medium, Medium, 29 Oct. 2013, www.medium.com/@hartconnections/4-strategies-to-overcome-fear-paralysis-93effc462dd.

Hoque, Faisal. "7 Methods to Overcome Your Fear of Failure." Fast Company, Fast Company, 10 June 2015, www.fastcompany.com/3046944/7-methods-to-overcome-your-fear-of-failure.

How to use humor effectively in speeches. (2016). https://www.write-out-loud.com/how-to-use-humor-effectively.html

"How to Design a Presentation." Lucidpress, 10 Sept. 2018, www.lucidpress.com/pages/learn/how-to-design-presentations.

Humphrey, Judith. "You Are Probably Making One of These 7 Mistakes in Your Everyday Speech." Fast Company, Fast Company, 7 Mar. 2019, www.fastcompany.com/90314736/you-are-probably-making-one-of-these-7-mistakes-in-your-everyday-speech.

Layton, Julia. "How Fear Works." HowStuffWorks Science, HowStuffWorks, 26 July 2019, www.science.howstuffworks.com/life/inside-the-mind/emotions/fear7.htm.

Lott, Tim. "Children Used to Be Scared of the Dark – Now They Fear Failure." The Guardian, Guardian News and Media, 29 May 2015, www.theguardian.com/lifeandstyle/2015/may/29/children-used-to-be-scared-of-the-dark-now-they-fear-failure.

Morgan, Nick. "How to Become an Authentic Speaker." Harvard Business Review, 2 Jan. 2019, www.hbr.org/2008/11/how-to-become-an-authentic-speaker.

Nediger, Midori, and Midori. "Presentation Design Guide: How to Summarize Information for Presentations." Venngage, 12 Nov. 2019, www.venngage.com/blog/presentation-design/.

Palmer, Belinda. "Fear Paralysis Reflex, Anxiety, and Panic Attacks." Friends and Family Health Centers Blog, www.homewoodfriendsandfamily.com/blog/2019/10/15/fear-paralysis-reflex-anxiety-and-panic-attacks/.

Parashar, Avish. "How to Add Humor to Your Speech-without Being a Comedian." Ragan Communications, 10 Aug. 2018, www.ragan.com/how-to-add-humor-to-your-speech-without-being-a-comedian-2/.

Ronnie Higgins. "Fun Activities to Spice Up Your Next Workshop (9 Ideas): Eventbrite." Eventbrite US Blog, 2 Dec. 2019, www.eventbrite.com/blog/9-ideas-to-spice-up-your-workshop-or-training-and-engage-your-audience-ds00/.

Ropeik, David. "The Consequences of Fear." EMBO Reports, U.S. National Library of Medicine, Oct. 2004, www.ncbi.nlm.nih.gov/pmc/articles/PMC1299209/.

Saab, A. T. J. A. L. C. (2017, October 27). What Happens in the Brain When We Feel Fear. https://www.smithsonianmag.com/science-nature/what-happens-brain-feel-fear-180966992/

Schmitt, Jeff. "10 Keys to Writing A Speech." Forbes, Forbes Magazine, 5 Feb. 2016, www.forbes.com/sites/jeffschmitt/2013/07/16/10-keys-to-writing-a-speech/#60cad69d4fb7.

"Single Post." Commanding presence, www.commandingpresence.com/single-post/2019/06/10/4-Tips-for-a-Commanding-Presence

Smith, Jacquelyn. "12 Tips for Overcoming Your Fear of Change at Work." Forbes, Forbes Magazine, 17 Jan. 2014, www.forbes.com/sites/jacquelynsmith/2014/01/17/12-tips-for-overcoming-your-fear-of-change-at-work-2/#10ec8c102735

Smith, Jacquelyn. "13 Public Speaking Mistakes You Don't Want to Make." Business Insider, Business Insider, 4 Feb. 2016, www.businessinsider.com/avoid-these-public-speaking-mistakes-2016-2#-13.

"Transitions in a Speech or Presentation." Manner of Speaking, 12 May 2019, www.mannerofspeaking.org/2019/05/12/transitions-in-a-speech-or-presentation/

van Mulukom, V. (2018, December 10). How imagination can help people overcome fear and anxiety. http://theconversation.com/how-imagination-can-help-people-overcome-fear-and-anxiety-108209

"Westside Toastmasters Is Located in Los Angeles and Santa Monica, California." Inspire Your Audience - Chapter 3: Preparation: The Source of a Speaker's Power, www.westsidetoastmasters.com/resources/powerspeak/ch03.html.

SIMPLE

SMALL TALK

An Everyday Social Skills Guidebook for Introverts on How to Lose Fear and Talk to New People.

Including Hacks, Questions and Topics to Instantly Connect, Impress and Network.

Gerard Shaw

Table of Contents

INTRODUCTION

What comes after, "Hello?"

Let me guess how you feel about small talk: You hate it. If you're reading this book, and you're like me, small talk isn't your favorite thing. I'm a guy who struggled with it his whole life. The good news: we're not alone.

Some of the most successful celebrities struggle with small talk. Professional tennis player Naomi Osaka is one of them. Like her, you get anxious and avoid socialization. And that's fine.

It is okay to be awkward with small talk just like Naomi, but it is *not* okay to remain that way forever. Just like I have, you've got to overcome your fears. Think of small talk as a life skill with immense benefits you cannot afford to miss. This skill is essential in helping you build friendships and relationships. That's why I wrote this book.

Unlike books powered by gimmick and offering little to no practical advice, this book is useful. There are *no gimmicks*. The advice is *real*, it is *actionable*, and *you will improve* your speaking skills.

What's more: I think you'll enjoy the process.

Think about when you were younger; try to remember the things you did effortlessly. More often than not, you did those things for the love of them. If you set aside the burden of perfection and learn to enjoy small talk, you'll undoubtedly improve.

The truth is, small talk matters, and it is the first step to most of our social interactions. Small talk is the first step for a job interview, a romantic relationship, making meaningful connections, and having exceptional conversations. You can even generate more sales if that's your line of work.

The world is all about conversations! Humans are social creatures. We all desire connections and a sense of belonging; it has always been this way.

Yet, somehow, isolation and loneliness are prevalent in today's society. Part of the problem is that, as interconnected as we are, we've lost the art of small talk. If you can overcome the challenge of making small talk, you will enjoy the power of human connection in an interconnected world.

After you read this book, which is my hope. You *can* overcome this challenge, and you *will*. As a result, perhaps you can go after your dream job or finally muster up the courage to ask out that person that has captured your attention.

This book was designed to enable you to create more authentic and fulfilling friendships that are valuable to you. However, to enjoy all these benefits, you must be willing to put in the work. Be determined to read and execute the ideas in this book.

As difficult as it may seem to speak with total strangers, that's exactly what this book teaches you to do. It may be painful—but remember the adage: "no pain, no gain" and, of course, "practice makes perfect." Clichés aside, this is the truth. The path to mastering small talk takes a little bit of pain and a lot of practice. Don't worry. I'm here to make the process as painless as possible.

Are you shy? Or probably, Socially awkward? Forget that stuff and read on.

I can't stress it enough. This book is about *action*. You must take action to be better at small talk. There are no shortcuts. Gimmicks don't work.

Now then, what comes after, "Hello?"

This book bundle comes with a FREE booklet on masterminding a winning routine to improve calmness and your level of confidence daily. Head to the bottom of this book bundle for instructions on how you can secure your copy today.

CHAPTER ONE

What Is Small Talk?

We will begin our exploration with the foundation of the discourse: the definition of "small talk". We'll ground it in the simple question: What is small talk?

Small talk is light and informal conversation commonly used when talking to someone you don't know very well. Small talk is also a way to converse at networking and social events to create a connection with new people.

I want you to know everything that pertains to small talk when you are done reading this book, so let us leave nothing to assumption.

In this chapter, I will break down the idea of small talk to its most granular components. You will also take on a fascinating yet important talk exercise that requires you to identify the errors in a small sample talk and correct such mistakes.

So far, our definition of small talk is a bit too specific. It's actually broader than I've suggested. Small talk doesn't relate solely to face-to-face interactions because we live in a digital world. This conversation style also pertains to communication through digital means (online messaging apps and platforms) as well. For example, when you chat with someone for the first time on the WhatsApp platform, when you send a sales email, or when you hop on a live chat with a customer service representative, that's small talk.

Think about small talk as a bonding ritual and a strategy for managing interpersonal distance. With little discussion, people can maintain a positive demeanor around others while connecting with them in a warm approach.

Do you work? Do you own a business, or are you a manager? Even if you are a student, so long you are surrounded by people, you will need to develop small talk skills. How did you become friends with your current *best* friend? You probably met him/her somewhere, stared at each other for a while, and then one of you made a move with small talk.

Today you enjoy the company of your friend and other amazing people because, at some point, you or the other person reached out. But aside from social connections, small talk is an important work skill that is the first step to establishing a relationship with colleagues.

Small talk is a starter for friendly conversations, and there is a proper way to go about it. A significant reason why some people shy away from small talk is that they don't use the appropriate method. Now don't worry if you previously fumbled, you are learning anew, and you will become excellent at it, so continue reading.

One thing's for certain, many of your friendships would not have succeeded had your small talk gone awry. The enemy of small talk is the awkward silence that follows when something goes wrong, such as bringing up a controversial topic. In other words, we must extend our definition of small talk by telling you what does *not* constitute small talk.

To succeed at small talk, you must become familiar with what is expected of you to say and what isn't. I am not saying you will have to memorize the ideas. This is not an exam. Instead, you should become familiar with small talk etiquette, practice intentionally, and it will come naturally to you when you converse.

Small Talk Mistakes to Avoid

Let's look at some of the small talk mistakes you need to avoid when making conversation.

Asking Locational Questions Beyond Where the Conversation Is Taking Place

Remember that the small talk is probably happening at an event or someplace new. You just met this person, and you shouldn't be going beyond your boundaries by talking to them about another place. For example, if you pick up your child from school and run into another parent while making small talk, keep the locational aspects of the conversation to the school setting.

You might run into that parent again or meet him/her somewhere else; then, you can broaden the scope of the conversation. The idea of small talk is to establish friendship without the pressures of divulging extensive information.

If you are talking to someone else for the first time in the office, try to keep all conversations about locations to the office space. When you take this initiative, you will be able to avoid awkward pauses and remain in control of the talk.

Discussing How Much People Make at Work

Within the office setting, people are always curious about how much money their colleagues make. So, some people try to get information from others through small talks by asking indirectly.

Don't do it! At least, don’t do this in a culture, such as American culture, where this is not an acceptable norm. This information can be personal. Avoid it until the friendship is better established. Even if the subject of pay comes up, do not segue into a personal question about another’s salary.

Offering Unsolicited Advice

This mistake often happens after the person you speak to says something, and you provide some advice or suggestions without their asking.

For example, if the person compliments your look by saying you look fit and healthy, don't then suggest that the person registers at your gym because you feel he/she is obese. This example captures the essence of not offering unusual (and, in some cases, rude) suggestions.

If you do get a compliment during small talk, accept it gracefully and move on to the next idea. If the person requests your advice, then you can offer it, but, even then, it should be polite and straight to the point.

Continuing with a Line of Conversation When the Other Person Isn't Interested

We all have that friend who can talk on and on about a topic even when we are not involved. This trait also tends to affect the flow of small talk.

If the person you are conversing with isn't interested in the topic anymore, move on to a new topic, or end the conversation! So, how will you know when to stop a line of conversation?

You will know from the person's responses, if the person was enthusiastic when talking about the coffee served and loses that enthusiasm when the issue of office furniture crops up, then that's the sign that he/she doesn't want to talk about office furniture. Read the room. If suddenly a person cannot offer so much as a nod, and you meet awkward silence, it’s time to talk about something new.

Not Taking the Cue That the Conversation Is About to End

As you would discover in the small sample talk we will consider later, a significant mistake people make with small talk is not getting the cue that the other person wants the conversation to end. If a person’s too busy, for instance, or has somewhere they need to be, often they'll hint as much by tapping their foot, looking at the time, or edging toward the nearest doorway.

In a later chapter, we will discuss body language and non-verbal communication. Before we get there, you should know that when the person wants to end the conversation, he/she will give a cue, and you must finish the conversation at that point.

Giving Your Opinion About Controversial Topics Is Not Ideal

Giving your opinion on controversial topics can be a double-edged sword. If you and the person you're talking to happen to share similar views, controversial topics can be a fast-track to a friendship. However, if the coin lands on the other side and the person has opposing views, you might generate animosity or argument. It's best to avoid controversial topics, such as politics, if you don't know how the other person feels.

If someone else presses a controversial topic, find a way to carefully steer the conversation to a safer topic. This way, you don't give the wrong impression.

Giving or Asking About Private Information from a Person

Private information about your life or the person's life is not ideal for small talk. Especially if you're talking with them for the first time, do you think he/she will be enthusiastic about sharing private (sensitive) information with you?

Just as you are not advised to share such information, don't put the other person in a weird position by asking. We are talking about small conversations! It isn't an interrogation or a way to get secrets from a person, so remember the K.I.S.S principle here: ***Keep It Short & Simple.***

To emphasize all we have discussed thus far, here is an example below of small talk between two people in an office setting.

Please pay close attention to the *flow* of words and observe how they both communicate; we will discuss what was appropriate and inappropriate in the discussion using the example.

After identifying the mistakes together, I will then show you the better way through which this conversation would have played out.

Sample

Woman: Hi, there.

Man: Hi. I haven't seen you around here. Have you been working for an extended period?

Woman: No, I've been here a few months. I work in the Human Resources section.

Man: You must make more money than I do. I'm in Sales.

Woman: Sale is an exciting job.

Man: It's okay. Hey, you look like you could have a coffee.

Woman: Yes, it's been a hectic week.

Man: Tell me about it! At least it is supposed to be a lovely weekend.

Woman: Yes, I heard they are calling blue skies.

Man: Say, did you watch the game last night?

Woman: No, I was working late.

Man: It was a good game. We won.

Woman: I don't even know who was playing. I'm not a sports fan.

Man: The Chiefs! Do you think they will make it to the finals?

Woman: I'm not sure. I will get back to my desk now.

Man: Speaking of desks, what are your thoughts on the office furniture?

Woman: It's beautiful, but I would instead get paid for my overtime hours.

Man: I think I'll be heading home early. Just in case it snows.

Woman: I know. I can't believe the cold weather. Hopefully, it will be springtime soon.

Man: I can't wait for springtime.

Woman: Me neither! My divorce will finally come through!

Notice much of that conversation felt forced or uncomfortable. Did you find some of the mistakes we discussed earlier? If you didn't, you could reread the small sample talk to try and analyze it for such errors. We will do that together now as well:

- The man said, "You must make more money than I do then," which is wrong for small talk because we are not supposed to talk about what people make in the office.
- Another mistake was when the man asked about the Chiefs and finals. Here, he continued with the subject even when the woman was no longer interested.
- Did you observe when the man kept talking about the "desks?" he didn't take the cue that the woman wanted the conversation to end.
- The woman also committed a small talk blunder by mentioning, "Getting paid for overtime hours." She gave her opinion on a controversial subject, which is inappropriate.
- The woman mentioned her divorce. A divorce is private and sensitive information that shouldn't be shared during small talk.

We have identified the mistakes and analyzed the errors, well done! Now I want to show you the exact small talk scenario with this sample. This corrected version will help you appreciate the value of little talks when done right and how you can ace it every time.

Corrected Sample

Woman: Hi there.

Man: I haven't seen you around here before. Have you worked here long?

Woman: No, I've only been here for a few months. I work in the human resources department.

Man: Oh, that must be why I haven't seen you around. I'm in sales.

Woman: Sales sounds like an exciting job.

Man: It's okay. I could use coffee; it's been a hectic week.

Woman: Yes, it's been a hectic week for me, too.

Man: Tell me about it! At least it's supposed to be a lovely weekend.

Woman: Yes, I've heard that they are calling for blue skies.

Man: Say, did you watch the game last night?

Woman: No, I was working late.

Man: I think I'll be heading home early today. It might snow. I better get going. See you tomorrow!

Woman: See you![1]

This chapter is a foundational one that has introduced you to the basic idea of small talk. Everything we will learn or discover in subsequent chapters will be linked to this section, so keep all we've discussed in mind.

---

[1]*Excerpts from small sample talk was derived from English Club.com. Please see the reference list for a direct link.

There are challenges with the idea of small talk! Some of these challenges are caused by the personality and behavioral traits of the individual. In the next chapter, you will find two such issues and learn how to overcome them.

CHAPTER TWO

Overcoming Fear and Shyness

A lot of us are very afraid to make small talks, especially the introverts who worry too much and think it will be awkward, boring, or maybe they will run out of what to say when they initiate the conversation. However, with the evolution of the world and with the way the world is now based on mostly connections, avoiding small talk is like avoiding seeing people; it is very difficult, people are everywhere, and you will surely see them and make conversations. Networking events, parties, or having lunch at work will always provide opportunities to meet people and exchange pleasantries.

You will get to understand that making small talk isn't as painful as it seems. Once you learn to overcome the obstacles surrounding you making it, you will be able to polish your skills and make a better impression.

Fear and shyness make some people feel inadequate when making small talk. In this chapter, we are going to start practicing how to execute excellent small talk by first getting rid of specific challenges, such as fear and shyness. Here, you will discover the importance of confidence, how to turn anxiety into excitement, and how you can focus on the present. Get ready to divc into a bit of stoicism as you learn how to discover yourself.

Fear in a person when he/she converses with another person means confidence is absent. This realization should propel you to want to build self-confidence as a necessary skill for executing successful small talk. We will talk about confidence a lot because it is a deal-breaker, but why is it so crucial?

Why Is Confidence Important?

Your confidence level influences your thoughts, which means that it can either boost the success of your small talk or defeat it. If you are less confident about approaching someone for small talk, if you are afraid of doing it, you will end up being boring.

Understand that you are a worthy person with a lot of exciting things to say. Sometimes the root of a lack of confidence lies within a feeling of unworthiness. When we feel like we are not worthy, we tend to feel less confident, and that is where problems begin.

Always keep this in mind: other people in the office or other social functions are just looking for someone to chat with. As such, you must relieve yourself of pressure that compels you to try and "impress" them.

Confidence is knowing that you bring something to the table and sharing your thoughts most articulately. If the person you converse with feels like you are not comfortable or confident, the conversation can end abruptly.

So how can you build such confidence when you make small talk?

Be Interested

To be a confident and attractive person, you must be involved in the person you are talking to and the subjects you both cover. This idea is not only a good step towards building confidence, but it is also crucial in helping you make great small talk. In addition, by showing interest, you feed into the self-confidence of your conversational partner. You may ask, “How can I show interest?” Let your curious side out to play! Maybe you’ll learn something new.

Be Relatable

It is also crucial that you don’t monopolize the conversation, which means you need to attempt being relatable. The other person shouldn’t just feel led on in the conversation but feel like a part of it and that they can relate to what you’re saying.

If the person mentions that they like being fit, you can add that you agree on the role that exercise plays in good health (or something like that). Inject your observations, share relatable experiences, and be calm.

Ask Questions

You don't have to ask deep-rooted questions that will require a lot of thinking. Ask simple questions, "How was your week?" "Are you enjoying the event?" and then listen for the answer. Don't ask questions because you feel compelled to without paying attention to the response.

To keep the flow of conversation going, you can also ask follow-up questions, which shows that you are listening to the person. If the person says they are not enjoying the event, for example, you may give a little chuckle to lighten the mood and ask why.

Be Present

You will show a higher level of confidence while conversing when you are 100% present. A smile wouldn't hurt, uncross your arms, and avoid looking over your shoulder (it makes it seem like you are bored and you want to leave).

More importantly, when making small talk, keep your hands off your smartphone or mobile devices.

Use the Twenty Seconds Rule

Dr. Mark Goulston, a clinical psychiatrist and communications expert inspired the twenty seconds rule, and it is crucial for successful small talks. Dr. Goulston recommends that when speaking, the other person will only be interested in what you say during the first twenty seconds.

Beyond that, the other person starts to lose interest. In addition, the other might mistake you for self-absorbed. Practice the rule to mastery.

Turn Anxiety into Excitement

Think of anxiety and fear as two sides of the same coin. With that coin, you might be tempted to flip it or leave it up to chance. Let's try a different strategy, however. You choose which side is face up.

When you are anxious or excited, your heart beats faster; you experience rapid breathing, mild trembling, sweaty palms, and an unusual tensed feeling. You also feel nervous, unfocused, and sometimes sleeplessness.

There are similarities between the symptoms of anxiety and those of excitement, so why not turn one (which is negative) to the other (which is positive)? Whenever you feel anxious, have a pep talk with yourself and get excited, let this be your reflex action whenever you feel uneasy.

Yes, it is possible to train yourself to always turn anxiety into excitement, and it is easier than you think. Until now, the goal has been to remain calm, i.e. to suppress anxiety. Rather, it might serve better to take all that energy and turn it into something more productive.

How do you do that? I want this process to be as smooth and natural to you. That's why I created an easy step-by-step guide.

Step One: Embrace Your Emotions

Don't try to fight off the anxious spells you feel, if you are nervous, allow yourself to handle it. Yes, it will be uncomfortable, but you've got to endure it and become aware of the sensations you feel. How do you feel? Are you restless? Trembling? Sweating? Embrace all these emotions, and they will not overwhelm you.

Step Two: Stop Beating Yourself Up

Next, stop beating yourself. If you allow self-sabotaging thoughts to obstruct you, you will under-perform. You might have noticed in times of success, during a presentation, for example, you never exactly stopped being nervous. Instead, you stopped telling yourself "*I can't*," and you just *did.*

Step Three: Tell Yourself to Get Excited

At this stage, you need to reframe your emotions by telling yourself to get excited. Acknowledge the feeling of excitement and *not* anxiety (this is where you choose). If you do as much, convincing yourself that you're excited, then you will be.

Step Four: Visualize a Successful Small Talk

The role of visualization is crucial! Imagine yourself doing what you are about to do impressively. Always inject details of the conversation you can see, hear, and feel in your imagination.

Most of the time, you will get what you replay in your imagination. If you envision a failed conversation, then you will fail at it. If you envision a successful small talk, you will get that—if your expectations are reasonable, of course.

Focus on the Present

The present is fleeting, hence the expression "no time like the present", which is why you must make the most out of it. Confidence will make you seize the present and not try to envision what could happen in the future.

This sounds contrary to advice about visualization, and, in some sense, it is. You're visualizing something that may or may not happen in the future. However, the point of remaining present isn't to forget about the future—after all, your goal is successful small talk. Rather, the point is that, in the moments that count, you're no longer daydreaming. You're there. You're present.

That conversational moment is what counts, so stop anticipating what could go wrong. Stop thinking if you will stutter, say the wrong thing, or do something with a terrible future implication.

Destructive thoughts serve only one purpose, which is to disorientate you and cause self-doubt.

Let's enjoy a little imaginative/mindfulness exercise, shall we? At this moment, imagine that there is no future, and there is no past, only the present moment. Forget about the experiences you had in the past, school, home, childhood, university, etc. and focus on the now.

How do you feel? Do you feel constrained when you have no past worries? Do you still feel pressure when you have nothing to worry about in the future? Now relax and connect to the present moment, and only focus on yourself alone.

Tell me. What do you feel? The answers will vary, but one thing is for sure, you will definitely be your most authentic self. You would say whatever you want to say and do whatever you want to do; you will be free! There will be no future consequence nor past regrets, and you won't have to bother about making great first impressions either.

Now the exercise above represents an imaginative utopia, but I had to express it to you so you can imagine the extent of freedom you will enjoy when you focus on the present. People who are shy often overthink and worry about what people will say about them afterward.

You need to set all these worries aside and be free, confident, and assured in the fact that you will do well. Don't forget that you may not get another opportunity to have that "small talk" with the same person again. When you meet him/her in the future, it will be a continuation of the first talk, and it inevitably wouldn't be tagged small talk again.

So, I'm telling you to relax and take it all one step at a time. Focus on executing the small talk at the office before thinking about the wedding ceremony you need to attend next week.

Take it all in one at a time, and you will do great. (One great way to put the above exercise to use is by practicing mindfulness meditation).

Know Thyself

Yep, time for some philosophy. One way to know one's self is through a philosophy called Stoicism. First developed in ancient Greece c. 300 B.C.E., the well-known Roman emperor Marcus Aurelius' adoption of the principles likely contributes to the popularity stoicism enjoys even today and the shift from more theoretical to practical applications of the philosophy.

Modern Stoicism teaches that virtue is happiness and our judgment should be based on behavior instead of words. This idea teaches us that we can only rely on ourselves and not on external events. This means that, when relating to someone else through small talk, you must understand that you cannot control the other person's narrative, you can only control yours. Modern Stoicism is a tool we can use to be better individuals who excel at our jobs, relationships and even while communicating with strangers because we are aware of the power in knowing ourselves.

Stoicism encourages a meditative process that allows you to take negative feelings and turn them into thoughts that give you peace and a better perspective on life. This philosophical idea helps you develop a better mindset and enables you to look inward by asking yourself questions about life. So how do all these ideas translate into you knowing yourself?

Well, when you spend so much time looking inwards and getting answers to the situations you find you will be honest with yourself. You will get to know how you think, the aspects to work on, and how you can relate on a better level with others (especially through small talk).

To know yourself, you need to ascertain the kind of social environment where you thrive. Yes, it is crucial to be able to adapt to any social situation, but it is essential for you to know yourself and know where you are most comfortable.

Stoicism will help you become better at knowing yourself, and in that state, regardless of your character type (introverted or extroverted), you will see the kind of situations you enjoy. For example, when you start practicing your small talk, avoid using locations you are not comfortable in and stick to the ones that come naturally to you.

What do you know about yourself? Do you like intimate gatherings? Large parties? Are you a very extroverted person? These are questions I cannot answer for you, and there are the questions that will lead the way in helping find yourself.

If you loathe large gatherings, then you would have a more difficult time with small talk. On the other hand, if you love smaller crowds, you will probably talk to almost everyone in the room before the party ends.

You can see that the dynamics of small talk changes based on who you are and your preferences. An introverted person will want to practice more privately before getting on the scene.

Philosophy may be a tool to help, but, in reality, there is no universal manual for socializing. Remember, perfection is the enemy of the good, as Voltaire said. Do what works best for you and maintain your flow while getting better. What stoicism can do is help you become excited about what you do because you know yourself. You know what you can do and ready to take on any situation.

When you meet a person who isn't self-aware or confident, you'll see that their conversations do not reflect their complete personality because they are unsure of themselves. I don't want you to read this book and try to implement small talk while being unsure of yourself.

Practice stoicism, be mindful, and enjoy the process of getting to know yourself.

What Is in Keeping with Your Character?

The concept of rationality and irrationality varies from person to person, and this applies to the idea of good and evil. This realization expresses a significant reason why we need to learn how to adjust any preconceived notions we may have about these ideals.

We must understand that what might be useful to you might be viewed as bad to someone else. If you meet that "someone" who sees your good as evil, will you change it for them? Can you stay true to your character despite the differences in opinions that occur in the world?

To be successful at small talk while fighting off fear and anxiety, you must keep in touch with character. The world is very diverse, and it is easy for anyone to lose their identity, especially when they don't know their character.

While at a social event, it will be much easier for you to allow irrational fears, and your opinions get to you. You will feel like you are following an invisible script, patterns, and instructions because you are under pressure to conform and maintain a specific social skill code.

But the more you get to know who you are, the easier it will be for you to become your compass. You will value your convictions and thoughts, holding them in high regard because they are yours. You will be comfortable sharing your ideas because you know such thoughts belong to no one else.

Character is powerful!

Your character is a tool that enables you to internally seek out what you believe in and know your interests because these are the distinguishing factors that set you aside from others. Since small talks are all about making authentic connections, you will need to trust yourself, hence why you must also know yourself. Your words and actions should reflect who you are.

When you initiate discussions, do you feel like yourself? Or do you feel pressure to speak in a certain way that will be pleasing to the other person? Do you change your opinions easily because you want to conform to another person's idea?

Your experiences with small talk will be a whole lot easier when you stay true to who you are and your character. You will also avoid toxic relationships, the wrong people, poisonous jobs, fair-weathered friends (they drain so much energy), and other ills that affect people who do not know their character.

Please note that this realization with character doesn't mean you have to embark on a journey of self-discovery. I am merely imploring you to ask yourself questions that will inspire a sense of awareness within you.

All forms of conversations are linked to connections, but the purpose of connecting with others will be lost if you don't hold on to who you are now. The people you interact with will meet a "different you" all the time because you have an inconsistent character.

Do you remember when you went for your first date? You were probably giddy with excitement while anticipating meeting your date. The reason for the anticipation is because you couldn't wait to learn more about this person.

Just as you anticipated spending time with a total stranger, you need to spend time with yourself. When you spend time with yourself, you will be able to align your interests and get to know the true nature of your character. Knowing your personality will, in turn, sharpen your level of confidence, eliminate fear, and allow you to enjoy the process of connecting with others.

Fear and anxiety only cripple those who lose themselves to others, what can you do to fix this? Take yourself out on dates, know who you are focused on the present, and turn your anxiety to excitement.

This process of self-discovery, dispelling of fear, and mastery of confidence is an important part of small talk. We're making progress! In the next section, you will learn all about the social code and how it relates to making small talk.

CHAPTER THREE

Non-Verbal Communication and the Social Code

Anxiety and fear-free people, as discussed in Chapter 2, will have no difficulty with this section. Here, you will learn all about the concept of a social skills code, which is closely related to the four sides model, also known as the communication square or four ears model.

This chapter will help you avoid misunderstandings. The concepts in this chapter will show you how to speak coherently and succeed at all small talk.

Let's look at a communication model developed by German psychologist Friedemann Schulz von Thun, an expert on interpersonal and intrapersonal communication. Based on his model, every message has four essential parts that are not the same but must be individually considered. The four aspects of the message include factual information, appeal, relationship, and self-revelation.

So, what's important about it in terms of small talk? Simple. Learning more about the nature of communication will make you better at it. The better you are at communication, the fewer misunderstandings you'll have.

To understand the four-side model well enough, we must start with the two people involved and the message component:

1. Sender

The sender is the individual who delivers the message; this is the person that says something. So if you were conversing with someone else, the time you spoke, you would be the sender.

2. Receiver

The receiver receives the message; this person listens to the sender.

3. Message

The other component is the message. These are the actual contents of what each sender says: the words and the tone.

When you engage in small talk, all three components will be present, but whether or not you're able to avoid misunderstandings depends on your ability to process all three components at the same time. Many misunderstandings come from a receiver only paying attention to one component without considering the others.

The four sides of communication introduced earlier help you see everything during small talk. Let's analyze each level:

The Factual Information Level

The first level of communication in the four sides model is the factual level. As the name of the level suggests, it's about the exchanged facts during communication: objective data devoid of subjective inputs. For example, if I say, "the laptop is $599.99," that's matter-of-fact. It's simply data.

However, factual information isn't always communicated matter-of-factly. Sometimes the receiver infers fact. Much of the information that's misunderstood is implicit, remember. Take this sentence as an example: "It took me a long time to get here. The drive was difficult." This might be interpreted as "traffic is bad." Is it? Is that what was said? Not necessarily. Even at the factual level, misunderstandings can happen.

The Self-revealing or Self-disclosure Level

During communication, the self-revealing level is information about the sender that's implicitly revealed (or at least thought to be revealed). If, for instance, I say, "Why do you even like sour cream"? You might infer that I don't like sour cream because I've asked you with incredulity.

But it's important to keep in mind that this is an inference. It may or may not be true. It's distinct from the factual level of the four sides model because it's not a fact but rather a conjecture.

The Relationship Level

When analyzing small talk, sometimes you'll find information revealed about the relationship between the sender and the receiver (or yourself and another). When a sender talks to the receiver, something they say might send a cue to the receiver that the sender feels a specific way about them. In other words, at the relationship level, the receiver determines: "He/she thinks *this/that* about me."

This is yet another inference based on implicit rather than explicit information. If I say, "What are you doing here?" to a friend who showed up unexpected or uninvited to a party, they could interpret that as "He doesn't like me. We're not good friends." Again, that's not necessarily proven or disproven.

The Appeal Level

At the appeal level, the receiver is trying to determine: "What do they (the sender) want?". Here's an example. Your boss says, "If we had these reports earlier, we could have reacted more appropriately." You could interpret this as the boss saying: "Don't be late on reports."

Each of the levels above can be misinterpreted individually between the sender and receiver, the intent of the message can be different, the same with their meaning. When people understand things differently, they also tend to react/respond differently, as well.

Below is an example of how the four sides of this communication style work:

Two people meet at the buffet stand during a party, one of them is the caterer, and the other is a guest.

Sender: "This pasta has proteins."

The potential intention of the sender based on the four levels is as follows:

Factual level: There is protein in the pasta

Appeal level: Tell me what kind of protein!

Relationship level: You should know what kind of protein

Self-revealing level: I don't like proteins in my pasta.

Receiver's perception/perceived intent through analysis (remember that the receiver is the caterer here)

Factual level: There is protein in the pasta

Appeal level: I can't cook what you like because it is a party.

Relationship level: Are you questioning my cooking?

Self-revealing level: You don't know what the protein is that makes you feel uncomfortable.

This pasta example shows just how easy it is for misunderstanding to occur between the sender and receiver. There is always the massive potential for misunderstanding during small talk, hence, the reason you need to know how to relate in a way that all levels are in-sync for clarity.

The sender always has an intention that is hidden/implicit in the message. The purpose of the word is what he/she wants to convey. The receiver, on the other hand, analyzes the information heard by matching it against his/her beliefs, experiences, and values. So think of the process this way:

Sender: Intention = Truth

Receiver: Perception = Truth

Sender's Truth = Receiver's Truth

Please note that the receiver's truth may not be the sender's truth. This process happens so fast, and most of it is subconscious. Some people have a default channel through which they send and receive messages due to past experiences, their belief systems, etc.

To avoid misunderstanding, you must know how to use the four-side model effectively when making small talk. Again, the only way you can make this work is through intentional and persistent practice. How can you start practicing to get better?

Below I'll show you how best to manage a small talk situation from both sides (as sender and receiver). You can practice with both ideas until you get it right.

Begin with the first phase of communication: *thinking*. If you are the sender, please think about what you want to say and your intention for saying it. What information do you want to send? If you are a receiver, listen for the exact information your partner is communicating and how else you can understand the message.

Next, as a sender, you've got to ensure that your intentions are explicit and not vague. Ask what the receiver heard and what they make of the conversation before saying something new.

If you are the receiver, ask if you understood what was said, you could say something along the lines of: "Do you mean…?" or "To clarify, do you mean …"

This exercise can be done repeatedly for all four sides of communication, and then you will be excited at the fact that all your messages are received without any misunderstanding. Through practice, you can make progress with using this model.

Understanding is crucial for the success of small talks, and it begins with knowing a lot about the varying aspects of speech, as analyzed in this chapter. Now you know how the four-side model works and how you can appropriate it to your small talk experience.

Can we move on to another exciting idea? I'll assume you that's a resounding "yes!", so let's consider the role of non-verbal communication next. The details of the next chapter take some inspiration from this chapter as non-verbal communication is important when trying to understand others.

CHAPTER FOUR

Using Body Language in Small Talk

Non-verbal communication is as old as man, and it is just as important as verbal communication. But why doesn't it get as much attention as verbal communication? Most likely because we were raised to listen to words and not observe body movement.

This chapter focuses on non-verbal communication as a vital part of making small talk. You will learn how to utilize non-verbal cues and observe peoples' body movements for responses while communicating. Let's get right to it then!

Have you ever said something without "saying" it? Think about it before answering.

If your answer is affirmative, surely you agree that non-verbal communication can be a swifter way of sending a message. Pointing, hand gestures, head tilts, and all the like can help communicate messages, and can even help avoid the misunderstandings discussed in Chapter 3.

According to a study by Professor Mehrabian, communication is 7% verbal and 93% non-verbal. The non-verbal component constitutes body language at 55% and the tone of voice at 38%. This means you can say one thing with your words, but that your body language can send a completely different message.

So, the goal for everyone who wants to excel at making small talk should be to improve their understanding and use of non-verbal signals so they can fully express what they mean without contradiction. If you don't want misunderstandings and want to build stronger relationships, your verbal and non-verbal speech must use the same language.

Due to the nature of the small talk, you may not have the opportunity to correct a misunderstanding by saying, "Oh, this was what I meant". Remember! This is a small talk. It's short, sweet, and meant to build relationships. There's little room for error. You have only a few minutes to pass your message across in the best way possible.

If your non-verbal signs agree with your spoken words, this increases clarity, rapport, and trust between you and the other person. When they don't align, it leads to tension, confusion, and mistrust. You need to be very sensitive to these ideas to become a better communicator. More so, your sensitivity has to go beyond the spoken communication to the non-verbal one.

Let's take this instance as an example of the powerful way of nonverbal communication. Imagine your best friend or spouse arrived at your house right before dinner. Her lips were tight, face red, and eyebrows furrowed. She refused to speak to anyone. After pacing back and forth throughout the room, she threw her bag on the couch and plopped down in the chair beside the window. After a few seconds of her glaring out the window, you asked, “Are you OK? I hope all is well?” She yelled, “I’m fine.”

Now, let me ask, which of these messages are you going to believe. Is it her verbal communication, which says she is fine or the nonverbal cues which consist of her tone of voice and behavior? I believe you will most likely believe the nonverbal cues she gave.

Below we will learn what verbal clues entail, specifically about the types for small talk and how you can use body language to succeed with excellent communication. Please note that with some of the ideas you will find below there are cultural implications as well, so I offer some explanations on these implications. We must be respectful to others while communicating.

What Exactly Are Nonverbal Cues?

According to Patti Wood, an author and expert in body language, nonverbal cues constitute most of the communication between people without having a direct translation. These cues can be in the form of nuances of the voice, body movements, body orientation, facial expressions, choice, and the movement of the objects that contributes to communication, and details of the dress. Space and time can also be nonverbal cues.

To simply put, nonverbal cues are how you show, express, and present yourself, and not just the words that come out of your mouth. These nonverbal cues are very important in your business, and at work because "perception is reality".

In communication, our senses play a vital role as "all good conscience, credibility, and proof of truth can only come from the senses. How we are being perceived or 'sensed' by other people will greatly impact our success in our businesses or workplace. If this is not the case, a lot of people will be misjudged. People with great ideas, the brilliant ones, and people with exceptional talent will be mislabeled, misjudged, and ignored because of the ineffectiveness of nonverbal cues.

Since nonverbal cues are mostly sent from the "emotional brain" and not the neocortex (also known as isocortex and neopallium). The neocortex is involved in higher functions like generation of motor commands, sensory perception, conscious thought, and spatial reasoning in people. This emotional brain helps to create a more honest answer and revealing messages during conversations.

According to Wood, nonverbal cues enables business owners to determine the motivation of others and analyze business interactions in a depth, better, and richer way than just relying on printed or spoken words.

Wood suggested that people who can understand nonverbal cues can assess what their customers, co-workers, and clients are actually telling them, just to know how to satisfy their needs better. "Employers can evaluate the messages their employees are sending to customers, clients or fellow workers and know whether that employee is hurting or helping business," He says. Employees too can learn to understand those subtle signs that their bosses send; this will help them adjust their behavior when needed.

Effectively using nonverbal communication is vital in your career development. When an employer is looking for a talent to hire, or promoting an existing employee, the traits they normally look for include professionalism, enthusiasm, and confidence. As an employee, to express these and all other leadership traits they might be looking for requires you to send the right nonverbal cues.

Let's dive into the types of nonverbal cues that will help you with small talks.

Types of Non-verbal Cues for Small Talk

Since we can't avoid sending nonverbal cues to people, it is important to train yourself to send the right ones. Below, we will be looking at the types of nonverbal cues that are essential for small talks.

Facial Expression

Did you know that the most expressive part of your body is your face? Oh yes, it is, and it is the first observable feature the person you talk to notices even before you start talking.

You can say a lot with your face, even more than your words. Have you ever spoken to someone before, and they had frown lines across their forehead? It might have felt disrespectful even if the person didn't intend to be rude.

You can convey countless emotions without saying a word, and unlike other forms of non-verbal communication, facial expressions are universal. A person smiling in China and a person smiling in America is usually the same message despite the differences in location. Of course, there are different types of smiles: some sinister, some greeting, some mirthful, some questioning—but research supports that the lines that create these expressions in our faces are more or less the same in spite of culture.

Across all cultures, facial expressions are the same. We express happiness, surprise, fear, and disgust in almost the same way, which shows the impact of this non-verbal cue. While building your level of confidence, getting rid of fear also make sure you pay attention to your facial expressions. If you are saying something pleasant, what should you be doing? You should be smiling! If you are considering an idea, you should tilt your head like you are thinking about it. Small talk will go exceptionally well when your facial expressions are in agreement with your words.

Tone of Voice

With the sound of the voice, you should know that it isn't solely about what you say, but *how* you say it. When you speak, the other person gets your voice in addition to your words, and your voice can mean something different from your words.

The words, “sit down” and “sit down!” are the same words but the exclamation produces a different tone. An exclamation usually implies increase volume or increase enthusiasm.

The timing and pace also matter. Faster speech usually implies urgency (or perhaps anxiety) whereas slower speech usually communicates calmness. In such ways, your voice can express affection, confidence, sarcasm, and much more. The sound of your voice can be overlooked when discussing non-verbal communicative cues because people merge it with speaking, but it doesn’t entail words, so it is non-verbal. Learn how to fluctuate your tone of voice appropriately to achieve exciting small talk experiences.

Eye Contact

The way you look at someone communicates a lot about you to them, and it is one of the most crucial non-verbal communication. Your eyes can express affection, hostility, attraction, interests, tiredness, etc.

If you want to maintain the flow of small talk and enjoy the process, you must pay close attention to how you use eye contact. We will extensively discuss how to make good eye contact in the next section of this chapter: How to Use Body Language When Making Small Talk.

The way you carry yourself is a reflection of who you are and how you want people to relate to you. You also communicate with how you sit, walk, stand, or hold your head, which is why posture is crucial here. Your posture should reflect how you feel, and for a first impression, small talk, it should exude confidence.

Gestures

Gestures are a part of our daily experiences. You might have even gestured while reading this book (without knowing it). Gestures are done with the hands, and there are varying types: waving, beckoning, pointing, or using your hands while speaking or arguing.

When you raise your hands to your face level a little bit while speaking, it means you are trying to make a crucial point. When you run your hands through your hair while speaking, it could mean that you are nervous or unsure. If you point, then you are trying to make the person see what you are talking about.

You should know that gestures have varying meanings per culture. The "Ok" sign made with the hand, for example, conveys a message of positivity in most English-speaking countries. But in some countries, such as France, Venezuela, Turkey, and Brazil, it's offensive.

Of course, you wouldn't know all the offensive gestures based on all cultures, but you can take a cue from the person.

Touch

We also communicate a great deal through touch because human connections also happen through contact. If two people gave you a handshake, for example, with one being weak and one being firm, you would most likely remember the one who gave a firm handshake more than the other one with a weak handshake.

What about hugs? If you are allowed to give hugs at that first meeting, you can give a bear hug and make the person feel more comfortable around you (or perhaps more uncomfortable in cultures for whom personal space is of higher value). In some other cases, you will be required to provide a pat on the back or a mild grip on the arm.

Be mindful of how you use this non-verbal style because you don't want to be too touchy with the person. In some cultures, touch while making small talk may be inappropriate, and then sometimes the occasion might not be one where you need to be touchy. This is especially true of communication between people of the opposite sex.

With this non-verbal communicative style, you need to apply a lot of tact and caution. But if you sense that you can use touch, be generous but careful with it.

How to Use Body Language When Making Small Talk

While growing up, I was in a rush to make friends. After some trial and error, I realized that making friends, building lasting friendships, and connecting with people takes time. Before you connect with people, you need to get to know them. Now I kick myself after realizing that most of the time I'd been forcing connections by inviting myself to parties or having conversations people didn't really want to have with me.

Building lasting friendships doesn't take a day, it is a gradual process that often starts with a simple smile or hello. Some of the steps needed can be harder than others, but you should feel comfortable when you use your body language to attract people and make small talk with people! Let's look at how to use our body language when making small talk.

Don't Cross Your Arms or Legs

Crossing your arms or legs while speaking is not ideal for fruitful discussions. When you cross your arms, you appear defensive, and you also look uncomfortable, which might prompt the other person to end the conversation.

Instead of crossing your arms, use them to gesture. Instead of crossing legs, maintain an open stance that communicates welcomeness (unless you're wearing a skirt). The idea is mostly to remain relaxed and comfortable.

Make Eye Contact, But Don't Stare

The eyes are essential when talking about non-verbal communication because we can say a lot with them. What you shouldn't do, however, is to stare at the person, making eye contact isn't the same as staring.

Staring can be considered offensive by some people, so refrain from doing that. When saying something to the person or replying to a question, you can look him/her in the eye. But also move your eyes around the person's face and occasionally around the room.

Making eye contact shows your level of confidence, and it also informs the other person that you are present during the brief yet impactful conversation. Don't worry about executing all these cues flawlessly; remain aware, and you will do just fine!

Relax Your Shoulders

You may not know this, but your shoulders speak loudly, and you've got to keep them in check. A tensed shoulder is a non-verbal sign that you want to leave the room, and you are done talking. While a relaxed shoulder is a signal that you are ready to enjoy the conversation.

An excellent way to relax your shoulders is to take deep breaths before approaching the individual because one of the reasons for a stiff shoulder is anxiety. You may not even know that your joints are stiff, but the other person can see it, so be mindful of it. Here is a tip, you will know that your shoulders are tensed when you feel the tension on your collarbone and neck region, whenever you feel that pressure, know that your shoulders are tensed and loosen up.

Nod

How do you feel when talking to someone else, and they nod in acknowledgment? A nod tells the other that you're listening. It's an effective tool to show that you're present and remain respectful to your small talk partner.

Sit up Straight (Don't Slouch)

If you are discussing with someone and you both get to sit, don't slouch. Slouching is signals that you are tired, disinterested, or want to go home.

Sit up straight like the confident person that you are and share your thoughts most concisely. When you don't slouch, you also get to pay close attention to the other person and minimize distractions.

Lean In!

When we say "lean in," we are referring to your ability to tear down the walls that may affect the proper connection between you and the other person. When a person meets you for the first time, within the opening seconds, they try to figure you out.

Leaning in is a way to drop your guard and signal we're available and present.

Ensure that you are a good listener who understands the meaning of what you are hearing. Keep your eyes on the person (but don't stare) while nodding as you listen. But always be aware of personal space. Leaning in too much, as former president Lyndon B. Johnson was known for with his so-called Treatment, can also be intimidating and overbearing.

Smile and Laugh (When Appropriate)

There are moments during the conversation when you should smile and laugh, comply with this step as it would help you maintain a positive flow of communication. Small talk is what it is, so there is no need for you to be all stiff.

If you sense a stiffness with the other person, try to create some ease by smiling, say something a little funny that gives way for a laugh.

Mirror Body Language

The essence of mirroring in communication is to improve the rapport between both parties. What you do here is to imitate the person's physical mannerisms and positions to bond with them.

Sometimes we practice mirroring without being conscious of it. Yawn! If you suddenly felt like yawning just from seeing the word, that's unplanned mirroring.

When conversing with a person and they smile, you can mirror their body language by smiling back at them. By doing this, you are keeping the flow of the conversation and maintaining a great connection with them.

When two people mirror each other, it shows comfort and trust. Mirroring works most smoothly when you've known the person for a long time; for example, romantic couples can easily mirror each other. But with small talk, you are probably talking to this person for the first time. As such, you will have to pay closer attention to them. You must observe them and then reply with non-verbal communication through mirroring.

So, if the other person smiles, please take it as a cue from them and smile back. If they appear to relax and you feel tensed, mirror their calm by being rested as well. Mirrors are mostly a non-verbal idea and something you can achieve by being present during the conversation. For you to become great at mirroring, you need to practice a lot with all your interactions and pay attention to others.

But the bulk of the work doesn't rest solely on you as the other person will also mirror you. You can ensure that you portray whatever you want the other person to reflect. Do you want them relaxed and calm? Then smile more often while injecting little laughs here and there.

If they take your cue and mirror you, the talk will move smoothly.

Respect Personal Space

Lastly, please respect the other person's own space. We are all different, but we will all agree that we love it when people appreciate our space. If you don't respect people's areas, you will make a wrong first impression that will affect follow-up conversation.

As you speak with this individual, try to maintain a reasonable distance, and don't initiate personal touches if you are unsure of how the person will react. For example, don't give unwarranted hugs, high fives, or touch their bodies.

You've just met this person, and you don't know their orientation about such things. It will be better for you both if he/she initiates it, then you will be on the safer side.

How Non-Verbal Communication Can Go Wrong with Small Talk in an Office (or Anywhere Else).

Within the office space or anywhere you go to regularly, people form impressions of others based on non-verbal communication.

A person may be intentionally trying to be great at small talk with all the "right" words and fail at it because of a lack of excellent non-verbal communication. Now, people avoid speaking with the person because his/her non-verbal skills are sending the wrong message.

We will analyze three personalities with great intentions for successful small talk with others. However, they struggle in their attempt to connect with others, and they are not aware of the wrong non-verbal message they communicate.

Meet, Andrea, Meghan, and John!

Andrea

Andrea looks excellent, and she's a good conversationalist but is also very distracted. She claims to be great at speaking, but when talking with someone, her eyes dart all around the room, thus giving the impression that she isn't present.

The people that Andrea talks to feel ignored after the first few seconds of meeting her. They think she is self-absorbed, even though she feels like she is excellent at communicating.

Andrea needs to learn how to strike a balance between her impressive speaking ability and how she uses her eyes to communicate as well.

Meghan

Meghan is a beautiful lady who wants to connect with eligible men (in the office and other social events). But she always has a difficult time maintaining small talk even though she thinks she's funny and exciting.

Despite her constant laughs and smiles, Meghan's voice is raised, and her body is stiff. When great guys are around her, they feel anxious and uncomfortable, so they quickly cut the conversation short, leaving Meghan confused.

Even though Meghan has got jokes, her body language says something else, and this will consistently be a hindrance to everything she tries to achieve with small talk.

John

John believes that he gets along well with his colleagues, especially the new employees he has had small talks with. But if you ask some of these new employees and his other colleagues, they will all agree that he is "tense" which makes it challenging to enjoy chatting with him.

Some of his colleagues claim that he doesn't just look at a person, he stares for a long time, and with handshakes, he squeezes too hard (it hurts). John, on the other hand, believes that he is trying to show interest in people, hence the reason he makes eye contact for too long.

Despite his efforts, his non-verbal signals make him appear awkward and keep people at a distance. John will struggle with making progress with communication at work because he is not aware of this non-verbal challenge. He is a lesson in moderation.

The examples above show the willingness of the individuals to communicate effectively (they've got good intentions). But they struggle because they lack awareness of how best to utilize non-verbal signals. With the tips provided above, you can make the most out of every moment mixing great verbal and non-verbal communication skills.

Non-verbal communication is always a fascinating topic, especially within the confines of small talk. People speak all the time using non-verbal cues consciously or unconsciously, what matters is if you are paying attention to what they are saying.

You can also communicate with someone else through non-verbal communication, and this chapter has expressed all of that. We are adding more layers to our learning experience; it has been exciting, coming from the basic ideas in section one to where we are now. But we are not done yet as there are still so many ideas to uncover. In the next chapter, we'll finally discuss what comes after hello.

CHAPTER FIVE

After Hello, Breaking the Ice

Saying hello to someone in a social setting or the office seems easy. Think about it. Anyone can say hello and move on. However, the aim of small talk isn't just to move on afterward. You will need to lay the foundation for a follow-up conversation with the person. Now, this is where the challenge begins for a lot of people that struggle with small talk; they wonder, "What should I say after hello?"

This chapter will teach you how to hold an exciting and memorable conversation after saying hello. You will learn the essential qualities of the best conversation starters. You will also discover how to make a good first impression.

Generally, what comes after hello is referred to as a conversation starter, which entails the things you say to the person that kick-starts the small talk properly. As easy as it may sound, some people get stuck because quite frankly, the number of things that can be said is practically infinite. Still, the question is, which is most appropriate?

Remember that small talk aims to strike a connection another and not just to talk excessively on nothing in particular. You've got to speak in such a graceful and concise manner that you can pick up the conversation with the person again another time, and it will flow naturally.

But please note that the tips for conversation starters I'll provide are not exclusive. They're not the only things you can or should say. This book is training you, but more importantly, the best way to learn practically about small talk is by, well, talking. So, don't worry! While the ideas here aim to sharpen your skills, sometimes you have to go with the flow and say what comes to mind.

For you to achieve a profound connection after saying hello, you've got to know some of the qualities of good conversation starters. These qualities are a guide on the content of your conversation starter should be, but don't worry. I will elaborate on them with an example, so you know how to apply them to your peculiar small talk situation.

Four Qualities of the Best Conversation Starters

1. Great Starters Deliver Confidently

The best starters are the ones you deliver in a self-assured way, making it easier for the other person to join in on the conversation. Confidence is likened to a magnet when you exude it; others catch on and are attracted to it. Confidence is one of the best qualities you need to speak to others from the start.

For example, when you walk up to a person, become aware that he/she isn't only anticipating your speech, but also *how* you communicate holistically—body language and all. So, you've said hello (which is essential) the next thing you say should be uttered confidently.

Even if you are saying something funny, silly, or random, say it most confidently by making eye contact and adding some excitement to the start of the conversation. When you do this, the remaining part of the small talk will follow suit. But if your starters are with anxiety and fear, it will ruin the process.

Always remember this simple yet profound rule: Start confidently, and you will finish excellently!

2. Starters Are Personal

We feel drawn toward talking about the weather first or something impersonal, but, if you are going to relate to people, you've got to have a personal touch.

When you start with something personal, you will get to learn more about the person, and they will also be interested in finding out more about you. If you don't know their names, ask, and then if you are in a peculiar space (maybe in an office), get to see the person's position.

Being personal is a great starter that enables you to say the next best thing because it will be a follow-up question. So, if you ask for their designation and they say, "Oh, I work in sales", you can say something about sales afterward. Then the person will have an opportunity to ask you the same thing and just like that the conversation is underway.

Be careful, however, not to confuse *personal* with *private*. Sometimes we say, "that's personal" to something when we actually mean that it's private. You'll recall from earlier chapters that it's taboo to discuss private topics during small talk. That brings us to our next point.

3. Starters Are Not Too Personal

Yes, you can be personal, but please don't be *too* personal. We gave two instances of how you can be personal, yet they're not the sort of personal questions we'd associate with private information. Don't ask a person if they are married, divorced, or single as a small talk starter. Such questions will be too personal. Great conversation starters know how to draw the line between private and personal statements or questions.

Imagine talking to someone and they ask what place on your body makes you most insecure. How would you respond? Not a great way to start a conversation, and it might ruin any good first impression the person may be trying to establish.

You've got to be careful even with jokes as starters. When you meet the person again for a follow-up conversation, you can be a bit more forward (if they are) because you've laid the foundation, but as a starter avoid being too personal.

4. Great Starters Show Genuine Interest

Another quality of great starters is the fact that the parties show real interest in each other. For example, you can show interest in the person by asking questions about things you like and suspect they may like. If you don't care about something and you add it as a starter to the conversation, you will struggle with the communication.

You will also not know how to keep the conversation interesting because you are not interested in the topic. If you don't know anything about soccer and you don't like sports don't ask about it.

If you make this soccer idea a starter, and the other person knows quite a bit about soccer, the conversation will be one-sided. Your eagerness to make a swift change of topics might be off-putting to someone who's still excited to talk about soccer.

Stick to what you are interested in, and you will do well. If asked about something you don't know, think for a few seconds, and say you don't know. Then ask the other person to "enlighten" you. It is better to be honest than to give a false impression of knowledge. Then, when you're ready, you can steer the conversation toward a new topic without causing too much offense, as the person knows you're unfamiliar with it.

The guide above expresses the qualities of good conversation starters, which means that it will be ideal for your starters to embody such qualities. But the lesson doesn't end there; you also need to know how to start a conversation smoothly.

For that, we need to know how to transition after "hello".

Smooth Ways to Start a Conversation

Ask a General Question

You can begin by asking a straightforward question then listening carefully for a response. Afterward, make a statement that relates to the issue and build up the conversation from there.

However, try not to be brash with too many questions because the conversation must take a natural path. Here are examples of how you can start with a simple issue:

"What brings you to New York this month?"

"What are we celebrating today?"

"Where are you from?"

"How do you know the host?"

With each of these questions, the other person can give an answer that will lead to other talks. Use the examples above as a guide.

Observe the Surroundings

Next, if your initial questions didn't provide ideas for where to go next, you can observe the area and ask about objects or surroundings to transition to new topics. Such questions are open-ended, yet they require a bit of description. If you are at a house party, you can comment on the house, make an observation about the music, or something relating to the environment.

You should be authentic and spontaneous with observational statements, yet don't be critical or start badmouthing. The essence of this starter is to get the person's opinion and build the talk from there.

"What do you think about the pink butterfly décor?"

"Do you realize how perfect the centerpiece is?"

Cold Read Something

A cold read is an educated guess about the other person based on some details you may have observed. Think about this step like making an observation yet stating an assumption. Now the fun part about this starter is that you don't have to be correct.

If you are correct, the person will be amused, and if you are not, you will be corrected, but it will add some humor to the conversation. Cold reading also shows your fun side and helps the other person feel relaxed while conversing with you.

To cold read successfully, you need to pay close attention to the person. That way you will get some essential details that will help your cold reading:

"You are not from around here, are you?"—if you spotted something different about the person's accent or dressing.

"You are quite passionate about sports, aren't you?"—if the person gave good sports predictions.

"You've been friends with the host for a long time?"—if you observe a close relationship between the person and the host of the event.

Share an Anecdote

An anecdote, or a story, will help you strike a connection with the person on an emotional level. If the person says something a bit off, you can share a humorous story, and if it engages the person, you will be off to a good start.

Here is an example of a typical conversation with a tremendous anecdotal start:

You: "Wow, what a lovely fascinator. You've got an exceptional sense of style."

Stranger: "Oh, thanks! I purchased it recently in London while out shopping with friends."

You: "You were in London? I was there a few weeks ago at this fantastic fashion store; you wouldn't believe what happened to me.

Stranger: "Haha, yes, that reminds me of what happened two days ago…

You: "Wow! That's like what happened to me…

When you start with a simple story like the example above, the other person will surely open up, and you both will have a new chat. Stories are a great connector because we all can relate to the stories other people share, so use them generously in your small talks.

Give a Compliment

Yes, we all love compliments, and these are some of the best conversation starters as well. A tribute is an excellent way of making someone else feel comfortable around you.

But you must be mindful about giving compliments because they must be real and from a particular place.

You: "Hello."

Stranger: "Hi (smiling)."

You: "You've got a lovely smile."

Stranger: "Thank you, so what brings you here?"

Bring Up Shared Interests

If you are about to talk to someone else and you observe that they've got shared interests, you can use that as a great starter.

Say you're at the coffee shop, and someone is dumping creamer endlessly into their coffee. You happen to do the same thing. You can use that as an opportunity to start a conversation.

You: "You seem to like a whole lot of cream in your coffee (little chuckle). I like it a lot too."

Stranger: "Cheers to cream in coffee (little laugh)."

Ask for Their Opinion

Another excellent option for conversation starters is to simply ask another for advice. After the initial hello, you can ask them a question that makes it easier for them to contribute to the talk from the beginning. Say you're traveling on a plane; you can ask the person seated next to you for their advice.

You: "I often feel nervous before traveling; is there something I can do to relax?"

Stranger: "Oh, that's sad; you can take deep breaths and don't focus on the flying experience."

Express Some Vulnerability

Sometimes a great way to start a conversation or small talk is through an expression of vulnerability. By vulnerability, we are not saying you should be excessively vulnerable with personal issues. We simply mean taking it upon yourself to share something with another person.

By expressing some vulnerability, you will be showing the person a side of you that he/she will want to connect with. For example, if you are at a party celebrating a product launch, and you don't know anyone. Start with this:

You: "I don't know anyone here; it is sometimes difficult for me to talk to strangers."

Stranger: "Oh, don't worry, I know most of the people here. You will find it easier to connect with someone. I'm Amy, by the way. You?"

Use a Celebrity Angle

Has someone told you that you look like a famous person? How did you feel? Flattered? If you see a person across the room, who looks like a celebrity, you can walk across to him/her and use that observation as a starter.

This approach is excellent because it is genuine in a fun and humorous way. The person will love the compliment and lighten up. If you are speaking with a woman, she will probably blush, and then a great conversation will ensue.

You: "Has anyone told you that you look like Jennifer Aniston."

Stranger: "Oh wow (laughs). Yeah, I think so, but I don't see the resemblance."

You: "You've both got the same hair color. Are you from around here?"

Stranger: "No, I'm from up-state. What about you?"

I cannot overemphasize the importance of smiling as an excellent tool for small talk but, more importantly, as a starter. The other person will smile back, and without saying a word, you both will have a kind of agreement, a silent acknowledgment that you've seen one another. Whether you or the other person decides to strike up a conversation is up to discretion, but at the very least, you've been connected in that fleeting moment.

Smile at the start of the conversation and then while saying the first few words. Listen, something is electrifying about a smile that sets the tone for a great discussion, especially at the beginning. In addition to everything else you have learned thus far, remember to smile from the start. Are you smiling now? Come on. Don't smile. Are you? There we go. Keep it up. (Works every time.).

If you start with any of the ideas above, the other person will open up to you, and then the conversation can continue. The examples above are guidelines to help you generate your own ideas. Try to experiment because every situation will not be the same. After all, it is better to be a little bit awkward than to be stiff, trying to be perfect.

Making A Good First Impression

Even though small talk starts small and seems like an easy way of communication, always remember that it is an art you must master. Small talk can open doors. Who knows where it will lead in the future? As such, you've got to make it count by making a great first impression. How do you begin?

1. Start with a small gesture (this is a building block)

Small gestures are building blocks, and they give great first impressions. Such small gestures include:

- A greeting
- A smile
- A compliment

These are little things you will always be remembered for because they lead to other in-depth parts of the conversation. A smile will lead to a "Hello," and then a "How are you," which would turn into a chat. Just start with these gestures, and you can take it from there.

2. Avoid filters

Filters are words that cause you to be excessively critical, and this kills potential in any conversation. Avoid being judgmental and trying to force your opinions down another's throat even when you know you are right.

If you tend to overthink things, please set that trait aside because this is small talk and not a philosophical conversation. Your words should be spot on, insightful, meaningful, funny, and relaxed.

Here is an example of a conversation between you and a lady who is a guest at a wedding ceremony. The talk will show how filters are used (which is wrong).

You: "Why are you wearing a white dress for the wedding?"

Woman: "Oh, white is my favorite color, and I love this dress."

You: "But this is not your wedding. Don't you think you are stealing the attention from the bride?"

Come on; if you were the lady, you would feel offended and not want to talk to the person again, right? But this wouldn't be you; I am optimistic that you will do much better!

3. You don't have to be brilliant, just kind.

People don't expect every word out of your mouth to be a revelation. To be perfectly honest, it would probably bother people.

All you really need to build connections is kindness. People feel comfortable when talking to others who are nice.

Ask questions, show some interest in the other person, be friendly, exciting, and try to focus more on the other person. Don't worry about "serious" topics or complete originality. Be nice, and you will make a great first impression.

4. What should you say?

To make an excellent first impression, you need to think about what you will say. This thought process should happen before speaking to the person, as it will give you substance for the conversation.

You can also achieve a good first impression using this tip by creating a conversation pathway. This pathway will help you quickly move from one point to another.

But first, you need to know what you are going to say, I advise that you plan your words around concepts like:

- How the person is connected to the event
- Holidays
- Mutual acquaintances

The examples above are just a few ways you can plan your starters, and then you will build from there.

5. Build the conversation.

Making a good first impression also relates to how you create a conversation. Conversations evolve quickly as you and the other party can move from one topic to another.

When you know how to build the conversation from start to finish, you will be able to connect with the person in such a way that he/she will want to discuss it with you again in the future.

Here is an example of how you can build a conversation:

You: "So do you have anything planned for the weekend?"

Stranger: "Yes, I intend trying out the new pasta menu at the Italian restaurant down the street?"

You: "Great, I hear they've got great pasta, and it reminds me of a vacation I took to Italy last year, beautiful county!"

Stranger: "Wow, you've been to Italy. Now you are giving me vacation ideas."

You: "Oh, Italy is great. You will love the picturesque view and the food. Have you had authentic Italian food before?"

You can see that from asking about weekend plans, you both progressed into talks about food, countries, vacations, and views. This is how you build a conversation. When you create a conversation, and it naturally flows, both of you will feel at ease.

6. Exit gracefully

The way you end the talk can also affect the kind of impression you give to the other person. Most of the time, we focus exclusively on what to say and forget how to end.

The most complicated part of making small talk with someone unfamiliar is winding down the conversation. Sometimes, finding a reason to leave can be helpful, but you've got to think about it before saying it.

When you are about to end, you can use any of the examples below or use them as inspiration for stopping gracefully.

- "There's someone close standing by the entrance I need to talk to; hopefully, we will speak again soon."
- "It's been a pleasure talking to you; I have to go grab a drink now."
- "I need to make a call now, but nice chatting with you. Please excuse me."

What do people like best when they meet someone for the first time? They like it when the other person shows interest in them. Making a good first impression is a way of building relationships with others, but it all comes down to how you make them feel.

First impressions are not about words; they are mostly about connections. People will forget what you said, but they will always remember how you made them feel. All big things start with small things, like a little talk, so make the most out of it with a memorable first impression.

Conversation starters are great because they are like the bridges that connect the first "hello" to the remaining part of the conversation. The only reason you wouldn't stop at hello is that there are conversation starters, and when you are used to such starters, you won't struggle with what to say or how to say it.

In the next chapter, you will find a guide to small talk topics and what you should discuss.

CHAPTER SIX

Guide to Small Talk Topics and What to Talk About

What am I going to discuss?

Knowing the start of a conversation is not enough (I wish it were, but it isn't). If a person is great at small talk starters but doesn't know the topics to cover while speaking, he/she will have issues.

You can start a conversation confidently now (we did this in chapter 5), but we are going to learn the kind of small talk topics that are appropriate and inappropriate.

First, we will begin with safe topics and topics to avoid.

Safe Topics

The Weather

Talking about the weather may seem too predictable, but it is a fascinating topic for small talk because it is neutral and universal. Anyone can talk about the weather, and everyone has an opinion about it as well.

You can talk about the day, season, or temperature. You can also practice your small talk using weather topics. Weather topics are great in helping you get out of awkward silences as well.

Hobbies

We all have hobbies, those things we like to do, and we want to share them with others. You can introduce hobbies right after learning the person's name, and knowing what they do as this topic can add a bit of friendliness to the conversation.

Listen to the person as he/she talks about their hobbies, and if you've got questions, ask so you are clear on the idea as well.

Work

Work is a popular small talk topic that goes both ways between the sender and receiver. Getting to know what the other person does will help you understand how to make progress with the conversation.

Focus on what you want to learn about the other person's work. Work (regardless of what it is) is a crucial part of life so that it will be a fantastic topic for small talk.

Sports

Some sports topics may include favorite teams, sporting events, tournaments, bowl games, etc. Stay updated on sporting games such as soccer, football, hockey, golf, etc., if those interest you, and you'll have a consistent topic for small talk. When it's World Cup season, everyone talks about it, so keep an ear out for information.

You will find sports prominently featured in other sections of this chapter because it is a universal topic for small talk. Always focus on games you love for the smooth flow of conversation.

Family

You can also ask about family, using such conversation starters as:

"Do you have brothers?"

"How are the kids?"

Always be open about family questions and answers because engaging in this type of talk shows the depth of your communicative skills, and it helps you learn about the other person.

Hometown

You might want to ask the person about his/her hometown, and you may be requested as well. You might be from the same place as the person or know something about his/her hometown. Show interest in such topics because people will want to share such information with you.

News

The news typically concerns us all in one way or another, and by being aware of the story, you should be able to maintain basic conversations. Small talk is about building a bridge between you and the other person, so the content of the discussion will determine the strength of the bridge.

In this digital stage, you don't have to rely on newspapers, as even on social media, you have access to the news to stay updated. One note, however: Be careful not to put a political spin on news topics. Keep your political opinions separate, if you can help it.

Travel

Some people like to hear and discuss vacations, so if you travel a lot, that will be an advantage for you. Ask them about the places they have visited and recommend travel destinations as well.

When you share experiences such as this, you will connect with the other person and build an excellent opportunity for a follow-up.

Arts and Entertainment

Yes, arts and entertainment topics are great for small talk! Movies, television shows, books, popular music, restaurants, etc., all make for good conversation.

This may not necessarily be the best conversation starter, but it is almost always a safe topic.

Celebrity Gossip

There are a lot of celebrities, so you don't need to know the latest with them all. However, it does help to have familiarity with the lives of some famous people.

This type of talk is appropriate for informal gatherings, casual parties, and other occasions that are not so serious. However, *do not* lead with this topic; if someone else brings it up, then go with the flow.

Topics to Avoid

Some questions are off-limits when it comes to small talk because such issues are offensive, inappropriate, or just not right. We will analyze some of these topics below in a bid to help you entirely avoid them while discussing it with someone else.

Finances

Asking the other person about how much they earn and money issues are inappropriate. It is okay to ask what a person does for a living and other positive aspect of their career, but don't ask them questions relating to their salary or bonuses.

Age/Appearance

Regardless of how a person looks, don't refer to their age or appearance. You can only do this when you know them well enough, and although age/appearance related topics may seem simple, they are also taboo topics. Don't ask the person, "How old are you?", or, "Are you pregnant?". Don't comment on the person's weight gain or loss. You can keep such observations to yourself and maintain positivity throughout the conversation.

Sex

Don't talk about sex, and don't ask questions about intimacy. Let's get real. Especially if you're talking to a stranger, you'll come off as a creep. Avoid talking openly about sexual preferences and don't make sexual references and allusions. All of these will make the other person uncomfortable and ruin the small talk.

Personal Gossip

Celebrity gossip is fair (come on, we all love a bit of Hollywood drama), but gossiping about those you know personally is off-limits. Don't gossip about others because when you do, it paints you in a bad light, and the person you are talking to may know the subject of your gossip.

Be a good person. Don't badmouth others. If you must talk about someone else within the conversation, then it should be done in good faith with positivity and kindness.

Politics

Politics poses a lot of threat to the success of small talk because you never can tell if the person you are speaking to has extreme political views. Unless you want to risk ending up in the middle of a heated and unpleasant conversation, please refrain from politics while making small talk.

Past Relationships

Past relationships could be a grey area for some people, especially if it didn't end on mutual terms. Asking people about their past relationships is being intrusive, and it can miff a lot of people.

Religion

Some topics are personal and potentially sensitive; as such, you must avoid mentioning them during a small conversation.

Regardless of religious preference, you've got to understand that people have their own, and you cannot impose your ideas on them.

Always remember K.I.S.S. (Keep it short and simple).

Death

Another severe topic you must avoid is death. During small talk, please don't bring up anything related to death because the topic is typically too heavy to weigh in front of strangers.

Some topics can be very upsetting such that the person(s) you talk to might not want to have a follow-up conversation afterward. But what if you're at a funeral?

Well, you can talk about the life of the person who passed on and try to be optimistic by being available for the person who is grieving. But don't talk about death because they are trying to get over it.

Offensive Jokes

They're called offensive jokes for a reason. You'll never know who will find the jokes offensive, even if you're clearly joking and mean no harm.

Jokes that include sexist remarks, racist comments, or stereotypes should be kept under lock and key around strangers. Yes, they may be funny to you, but that doesn't mean they won't be hurtful to others.

Topic for Friends

Yes, friends are great, and you can talk to them whenever you want, but should you find yourself without a topic, here are some ideas.

Truth or Dare Questions

Truth or dare questions are also fun questions to ask friends, especially at a party or a fun event. You can enjoy entertaining banter that goes back and forth with truth or dare questions.

Some examples:

"What was your nickname in school?"

"Did you ever not make it to the bathroom in time?"

"What's the worst thing you've ever done?"

Try not to use these questions as starters also because ideally, they should come in when the talk is at its peak, and you and your friend are very comfortable with each other.

Deep Questions

Although you are talking to friends, there can also be room for some deep questions that relate to serious issues. These are the questions you ask to get an in-depth idea of how your friend is doing, especially in challenging times.

Here are a few examples:

"How are your parents?"

"What do you struggle with the most?"

"What do you think about an added degree?"

Please note that some of these questions are not great small talk starters but can be injected into the conversation while it is ongoing. Ensure that the questions asked are at the right time and that they are appropriate for the occasion.

Would you Rather Questions

Some would-you-rather questions are humorous and witty. Such issues can also be a part of other conversations as a way of lighting up the mood. Some examples include:

"Would you prefer calls or text?"

"Would you dance uncontrollably or sing at random times of the day?"

"Would you rather get rich or marry happily?"

These questions can add a lot of fun to any conversation with your friends.

Fun Questions

Who doesn't like a fun conversation? We all do! Fun questions make us laugh, giggle, and feel relaxed while exchanging information. There are specific kinds of issues that can trigger a lot of fun.

Some examples include:

"What is the funniest memory you have from camp?"

"If you were the leader of a music group, what would be your band's name?"

Casual Questions

Causal questions are regular ones that people ask without the pressure to think about an answer, but they are also great for small talk between friends. Casual questions include everything from movies to the days of the week.

Examples are:

"What is your favorite color?"

"Have you seen any good movies lately?"

"What activities do you do in your spare time?"

"Do you watch America's Got Talent? Who's your favorite contestant or judge?"

The questions above are strategic in helping two friends engage in small talk that will lead to them also getting to know themselves better. As your friend opens up to you also share your thoughts as well.

Workplace Topics

Small talk in the office or workplace seems like the easiest thing to do, right? Yet it can be challenging for some people who feel side-lined when their co-workers are discussing specific topics.

Maybe everyone is talking about football, a TV show, or an upcoming event, and you feel lost. Here is some cheerful news: You are not alone! You can change that situation at the office with the tips below and establish common ground with your colleagues.

Even if everyone is talking about something you are not familiar with or something you don't like, you can turn the tide of the small talk around to suit you. All you have to do is take charge by asking the kind of questions that suit your conversational style.

But first, you need to know some of the areas to cover, and that is what you will find below:

Please note that the tips below are questions that will help you get started on the conversation.

Pop Culture

Everyone loves pop culture! An excellent way to talk about pop culture is through the movie scene, which can help strike a conversation fast. Even if you haven't seen the Netflix series The Crown, you can nod along politely when the other person talks about or bring up a series you've watched or one you love.

Try any of these:

"I just got my Netflix subscription. What movie would you recommend I add to my list?"

"I need to binge-watch a new show. Got any recommendations?"

"I'm seeking new music to add to my Apple Playlist. What are you listening to currently?"

What do you have in Common?

Regardless of what you do within the office, you will surely have one or two things in common with someone else. You probably eat with your colleagues, commute with them, and do other things together, so there are easy ways to start small talk with this idea.

Try any of these tips:

"What is your favorite place to lunch around here?"

"I see you prefer the printer in the storage area to the one out front; I do too."

"Do you know how I can avoid walking through the construction mess on the main street?"

Office Life

Office life is something you and your colleagues have in common. This kind of topic resonates with everyone.

Try these tips:

"What's up with the smell coming from the photocopier?"

"How awesome is the new games room?"

"Please tell me I'm not the only one who has gotten stuck on the fourth elevator and almost experienced a panic attack?"

"Do you always find good parking downstairs?"

Talk About Yourself

An excellent way to engage in small talk at the office is to be yourself. Be real by talking about some of the funny yet honest issues you have that others may experience but don't want to discuss. Stop trying to be "cool". We all want you to be real so people can relate to you quickly.

These are helpful tips:

"Is anyone as obsessed with the lemon cake we get for lunch as I am?"

"I love Fridays; I tend to count down to it from Monday. I can't be the only one who does this."

Travel

Most colleagues at the office will surely want to talk about vacations (past trips and future aspirations). Vacation topics are great for small talk at the workplace.

If you have traveled a lot, don't try to rub it in with your colleagues; be modest yet excited about sharing your experiences. Show enthusiasm when they also share their experiences and try these tips:

"Where is the last place you traveled?"

"What's the next trip you have planned for summer?" "If you could take a sabbatical, where would you go, or what would you do?"

Small Talk for Business/Sales

Small talk is a vital aspect of sales, and when you add some creativity to it, you can boost your numbers. If you are in sales, or if you are an entrepreneur, you will agree that some customers are emotional buyers.

These emotional buyers understand the importance of your product to their lives but still require some connection with the seller before making a purchase. Such customers are never tired of reassurances, and when are such reassurances given? During small talk!

Small talk helps you establish a connection with clients and prospects, which in turn buys the time you need for the candidate to decide after listening to your sales pitch. The challenge with small talk for sales is knowing how to use it effectively and how to build momentum with it. You've got to know how to satisfy the prospects through a question-answer approach.

So how can you make this happen?

1. Be brief and substantive.

In the world of business, time is an essential factor, and if you want to get peoples' attention, you must show that you respect their time (even with small talk). Prospects don't care about your lengthy commentaries on how great your business model or product is, so stick to substance over long conversations.

Everything you say should be brief with specific and insightful information that will keep the attention of the prospect on you. If you do this well enough, you will have another opportunity to have an extended follow-up conversation.

2. Ask questions about the prospect's business.

By asking questions about the prospect's market space, you will be allowing him/her to lead the conversation (don't worry, you will get the right time to make your sales pitch).

When you ask about the prospect's business, it gives you an advantage because the person will feel much more comfortable with you. This step and others will provide you with an early lead for high sales.

3. Go from general to specific.

After asking about the prospect's business, you should move on from a general idea to a specific one. By "specific," I am saying you should strike a *subtle* connection between what you are offering and what the prospect will need in business.

Here is an example of a company you work for or work with that sells kitchen equipment, and you are the sales manager of the company. Your team has to sell to restaurants and families.

While making small talk with the manager of McDonald's, for example, with this step, you can draw a specific connection between the new grill set you are marketing and how it can help them at McDonald's achieve a perfect beef grill.

The general idea is "kitchen equipment," and the specific item is "grill set." I am saying that you should move from the general to the particular, as this will boost sales and help you achieve excellent small talk.

4. Ask for the prospect's views

Next, you should ask the prospect for his/her opinions on the line of business and the industry. The reason you should take this step with small talk for sales is that it will give you an insight into the possibility of closing the deal.

Discover how the prospect feels about the new product. Is the product going to solve his/her problems? When you ask this type of question, you will be getting the prospect's honest opinions, which will also contribute to your sales data.

5. Present your preposition

When your potential client is relaxed, you can shift the pathway of the conversation and move ahead into your sales presentation. Now at this point, the prospect already has an idea of what you want to say.

But you must take the initiative by presenting useful information and by showing respect for his time by being straightforward. You will find that it will be easier for you to complete the sale on a positive note using this approach.

Small Talk Questions (Bonus Section)

In this section, you will find some random short talk questions that are a valuable addition to everything else you've gained thus far. These questions incorporate varying topics.

1. What's the best career advice you've received?
2. What's your favorite restaurant?
3. Have you been to Africa before?
4. Who is your favorite person on Instagram?
5. What's your go-to comfort food?
6. If you could fly anywhere, where would you go?
7. Do you have any podcasts suggestions while we commute?
8. Are you reading a book right now?
9. If you could watch a movie repeatedly, what would it be?

Now, these are questions that are not starters but build-ups for the conversation itself. You can always change the words to reflect the particular situation you will be in, but the point is that these questions will help you practice and what do they say about the practice? It makes perfect. Knowing the current topics and those that are off-limits are probably the most crucial aspect of small talks. This realization is because a more significant part of the conversation will be on the topics you and the other person discuss.

Just as we learned what to focus on, we also unearthed what to avoid for a balanced perspective. You have done well thus far, and you must keep up with your momentum because there are still so many parts of this discourse to unravel. The next chapter is a guide on how to keep the conversation going; this should be easy because you know the topics to focus on and what to avoid, so let's get to it.

CHAPTER SEVEN

Keeping the Conversation Going

Some people will agree that starting a small talk is quite easy, especially if a person has been practicing, but how do you ensure that the conversation keeps going? How do you keep up with the other person? How can you tell what the other person will say that changes the conversation?

Well, these questions are crucial, and you will find answers to them in this chapter. Here, we will learn how not to run out of things to say (so you can maintain the flow of the conversation). You will also find the meaning of the FORD and ARE methods, respectively.

The point of all of this: avoiding awkward silences. We will begin with ideas on how not to run out of things to say.

How to Not Run Out of Ideas While Conversing

We've all had those moments during conversations when our minds go blank right in the middle of the talk. You frantically search your brain for something to say, anything, and the harder you try, the more difficult it becomes.

Awkward silence creeps in, and then you start to overthink:

"Am I incompetent at small talk?"

"What will this person think about me?"

"What's wrong with me?"

If this has happened to you in the past, you will agree that it sucks! But don't worry, now we are going to handle it (just as we have been doing thus far). You ran out of what to say because you haven't practiced well enough, and you probably got distracted while the other person was still speaking.

Practice and presence are two crucial things you must remember while building a conversation. When you are present, you will be able to utilize the ideas on how you can never run out of what to say that I am about to share with you now.

Below, you will find three major social strategies that will be very helpful.

First strategy

The first strategy is the "quick scan" approach, which serves to help you stay ahead with news and information. Every day before you head out, scan social media, online newspapers, and other exciting platforms for recent information.

The reason you are making this effort is so you can use the headlines or topics (the ones that are not sensitive or radical) as conversation starters. With this method, you have a safety net that allows you to introduce something fresh and new to the conversation.

For example, at the office you can start with:

You: "So I saw this post by Serena Williams on Instagram just before I left the house."

Stranger: "Really? What was it about?"

You: "She just launched her clothing line."

Stranger: "Wow, I've always loved Serena. Can't wait to view the collection."

With the example above, it is evident that the other person loves fashion. This method works best with people in the office or some other person that you may have an idea of what they like (sports, fashion, etc.).

Second strategy

The second strategy is the “spokes” method, which enables you to connect with anyone on varying topics. The word "spokes" for this method comes from the spokes on a bicycle tire. The spokes say that even when you don't know much about the topic of the discussion, you can roll with it. You know, like the spokes.

The small talk is the center, the spokes (topics) radiate from the center. The spokes may be different, but the conversation has to keep going, and you can introduce an issue you like if you are not familiar with the current one.

Don't stonewall the other person if they talk about hiking, for example, and you don't know anything about hiking. You don't have to continue with the hiking topic; instead, think around the issue and mention something similar to hiking that you are familiar with.

You can also play the beginner role by asking questions about hiking, as the person fills you in on the information, you will be able to flow. Overall, the spokes method teaches you that you can strike a conversation with anyone about anything.

Here is an example:

Stranger: “So have you gone hiking lately?”

You: “Wow, do people go hiking in this weather?”

Stranger: “Yes, they do.”

You: “Oh nice. I prefer mountain bike races. Have you gone on one before?”

Stranger: “Yes, I have, and I enjoyed it.”

The reason the spokes method works is because it is a win-win for everyone; you get to engage in great conversation without silences and awkward pauses.

However, you must always resist the urge to self-edit what you say, especially after you’ve said it. Let the conversation take its natural course, as it doesn’t have to be perfect; it just needs to be good enough.

Third strategy

The third strategy is known as the "quick win" strategy, which teaches you not to overthink things while making small talk and that you shouldn't hesitate when responding to the other person. Hesitation will cause you to overthink, and then you will give responses such as "I can't say that" or "I don't have an answer for that." Likewise, it might lead to missed opportunities, as hesitation allows the other to dominate the discussion. As it moves forward, what you had in mind will likely become less and less relevant.

When you stop overthinking and start taking action, you will learn and grow faster. So how does this strategy work?

First, introduce yourself to any new person or people if it is a group. Then catch up on the current topic by offering your opinion.

Next, bring up interesting topics that are similar to what to the central discourse.

Maintain a state of curiosity about them, which will help you become interested in knowing them.

Using these steps above will enable you to achieve a quick win with your small talks. You will have more engaging conversations with a lasting impact that becomes a part of you. Such that, whenever you engage in discussion, you won't struggle with what to say.

Building social confidence is very crucial to achieving your desired goal with small talk as well. As opposed to popular opinion, everyone and anyone can build social trust, all you have to do is stick to the TWO GENERAL ideas I mentioned earlier (practice and presence).

With consistent practice and intentional presence, you will always keep up with any conversation; it will all come naturally to you with time.

The FORD Method

The letters of the FORD method represent topics that can be used in a conversation as starters with anybody.

F: Family, here you can ask about family as a way of getting to know the other person better. Now it is possible that later in the conversation, you both will make reference to family again, and if you have built a good foundation with it as a starter, it won't be awkward.

O: Occupation, remember what we mentioned in an earlier chapter? People like to talk about their work. Another way to keep the conversation going is by asking them questions about their work.

R: Recreation. Fun! We all love to talk about fun, and it is a great topic to keep the conversation going.

D: Dreams, this idea relates to speculation about the future, ambitions, and the kind of things the person will want to do. Most people feel relaxed when asked questions about their dreams, so use this as an opportunity to build great conversations.

If you want to cut off awkwardness entirely from your conversation, you must be a great listener. If the person said something, you didn't get or something you didn't understand, politely ask them to repeat it so you can grasp what they are saying. Be open to sharing just as you ask questions!

The ARE Method

The ARE method, developed by Dr. Carol Fleming, a communications expert, is excellent for small talks. This method is a three-part process with each of the letters representing the specific steps.

A: A represents "anchor", which is something that connects you with the other person. Having just met the person, the starting point of the conversation should be a comment about what you both can see and experience.

The anchor is a way of striking an instant connection with the other person by using the events or present circumstances surrounding both of you. At this "A" stage, you don't have to worry about coming up with something bright or grand. A pleasant and straightforward opening will do.

For example, if you both are at a birthday celebration for an older man, you can say, "What a beautiful night for an 80th celebration!" The "A" in the ARE method will help you start well and keep the conversation going as well.

R: R stands for "reveal", which relates to you revealing something about yourself. What you tell about yourself must correlate to how you anchored the conversation.

After the first statement about the night with the first part, you can say, "I attended some events like this last year, but the weather wasn't this beautiful."

E: E stands for "encourage", which relates to how you can encourage responses from the person by asking a question. When we do a poor job at keeping the conversation going, it is because we don't allow the other person to inject his/her opinions. Following up with our example, you can ask, "What about you? Have you attended such a celebration of life before?" When the person gives a response, the next step is to keep the ball rolling. How can you do this?

You can keep the ball rolling by asking more questions and giving follow-up comments. Always strive to strike a balance between explanations and questions as too many comments from you will restrict the other person from commenting. More so, too many questions from you will make it all seem like an interrogation.

You may ask, what if there's a lull in the conversation? Well, this is what you can do: remember the pneumonic FORM!

Yes, we've got another acronym, and it means:

Family: You can ask the person to tell you about their family. Have they had children? Grandkids?

Occupation: You can also ask them what they do for a living, what they love the most about their jobs and some other information about their profession (not in an intrusive way).

Recreation: Recreational topics can be in the form of asking questions about vacation, what's on his/her bucket list, etc.

Motivation: With motivation, your goal is to motivate the other person to share more with you. "Do you intend on attending other such events later?"

The FORM method aims to help you avoid the typical way of carrying on with small talk, which entails annoying questions and statements such as "Hi, how are you?", "How was your week?" "I'm good". This helps you do better.

Even if you must go with this typical approach, try to fill them up with more interesting answers.

A few pointers for you:

Mention your name more than once because it is easy for the person to forget your name amid a discussion. Repetition, in this case, aids memory, and it will be a great way of making a first impression.

Always avoid one-word replies such as "Yes," "Yeah," "No". These are too abrupt, and it makes it seem like you are not willing to engage in a conversation.

Lastly, always make a clean exit by using the phrase "I need to ...", as in, "Excuse me, I need to make a quick phone call," or, "It was nice meeting you, I need to get some food now". You can also give some parting commendations such as "I enjoyed your travel stories. Hope to talk to you soon."

A very striking feature about small talk is that there is a pattern to it, and once you know the model, you can achieve success with it regardless of who you are talking to. The concepts in this chapter revealed some of these patterns and using them in addition to every other thing you've learned thus far can be very beneficial to you long-term.

We are approaching the end because the next chapter is going to be all about how you can end small talk gracefully with the other person. What can you do when you are done talking? Do you walk away? Smile and wave? How exactly should a person end small talk? Let's find out in the next chapter.

CHAPTER EIGHT

Planned Exit - Ending Small Talks Gracefully

Not many people are aware that we all need to practice how to end a discussion gracefully. As a result, people learn about the tenants of the conversation itself but fail to plan for the exit.

Yes, it is good to make an excellent first impression, but what about an excellent last impression? What should you say when the conversation winds down? How do you say it? What about the concept of a graceful exit? Is it possible to be remembered for making a fantastic lasting impression? Let's find out.

What to Say and How to Say It

There are reasons a person will want to end a conversation. They might want to end it because they have to get back to a task before or they want to run errands. It could also be that they are no longer in a chatty mood, or they want to keep things short.

Also, the way you finish off a conversation depends on the context. Maybe you ran into someone else, or perhaps you received an unexpected phone call. Generally, when you start talking with someone, it is always advisable that you have a time in mind for when you will end the conversation.

If you time yourself, you will be able to make a perfect ending. However, timing is never set in stone, especially when the conversation becomes fascinating, and you feel comfortable with the other person. Keep the conversation for as long as you can and end it well.

So, what should you say to end the small talk?

End quickly and cleanly

You don't have to say something formal to end the chat or make a grand statement. A big statement isn't called for because it will lead to you dragging on the conversation, which will ultimately make things awkward for you and the other person.

Say your goodbyes promptly cleanly and quickly, such that there is no room for an additional talk that will ruin the entire experience for you both. It is okay to say you want to go without any other window dressing. Here are some examples below:

"I have to run now. Good talking to you."

"(During a phone call) Well, that's my cue to run along now. Talk to you later?"

"Alright then (agree to what they say)."

"Enjoy the rest of the party. Goodnight".

The examples above reflect how you can end a conversation swiftly without additional comments. This step is just one way through which you can finish a discussion (we will highlight many others as we move on. The point here is that you can end quickly and cleanly.

Just leave a group discussion

The rule for a group discussion is different because you are not required to say anything in particular. If you joined a group chat at a party, then you can decide to leave after a few minutes.

All you have to do with this situation is to walk away. With group discussions, people drop in and out without obstructing the conversational flow. But if silently walking away will be too awkward for you, quietly indicate that you are leaving with a little nod or a wave.

You can also nudge the person standing next to you because they are within your reach and notify them that you are leaving.

Summarize all you've said

Another way to end the conversation in a memorable way is to summarize all you've said. This method is an excellent way to transition from the small talk to the conclusion gracefully.

Comment on the recent topic and then make a quick summary of the discussion before you indicate your exit. Here are some examples that will serve as a guide:

"Yes, clearly a lot has been happening with the company. Anyway, I should get going now. We will catch up at another time."

"You said it all; the interior designer could have done better. Let's hope it's better the next time we come to the convention. See you later."

Leave without saying too much

Don't clog the end part of a conversation with excessive discussions about irrelevant things and try not to bring up new ideas that will spark further discussions. Remember that you are at the end, and you are ready to close, so do just that without making it complicated.

Exit gracefully

Sometimes ending a small talk conversation can be tricky, which is why you should be concerned about how you complete your small talk. We will consider some tips and ideas you can implement below:

You are not the only one thinking about ending the conversation

If you are eager to end the talk, you should know that you are not alone, as the other person may also be thinking about the same thing. Most people who engage in small talk know it will end and are willing to end it at the same time you intend to.

For you to make a graceful exit, don't worry about hurting the other person's feelings when you need to end the conversation.

Knowing that they may be thinking about the same thing will help you relax and get it done with ease.

Foreshadow the end

When we are about to end something, it is good to hint at it beforehand. Yes, small talk is not a very serious issue, but if you are great at it, the fact that you are about to end it might be disappointing to the other person.

For you to end gracefully, you need to cushion the impact of your departure by previewing the exit before its time. When you do this, you also program the person's mind to be prepared for the end of the chat. There are several ways to foreshadow the end of small talk; the examples below can serve as a guide.

"I promised the bride that I would introduce her to a special guest, but before I do that, let me hear your thoughts on."

Now with the example above, the speaker has foreshadowed the end of the chat already by informing the person that he/she will be heading the bride's way soon (we are assuming this is at a wedding). Some other examples:

"I can't wait to go try the pastries over there, but what do you think about the décor?"

"I will be visiting the display stand right after you tell me all about the new product your firm launching next week."

Make an introduction

Another way to end small talk gracefully is by making a very organic introduction. This step enables you to make a smooth exit by introducing the other person to someone else, then ending the conversation.

Here, you give the person you were chatting with an opportunity to connect with someone else as you make your graceful exit.

But you must be mindful because you are not expected to introduce just about anybody, you must add someone who is within the discourse and someone who can be a mutual contact to you both.

If the other person is talking excitedly about the decoration or interior design at the event, for example, you could introduce him/her to the interior designer. Now the right way to execute this is by being conscious of timing, presence, and the person you will introduce.

Please don't walk away from the person entirely to bring the person you want to introduce. This step means that if you are going to use this pattern, you will have to start scanning the room for possible introductions while still chatting with the person.

Some examples you can utilize includes:

"Hey, there's the chef. Want to meet him?"

"You need to connect with this DJ, so he can show up for your next party."

Give a rationale for ending the talk

With motives, you will be explaining why you are going off and indicate that you have enjoyed the chat. Here, you can signal the end of the talk and increase the odds of a follow-up conversation in the future.

Examples:

"I love this conversation, but I just noticed it's 8:30, and I have to be home by 9. Can we continue with this some other time?"

"Oh my, the weather just changed, and, if I don't leave now, I will get drenched by the rain."

From the examples above, we can agree that the rationales provided by the speakers express their disappointment at ending the chat, signals their exit, and also shows how regrettable it is for them to leave. Using this method is graceful and will help you achieve a great connection with the other person.

Use immediate surroundings

You can also use your immediate surroundings to construct your ending organically. For example, if there is a drink stand by where you are standing, you can encourage the other person to grab a drink, knowing that you both will get mixed up in the crowd or encounter others for a chat.

If it is a pool party, for example, you may suggest that you both head out to the pool area, and, by doing this, you can move on gracefully from the small talk. But before using this style, make sure you have said all you need to say, and you are ready to end the conversation as well.

Making an Excellent Last Impression

People remember the beginning of a thing and the end as well, but typically have trouble remembering the middle. Think about when you read a novel, and it started with a lot of suspense; you will remember all of it after reading—but as time goes on, you'll likely only remember the beginning and end, and, perhaps the climax.

The novelist created balance with the beginning and end, and you must do the same. Don't spend so much time thinking about how to make a first impression while ignoring efforts to make a good last impression. You will find tips that will help you make a good final impression.

1. Make physical contact twice before leaving.

In most or all cases, making physical contact with the person just before leaving aids bonding between the two parties. A handshake is a sign of great rapport and makes you memorable; it also contributes to making you very likable.

Give a warm yet confident handshake just as you are about to part ways, and, if the person is someone you are familiar with, you can give a subtle hug. In some cultures of the world, pecks on the cheeks are ideal when meeting strangers (so be conscious of cultural implications as well).

Your handshakes should be firm (this will make it a very memorable handshake). Ensure to connect your fingers, and they should be flat rather than cupped so you can touch their palms. There is so much power in a firm handshake.

2. End with eye contact and a smile.

We have talked about the importance of making eye contact and smiling in previous chapters, and these non-verbal signs are vital while ending the discussion.

Always look at the person in the eye directly and give them the impression that you are open, warm, and straightforward. As you make eye contact, smile warmly, and let that be the image of you the person holds in his/her mind about you.

Making eye contact also enables you to internalize the person's facial features such that when you see him/her somewhere else again, you would remember the small talk and take it up from there. A smile is a tremendous non-verbal communicative tool for a memorable last impression.

3. Move with intent.

Avoid standing there, shifting your weight because you are hesitant to leave. You've got to move with some intention by being friendly yet firm with your goodbye. Know what you will do next, so you could mention it subtly as you prepare to leave.

By moving with intent, I mean that, if you need to move across the room to talk to someone else, you should know it. When you are unintentional about leaving, it will lead to a lot of awkwardness, which will also ruin any attempt on your end for an excellent last impression.

Some examples include:

"It's been a pleasure talking to you; now I need to get to my car. Thank you."

"Wow, what an experience you had! I hope we get to talk about this again. I need to catch up with the groom over there. Thank you."

4. Don't cut the other person short.

Sometimes, when we are ready to end a conversation, our minds get so one-tracked that we inappropriately cut the other person off even while he/she is still talking. Yes, we know you are in a hurry, and you want to leave, but you also want to leave a tremendous last impression, which requires you showing respect for the other person.

For you to avoid cutting people short, you must take control of the conversation by giving signals that you are ready to leave. If the person still talks afterward, allow him/her finish, and then end the talk (but don't cut the person off).

Cutting the person off will send a wrong signal to him/her about your personality, and it is generally a rude approach. I know some people might go on and on talking, but then you've got to be tolerant.

However, if you MUST cut them off (this is in rare cases when you need to leave, and the person wouldn't stop talking) then you can use the ideas below:

"I hate to interrupt your stream of thought, but I have to leave."

"Sorry for butting in, but if I don't talk to the principal now, he will leave the premises."

"What an inspiring story, it's so sad I can't stay to hear it all."

5. Thank the person.

As you get ready to end the conversation, remember to thank the person by looking them in the eye and saying, "Thank you." More specifically, you've got to thank them for their time, or a great chat.

Now you can say thank you twice: when you realize that you are about to end the conversation and when you intend leaving the scene. As you say thanks, make the other person feel like you have had a great time.

Some examples are:

"Thank you for your time this evening; it was lovely chatting with you."

"Thank you for your wonderful food suggestions; I will have a great time with the recipes."

6. Keep open-ended conversations.

Another way to make an excellent lasting impression at the end is to keep an open discussion, so the next time you meet this person, you both will have significant common ground to pick up from where you left off. The other person will be excited about continuing the conversation and even ponder on how the next discussion will be. Now, keeping the conversation open-ended may not apply to all situations, but if it does apply to yours, make it count.

We have achieved a balanced narrative thus far with how to start and how to end the small talk with anyone gracefully. Listen, if you stick to all these ideas and concepts, you can hold a conversation anywhere. We're getting close to the end, but there's still more to discuss. In the next chapter, we focus on how you can make genuine connections with people.

CHAPTER NINE

Making Genuine Connections with People

The experiences we have with people are based on the connections we build with them. When we make great connections with people, everything else relating to how we converse with them becomes more comfortable. You can initiate small talk now, and you can end it, but the question is, can you make a *genuine* connection with people—the kind that builds lasting friendships?

Do you know the kind of questions that will lead to deeper connections? What are the signs that you are connecting with someone? Can small talk become even more meaningful?

If you observe the pattern with this book, I tend to ask you a lot of questions because that is one of the quickest ways to learn a lot about life. Questions teach you two things:

1. What you know
2. What you don't know

When you answer a question correctly, it means you understand the concept, and when you don't, you know what you should get to know. With the questions I have asked, you will be able to decipher if you know these concepts and if you don't.

We will begin with small talk perspectives/approaches that will help you strike a connection with people.

Small Talk Perspective/Approaches

Small talk is one of the swiftest and most organic ways through which you can strike a connection with people. As you know, there are varying ways through which you can use small talk that can be advantageous to you, but we are not going to go through a repetitive circle again.

What this section aims for is to show you some approaches to establishing genuine connections between people. Using these ideas and all other concepts you've learned thus far can help you become a much better communicator while connecting with others. Shall we begin?

Use what they say

An excellent approach for small talk is to use what the person says as an anchor for the conversation. This approach puts the spotlight on the discussion on the other person and helps you retain a perfect relationship with him/her.

Always look to intentionally use what they say as a catalyst for the conversation going forward and help them maintain a lead on the conversation by using their words and suggested topics.

Find out what makes them special

We all have qualities that make us special, distinctions that set us apart from others. When someone identifies this exceptional quality in us, we feel welcomed, loved, and appreciated.

You can genuinely strike a connection with someone else just by identifying what makes them unique and commending them for it. It doesn't have to be something based on character (you just met the person); it can be personality-based or a visible attribute they portray.

Don't push people to see and embrace your perspective

Another perspective you must consider is to avoid imposing your view on other people. Yes, you have strong opinions, and you want the whole world to hear you. Nonetheless, small talk is not a place to indoctrinate people. It's a place to build connections, one to learn—not teach.

Always give room for the other person's opinions and seek common ground with him/her. We will discuss more on common ground in another section in this chapter.

Reveal something personal

Yes, this is an approach of small talk that will help you make genuine connections with people. When you share something personal, you are sending a message to the person that you are open to a relationship, which is the essence of great small talk.

But please be mindful of what you share (if you go with this approach). Don't share overly personal things (for example, a miscarriage or the death of a child). Avoid sharing painful memories as soon as you meet a person. Get to know them first. You could share challenges at work or your struggle to buy a good piece of property. You mustn't scare the other person away by revealing too much too soon.

Questions leading to deeper connections

Not all inquiries lead to deeper connections, some are "yes" or "no" questions, and some others require only succinct direct answers. But if you are keen on getting connected with someone else, you must intentionally ask questions that will lead to deeper connections.

Below, you will find some of these questions which go beyond the surface and help you reach the person at a well-connected level.

1. "Why do you live in this neighborhood?"
2. "What is your vision for this non-profit?"
3. "How do you feel about your life situation?"
4. "Which new skill would you love to learn?"
5. "Who do you admire in history?"
6. "What would you be known for if you were a celebrity?"

Ways to Make Small Talk More Meaningful

Whereas some discussions are meaningful, others are simply exchanging pleasantries. You should strive to make discussions meaningful, and cast aside the stigma that small talk inherently has: that it's simply a waste of time. It's not—not if you're striking up a substantive conversation. This isn't always best, however. For example, you might have no intention of striking up a conversation with a stranger in the future (for reasons best known to you), in which case, you will want to stick to an ordinary and drab conversational style.

But if you seek a relationship with the person and you want to continue with the conversation, you will have to do more. By more, we mean take a cue from the examples below because they can be helpful.

Celebrate successes

If you want to make small talk with others more meaningful, you must celebrate their progress as they share them with you. By success, I am referring to the little bits of information they share with you that are an indication of their progress.

You can inject some exclamations that show your excitement for them; some examples include: "Wow," "Amazing," or, "That's so good." If a person tells you that he traveled to the Vatican City for vacation and met the Pope, don't let it slide. Respond to the information by celebrating his/her success through such exclamations.

Focus on engagement

You can also get a more meaningful conversation by focusing on engagements between the two of you. What are the points of the discussion that you both seem to enjoy the most? Focus on those points and dig further into them.

You will find that your small talk is even more meaningful because you are not conscious of what gets less attention from both of you.

The gift of going first

For you to have a more in-depth conversation, you need to give the gift of going first by choosing to share something personal or vulnerable. When you do this, the other person will take your cue and do the same. Sometimes, between both parties, one person is waiting to see if the next person will take the first step.

By sharing something deeply, you will be having a more meaningful conversation with a deep-rooted connection such that the follow-up talk will flow naturally. People often respond in kind to such gestures, so take the step for a more rewarding and bonding experience.

Don't (always) fill a silence gap

You mustn't superimpose your words by filling the silence gap all the time. If you do this, the other person will become lazy and would leave you to take the lead, ultimately making the conversation one-sided.

Give room for the person to take the lead as well and be content with following sometimes. Even if you know what to say every time silence creeps in, resist the urge, and allow the talk flow naturally.

Encourage elaborate descriptions (if you've got time)

If you've got time for small talk, you can allow the other person to give detailed explanations, which will also aid a fascinating conversation. Encourage the person when he/she is showing enthusiasm about a topic by using sentences like "Go on," "This must be interesting," and "Wow, I didn't know that."

Remember that the caveat with this step is that it should be used when you are sure you've got time for it. It wouldn't make sense for you to lead the person on and cut him/her off halfway by saying you want to leave.

Signs You Are Connecting with Someone

How can you tell that the above ideas work? How will you know when you have connected with someone in the course of the conversation?

In this final section, you will discover the signs that show how well you are connecting with someone else.

Please note that for some of the ideas below, there are exceptions, and I will indicate these exceptions (if any).

1. Notice a slight smile

A great way to tell that you are connecting with someone is if he/she gives you a little smile while you speak. That smile is a sign that they genuinely enjoy your company, and they love conversing with you. Make sure to return the favor by smiling while they speak, as well.

2. Do you both have some common ground?

Even if you both have little disagreements, at some point during the small talk, you should have moments of common ground as this is a sign of great connection. Most of the time, social setting contributes immensely in providing common ground because you both can draw on the surroundings for talking points.

For example, do you both like the party setting? Are you both colleagues at the office? If the people around the venue are there for the same reason as you, then there is a higher chance of you both having common ground.

If you struggle to achieve common ground with the other person, then it might mean that there is no connection between the two of you. But all hope isn't lost, you can lean in with them by taking what they say and endorsing it to aid common ground (this step can be utilized if you are keen on striking a connection).

3. Is the person making eye contact?

Eye contact is significant when making small talk because it is a visible sign of connection. Of course, by now, you know the difference between eye contact and staring, so while we don't want the person staring at us, we certainly don't want them looking away either.

If the person intentionally avoids making eye contact, then he/she hasn't connected with you. You can help the person at some point to mirror you by also making eye contact with them, but if they don't reciprocate, it means they don't want to talk further.

4. Are they digging deeper into the conversation?

When you start talking, try to find out if the person is making attempts at getting to know more about you or what you are talking about. After the initial "hello," you should track the individual's responses to questions you ask and how they answer yours.

If you do all the talking and they don't ask further questions, then it means they are not interested in the conversation. However, you can be sure of making a connection if, after the first three minutes, they are responding well to you.

5. Are they willingly sharing information with you?

When a person willingly shares information with you without you asking, it is a sign that they are connected to you. It's a sign of comfort level as well.

On the flip side, some people withhold information even when you ask, and it could be a sign that they are not comfortable with you—or simply that they are not as well-versed in small talk. If you sense this withdrawal, you can reach out to them by also sharing information and watch to see how they react.

6. Do they mirror you?

Mirroring is crucial, and while speaking, you should pay attention to the other person's body movements. Do you remember when we talked about mirroring in a previous chapter? According to studies on communication, humans tend to reflect each other when they are interested or when they have made a connection with someone else.

Sometimes we become so comfortable with the person that mirroring becomes a subconscious act. Mirroring helps us reassure the other person that we love being around them. But if you are making hand gestures and the other person stays stiff, it could be a sign that they want to end the conversation.

7. Are they following the details you share?

Another sign to look out for is if they follow the details you share. When conversing with a person, if he/she often forgets what you say, then it is a sign that you haven't connected with him/her.

But if the person is enthusiastic about your narratives, stories, and opinions, then you've got yourself a great small talk buddy. To check this sign, you can say something repeatedly and then ask them. If they don't understand, then they haven't been listening, and that also means you haven't struck a connection with them.

8. Do they make body contact?

Yes, when people have struck a connection with you, they start to feel comfortable enough to make body contact. Some people, regardless of what you do, will never make body contact because they seek minimal interaction with you.

So, such people will not give you a handshake, hug, or even touch you slightly. If you extend your hand, they may take it less firmly than expected. But, on the bright side, if the person has made a connection with you, they will not shy away from professional body contact.

Please note that in some cases, a person might be pleased with you but has issues with making body contact with strangers. So please don't take it personally when a person doesn't reciprocate your body contact gestures.

9. What about the "feet rule"?

There is an old rule that states that when a person is interested in you, he/she will point their feet towards you while speaking. Yes, it is an old saying, but it still holds a lot of truth. While conversing, take a split second to look down if the person's feet are pointed in your direction. If it is so, then it is a good sign; it means the person is mirroring you successfully and is ready to move in whatever direction you take the conversation.

On the contrary, if their feet are pointing in another direction, it means that they are no longer interested and want to end the conversation. Please note that this is an old rule, and it is not set in stone (people can adjust their body parts as they deem fit), which means it may not apply to every situation.

10. Do they drop their guard around you?

A good sign that you have made a connection with some is when they drop their guard around you. With some people, you can feel the walls around them still intact, such as folding their arms across their chests, stiffening their shoulders, or crossing their legs.

But once you spot a fully relaxed person around you, then you know that they have dropped their guard and they are free with you. This sign ultimately translates into a great connection with the person.

Connecting with people is an enriching experience. It's how we ultimately make all of our lifelong friends. So now you know how to build such authentic connections, which will also enable you to succeed at making small talk with anyone anywhere.

The next chapter is the last one in this book. You've got the foundation. You've got all the skills you need. Now we simply need to perfect those skills. We're talking about mastery.

CHAPTER TEN

Mastering the Art of Small Talk

We have learned the most basic and in-depth ideas on the art of small talk, which has contributed immensely to helping you know how to begin the conversation and how to make the most out of it long-term. I've always encouraged you to put your skills to the test, making small talk in the field. Still, even if you feel like a pro, there's always more work to be done to become a master at something.

We'll begin with a reminder of why we make small talk. What makes it worth your time? And of course, we'll discuss what you can do to master it. Some of the ideas you will discover below may sound familiar, but we will be considering these concepts from the standpoint of gaining mastery.

The Art of Small Talk and Why It's Worth Your Time

For you to gain mastery of anything, you must know its worth! Of what importance is this discourse to you? When you fully understand the reason small talk is crucial, you will start to make conscious efforts towards ensuring that you gain mastery.

Think about all the non-familiar relationships that became familiar ones. What was the tipping point for such connections? How did such people move from being strangers to best friends? The answer is quite simple: small talk!

Now, in addition to being able to help you retain perfect friendships, the benefits of the small talk below will also empower you to take the concept of mastery seriously. Let's discover more, shall we?

1. Small talk is spontaneous.

One of the benefits of small talk to you and the reason it is worth learning is the fact that it is unplanned. With speeches and other communication patterns, you will be required to carry out some preparatory exercises because you are expected to meet a certain standard.

However, with small talk, you must be as good as the last one you had and build on it consistently. The spontaneity of small talk also removes whatever kind of pressure you may feel to be anything other than yourself.

2. Small talk can inspire new ideas in you.

Yes, with small talk, you are consistently inspired with new ideas because you will be interacting with new people who have varying opinions about life and work.

If you pay close attention to the content of the conversations, you will agree that there is always something new to learn. Your perspective on specific topics will also often change because the interaction is the foundation of education.

3. It helps you embrace your real value.

When you are engaged in small talk, you will get to see yourself through the lenses of another person. As the person commends you and points out the value in what you say, you will start to embrace your real value.

Most people trivialize their opinions and their view of the world because they erroneously think they are insignificant. However, when you chat with someone for a few minutes and he/she says "Wow, you've got an amazing perspective", you will learn to value that comment, which affects how you see yourself.

4. You become a better admirer.

Small talk also empowers you to become a better admirer of others. Some people are not great at connecting with others because they don't engage in what they perhaps believe to be a fruitless conversation, and they are isolated.

When you start sharing your thoughts with others, when you begin to connect with people, you will fall in love with the diversity and uniqueness of human nature. This idea also influences your ability to be a better admirer of people who acknowledges their flaws but respects their opinions.

5. It helps you create lasting impressions.

We dedicated an entire chapter to learning how to create lasting impressions because it is essential. Those lasting impressions become the springboard from which follow-up conversations are birthed and relationships formed.

6. You also become a people's person.

One of the hallmarks of leadership is a person's ability to be a people's person. As a people person, you can relate on any level, and this will help you lead with purpose.

Imagine being a manager who has occasional small talk with subordinates at the office. You will agree that through those little conversations, you will get to know more about the people who work for you and know how to harness their abilities for the good of the firm, and better yet, for their good.

7. You wouldn't struggle with holding a viable conversation.

The struggle to maintain an excellent discussion with new people is real, especially in this digital age. But a person who is proficient in the small talk will not struggle with conversational patterns. Such people will not only be great with small talk starters, but they will also know how to take other people along.

Small talk helps you build a conversation from start to finish without awkward silences and other mannerisms that affect the flow of a proper conversation.

8. A great career booster.

Within the corporate world and other workplaces, those who are great at small talk are those who get to move up the ladder quickly because they are good at connecting with people.

Such people will get the attention of top management because every company will consider both your hard and soft skills. What you do for the company/business is your hard skill, and your ability to communicate effectively with your colleagues and those you lead constitute your soft skills. A combination of both skillsets will serve as a significant career boost!

Best Practices to Improve Your Conversational Skills

If you ever struggled with conversational skills, you would need to start indulging more in small talks. As you apply this principle, you will notice a significant improvement in your communication skills and your ability to reach out to strangers.

Small talk completely transforms the way you view communication. You will move from seeing it as a stressful process to embracing it as a bridge that connects you with others. It is, for this reason, you must become intentional about mastering the art of small talk.

We have laid the foundation for mastery with the worth of small talk and its value to your experience. Now we will move on to learning all about good practices that will improve your conversational skills.

The practices you will discover below are not ideas you should implement once and forget. These are ideas should be repeatedly utilized until they become a part of you. You can come back to this chapter every time you feel the need to upgrade your small talk skills.

Think of the ideas below as habits that can only become a part of you when you do them consciously. No one was born with an excellent ability to execute small talk; we all must deliberately learn and trust that the more we put in the effort, the better we become.

1. Face your fears.

Introverts are not the only ones who struggle with making small talk, as it can be intimidating for anyone. However, due to how important it is, we must all learn how to make it work, and the first step to doing that is by facing your fears.

You've got to highlight the major reason why you don't like small talk and then plan to conquer that fear. It could be that you don't feel comfortable around strangers, so what can you do if that's the case? Spend more time with the people you don't know!

When you face your fears, they can no longer limit you!

2. Use a friend.

To master the art of small talk, you've got to practice a lot, and you should work closely with a friend so you can feel comfortable. When you visit your friend, engage in small talk over a wide range of topics that may cut across the weather, food, vacation, etc.

Use this step whenever you have the opportunity, and you will find that you are gaining mastery over time. Talking with a friend will help you handle the sweaty palms and knotted feeling in your stomach caused by anxiety over making small talk.

3. Ask questions.

When you make it a habit to always ask questions, you will do the same whenever you are making small talk. If you get to a new place where things are very different, learn how to ask questions, as this will help you build confidence.

Regardless of where you are (with a larger or smaller group) or a one-on-one conversation, if you ask the right questions, you will build your skills. Questions help you move the conversation from the surface level to a real place where a relationship can thrive.

4. Set your mind right.

Your mind plays a crucial role in the success or failure of small talk. If you always hold the opinion that you cannot make small talk successfully (maybe because of past mistakes), no matter how well you practice, you will struggle.

So set your mind right by telling yourself that you can do it! Don't allow the failures of the past to get in the way of your commitment. Before going for an event, make up your mind that you will make small talk and tell yourself that regardless of who you speak to, it will be successful.

5. Make a game of it.

Sometimes for you to master a concept, you've got to play with it so you can enjoy the process. Trick yourself into seeing small talk as fun, and commit at least an hour to meet someone new and learning something about them.

Your mind will experience a shift, and the more you engage in this kind of game, the more natural small talk becomes. Give yourself points every time you get it right with someone and build on your previous success to get better.

6. Be yourself!

Don't try to be someone else who is excellent at small talk in the office because you think he/she is better than you. You didn't read this entire book so you could imitate someone else now, did you?

You read this book to empower yourself, and you have gained that empowerment. What's next? You've got to be authentic. Don't fake an accent because you want to "appear" relatable to the other person. All you have to do is to be you. Be original and be excellent!

7. Lower your expectations.

You have read this book that has prepared you for the future with small talk, but other people don't have access to such publications; as such, they still deal with specific conversational challenges.

It will be wrong for you to show up to discuss with such people and expect them to be as good as you. Please minimize your expectations of others and go with the flow of the talk.

Don't add to their awkwardness by laughing at their mistakes and putting a stop to the conversation because you don't find them "interesting." Keep expectations at a minimum, and you will be able to gain mastery of small talk.

8. Don't be on the sidelines.

Being on the sidelines means sticking to someone else and standing behind them (hiding) while they make small talks. You are too good to be standing on the sidelines, and you have been groomed to do better.

Don't be a sidekick. Don’t be a wallflower. Don't stand in another person's shadow because if you do, you will never gain mastery. You may have accompanied your friend to an event, but after a few minutes of arriving together, find your way around the venue and make contact with new people.

9. Take responsibility for the process.

You must take responsibility for the conversational process whenever you are talking to someone else, so you learn how to take charge of small talk. Don't blame the other person when the conversation becomes dull; don't attribute it to something the person said or did.

If you must gain mastery of small talk, you must be willing to take responsibility. Taking responsibility will propel you to give your best and utilize all the ideas shared thus far in this book.

10. Don't stop practicing.

Above all, don't stop trying! I am still harnessing the power of small talk even today because I am always practicing for varying scenarios. When you practice well enough, you will become confident, and this will empower you to set the tone for your conversations.

Consistent practice is the key to mastering the art of small talk, and with the ideas shared in this chapter, you can rest easy knowing that you are on the path to being an expert in it.

Oh, what a moment it is right now! We have finally come to the end of a fantastic journey, and it feels rewarding. You have been such a good sport, and I believe you deserve a pat on the back. We will round off this journey with a concluding section that will propel you to action.

FINAL WORDS

Now you know what to say next after hello!

The key message for this book is how you can engage in small talk while building better relationships. We started like we were on a journey by analyzing some of the key reasons why people struggle with making conversation with strangers. Fear, anxiety, and shy personas were some challenges we discussed, and then we moved on to solutions.

This book has taught you the definition of small talk as a foundational part of the discourse and how you can overcome shyness as an individual. You unearthed the value of the social skill code while gaining insight into the concept of non-verbal communication.

Knowing what comes after hello is crucial for the success of small talk. You wouldn't feel stuck while communicating because you know how to maintain conversations.

Planning a graceful exit is also vital because as much as you want it to end, you also want to be remembered fondly. Overall you have gained in-depth insight into how to master the art of small talk, and this is the biggest lesson to glean from this material.

From the start, I promised you that you would enjoy the process and become enthusiastic about small talk. I hope that's true now, but what you gain from this text is ultimately up to you. It's out of my hands.

The solution mentioned at the start was encapsulated in one word, "Enjoy." Now, if you enjoyed reading, you will surely enjoy making small talks, which ultimately will help you get better every day. I'll say it again: Perfection is the enemy of the good. Don't expect it immediately after reading this book. Seek it. Strive for it. Then learn to let it go and accept good enough.

You'll see progress if you practice. Remember that this isn't magic. This is a process. You must engage with it as it engages with you. Over time, you'll improve.

Pressure will pave the way for disappointments. That is not in the spirit of this book. I want you to feel comfortable and relaxed knowing that it will take consistent practice for you to become a master.

Nonetheless, if there's one thing that's most important about this book, what do you think that would be?

It's this: You can hold a conversation (small talk) with anyone, anywhere. I want this idea to be palpable to you; it should be within your mind all the time, so you are prepared. Remember this message when you are at a party wondering if you can strike up a conversation with someone standing next to you.

You can start small talks with people you've just met, and you can do it without fear of the unknown. You are ready to build new friendships with people that will add color to your world.

Small talk is an integral part of everyday life. It's easy to dismiss it as something pointless, something that will get you nowhere. In truth, though, it contributes to your well-being and happiness. You will probably miss out on meeting your soulmate if you have a fear of small talk. Yes, your soulmate!

Also, remember that the principles discussed in this book do not only apply to face-to-face interactions. This is the digital age, and, as such, much of your communication will happen online. You can socialize just about anywhere these days: Facebook, Instagram, YouTube, email, Snapchat, Kik, WhatsApp, text messages, etc. Through such social platforms, you can build confidence and master the art of conversing with others.

As we round off this journey, I want to reinforce the power of confidence. You need to build confidence to fight off the impact of negative thoughts. They are not the reality you make them out to be. To put it in perspective, when you think positively, you become excited about meeting someone and learning from them.

That positivity transforms into self-confidence because you are in a great mental space for interaction. Don't worry about being boring; you are a worthy person who has got a unique point of view and a particular way to say it. More so, the people you speak to could also be as shy as you are, so why not make the best out of the situation?

Whenever you feel nervous or anxious before meeting people, get excited about the encounter, and visualize a successful talk. Happiness will turn your trepidation into something positive while leading the way by interacting, engaging, and learning something new.

The fact that this book ends here doesn't mean I can't give you additional tips for success. I want you to go into the world, feeling empowered and ready to speak passionately.

Here's another great idea for you; try practicing stoicism as a way of seeing things from a more rational viewpoint. We all wear pants the same way, one leg in at a time, so don't try to rush things. Focus on the present moment when you are conversing and avoid getting caught up on past awkwardness and what-ifs that birth irrational fears.

You will achieve more with your practice when done in a familiar environment. Don't start by attending social events you are not interested in and stick to settings where you can thrive easily. The aim is for you is to have fun and enjoy the process, so ask yourself, what are my interests? What do I believe? These questions will make it easier for you cultivate relationships with like-minded people.

Recall our discourse on the four-ears or four-sides model that provides you with the idea that a statement made by another person can mean different things. The message is:

1. Factual Information: Desire to accurately state information.
2. Appeal: To appeal to you or seek command or receive advice from you
3. Relationship: To refer to an aspect of your existing relationship.
4. Self-Revelation: Divulge something about themselves (motives, values, emotions, likes/dislikes, etc.)

Don't forget to interpret non-verbal clues and body language of the people you interact with at events. Keep an eye on their gestures, facial expressions, tone of voice, and posture. You should also soften your body language while in conversation, so your communication isn't misinterpreted as aggressive.

You must seek to provide a positive experience both for yourself and the other party. Smile more, sit up straight and show excitement (this is so important), would you enjoy small talk with someone who looks bored? Of course not!

In addition to excitement, be interested in what the people are saying by listening emphatically. Be an active participator, be positive, friendly, and be a warm person. Be the person that everyone loves to connect with.

Another way you can win with small talks is to keep the conversation going by asking open-ended questions. Questions about the weather are not open; they are direct questions that will not lead to exciting discussions. Also, avoid controversial topics that will lead to overly passionate outbursts (examples of such issues are politics and other adverse problems).

Please don't get confused. Here is a piece of advice that can help you strike a balance; tie in the conversation starter to the occasion, event, or location. Talk about the décor, the colors, the main reason for the game, the organization, etc. This way you will be on the safe yet exciting side.

Get to talk about hobbies, art, what brought your acquaintance to the event, and how they know the host. These are topics that will inspire a fascinating conversation between you and the acquaintance. Prepare conversation starters ahead of time as well to avoid stress. By preparing, you will be ready for anything. Don't focus solely on the content of the conversation and forget how to end it properly. When you end correctly, you open an opportunity for future discussions. If you meet the person again, you both can continue from where you left off.

You can be proactive with message continuance by sending a follow-up message soon after to maintain the connection. With proper follow-up, you can build new and lasting relationships as an adult in the digital age.

We have shared so much thus far, and I hope you are pumped up and ready to go! Above all, take great pride in executing the knowledge gained because think about it, what is the usefulness of information if it isn't applied?

This should be your formula going forward: READ = INTERNALIZE = EXECUTE = REPEAT!

Best wishes.

RESOURCES

English Club, (2019), Small Talk Practice 2: At the office Retrieved November 4, 2019 from https://www.englishclub.com/speaking/small-talk_practice2office.htm Bridges, F. (2019, April 25).

What to Say After "Hello" Retrieved November 4 2019, from https://www.nicknotas.com/blog/what-to-say-after-hello/ Frost, A. (2019, July 24).

The Ultimate Guide to Small Talk: Conversation Starters, Powerful Questions, & More. Retrieved November 4, 2019, from https://blog.hubspot.com/sales/small-talk-guide Callahan, J (2018, May 31)

10 Nonverbal Cues That Convey Confidence at Work. Retrieved from https://www.forbes.com/sites/jacquelynsmith/2013/03/11/10-nonverbal-cues-that-convey-confidence-at-work/#1f5b763f5e13 Smith, J. (2013, March 11)

Stop overthinking and Never Run Out of Things To say Retrieved November 4, 2019 from https://goodmenproject.com/featured-content/stop-overthinking-never-run-out-things-say-lbkr/ Schiffer, V. (2019, June 13).

The Art of Misunderstanding & The 4 Sides Model of Communication. Retrieved November 4, 2019, from https://www.medium.com/seek-blog/the-art-of-misunderstanding-and-the-4-sides-model-of-communication-7188408457ba Amintro, (2019, July 30).

The Art of small talk: how to start and keep a conversation going, Retrieved November 4, 2019 from https://www.amintro.com/life/art-small-talk-start-keep-conversation-going/ Hertzberg, K. (2017, June 20).

Small Talk 101 for Shy People in the Office. Retrieved November 4, 2019, from https://www.grammarly.com/blog/small-talk-tips-for-introverts/ Eduard, (2012, April 30).

The Best Conversation Starters Retrieved November 4, 2019 from http://conversation-starters.com/ Khuu, C. (2018, October 8).

15 Tips to Get Better at Small Talk. Retrieved November 4, 2019 from https://www.success.com/15-tips-to-get-better-at-small-talk/

The Art of Small Talk. Body language. Retrieved November 4, 2019, from https://www.the-art-of-small-talk.com/bodylanguage.html Sedghi, A. (2019, February 11).

37 Conversation Starters that make You Instantly Interesting, Retrieved November 4, 2019 from https://www.readersdigest.ca/health/relationships/interesting-conversation-starters/ Johnson, P. (2016, August 11).

7 Ways to Make a Big Impression with Small Talk, Retrieved November 4, 2019 from https://www.heysigmund.com/7-ways-to-make-a-big-impression-with-small-talk Hey, S. (2019).

Small Talk Practice 2: At the Office, Retrieved November 4, 2019 from https://www.englishclub.com/speaking/small-talk_practice2office.htm

How To Be Better At Small Talk, Retrieved November 4, 2019 from https://www.forbes.com/sites/francesbridges/2019/04/25/how-to-be-better-at-small-talk/#318291135ca5 Holiday, R., & Hanselman, S. (2016).

Small Talk for Big Sales, Retrieved November 4, 2019 from https://www.sellingpower.com/2010/02/02/8361/small-talk-for-big-sales Craig, B. (2010)

Keep Conversations Flowing With the FORD Method, Retrieved November 4, 2019 from https://curiosity.com/topics/keep-conversations-flowing-with-the-ford-method-curiosity/ Ashley, H. (2018, February 8).

Stop Overthinking and Never Run Out of Things To Say, Retrieved November 4, 2019 from https://goodmenproject.com/featured-content/stop-overthinking-never-run-out-things-say-lbkr/ Jeff, C. (2018, May 31).

ALPHA ASSERTIVENESS GUIDE FOR MEN AND WOMEN

The Workbook for Training Assertive Behavior and Communication Skills to Live Boldly, Command Respect, and Gain Confidence at Work and in Relationships

Gerard Shaw

Table of Contents

INTRODUCTION

You want better things in life. Perhaps a better salary, higher social status, or more respect from the people around you. You want your today to be better than yesterday, and tomorrow to be better than today. And, you deserve it. Really!

Not because you have been dreaming of it for so long, but also because you've been working to achieve it. Yet, you somehow miss the train every time. You constantly ask yourself what it is you're lacking. Or is it just bad luck?

Bad luck? Hardworking people are the creators of their own destiny, and you are not an exception. You're also an all-around nice person, very genuine and kind.

So, why aren't you getting what you deserve?

Maybe you are too generous, and your generosity is working against you. Or perhaps you never ask for what you really want, or you're unsure how to ask for it. All this, when added up, is preventing you from achieving what you desire in life, and what you deserve.

Nevertheless, it doesn't mean you can't get it NOW! You can, without losing your self-identity, your generosity, or your self-respect.

You only need to discover the most effective way to communicate and express what you want in your relationships, at work, with your family, friends, and life. Sound tough?

In this book, you'll find the blueprint of an effective communication style that equips you with the skills of expressing, asking, and receiving what you want in life. Best part?

The lessons imparted in this book are actionable and adaptable to your everyday life. You will find it easy to identify situations you can relate to and apply the knowledge you will learn in your day-to-day life.

I have been studying different communication techniques and picking out a few that will equip anyone to be a winner in their life. However, the assertive style of communication has always stood out. I have been using this communication style every day, trying to better understand how it is best executed in each aspect of my life: work, relationships, family, friends, and personal development.

To tell the truth, I feel empowered in every aspect of my life when I started being more aware of using more assertive style of communication. I feel constantly increasing power to have more control over my life.

And now, I want you to experience the same! I want you to seize control of your life; to be empowered to control your life situations.

Reading this book will take you on a unique journey where you discover a new self. You will work with your strengths rather than lamenting your weaknesses. It will shift your entire perspective to what you *can* do to achieve what you have been aiming for.

It will give you a balanced perspective of your life, a solid idea of the know-how and essential techniques to achieve what you want in your life through assertive behavior and communication. It will guide you through understanding assertiveness in the right context, the skills to use it appropriately in your personal life, and some workable techniques to develop these skills of communication into an empowered lifestyle.

If you ask me one thing I can share from my expertise as a communication coach that will help you to lead a happier and more fulfilled life, I will always tell you to discover the power of assertive style of communication to express your wants and needs. I always advise people looking to learn effective communication skills to learn this assertive style.

Imagine people getting that pay raise or promotion after applying the techniques they learned in this book. Or, the couple whose marital success can be attributed to the style of communication they learned here. These are only some of the success stories I heard. What will your success story look like after reading this book? Imagine what it will look like - and share it with me. I eagerly await it.

Also, I promise that whatever you imagined will soon be a reality, provided you follow this blueprint. Along this path, you'll gain knowledge, wisdom, and the art of building your power. Not your physical power, but the inner potent power of assertiveness. This may be the only power you lack to get the life you want.

The lessons you'll learn along this journey will give you techniques to look inward, discover your strengths, and feel empowered. It will teach you how to use assertiveness to reach your end goals, whether in relationships, business, career, or just in everyday life.

The big question is: Why should you learn the assertive style of communication? The answer lies in the life situations where you currently feel you are stuck. Or might be stuck soon, if you don't learn these communication techniques now.

You may be feeling frustrated with your job, health, relationships, or financial security – that's enough to make you wonder what's wrong.

If you really wish to move ahead and stop feeling stuck in life, you need to take action today. You already know deep in your mind that something needs to change, and that change must happen now.

It's high time you stopped playing victim to your circumstances. It's time to be the master of your own destiny. If it doesn't happen now, it probably won't much later. So get up, and get ready to take charge of your life. Speak up and stand up for yourself and take the first step. Learn the how.

I know it's not the first time you have realized the need for a change. You've realized this many times before. However, something was holding you back. You either didn't find the right techniques to change or didn't have the courage to do it. That's okay. This book will equip you with the right skills to change your life, skills that will work to your advantage rather than others taking advantage of you.

Every change, even a small one, seems tough in the beginning. That's because we are creatures of habit, and we like living inside our comfort zones. We might not be satisfied with where we are, but still haven't mustered the courage to make a change.

However, let's find you the courage to take your first step towards change. If you want a new and unique way of restarting your game and taking charge of your life, start here. It's the easiest first step and it's worth it.

Know what you want, say what you want, and get what you want. It may sound as simple as that, but it CAN be. Learn "how" here.

This book bundle comes with a FREE booklet on masterminding a winning routine to improve calmness and your level of confidence everyday. Instructions on how you can download this booklet for free can be found at the bottom page of this book bundle.

CHAPTER ONE

Assertiveness in a Diverse World

So, what's this 'assertiveness'? People commonly see assertiveness as being rude, domineering, or aggressive. However, the actuality is different.

Assertiveness is a social skill. It is a way of communication where you clearly and respectfully express your wants, needs, positions, and boundaries to others. This communication happens irrespective of your position. It's not being selfish, not being rude, but rather simply being firm and clear in your ways of communication.

Being assertive is standing up for your rights calmly and positively without being aggressive or accepting the 'wrong'.

Assertiveness in Psychology: Cognitive, Behavioral and Social Standpoint

An assertive person thinks, behaves, and speaks differently than others. He is calm, relaxed, and less anxious, even under stressful situations. That's natural, because when you are clear about what you want and know how to communicate it to others, frustration and anxiety won't build up. You won't be fearful in your interpersonal interactions, and can easily achieve your goals.

On the other side, people who lack assertive skills are more neutral and anxious. They fear the outcome of expressing their thoughts. What will others think of them? What if they lose their approval? In short, non-assertive people are controlled by others and lack control over themselves.

Assertive people are firm without being rude. They equally regard other's opinions, thoughts, and wishes, as well as their own. They always react towards positive and negative emotions in a balanced way, without resorting to aggressiveness, shouting, or passivity. Assertive behavior has also been linked to lower levels of stress and depression.

Assertiveness also leads to transparency in your interactions. Such people know how to communicate their wishes and set boundaries, yet are not demanding, nor get furious when requests are not met.

They confidently put their point of view in front of others and may even influence them to see their side. Yet, they respect others' opinions even if it differs from their own. They are open to constructive criticism.

So, considering assertiveness from different aspects, what can you conclude?

It's clear that assertiveness is about controlling your own behavior, not others. With assertive behavior, you can acknowledge your thoughts and wishes honestly. You won't expect others to give in to your demands.

You listen to others' feelings and opinions, respect them, but ultimately you choose to go along with them or not. Even if you go along with them, it's ultimately your decision. A decision that won't be made out of compulsion or helplessness. You won't be a people-pleaser with assertive behavior.

However, every great concept comes with a word of caution. Such is the case here. There's an optimal level of assertiveness to use, especially if you are a leader. Too much, or too little, and assertiveness will lose its desired effect.

Now, we'll explore in-depth the other communication styles besides assertiveness…

Assertiveness in Communication: The 4 Basic Styles of Communication

If I had to categorize people based on their style of communication, I'll place them in one of the following categories.

Passive communication

What do you think about these statements?

"I don't know about my rights."

"I can't stand up for my rights."

"People never consider my feelings."

They reflect a weak, depressed, even resentful personality. One who does not stand up for his own needs and feelings. This failure is a consequence of not identifying and expressing their needs and opinions.

And what happens when you don't express those ideas or needs?

You'll suffer silently while all that anger, hurt, and resentment builds up. Finally, it gets expressed as an emotional outburst, usually out of proportion to the triggering incident. You might feel embarrassed or guilty after the outburst, but still return to the passive style of communication.

Passive communicators rarely make eye contact while speaking and exhibit a slumped body posture.

Do you know how passive communication affects your life?

Passive communication can lead to:

- Anxiety and loss of control over one's life
- Hopelessness and depression
- Stress, resentment, and confusion
- Allowing others to take advantage of you or infringe on your rights
- Low self-esteem and confidence
- Poor decision-making

Aggressive communication

The exact opposite of the passive style is aggressive communication. An aggressive person expresses his feelings and advocates for his needs abusively. He is dominating, impulsive, and easily gets frustrated.

He humiliates others, criticizes, violates their rights, looks down upon them, and behaves rudely without giving heed to their feelings or opinions. Not only verbally, but their body language is also overbearing and aggressive.

It's only natural to think ill of such communicators who instill fear and hatred in others, and thus, typically lack true friends or a social circle.

You'll hear aggressive communicators saying things like, "I'm superior and I'm right" or "I'm the boss" or "I know better than you" or even "I'll get my way no matter what."

Passive-aggressive communication

Ever seen people muttering under their breath, maybe after a confrontation? They are the people who have a hard time speaking up, voicing their opinions face-to-face, or confronting issues directly. They'll appear to be passive on the surface but exhibit anger or aggressiveness in an indirect or subtle way.

Such people do not have the power to deal directly with their object of resentment. So they'll show cooperation and acceptance on the surface, but will indirectly express their anger through taunts, sarcasm, and games.

The impacts of passive-aggressive communication can include:

- Feeling alienated from others
- Feeling powerless and stuck in life
- Incapability to address the real issues in life

Assertive communication

Assertive communication is a style where you clearly communicate your feelings and opinions, and advocate for your rights without violating others' rights.

In other words, you don't keep it all inside, or have emotional outbursts, nor do you fabricate things. You value yourself, your time, and your physical, emotional, and spiritual needs, as well as those of others around you.

Besides being a clear communicator, an assertive person is also a good listener. They establish eye contact when speaking to others, maintain a relaxed body posture, speak in a calm and clear tone, feel connected to others, and listen without interrupting.

Know why it's my favorite?

Because an assertive person:

- Feels competent and in control of his life
- Can address problems with confidence

- Creates a respectful environment for others to grow and mature
- Can take good care of himself, physically and mentally
- Can establish true, healthy, and long-lasting relationships

These are a few of the statements I've heard from assertive communicators:

"We can communicate respectfully with each other."

"I am 100% responsible for my happiness."

"I always have a choice in life."

"I respect your feelings and rights."

However, the point to remember here is that we don't use a single style of communication in every interaction. The assertive style of communication is more likely to lead you into respectful and long-term relationships. So it should be the preferred choice at most times.

Sometimes the situation may demand a passive or an aggressive style of communication. For example, the passive style would be a safer option if the situation is likely to escalate to violence. Similarly, if it's a question of your safety, aggressive communication will prevent the situation from getting worse.

Therefore, in every situation you must use your discretion to choose the best style of communication. If you feel your opinion might be better delivered by using another style of communication, choose that 'style' for that situation.

When you use one style of communication frequently, it gets embedded in your personality type. You become either a passive, an aggressive, or an assertive person.

What's the best way to identify these personalities? Let's explore some of the characteristics of each.

Characteristics of an Aggressive, Passive, and Assertive Person. Which one are you?

Each personality type has its own traits that make them different than others. Here's a synopsis of the personality traits of aggressive, passive, and assertive individuals. Which one do you fit in?

Characteristics of an aggressive person:

- He places his own needs over others'. He wants his desires fulfilled right away.
- Talks over other people
- No control over his emotions
- Blames other people for his failures
- Criticizes, humiliates, and talks ill about others
- Believes that a strong offense is the only way to defend himself

- Feels that speaking in a calm and friendly manner is a sign of weakness, and makes you prone to be taken advantage of. He thinks you have to be loud and strong to win.

Characteristics of a passive person:

- Sulky
- Withdrawn
- No eye contact
- Fearful to speak his mind lest he makes enemies
- Submissive because he hates conflict
- Appeasing to win people's approval

Characteristics of an assertive person:

- Calm, composed, and confident in a variety of situations
- Speaks clearly. His message is not exaggerated
- In control of self
- Can modulate himself when necessary

To summarize, the 3 C's of an assertive person are: Confidence, Clarity, and Control. But, how does an assertive person benefit in his life?

Why is assertiveness so important?

You'll get the answer shortly. Assertiveness leads to many benefits in your personal and professional life.

Assertiveness in your personal life helps to:

1. Be your own master. No matter what, you can hold on to your own and not be trampled by anyone.
2. Have your own way without being rude or creating a brawl, unlike aggressiveness, which is about forcing others into submission.
3. Better manage stress because of clarity in interactions. You know what to accept and when to say "no" thus setting clear boundaries for yourself and others.
4. Improve your self-esteem and confidence. Only an assertive individual has the confidence to speak up for himself.
5. Enhance your decision-making skills. Both passive and aggressive people make decisions based on emotions. On the contrary, assertive people tend to have a more neutral stance, keeping emotions in check and basing their decisions on facts.

Assertiveness in the workplace is important for:

1. Healthy and long-term relationships with your colleagues. When you are clear and transparent in your interactions in the workplace and speak politely with everyone, relationships are bound to be good.
2. Enhanced productivity of your team. Imagine a team leader who is aggressive and dominating toward his teammates. How would you feel to be on his team? Resentment and

hatred, right? But if he was assertive? Valued your opinions and suggestions? The entire scenario would change. You would love working with him. The performance of the entire team would improve.

3. Better negotiation skills. You will never settle for less. You are also ready to modulate yourself where necessary.
4. A peaceful and friendly workplace where every individual, their feelings, and their opinions are respected. This will create a safe working environment for anyone and also leave room for new ways of thinking.
5. Achievement of your career goals. With all of these positive outcomes unfolding at the workplace, success will be yours!

Assertiveness in relationships

Success in relationships depends on honesty, clarity, and respect for each other. An assertive person will be well-versed in these behaviors, leading to successful relationships.

It's easy to see how important assertive behavior is; in personal life, work, and relationships.

Before proceeding to the techniques to create assertiveness in your life, it's time for some self-assessment.

Assertiveness self-scoring inventory

We have two essential components of assertiveness:

1. Express your wants, needs, and thoughts, even when it's difficult.
2. Respect what others want, need, and think, even when it's difficult.

To measure your proficiency in these two components, we have designed this Assertiveness Questionnaire to determine your level of assertive behavior in your day-to-day life.

Assertiveness Questionnaire

Please choose one response from below that best describes you. The responses vary on a scale from 1 (Not very like me) to 5 (Very like me).

Be honest! The information will be used to help you learn assertive behaviors in your work and relationships. There are no right or wrong answers. Just rate yourself on the scale from 1-5.

Key: 1 means very rare; 2 means sometimes; 3 mean usually; 4 means often; 5 means always

Questions→	Not very like me →→→ Very like me 1 2 3 4 5
1. I stand up to people if they are doing something I'm not comfortable with	
2. I speak up when someone doesn't respect my boundaries like "no cheating on me" or "I don't let friends borrow money"	
3. It's often hard for me to say "No"	
4. I express my opinions even if others disagree with them	
5. After an argument, I often wish I would have said what was on my mind	
6. I tend to go along with what my friends or colleagues want, rather than expressing my thoughts	
7. I sometimes fear asking questions to avoid sounding stupid	

8. I bottle up my feelings rather than talking about them	
9. If I disagree with my boss, I talk to him or her	
10. If a person has borrowed money and is overdue in returning it, I'll talk to the person about it	
11. I'm usually able to tell people how I'm feeling	
12. If I don't like the way someone is treated, I speak up about it	
13. I speak up about things I really care about	
14. I am careful to avoid hurting others' feelings, even if they have done wrong to me	
15. I have a hard time controlling my emotions when I disagree with someone	
16. I avoid attacking others' intelligence when I disagree with their ideas	

17. I listen to others' opinions, even if I disagree with them	
18. In disagreements, I make sure to understand the other person's point of view	
19. During discussions, I communicate I am listening through body language	
20. Even in an argument, I don't interrupt the other person	

How to interpret the results

When you complete the questionnaire, you'll be tempted to add up your score. However, the total score has no meaning. Assertiveness must be assessed in terms of the person and the situation.

To analyze your responses to the Assertiveness Questionnaire, follow these steps:

1. Look at your responses to questions 1, 2, 4, 9, 10, 11, 12, 13, 14, 16, 17, 18, 19, and 20. These questions are oriented towards assertive behavior. Do your responses to these questions tell you that you always speak up for yourself or others'?
2. Look at your answers to questions 3, 5, 6, 7, and 8 which are oriented towards passive behavior. Do your answers

reflect you are more submissive and let others take control over you?

3. Look at your answer to question 15 which suggests you push others around you more than you realize.

Chapter Summary

- There are 4 styles of communication - passive, aggressive, passive-aggressive, and assertive. Assertiveness is the most important and beneficial style of communication. Remember the benefits it pays you in personal, professional, and social life.
- There's an optimal level of assertiveness to use. Too much or too little, and you'll lose effectiveness.
- Did you complete the questionnaire to determine your style of communication? What's your level of assertiveness? Low or high? Why do you want to learn and improve your assertiveness?

Answer these questions before you move on to the next chapter.

In the next chapter you will learn:

- Why some people can't be assertive.
- The major barriers to the practice of assertiveness.
- How you see yourself and how others see you, and which one matters.
- Skills to build a positive self-image.

CHAPTER TWO

Self Discovery: Regaining Control of your Life

I'm sure some of you scored lower than you would have liked on your assertiveness self-assessment. That's okay! Most of us have been brought up that way, to see assertiveness as unimportant. Even if it were, we often lack the courage to use it.

Why? Why can't some of us be assertive? After all, we have the right to express our feelings, opinions, and beliefs. Yet still, we don't do it.

Who we are and why some of us are not assertive?

Each one of us is endowed with basic human rights that must be respected and upheld. These include:

- The right to express feelings, opinions, values, and beliefs
- The right to change one's mind
- The right to make decisions for ourselves
- The right to refuse if you don't know or understand something

- The right to say "no" without feeling guilty
- The right to be non-assertive
- The right to personal freedom
- The right to privacy

When you respond passively, you neglect or ignore others' rights, and allow others to infringe on them. In contrast, aggressive behavior abuses these rights of others. Assertiveness is the best way to balance upholding your rights as well as respecting those of others.

But assertiveness doesn't come easily to everyone, because of the following reasons:

Low self-esteem and confidence

When you feel poorly about yourself, you deal with people passively. That's because you believe that others' opinions and feelings are more important than your own.

Consequently, you give others the ability to make you feel lower and further lose confidence in yourself. This vicious cycle continues to reinforce low self-esteem and low self-worth.

Low-status work and gender roles

Low profile jobs (such as clerks, sweepers, etc.) and women are usually associated with non-assertive behavior. These people are placed under tremendous pressure to conform to their roles that often demand passiveness. Imagine a clerk who is less likely to be assertive to his boss than his co-workers or subordinates.

Past experiences

If you have been taught to behave in a non-assertive way, either by parents, role models, or past experiences, it's difficult to change your ways and begin to behave assertively.

Stress and anxiety

When under stress, you often feel a loss of control over your life situations. Stress and anxiety usually result in the expression of thoughts and feelings in a passive or aggressive manner. This further increases your stress and the stress of those around you.

Personality traits

Some people are born with personality traits that are more passive or more aggressive. There's little they can do to change themselves. However, anyone can learn to be more assertive, while remaining true to the personality they were born with.

Unawareness of rights or wants

When you don't know what your rights are, or what you even want in the first place, you'll definitely find it difficult to exhibit assertive behavior.

Can you spot what's stopping you?

In the previous section, I listed the most common barriers that stop people from being assertive. Can you spot what's stopping you? Additionally, there are some individual needs and behaviors that pose a threat to the practice of assertiveness.

Here are some examples of such behaviors:

Desire to be loved at all costs

Every human being wants love and affection. However, in the workplace, this desire can quickly turn into a kind of dependency. Rather than being assertive and exercising your rights, you behave to please others and gain their approval.

Being kind to everyone

Being kind is good, but if it exceeds the threshold, it makes you too sensitive to the opinions of others. This can cause you to lose your independence. Also, people may start taking you for granted.

Intolerance to disagreements

Trying to convince others of your opinion at all costs is impulsive. Give others the freedom and the right to disagree. Staying detached from your opinion and giving others a chance to speak usually leads to progress, and even breakthroughs.

Seeking to control all situations

Humans are powerful beings, yet, we can't control everything and every situation. Nor can we control other people's behavior or way of thinking. But, when you try to do so, you end up being aggressive and forceful over others.

Obsession with perfectionism

Imagine a boss who wants everything to be perfect. He can't tolerate a single mistake from his employees. If that's his obsession with perfectionism, what will the workplace be like?

That's what happens when you seek perfectionism in every single task. You behave aggressively, not assertively. As a result, you push people away from you rather than establishing good relationships.

Trying to gain sympathy by overworking

When you overwork to show off or get sympathy from others, you don't challenge your limits, rather, you are seeking approval from others.

Intolerance to failure

When you say, "I don't have the right to make mistakes," you forget that mistakes are a part of being human. One who has never made mistakes has done nothing at all.

Setting contradictory goals for yourself

Setting goals that contradict your values and needs (professional and personal), or taking up responsibilities while hoping to avoid any conflicts, is preparing yourself for disappointment. It's more useful to set realistic and relevant goals for yourself, and plan the steps you need to take to achieve them.

After analyzing all the barriers to assertiveness, one thing is absolutely clear. Everything comes down to what others will think of you. You fear losing others' approval and appreciation, or want to control them lest they might think you are incompetent.

But, do you correctly judge what others think of you? Let's find out in the next section.

Metaperceptions – how you see yourself and how others see you

If you say "I don't care what others think of me" you are only fooling yourself. Because ultimately, as humans, we all want to fit in with the social universe. The feeling of exclusion or rejection by a group leaves us anxious, irritated, and depressed.

To fit in socially, we need to connect with others. And to make good social connections, it helps to understand what others think of us and modify our behavior accordingly.

Knowing and perceiving what others think of you is called "metaperception." In other words, metaperceptions are how you feel about how others feel about you. Often these metaperceptions revolve around our perception of self – what we think about ourselves.

Mark Leary, a psychology professor at Wake Forest University in North Carolina says, "You filter the cues you get from others through your self-concept." This self-concept is fundamentally shaped by your mother. The way your mother responded to your first cries and gestures influences how you expect to be seen by others. Children with unresponsive mothers behave in ways that make people want to keep their distance, whereas those with responsive mothers are more confident and connect well with peers.

Though the self-concepts forged in childhood don't always carry on to adulthood, if they do, it takes a bit to change them, specifically the negative self-concepts. William Swann, a psychology professor at the University of Texas, conducted research that shows people with negative self-concepts drive others to think negatively of them, especially if they suspect that others like them.

You all have a fairly stable view of yourself, but it's not always easy to determine what others think about you. Therefore, your metaperceptions are often inaccurate. Why?

First, every person you meet will perceive you through their unique lens. For example, if a person generally criticizes everyone, he will do the same with you, even if you are genuine. Second, people are sometimes not direct in daily interactions. They might fake their expressions.

However, you can make your metaperceptions more accurate by following these steps:

Be curious to learn new things and open to new experiences in life. As you take up new challenges, you'll meet new people from whom you can gather clear data about how you are perceived by others.

Take care of how you present yourself to others. Have a sense of your voice, tone, clothes, and body language. This way you can help control the impression you give and make your self-perception more accurate.

Learn to regulate your emotions and gain an upper hand in knowing what others think of you. If you are overwhelmed by your feelings or can't express them at all, it becomes difficult to interpret how others feel about you.

On the other hand, prickly and hostile behavior, bursting into tears at the slightest provocation, and narcissism block accurate metaperception. Such behaviors encourage others to become guarded, or even lie to you.

If you are socially anxious, you block accurate metaperception. You fail to ask others about themselves, and fail to put others at ease while interacting with you.

So, being accurate in your metaperceptions is crucial. It rewards you by giving knowledge about how others perceive you, and helps you fare better socially.

Others judge you on two types of traits—visible and invisible. People notice your visible traits more than you yourself. On a scale of physical attractiveness, others will almost always rate you a point higher than you would rate yourself.

Talking about the "invisible" traits, they aren't entirely invisible—at least not to your close friends. They can easily make out when you are anxious or worried. Your negative traits might be "invisible" for most, but if someone knows you really well, they can recognize them, too.

However, no one wants others to perceive their negative traits. We don't even acknowledge them, despite being aware of their presence, and modify our behaviors in order to avoid their disclosure.

Here's where self-awareness works against you and you get stuck with what you are, and your negative traits. Another realm where self-awareness acts as a curse is by overanalyzing others' reactions to you and misinterpreting them.

Unpleasant emotions like embarrassment, shame, and envy are also felt through self-awareness. These emotions are meant to motivate us and cut down our potentially self-destructive behaviors. However, when you get overly concerned about what others think of you, it can stifle your spirit and constrict your behavior.

Do you really want to know how people see you?

Report cards and annual reviews can track your performance in school and at work. But finding a straightforward critique of your character is difficult unless someone blurts out something in a heated argument.

You can always ask a family member or a close friend to tell you honestly what they think of you, but the question is: Are you ready to listen to their perspective?

This is because we all want to hear good things about ourselves. We can't tolerate anything negative. It hurts our ego. It hurts our self-image. We might even land in a conflict with our loved ones to protect our own perspectives.

But sometimes you really need accurate feedback, like when deciding about a job change or a marriage proposal. That's where you need to learn how to see things from others' perspectives.

Perspective matters! The importance of seeing another perspective

Depending on where you stand, the view of your room can look very different. If you stand on one side of the room and your partner stands on the opposite side, you both will describe the same room, yet your descriptions will be different, simply because you are looking at the room from two different sides.

Similarly, perspectives in subjective matters can vary. The same fact will have a different meaning for people with different viewpoints. Like how a single divorce case can be viewed quite differently by different advocates. And sometimes, two opinions may be entirely opposite, yet are still both valid.

However, conflict arises when you fail to understand other perspectives. What makes sense to one person may sound absurd to you, because you can't see their point of view. You can't take in other people's perspectives if they differ from yours.

Why? Here's the kicker!

Reality is how things are. But, for any person, what they think and feel is the reality for them, given the circumstances. What they think and feel further drives their actions.

Behavioral science research proves that we don't see things as they actually are. We filter them through our self-concept. Our personality and the way we are affected by the situations build up the way we see things. We interpret them according to what we believe is true about ourselves, about others, and our past experiences. All this builds our perspective about self and others which, once formed, is difficult to change. This tendency in humans is called confirmation bias. We see what we want to see, and thus, interpret information in a way that confirms our perspective.

That's why it's hard to truly understand another's perspective that is different than ours.

So even if a decision, event or statement is the same, it can have different meanings for every individual or the group. And each of us may feel that we are right. However, that's the beginning of all misunderstandings, disagreements, and arguments.

If ONLY we could see things from another's perspective, we would have fewer conflicts and more productive conversations to combative issues. All the more, we would be more cautious with our words and actions in difficult situations to avoid making them worse.

For example, Theresa May's failure to get her Brexit deal through the House of Commons three times has stretched the Brexit drama far longer than most British people expected.

On such issues, can you keep your own perspective at bay, and try to see things from the other side?

The day you do so, you may find your own perspective not as accurate, or not the only "right" way. It's not that your perspective is wrong or you shouldn't stick to it for good reasons, but now, you better understand the other perspective.

Mistaking a perspective

However, there's a catch when trying to see things from another's perspective. You must avoid these two mistakes.

First, don't be overconfident that you have succeeded in interpreting a different viewpoint. Have you really seen it the way he thought/wanted? Are you sure you are not mistaken?

Research shows that when you infer the thoughts and feelings of a person by observing his face or the way he behaves, it's mostly inaccurate.

Next, avoid being easily pleased by the other person's perspective, and base your argument over it. Understanding another person's perspective doesn't mean you can't question it politely. When you base the perspective on wrong assumptions, you often make a misleading conclusion and miss the real issues.

For example, in the case of the Brexit deal, one may suspect that the leader is corrupt or faulty. If this speculation is accepted without raising a brow, the disagreements would eventually result in false judgments without addressing the actual problem.

How to take other perspectives in the right way

While taking another person's perspective into consideration, it's crucial to follow these three habits.

First, consider each perspective that differs from yours. Honestly include each of them. While comparing the different perspectives, you may come across some similarities. Plus, you may see how different perspectives can compensate for each other's strengths and weaknesses, and you may walk away with a new and better perspective.

Inclusivity also plays an important role when disagreements between perspectives are based on strong values and principles. If you pursue your own perspective driven by one of these values or principles, could it be that others are also motivated by some of these values and principles that are dear to you? So consider the values or principles that back up a specific perspective, and how relevant they are.

Secondly, interact with people. You can't just imagine what the person is going through unless you have a conversation with him. You must interact with the person, ask questions, and listen to what he feels, his concerns, and ultimately his perspectives. When you are involved in such interactions, everyone is more likely to express their true feelings rather than simply saying the things that others want them to. This results in a better understanding of others' feelings, worries, and positions. Over time, such quality interactions also build trust and social collaborations.

Finally, strike a balance between your individuality and other's perspective. You must empathize with them, including their emotions and subjectivity, but also don't get carried away by them. Stay slightly detached so you can properly evaluate the situations and perspectives. Detachment doesn't mean to become feelingless, but to resolve the issue without getting entangled. In terms of opinions, detachment means you don't necessarily agree with others each time, but you always understand their perspective.

If you can be more considerate, interactive, and detached to manage arguments or disagreements, many differences will disappear. New pathways will open up that lead you towards common goals.

If you learn to appreciate another's perspective and use it appropriately, you can prevent misunderstandings, enable productive conversations, and achieve your common goals.

So ultimately what matters: How you see yourself or how others see you?

If you have followed me until here, it won't be difficult for you to answer that. It's legitimate to conclude that both have their value. Neither can be left out for the other. However, you should take everything with a detached mindset.

If you collect other's perspectives about yourself to improve your self-image or be a better version of yourself, it plays a positive impact on your life. Otherwise, if you get bowed down by other's viewpoints, it stifles your own character.

I'll talk more about building a positive self-image in the next section.

Building positive self-image

Self-image is how you see yourself, your personality traits, abilities, and what you believe others think of you. If you feel good about yourself, and recognize your strengths while being realistic about your shortcomings, then you have a positive self-image. Conversely, if you don't feel good about yourself, and focus on your faults and weaknesses while exaggerating your failures, you have a negative self-image.

You assess yourself both objectively and subjectively. Objective assessment is not influenced by personal feelings and represents facts such as your height, weight, hair color, IQ, etc. Subjective assessment includes traits such as care, affection, generosity, humor, patience, etc., and is influenced by your personal feelings. Since self-image is a collective representation of your self-assessment, it ultimately becomes more subjective than objective. People are generally more critical about themselves, and place a greater emphasis on their flaws rather than their goodness. Therefore, their self-image becomes biased.

A person's self-image is more or less resistant to change. However, it gets influenced by one's life experiences and interactions with others. Life experiences, both positive and negative, and interactions with family members, peers, and friends play significant roles in shaping self-image. For example, if you fail at a task and the people surrounding you also criticize and reject you, you may develop a negative self-image. Contrary to this, if your family and friends are supportive, they'll reinforce your positive attributes and help in developing your positive self-image.

As your experiences and relationships affect your self-image, so does self-image shape your experiences and relationships. If you have a positive self-image, you'll have a generally optimistic attitude. When you interact with others with such an attitude, they'll be uplifting and rewarding, thus contributing to a constructive relationship. These constructive relationships will further feed your positive self-image.

Your self-image is also closely connected with your self-esteem and self-confidence. Self-esteem is how you value yourself. Self-confidence is the trust in your knowledge, judgement, and abilities. Poor self-image will lead to low self-esteem and self-confidence. So having a positive self-image is important as it affects your thinking, behavior, and how you relate to others around you. It enhances your physical, mental, emotional, and spiritual well-being, and gives you more confidence in your relationships. Even the people around you are influenced positively by your positive self-image.

However, the question is: How do you build a positive self-image?

Because, today, we all are the products of what others expect from us. We have often lost touch with what we "actually" are.

Each one of us knows ourselves better than anyone else. We know what we think, what we feel, what we like and dislike, yet we still compare ourselves with others. This reflects our dissatisfaction with ourselves. And we are dissatisfied because we are far from being our true selves, which leaves us unhappy and emotionally drained.

So, follow these steps to uncover your real self:

Follow your passion. Be yourself by feeding your spirit, mind, and soul.

In modern times, money and wealth have become the metrics of a person's success. Consequently, you see young professionals taking up higher-paying jobs to make others feel proud of them.

The job might not be enjoyable for them, but since it pays well and earns them more respect, they prefer it. They pretend to be happy but may actually feel quite hopeless.

Sadly, people today often view each other in terms of their titles and salaries. These have become the determinants of one's self-worth. Instead, you should concentrate on just being yourself, which in turn will feed the mind, spirit, and soul. Cultivate your passion and find work you enjoy doing.

Never let your inner child die.

What can you best learn from a child? Being carefree!

Children don't care what others think about them because they're happy with themselves, with their lives. They are their own person because they haven't been modeled to fit into society and its funny norms. They enjoy running, playing, and jumping wherever they are and don't care what anybody thinks.

However, as you grow, you cast yourself as per other's expectations and lose touch with your inner child. Tickle your inner child again and become free by enjoying the moment and having fun.

Find your inner strengths.

Embrace yourself and your personality no matter how different you are from others. You could be an extrovert who's spontaneous or an introvert who's a bit awkward. Shed these labels that aren't important. You are what you feel and think. Get rid of all the pretending because you want to fit in. Just be yourself, and find your strengths. If other people are genuine, they'll accept the "real" you.

Tune into your feelings.

Acknowledge your feelings, good or bad. When you are in touch with your feelings, you understand more about yourself. Plus, it gives you the strength to deal with sadness, happiness, fear or anger without getting stressed, and help you enjoy a peaceful state of mind.

Be more aware of your thoughts.

It's incalculable how many negative thoughts run through your mind every day. And after a period of time, these negative thoughts can start to turn into reality. Because that's the law of nature. Every thought manifests into a reality. So, you must take extra care of your thoughts and their quality. Regular meditation helps you become more aware of your thoughts and gives the power to change them. Then, throughout the day, continue to observe your thoughts. By becoming more aware of them, and changing those thoughts when needed, you'll focus more on your present.

Trust your intuitions.

It's always advisable to follow your intuition. It's one of the most essential parts of being you. As you begin trusting your intuition, you transform into your most authentic self, which is the "real" you.

You may believe that a wise decision is practical and serves more purpose, but this isn't always true. Practical decisions are made on what is thought to be right, and not what is felt to be right. When you make a decision by following your intuition, your soul will be satisfied.

Get out of your shell.

While learning to be yourself, you may feel tempted to do everything at once. You want to get rid of all the masks, pretentions, and become totally authentic overnight. However, it doesn't work that way. First, you should identify the ways you're socially inauthentic and then correct them one at a time. Get out of your shell gradually to be more authentic in your life. Start by setting small goals to change and work gradually and consistently to achieve them one by one. Small steps lead to a big change. You'll achieve your goals soon, and find yourself behaving entirely different than before.

Calm down. Be assured that it's okay to be yourself.

Many people feel tense or anxious when trying to be themselves. If you are one of those, first, calm down, and assure yourself that it's perfectly alright to be "myself." The ONLY way to do this is through self-talk. Sit in silence for a few minutes, observe what's going on in your mind, and make it understood through inner dialog. Just like we would make a child understand, in an assuring and convincing way. Do the same with your mind now. You need to tell yourself that it's okay to be your real self. If others don't like it, that's their problem. This self-talk will relieve your tension and anxiety and help you interact better in social settings.

Deal with your anxiety

Go a step further and read some books on how to deal with anxiety. Your lack of positive self-image might be more than just a little lack of confidence. It could stem from some serious social anxiety. Taking steps to handle social anxiety will prove beneficial in discovering your true self.

Once you connect with your "real" self using these steps, I assure you that you'll start feeling good about yourself. You'll learn to accept and love yourself as you are. And when that happens, others also start accepting you as you are, too.

Case Study: The Power of Perspective and Positive Self-Image

John is excited to go out on his first date. He really likes the young woman he is going out with, so he is really keen to make a good impression and connect with her. However, over the course of their discussion on the date, he learns that she is motivated and driven by completely different values. She has very different tastes in almost everything. Now, what does John do to make a good impression?

He respects the woman's opinions and values, but also offers his own. Instead of blindly following her opinions on things, he isn't afraid to disagree with her openly, yet respectfully.

His positive self-image and high self-esteem allow him to stay true to his values and easily communicate with others, even when they don't agree. That's because John believes more in behaving authentically than focusing on getting his date to like him.

So, what do you think about yourself? Do you have a positive or a negative self-image for yourself? Let's find out with the next questionnaire.

Self-assessment for self-discovery

Yup! I am back again with yet another self-assessment activity for you. I promise it'll be fun and deliver real insight, something that is very critical in seeking to be the master of your life.

So don your thinking caps and answer the following questions honestly:

1. What are your strengths?
    a. List 5 things you love about yourself.
    b. List 5 abilities, skills, or talents you have.
    c. List 5 life achievements or instances you "win" in your life.
    d. List 5 difficult situations you overcame.
    e. List 3 - 5 people who are your best supporters.
    f. List 3 - 5 people you have helped in some way.
    g. List 5 things you are grateful to have in your life.
2. What are your major barriers to assertiveness?
3. What are the areas you need to shift your perspective in order to change your life?

Chapter Summary

- Low self-esteem, low self-confidence, unawareness about one's rights, stress, and anxiety are the major barriers to the practice of assertiveness in daily life.
- Building a positive self-image and giving due consideration to others' perspectives (different) are the keys to use the assertive style of communication.

- Follow your passion, tune in to your feelings, be aware of your thoughts, find your inner strengths, trust your intuitions, and get out of your comfort zone to discover your real self and build a positive self-image.

In the next chapter you will learn:

- What is personal empowerment and how to achieve it?
- What does personal empowerment feel like?
- The relationship between assertiveness and empowerment.
- How to assert yourself positively.

CHAPTER THREE

Using Your Personal Power

As discussed in the last chapter, building a positive self-image allows you to be the master of your life. In short, it makes you feel empowered.

But, why do we all want to feel empowered?

Because without empowerment people lack control over what they do. They lack confidence in themselves and their decisions, and thus, rely on others to make decisions for them – their spouse, colleague, children or peers. They might be dominated by their colleagues, friends or family, or overwhelmed by the demands of their job.

In contrast, empowered people are fully in charge of what they do, what they want in life, and how to achieve it.

What is personal empowerment?

"Empowerment" literally means "becoming powerful." That doesn't mean growing in strength like a Sumo wrestler or attaining the most influential position at your workplace. True empowerment requires you to set meaningful goals by identifying what you want in life and then taking action to achieve those goals, thus, making a significant difference in this world.

Therefore, personal empowerment is to take control of your own life, and not allow others to control it for you. Also, be clear that "empowerment" is not the same as "entitlement." Entitled people believe that all the benefits and privileges should come to them automatically. On the other side, empowered people achieve success through hard work, reflection, and cooperation.

As easy as it sounds, the process of personal empowerment is complicated. To empower yourself, you need to develop your self-awareness, which helps you understand your strengths and weaknesses. Plus, you must be aware and understand your goals, how they differ from your current position, and what behaviors, values, or beliefs you need to change in order to achieve them. The degree of this change required varies from person to person.

But, I did promise to make complex issues easier for you!

So, I have outlined an eight-step process for you to develop personal empowerment easily. Let's dive in to learn the process step-by-step.

Identify a goal focused on power

This might be, for example, a housewife seeking financial independence from her spouse, or someone looking to have more influence over their teammates.

Increase your knowledge

The next step is to understand more about the goal you have set. For example, if you don't want to be financially dependent on your partner, you need to understand the various ways to earn money by working from home. Also, open yourself up to the different possibilities. The more open you are, the more creative you get, and the more possibilities appear for you to succeed in.

Increase your self-efficacy

Before you take action to achieve your goal, you need to believe that you can achieve your goal. Having information about your goal is one thing. But you must also understand your strengths and weaknesses. That's what self-awareness is all about. It also includes being aware of your values and beliefs, and their critical examination to ensure they are fully valid. This will help you assess where you are most likely to achieve.

Work on your skills and competence

You may need to enhance your skills to become more influential. These skills can be acquired through experience, education, training, or practice. However, as you start interacting with more and more people, and try to influence them, you will rapidly learn what works, and further develop your skills.

Act and keep taking action

The road to personal empowerment won't be smooth. You will encounter bumps along the way. However, instead of getting "knocked back" by the first obstacle you encounter, you should maintain the resilience and persistence to keep moving and seek other ways to achieve your goals.

Run your own race

Don't be bowed down by the competition. Don't worry if the grass seems greener on the other side. It doesn't equate to your failure. Focus on your grass, on the opportunity that is in front of you.

If you worry about the competition, what others are and are not doing, then you'll lose track of the importance of what you're doing. Empowerment has nothing to do with competition, it has everything to do with what you contribute to the world.

Assess your impact

Empowerment is also about changing the impact you have on others and your life situations. Therefore, it's important to also assess your impact. At first, you may not see huge changes, but even small changes count as your success.

Expand your network

Empowerment comes from collaboration, not competition. Success is never a one-man job. One of the smartest ways to develop personal empowerment is to network. Build a network of people who have strengths to fill in your limitations. In collaborative environments, success is shared, and each person empowers the other.

Competition divides us, and may sometimes lead to jealousy or anger, none of which will help you build long-term relationships or be more successful.

How does language affect your personal empowerment?

The way you express yourself, both verbally and non-verbally, to others can empower you as well as the people with whom you communicate. For example, using a positive and active language like "I will" and "I can" is empowering whereas the opposite implies passivity, lack of control, and lack of responsibility for your actions.

While introducing yourself to others, use your own words to describe yourself, and not how others define you. Otherwise, people may persuade you to conform to their demands.

Never criticize a person to their face. If criticism is absolutely necessary, exercise it with extreme caution. Use positive and supporting words and phrases to offer criticism in a constructive way. For example, if your teammate is always late to work but is a very hard worker, praise his hard work. Tell him if he can work so hard, he can also be punctual. Your words will work like magic. They'll empower him to at least try to be on time.

That's how your language can play a significant role in your personal empowerment and those of others. Now, let's see what personal empowerment feels like by walking through an example.

A Case Study: What does personal empowerment feel like?

Amara and Shira are best friends. They both divorced their husbands within one year of marriage. They sincerely tried to make their marriages work but didn't succeed. Nor did they receive the required alimony from their husbands.

Do they feel empowered?

In Amara's case, she actually is. Though she was sad for a few days after the divorce, she decided to move on. She didn't want to be stuck. She took up a job of her liking, made new friends, and is now preparing for her second marriage.

Shira, on the other hand, is depressed, frustrated, and full of tears. She is convinced that her life has come to a standstill since the divorce. Every day she keeps blaming her husband and reiterating how he did not treat her well. She wants to work, she wants to meet new people, but she is afraid to be rejected because of her divorce.

Amara knew what she wanted from her life. So she made a decision and acted on it. Shira, in contrast, feels powerless to change her situation, so she doesn't even try. She lacks confidence and empowerment to achieve what she wants. This becomes a vicious cycle. Because of the lack of empowerment, she doesn't try. And because she doesn't try, she doesn't achieve to feel empowered.

However, empowerment doesn't only come from achieving. You must speak up and take a stand for yourself to feel empowered. In other words, you must be assertive in order to feel empowered.

Let's explore the relationship between assertiveness and empowerment in the next section.

Assertiveness and empowerment

Consider the following situation:

Nancy works in the HR department of a company. She's a young, beautiful, married woman. Her company has organized an office trip to Goa. All her colleagues are going except her. That's because her husband feels she can't go on a trip without him. He thinks she can't take care of herself without him.

So Nancy suppresses her excitement for the trip and goes along with the situation. A few months later, Nancy's boss throws a lavish party at his home, inviting her and her husband. But again, her husband refuses to go to the party, giving some lame excuse, and doesn't allow Nancy to go, either.

Time and again Nancy has had to suppress her feelings because of her husband.

Does that sound like your story?

Well, that's because Nancy and you choose to suffer in silence rather than expressing your feelings. You behave passively, lest you hurt others' feelings. This might seem using your powers for good, not hurting others' feelings, but that's an illusion.

Being passive makes you feel like a victim, one who is trapped in their life situation and can't get out of it without the help of others. Playing a victim will never let you feel empowered. You'll always be at the mercy of others.

Contrastingly, Nancy could have become aggressive, by shouting or yelling at her husband. Aggressiveness usually develops out of a sense of entitlement and is another common way for people to assume a sense of power, or to feel powerful. Such people believe that aggressiveness is the justified way to deal with situations like these, by controlling others. However, the power of aggressiveness is unhealthy and can severely damage your relationships. If it becomes your regular method of gaining control over situations, it will alienate you from others and may even create anxiety in people involved.

Besides the passive and aggressive approaches towards controlling situations, some people take the passive-aggressive approach. It's a deadly combination of two unhealthy approaches. When two people are in a relationship, this passive-aggressive behavior makes things much more complicated.

In Nancy's case, she may conform to her husband's demands on the surface but punish him silently, for example, by not cooking good food for him. A person with passive-aggressive behavior feels they are powerful, but, in reality, they lose their integrity and reduce any possibilities of healthy empowerment.

Healthy empowerment and how assertiveness plays a role

So how do we differentiate healthy empowerment from unhealthy empowerment?

That's simple! Healthy empowerment doesn't allow people to act at the expense of others. A person with healthy empowerment knows how to navigate his life with confidence and purpose. If an empowered person does commit a mistake that hurts someone, he'll apologize and seek healthy ways for resolution, considering the other person's needs.

Additionally, an empowered person lets the other know if he feels tread upon or taken advantage of. Love and respect for self, and others, are the life mantra of an empowered (healthy) person.

When you feel empowered, you also feel liberated. You take responsibility for your actions, which are unaffected by how other people behave. Here are four tips to help you become more assertive and feel empowered in your life:

Be friendly, not accommodating

There's a difference between *being friendly* and *accommodating people*.

Friendly means taking care of your loved ones and helping them in times of need. On the other hand, you accommodate people when you care for them at the expense of yourself. You simply don't know when to say no. Consequently, you build up anger and resentment inside. You feel that people take undue advantage of your inability to say "no."

So, the choice is yours: whether to be friendly, or whether to be accommodating to people. When you choose "being friendly," you not only befriend others, you're also being friendly to yourself.

Understand that taking care of others' needs doesn't mean sacrificing your own. For example, if your friend asks you for financial help with something you can't, simply refuse or ask to be reimbursed. This way you won't feel like the victim of other people's demands.

Speak up, not out

When you don't know what assertiveness is, you picture someone who is overly harsh and demanding. However, assertiveness is about speaking up, not speaking out. Speaking out is getting angry when your needs are not met, or yelling and blaming others when they manipulate you.

Speaking up, on the other hand, is making people aware of your needs upfront. You don't shout at or blame others, rather you proactively set reasonable expectations and boundaries. Communicating with others what you need helps build healthy, strong relationships, as well as your self-esteem.

Define your boundaries

Boundaries are important, and it is equally important to keep them defined. Despite setting the boundaries, some people will try to cross them. Then what?

Keep your boundaries well-defined and reinforce them with those that try to cross them. Come what may, never give in to the demands of those people. Otherwise, you'll invite them to walk over your boundaries again and again.

Let go of the selfish "friends"

You know who your selfish "friends" are! They're warm and complimenting but will interact with you only when you give something in return.

Can you call these individuals your "true" friends? Will they not trample your boundaries and expect you to give in to their demands?

If you worry about losing them, relax! You don't have to tell them that things aren't working out. They'll automatically leave you when they realize you won't do anything for them anymore. Some may try to make you feel guilty but try not to listen. Don't fret over losing selfish friends. It's good that they leave your life. You deserve the true ones.

Thus, the lack of empowerment makes you feel helpless. Your life is in the hands of others. They can make you dance like a puppet on their whims and fancies. This creates anxiety and resentment.

However, becoming more assertive puts the power and control back in your hands.

How to assert yourself positively

There's a fine line between being assertive and being aggressive. And if you seek to feel empowered, to feel more in control of your life, and to lead a happy, positive, and fulfilled life, you need to be assertive.

Yet, the question remains! How do you assert yourself positively?

People generally consider themselves as assertive, but in reality, they've had situations where they let things just slide by. They didn't stand up for themselves. Result? Anger, resentment, frustration, and guilt get bottled up.

Some people, when they confront a difficult situation, feel that it's easier to run away rather than facing it head on. That's because they lack the inner power; the empowerment we've been talking about.

However, it's much more effective to be a strong and mighty lion than a timid mouse, running away from danger. It's time to take a closer look at assertiveness and learn the steps to be a "lion" in your life.

But, why only the lion? Because the lion symbolizes strength and power, which you ultimately want and will help you achieve your life goals.

Here are the seven easy steps for asserting yourself positively:

Create an image of strength in your mind

Consider the example of the lion I gave above. Hold that image of yourself as a lion in your mind, and relive it when faced with a situation where you need to assert yourself. If a lion doesn't seem feasible to you, choose whatever image conveys strength and power to you. Come back to it when you need an assertive boost. Creating and commemorating the image of strength in your mind keeps you alert on being assertive. It also gives you the confidence that you can assert yourself positively.

Believe in yourself and your values

The first step to being assertive is to believe in yourself and what's important to you. Without this self-awareness or a firm sense of self, it will be difficult to stand up for yourself and be assertive when necessary.

You have to know who you truly are, and what you believe to be a truly assertive person. Start working on developing your self-awareness today. Find your strengths to make the most of the situations where you need to stick to your beliefs.

Understand your own boundaries

You can't be assertive unless you know where your boundaries lie, and when someone crosses them. It's essential to define and communicate to others what makes you uncomfortable.

You have to be clear as to what you'll tolerate and what you won't. But before communicating this to others, you must be clear with yourself, otherwise, you won't know when a line has been crossed.

Understand your needs and your purpose of assertiveness

What is that you want to achieve by asserting yourself?

It might be to stop another person's unpleasant behavior or to reach a specific goal. You must know this: what you want and what purpose you wish to fulfill by asserting yourself positively. That's because your purpose might get lost in the heat of the moment. So make sure you remember your values when trying to determine your goal.

Respect others (and yourself)

We've established that there is a fine line between being assertive and being aggressive. You can be assertive without humiliating others. You can be assertive without putting others (and yourself) in a vulnerable or uncomfortable position.

How? Be respectful. You can behave with respect and kindness even when being assertive. Put yourself in their shoes, and think about how you would like to be treated. Assert yourself while keeping this in mind. Being respectful of others will also make you maintain your integrity and conduct yourself in a manner that you can be proud of.

Express expectations clearly

To be assertive in any situation, it is imperative that you clearly express what you expect from others. Because if you are not clear about what you want, it will be very hard for others to give what you want.

While expressing your expectations, use clear and direct language. Avoid using vague terms or words that may be confusing. It might feel hard to be direct sometimes, but if you're clear about what you want, you are more likely to get what you want.

Remember: no one is omniscient and can read your mind or know what you want. You have to express it clearly.

Practice assertiveness often

You all have heard this before: practice makes perfect!

So if you want to improve your assertiveness skills, you have to practice them often. That doesn't mean insisting on getting your way all the time, but rather realizing your needs and valuing them just as much as those of others.

Think of the situations where you could have been assertive, but weren't. Think about if similar (or worse) situations arise in the future, how you could positively assert yourself. Rehearse it! Practice it as much as you can.

Rebuilding your life from a foundation of respect

One question that still pervades your mind: how do I respect my own needs and that of others at the same time? Don't I have to compromise my own needs, in order to create peaceful relationships? Isn't it easier to remain quiet than expressing my needs?

Short answer: NO.

You don't have to be a people pleaser to create better relationships. Or, meet this need by silencing your self-expression. This leads you to be passive and bottle up anger and resentment. The key is to refocus on your needs and respect them. This is called self-respect; it is your ability to see the "self" having the same basic rights and dignity as others.

In the last three centuries, the world has witnessed an immense increase in people's civil rights. The Declaration of Human Rights, signed by most countries, ensures equal dignity and basic rights to people irrespective of their social class, gender, religion, etc.

However, it's surprising that people still do not claim their rights or assert themselves, though they possess these rights. Like people who are mobbed or bullied and silence themselves instead of protesting against injustice. Some people accept less pay for their work even if their performance is the same as others.

And why does this happen? Research shows that when people perceive themselves as equal to others, they expect equal treatment. But, when they don't, they consider unequal treatment as just and protest as inappropriate.

Thus, to claim one's rights or behave assertively, one must view oneself as equal to others. In other words, they must have a good amount of self-respect.

But, what does it mean to perceive yourself as equal to others? How do you respect your own needs and that of others at the same time?

Let's understand this with a few examples.

Suppose you're at a restaurant and unhappy with the service. A passive response would be to stay quiet. An aggressive response would be to yell at the server. An assertive response would be to kindly let the server know what you'd want. Here, you're speaking up for your needs while also respecting the server.

Let's see another one.

Your employee is a bit lazy and doesn't complete their assignment on time. Instead of shouting and scolding, an assertive response would be to set clear expectations with your employee.

We can respect others' needs and our own by making "requests" rather than "demands." Demands don't consider the other person's needs or opinions, and usually backfire. Requests, on the other hand, consider the needs of both parties in question. People are more likely to respond to requests as they feel connected and have a choice to agree or not.

If you can't hear a "no," then it's a demand. If you are open to finding strategies that work for both of you, it's a request. Requests increase the possibility of what the other person is willing to do.

So respecting others' needs doesn't mean compromising your own, or remaining silent, or letting others take advantage of you, or becoming a people pleaser. Rather, it is about compassionately and acknowledging others' needs and making requests (not demands) to meet your needs. After all, you deserve to have a voice.

Chapter Summary

- Personal empowerment and developing self-respect are the necessary requirements to develop assertive behavior.
- Set a powerful goal for yourself, acquire knowledge, work on your skills and competence, and keep working to achieve your goals. This will help you feel empowered from within.
- Believe in yourself and your values, understand your needs, your boundaries, and set clear expectations with others to assert yourself positively and develop your self-respect.
- You deserve to have a voice. Compassionately and clearly acknowledge others' needs and make requests (not demands) to meet your own.
- I would appreciate it if you could answer the questions below before we get into the nitty-gritty of developing assertive behavior.

    1. Do you view yourself as equal to others? Why or why not?
    2. List any 3 situations in your life where you feel you could have been assertive but didn't.

3. What are the areas you feel you lack empowerment? How can you feel empowered in these aspects of your life?

In the next chapter you will learn:

- Why assertiveness is a learned skill
- Three keys for assertive behavior
- The various categories of assertive behavior
- How to handle criticism assertively
- How to speak up for yourself

CHAPTER FOUR

Getting Started: Developing the Assertive behavior

Now you are familiar with what assertiveness is and what qualities you need to develop assertive behavior in yourself. The real (and the fun part!) starts now - how to develop assertive behavior.

Assertiveness is a learned skill

Assertiveness is not only a style of communication, but a characteristic mode of behavior that involves expressing your thoughts, feelings, beliefs, and opinions openly, without violating the rights of others.

And any mode of behavior can be learned through consistent practice. However, the practice of assertive behavior is associated with the following dos and don'ts:

Dos of assertive behavior

1. Expressing your needs clearly and directly
2. Expressing your ideas without feeling guilty

3. Standing up for what you believe even though others may not agree
4. Knowing your rights and how to get them
5. Effective communication
6. Conveying your feelings to others with confidence
7. Self-reliance and independence
8. Persisting until your needs are met
9. Analyzing a problem and pinpointing the area of responsibility before taking an action
10. Having a positive attitude at all times
11. Being strong when others are weak
12. Taking pride in your accomplishments
13. Having the courage to dream and developing the skills to turn them into reality

Don’ts of assertive behavior:

1. Beating around the bush before expressing your needs
2. Feeling guilty or afraid to express your needs
3. Agreeing with others no matter how you feel
4. Ignorance about your rights
5. Ineffective communication
6. Begging for what is legitimately yours by law

7. Dependence on others

8. Giving up when you face problems

9. Giving in to defeat

10. Easily swayed by others

11. Uncomfortable about your accomplishments

12. Fear to dream

Practicing assertiveness is not a new concept. Many people and organizations have achieved their objectives through assertive techniques for decades. Here are a few examples of individuals who have "won" and reached their goals by being assertive:

- Susan B. Anthony, whose persistence in the long struggle for female suffrage won American women the right to vote in 1919.

- Mohandas K. Gandhi's determination freed India and inspired subjugated people all over the world to emulate his nonviolent methods to gain freedom.

- Carol Mosely Braun, who shook up Illinois politicians when she defeated the "undefeatable" Alan Dixon in the Illinois Democratic primary for U.S. Senate.

- Jane Bryne (former Chicago mayor), whose outspoken assertiveness got her fired from her job in City Hall, but a year later, she was elected as the head of the City Hall.

- Patrick Henry. His assertive quote, "Give me liberty or give me death" became the rallying cry of the American Revolution.
- Jesse Jackson's positive attitude overcame discrimination and poverty to become a powerful national leader.
- Joan of Arc, whose courageous assertiveness inspired a defeated French army to victory.

The people who stand out as doers, movers, and achievers are all assertive people, though their specific styles may differ.

Indeed, we are all born with an innate temperament to assert ourselves. But, as we grow up and socialize, it may either reinforce our innate tendencies or curtail them. The responses we receive from our family, peers, co-workers, and authority figures as children play a significant role in shaping our innate tendencies.

For example, if your family dealt with conflicts by yelling or arguing, you'll learn to deal with conflicts in the same way. On the other hand, if your family or peers believe in expressing your thoughts while respecting those of others, you'll likely develop the same habits.

When you grow up as an assertive individual, you tend to be emotionally balanced and have better health outcomes. However, being assertive doesn't guarantee that you'll ALWAYS get what you want. Sometimes you will, sometimes you won't, and sometimes you'll agree upon mutually satisfactory action.

I know what you must be thinking. You haven't grown up as an assertive person. People around you always taught you to put others' needs before your own, to please others before yourself. And now you find it hard to assert yourself. Relax! As I said, assertiveness is a skill and it can be learned at any stage of your life. Even now! So, let's dive in to learn more about how to develop assertive behavior.

We have already gone over the difference between passive, aggressive, and assertive styles of communication. Now, let's inspect these three different styles.

Behaving *aggressively*, even if you are right, communicates to others, "What I want is more important than what you want." You put others' needs at stake, in fact, outwardly disrespecting them. As a result, the recipients of your aggression feel resistant and often counterattack in anger. This can lead to conflicts, arguments, stress, and even hatred in relationships.

Being *passive* is not any better. It's living a lifestyle devoid of the word "no," which is like driving a car without brakes. When you say "no" you set appropriate limits to what you accept and what you don't. Without these limits, your life will be out of control and full of stress, anger, and resentment. Saying no at the right time and for the right reason is healthy, proper, and good. That's what assertiveness is all about!

Assertive behavior is the positive and controlled expression of your legitimate needs. It's a healthy way to communicate where you maintain your self-respect and also earn respect from others.

It's a healthy way to deny something with dignity. Being assertive allows you to get what you need without hurting others. It's a perfect balance between aggressive and passive behaviors.

Assertive behavior allows you to lead a life of peace, respect, and cooperation. An assertive person advocates for himself, but in a respectful and determined way, yet, acknowledging the feelings and rights of others.

The messages with the use of "I" typically reflect assertive behavior.

For example:

- I can't make it to the meeting today.
- I would appreciate it if you can help me with this.
- I am really not in the mood to go to the party.
- I am sorry, I already explained the consequences for being late to the office today, and now you have to face them.

Contrary to what many believe, assertive behavior evokes respect from others, whereas the other styles do not.

When you behave assertively, people know that "you mean what you say" and it's not an exaggeration or bluffing. Your "yes" means "yes" and your "no" means "no." Such clear communication is beneficial for all parties involved and builds trust and cooperation.

People feel more comfortable with those who are transparent and open about their thoughts and feelings. An assertive style of communication includes how you think, speak, and conduct yourself.

Behaving assertively also reduces your stress levels. Passivity is synonymous with the feeling of powerlessness and being overwhelmed. Aggressiveness often encounters resistance and counterattacks. These are extremely stressful.

In contrast, an assertive individual takes a balanced, calm, yet determined approach to get what he or she needs. Assertive behavior is the least stressful path.

Let's understand assertiveness with a true story.

Julie appreciates when her husband Jack refuses to help her with household chores. She knows when he can't or doesn't want to do something. Plus, she knows that when he does say "yes" to something, he actually means it, and will follow through.

Jack's assertive behavior towards Julie is an act of respect and honesty. If Julie doesn't agree with Jack about something, she knows she can, in turn, respectfully disagree with him. So together, they can resolve their issues, and arrive at a mutually agreed-upon plan of action.

The three keys of assertive behavior

The three keys of assertive behavior can be related to a three-legged chair. You can sit on a three-legged chair without worrying about falling, but not on a two-legged chair. Assertive behavior is also characterized as having three legs.

The three basic components of assertive behavior are:

1. **Know what you want**. Be clear as to what it is you want.
2. **Say what you want**. Communicate your intentions, needs, and desires to others clearly without using any vague or confusing language.
3. **Get what you want**. With respectful, determined, and controlled means of communication, increase the likelihood of achieving your reasonable and legitimate goals.

Categories of assertive behavior

Before you even open your mouth, your body language says a lot about you. It announces to others if you are confident about yourself or not.

Body language that shows confidence:

- Standing up straight and making eye contact when speaking with others
- Sitting in a relaxed, but professional manner
- Taking an initiative to greet others at a meeting and in opening the conversation

- Confidently sit next to the most powerful person in the room
- Not waiting for permission to speak before speaking up
- Organized in work and has the needed information at their fingertips
- Dressing appropriately
- Courteous and pleasant during discussions

Body language that shows a lack of confidence:

- Slumped posture when standing
- Afraid to look at people when talking to them
- Sitting down as though sitting on eggshells, too self-conscious to move
- Afraid to take the initiative in greeting people and waits for others to give permission to say "hello"
- Sitting inconspicuously
- Afraid to speak unless spoken to and given specific permission to speak
- Seldom carrying information or materials to meetings
- Under or overdressed for a picnic or a party
- Getting unpleasant, argumentative or rude when expressing a viewpoint

An assertive person communicates with confidence, both in body language and verbally. There are three categories of assertive behavior:

Refusal assertiveness is saying "no" at the right time and in the right way. Saying "no" helps you establish healthy boundaries and allows others to know what they can expect from you. It also makes you feel empowered and maintains strong relationships.

A useful strategy to help you say "no" with ease is to gain clarity about the types of things that you wish to say "yes" to. Jot down your top three priorities (which might change over time) in a diary or notepad, and always keep it handy. When someone asks you something, check to see if it aligns with your priorities. If yes, feel free to answer the inquiry affirmatively. If it is not in line with your objectives, say no.

Follow these steps to say no in the right way:

- State your position, like if you can't take up a task, "No, I can't."
- Explain your reason: Give a valid reason for your inability to take up a task, for example, if you are occupied with other important issues.
- Express your understanding for the other person.

If you don't have an immediate answer to someone's inquiry, ask him to give you a certain period to think over it and provide a deadline by which you'll answer. This keeps you accountable and ensures you value the relationship and yourself by providing a concrete reply in the desired time frame.

Expressive assertiveness is telling people how you feel. Expressing your feelings is an essential component of effective communication.

10 times where you must express yourself:

- When you love someone.
- When you feel strongly about something.
- When something bothers you.
- When you feel like you can't cope, speak up and ask for help.
- When you disagree with someone.
- When you're not happy in a situation.
- When someone has done something great for you.
- When you have a question, always ask it.
- When you have an answer, always give it.
- When you have good news, always share it.

No doubt you must express your positive, as well as your negative feelings. However, gloomy feelings must be expressed with a word of caution. You must take ownership of those feelings rather than blaming others.

For example, if your friend arrives late for dinner, you might say, “You made me angry by arriving so late for dinner.” Your friend might have arrived late, but they are not responsible for your reaction. Your feelings, in reality, are the result of your own expectations and hopes. If you express them in a way that puts the blame on others, it’s more likely to meet a defensive response. The other person may not acknowledge your feelings, and then the issue remains unsolved.

If I were in your place, I would express my feelings as “I was so angry when you arrived late for dinner, because I had hoped to spend some quality time together.”

See the difference? I took responsibility for my own feelings. When you clearly express your feelings without assigning blame and express why you feel that way, it enables the other person to understand and acknowledge your feelings.

Request assertiveness is to get the information, its clarification, and ask for what you want. When you lack the skill to make assertive requests, you make life unnecessarily hard for you and others. You may miss out on opportunities, take longer to complete things, or make them more complicated.

In contrast, when you learn to make requests assertively, you respect yourself and others. By asking directly, what you need, you say, "I have value" and "I value your help." So, it's essentially a compliment to the other person.

What stops you from making assertive requests?

See if any of these beliefs resonate with you:

- If someone denies my request, it means they don't like and/or respect me.
- Asking for help puts me under an obligation to them.
- Asking for help means I am weak OR other people will see me as weak.
- It's better to do it myself than risk rejection.
- I will annoy or upset others by asking for help.
- I don't want to be a burden/add to their stress/workload.
- I don't deserve to ask for help.
- I shouldn't have to ask; people should know I need help.
- Other people will help me only if I'm excited about it.
- People should help me as I'm more important or more stressed than they are.

These beliefs make it hard to ask for help. And even if you do, you'll likely encounter resistance. However, the point to remember is that these beliefs might be just your feelings. Just because you feel them doesn't make them true.

In addition, if you ask for help, you might get something done faster, more smoothly, or more easily. You might get a better job, learn something new, share your experiences, or get to know someone better. This will help you build better relationships and show people who you are (your authenticity).

So, here's a simple formula to make an assertive request:

Ask the person directly. Address them by name, and give the reason why you need help. Give a clear, short message about what you need from them. Make sure to stay calm, keep eye contact, and speak sincerely. Avoid being flattering to convince the person for help.

Be prepared to have a conversation until you both are satisfied. The other person also has the right to say "no" and ask for clarification, negotiate, or let you know about the problems your request might cause them. Be prepared for this.

Making requests assertively saves us from manipulating others or throwing our weight around and demanding assistance. It also builds our confidence and self-esteem. However, remember not to take the person's response to your requests personally.

Tips for being assertive

- EYE CONTACT – Look at the person to whom you talk most of the time, but don't stare at him 100 percent of the time.
- BODY POSTURE – Stand or sit up tall facing the person, but avoid being overly stiff.

- DISTANCE/PHYSICAL CONTACT – If you can feel the other person's breath, you are probably too close. Keep a comfortable distance from him.
- GESTURES – Use hand gestures to complement what you say, but remember you are not conducting an orchestra.
- FACIAL EXPRESSIONS – Ensure your facial expression matches your emotions and what you are saying. For example, don't laugh when you are upset or don't frown when you are happy.
- VOICE TONE, INFLECTION, and VOLUME – To make sure your assertive message is heard, pay attention to the tone of your voice, the inflection of your voice (emphasis on syllables), and its volume.
- FLUENCY – It's important to be fluent and let your words out efficiently.
- TIMING – Timing is important, especially when expressing your negative feelings or making a request to someone. Doing this several days later or immediately in front of people may not be the right time. Do it as soon as there is a time for both parties to resolve their issues alone.
- LISTENING is an important, yet often neglected part of assertiveness. When you express your feelings without infringing on the rights of others, you also need to give the other person a chance to respond.

- CONTENT – Depending upon what purpose you want to accomplish with your assertive behavior, the content of your message will be different.

How to handle criticism assertively

There are three ways to help you deal with the criticism and make a decision about which behavior, if any, you will change. Remember, people criticize your behavior - what you say and do, not who you are.

The three ways of handling criticism assertively are:

1. Agree, if it's true - It's always possible that there is some truth in what others say about you. For example, if someone says, "You always overthink petty issues," admit it, saying "Yes, sometimes I do tend to overthink on small matters."

2. If you made a mistake, accept it. Here, you are only saying about the mistake and nothing about yourself as a person. For example, your boss says "What's the matter with you, the file was supposed to be in .pdf" You admit your mistake and promise to correct it as soon as possible.

3. If somebody criticizes you unnecessarily, ask what exactly bothers him. For example, if someone criticizes your decision about late marriage. You agree that the marriage must happen at a certain age, but the person continues to make a big deal out of it. At this point, ask what it is exactly that concerns him.

Using any of the above three techniques for handling criticism assertively, you help yourself sail through an unpleasant situation without feeling guilty or dumb. Knowing that you can handle criticism without shouting or name-calling, it will allow you to become closer to the person you want to be.

Speak up for yourself and start thinking for yourself

Do you realize you are a unique, one-of-a-kind person? So you should learn how to feel comfortable in your skin, about the style in which you assert yourself. Some people speak loudly and enthusiastically, but people hear them clearly. But some speak more softly and infrequently, they are heard equally clearly.

So don't change your style. The key is to put into words exactly what you want or need. So how can you make yourself heard?

- Look into the eyes of the person you talk to. If you are short or use a wheelchair, draw attention to yourself by speaking directly to the person. If the other person seems unwilling to look at you, find a clever, yet polite way to say, "I'm right here!"
- Speak clearly and distinctly. If you have a speech disability, calm your anxiety. Relax the body muscles, take in a deep breath and exhale slowly. Speak slowly and as distinctly as you can. You can visualize a soothing image such as a mountain stream to help you relax the body. When you are calm, the other person will also relax and concentrate on what you are saying.

- Be courteous and polite, but not obsequious.
- If the other person addresses everyone around except you, tell him nicely and firmly that you would like to be addressed directly.
- Think about what to say and how to say it, *before* you begin speaking.

Self-assessment: What's your style?

If being assertive is not your style, then what is? Pick any one option from below:

- The **Nice Guy,** who is afraid to say or do anything that might offend others.
- The **Whiner,** who constantly whines and complains about the things they need and are not receiving, how others treat them when they ask for anything, or how bad everything is, but never does anything about it.
- **Adherent Vine,** who expects others to stand up for your rights and intervene on your behalf.
- A **Silent Victim** who sulks silently and believes there's nothing they can change about their life.
- The **Fairy Princess** that expects everything to be delivered without any effort on their part.

- The **Waiter,** someone who is waiting for a miracle to happen. Who waits, waits, and waits for someone else to do something.
- The **Bombshell,** who sporadically fires angry missiles.
- The **Scared Cat,** who fears others will get onto them if they took the trouble to do something.
- The **Appeaser,** who settles with compromising his needs.

How do you view yourself when others criticize you?

What are your expectations when you ask someone for help?

Write answers to these questions before you learn more about assertiveness in the next chapter.

Chapter Summary

- Assertiveness is a mode of behavior and communication skill that can be learned and practiced to achieve what you want in life.
- The three keys to assertive behavior are: Know what you want, Say what you want, and Get what you want.
- Your body language speaks volumes about you and your confidence, even before you open your mouth. Make sure you exhibit confidence and assertiveness with your body language.
- Expressing your feelings, thoughts, and opinions, both positive and negative, saying "no" respectfully to certain

requests, and asking for help when needed are the significant elements of assertive behavior.

In the next chapter you will learn:

- Why it's hard to say "no" to others
- How can you get better at saying "no" in life and business scenarios
- The right way to say "no"

CHAPTER FIVE

The Art of Refusing

One important aspect of assertive behavior is the ability to say "no" at the right time and in the right way. You know the benefits it has to you as a person and in your relationships. But, does knowing the benefits make everything easy?

You can't say "yes" to that! Right?

Why? Why is it hard to say no?

Jennie wasn't quite ready to get married. She knew her age was completely appropriate to tie the knot, but she wanted to focus on her career and think about marriage a year later. Her parents brought up the issue almost daily, "You are thirty-four now," they said. "If you delay, you won't find a good match. You'll have to spend your entire life alone. So why don't you think of getting married now?" Jennie knew her parents were probably right. However, somewhere inside, she wasn't completely convinced by the idea of marriage at the moment. And she didn't know how to say this to her parents.

Susan's friends were going to an expensive club. She couldn't afford to pay for a night out drinking, and also, didn't really want to get wasted, which she knew would be the end result of the evening. But she could not figure out how to get out of it without irritating all of her friends.

Susie had recently divorced her husband. Her parents and friends were pressuring her to sign up to a matrimonial site. But Susie was reluctant. Her problem was not if any guy will be interested in her or not, but what if she's not interested in them? She couldn't reject someone politely. She could not hurt other people's feelings. It was hard for her to say "no" to someone.

Do any of these situations seem familiar?

Many powerful men consider "no" to be an important part of a successful life strategy. For example,

Steve Jobs: *Focusing is about saying no.*

Warren Buffett: *We need to learn the slow yes and the quick no.*

Tony Blair: *The art of leadership is saying no, not saying yes. It is very easy to say yes.*

Despite these famous quotes by powerful men, it's not easy for us to develop the art of saying no. Why?

Here are the reasons:

Fear of conflict

Most of us are afraid of conflict. We don't like others to get angry with us or be critical of us. Therefore, we don't say "no" lest it might put us into conflict with someone else. Someone else may be our partner, a colleague, a friend, or the boss.

Many parents want to avoid battles with their children, and thus, fulfill all their demands, even if they know they shouldn't. They feel that if they said "no" to their children, their children will stop loving them.

However, this fear of conflict is taught to us as children. We are always taught and expected to do what parents, teachers, and others in power tell us. They show us the fear of punishment or losing their love if we don't obey. And this worry of conflict gets carried with us into adulthood.

Besides, the desire to fit in and be liked by our peers also prevents us from saying "no." Research shows that men and women have a tremendous need to belong to a peer group. We want to be accepted by our friends or the people we want to be friends with, and thus, stay mum.

Don't want to disappoint or hurt someone

Sometimes we do things that make others feel better, even if it's not what we want to do. But, just to make others smile, can you compromise your own? Imagine you have to submit an urgent project the next day but you can't say no to your relative for the party because you don't want to disappoint them.

Doesn't seem politically correct

For some, the idea of turning down someone's request is not politically correct as it presents you being selfish and unconcerned.

Harder for women

Women often find it difficult to say "no" to men because they want to get along, want to be nice, and don't want to hurt their feelings.

It's a sign of weakness

Saying "no" is perceived by a few people as a sign of weakness, either in their own mind or in those for whom they work.

People don't expect you to say no

When someone asks you to do something, they already assume that you will say yes. So they already have a psychological advantage over you, and you don't wish to let down their expectations.

For example, let's say your mother asks you to cook dinner before you leave for the party at your friend's house. She knows you are running late, but she made the request because she wasn't feeling well that day. That seems okay! However, the problem arises when she asks you to cook dinner each time you have to attend to other important issues, even if she is feeling well.

How others will perceive you if you say no

You're afraid that if you say no, you'll be seen as someone who's difficult to get along with or someone who doesn't play well with others.

Well, your interests and the interests of those you work with might be radically different. But you give in to their interests and compromise with your own values so that people don't think poorly of you.

Saying yes is natural to you

Maybe you're just a "yes" type of person. That means it's consistent with your values. You don't agree with your boss just because he or she is your boss. Rather, it's embedded in your giving personality.

You like to be as helpful as possible whenever you can. You tend to think of others, their needs and their time as being of greater value than your own. And so, it really doesn't matter what the request is. You'd simply rather say yes.

Though it seems to be a nice attitude, when taken to the extreme, can grind you down. It's always good to take a balanced approach and preserve your time and energy as well. Only then you'll be able to help others in the way and to the extent you want to.

Saying yes is more positive than saying no

The world today is getting very negative. To have positivity in your life, you have to put it there, and so, you have to go out of your way to say no to the things you don't want to commit to.

Everyone else is saying yes

Now, what does that mean? Suppose you are at an office party and everyone is enjoying alcoholic drinks, except you. Because that's against your values. You don't drink alcohol at all. However, to avoid not fitting in with your colleagues, you trample your values. You can't dare to say no.

Inability to recognize the extent of the commitment

Suppose you keep taking on projects at your office. You didn't say no to any of them, thinking that you'll finish them all by the weekend. That happens because things seem super easy on the front end, but when you actually sit down to work on them, they're far more complicated.

To return a favor

Anytime someone does you a favor, you feel obligated to return it in some form. That's human psychology and the power of reciprocity. Now, there's nothing wrong with asking for or returning a favor. But you need to think over how you return it. You don't want to do something that's beyond your capacity or beyond the time you ought to spend on it.

To prove your worth

People with low self-esteem or insecurity in their jobs are usually more inclined to say yes to prove their worth.

Thus, you need to think before you accept any request, each and every time.

However, the point to remember is that these stated reasons are not facts. They are just the thoughts or opinions you have learned and grown up with. Each of these can be replaced by a powerful and true opinion about saying no.

What's the truth about saying "no"?

Replace your old thoughts and opinions about saying no with these:

- Others have the right to ask and I have the right to refuse. Don't be afraid that other people will get upset if you decline their request.
- Saying no is refusing the request, not rejecting the person.
- When I say "yes" to one thing, I actually say "no" to something else. I always have a choice.
- Problems arise because I overestimate the difficulty that the other person will have in accepting my refusal. But, if I express my feelings openly and honestly, the other person will also feel liberated to express his own.
- Saying "no" to someone's request doesn't mean he/she can't make further requests.

How you can get better at saying "no"

Once you have identified the personal reasons that stop you from saying "no," it's time to deploy these techniques:

- Practice saying "no" in small or unimportant situations, like not buying something at a drugstore.

- Stop for a minute and take a breath before saying "yes." This gives you a little space and time to assess and respond to your own needs.
- Seek other's advice if you need a backup for your own position. I'll talk more about this in a moment.
- Don't get trapped in the pitfall of "everyone else." It's almost universally true that everyone else is doing the same thing, or wants you to do whatever is being asked for.
- Take a minute and ask yourself if you'll feel guilt, anxiety, disappointment, or any other emotion if you don't do what's being asked for. Can you tolerate it? Is it worth it to accept the request in order not to feel those emotions?
- Assess the outcome. How bad will it be? Is it worth it to give in or not?

To get better at the art of saying no, remember that you can change your mind in most cases. Don't feel you only have one opportunity. There will be many more.

Getting a backup to say "no"

Most of us feel much better about saying "no" to someone if we have the backup of some buddies or the people we trust.

Continuing with the above examples,

Jennie talked to her friends about her parents' behavior towards marriage. They helped her to understand her parents' concerns but also taught her how to put into words how she feels about the issue.

Susie's friends offered her a variety of techniques for saying "no" to guys, like not answering their calls or giving some excuses to not move forward, but she didn't agree with them. She realized that saying "no" nicely but firmly is just a part of the process and doesn't make her a mean or bad person.

Susan also talked to a couple of friends who were not a part of the drinking group. They supported her decision that it's a waste of time, and you spend a ton of money on something that leaves you feeling miserable and affects your performance the next day. They told her that her friends won't even notice if she didn't go. They just want company.

Susan simply refused her friends, and after a couple of tries to change her mind, the girls left her alone. And there was no change in the way they treated her at work.

But, the toughest part comes now!

What's the right way to say no?

Even assertive people find themselves in situations where they say yes to things they really don't want to do. This can be appropriate in some situations. For example, if your boss asks you to do something, and you really don't want to do it, you can't practice your assertiveness skills and say no to him - you don't want to get fired!

But, suppose your friend asks you to do something that you just can't take out time for and you say yes, you'll find yourself over-loaded.

Now, let's take a look at some of the effects of not being able to say "no":

- You invite resentment and anger towards the person you have said "yes" to, though they have done nothing wrong. This resentment builds up over time to the point you can't tolerate it anymore.
- You become increasingly frustrated and disappointed with yourself.
- You can get overworked and highly stressed if you take more than you can cope with.
- In the long-term, you may have low self-esteem, depression, and anxiety.
- Under different circumstances, some people are able to say "no," but in an aggressive manner, without considering or respecting the other person. This may cause people to dislike and alienate you, which is not good assertive communication.

There are some basic principles to keep in mind when you want to say "no":

- Tell the person if you find it difficult to accept the request.
- Be straightforward and honest, but not rude.
- Be polite. Say something like "thank you for asking, but..."
- Keep your message brief. Don't over-explain your actions and reasons for saying no.

- Speak slowly with warmth and compassion.
- Don't apologize or give elaborate reasons for saying "no."
- Take responsibility for saying "no" and don't blame others or make excuses.
- If need be, provide alternatives to solve the other person's problem.

Remember, it's your right to say no if you don't want to do things. Plus, it's better to be truthful at the beginning than breed anger and resentment in yourself by saying "yes."

Suitable ways of saying "no"

There are a number of ways you can say "no" which are more appropriate according to the particular situations.

- **The direct "no"** - When someone asks you to do something you don't want to, just say 'no' without apologizing. Though forceful, this technique is quite effective with salespeople.
- **The reflecting "no"** - Here, you acknowledge the content and feel of the request, and then add your assertive refusal at the end. For example, "I know you're excited about the Goa trip, but I can't come."
- **The reasoned "no"** - In this technique, you give a brief and genuine reason for your refusal. For example, "I can't come shopping with you because I have to submit this assignment tomorrow."

- **The rain-check "no"** - It is not a definite "no." You may refuse the request at the present, but leave room for saying "yes" in the future. However, only use it if you genuinely want to meet the request. For example, "I can't come to meet your parents today, but I could make it sometime next week."
- **The enquiring "no"** - It's not a direct "no" but opening up the request to see if there is another way it could be met. For example, "Is there another dress I could buy for you?"
- **The broken record "no"** - Can be used in a wide range of situations where you repeat the simple statement of refusal over and over again. Without explanation, without apology, you keep repeating the refusal statement. It's particularly helpful with persistent requests.

How to say no in business scenarios

Ever notice how many times you accept a project and regret your decision later? Do all those projects actually align with your business goals?

If you can't refuse such projects, you'll pay the price. Missed deadlines, lost clients, physical and mental exhaustion, frustration, and stress. When you are habitual in accepting each and every request that comes your way, you lose focus and get unaligned from your goals. That's too high a price to pay.

So learn how you can protect your time and energy in these typical business scenarios by knowing the right way to respond.

The freeloader is a pushy prospect who tries to persuade you and get his work done for free. Instruct him on the value of your work and how they can pay it.

Set up a formal consultation with the prospect, show your work plan, and determine whether you can work together. If things don't work out your way, still, stay professional and friendly. You can share other resources in your network or recommend books, blogs, or courses. Your honesty and assistance will be appreciated by the prospect. Otherwise, there's nothing to lose as the prospect never intended to buy from you in the first place.

What do you call a client who always makes changes to the project? Even after signing on the proposal. A scope creeper! Such people often request changes that threaten to disturb the project's schedule and your sanity.

In such cases, be firm, clear, and upfront in the first meeting. Set clear boundaries for any ad hoc requests. Explain what your policies are on the post-signing of the project (such as rejection, time penalties, high cost, etc.). This ensures that the prospect will think twice before making any post-sign off requests.

The dead-end meeting. Incidental meetings clutter your calendar, are time-consuming, and leave you mentally exhausted. Before saying "yes" to any such meeting, assess how it will help in the progress of your project.

Take a minute to consult your schedule, analyze the pros and cons of the meeting, and then respond to the requestor with a confident answer. If it's not worth your time, simply say "no."

Or, if saying no is difficult or you want more information to make up your mind, seek it out before you commit. And finally, if you agree to a meeting, decide the time limit for the discussion.

How saying no helps you in a business setting

You gift yourself by saying "no" to the things you don't want to do. It reduces your calendar clutter and your anxiety, and you can focus -- both physically and mentally — on the things that really matter to your business. By saying "no" you protect your energy and the most important resource: TIME.

Saying "no" is a valuable asset.

Homework for you

Before you continue to the next unit, here's your homework:

1. Elaborate on one (or more) situation of your life where you want to say "no" but aren't able to.
2. Write one (or more) reason that stops you from saying "no."
3. Recall the conversation where you gave in to the request. What made you accept it? Then, imagine the same conversation and practice saying "no" with confidence.

Chapter Summary

- Saying “no” to others’ requests at the right time and in the right way is crucial for your health, well-being, and for maintaining strong relationships.
- However, we fear saying “no” to others because we are afraid of conflicts, or that we might hurt or disappoint them by saying no.
- Anger, resentment, frustration, stress, depression, anxiety, and low self-esteem result from our inability to say “no” at the right time.
- Assertiveness teaches us how to respectfully say “no” to others while respecting our own needs.

In the next chapter you will learn:

- What boundaries are
- Why you should set boundaries for yourself
- Areas to set your boundaries
- How to set healthy boundaries?

CHAPTER SIX

How Are your Boundaries?

Unfortunately, the boundaries we set for ourselves aren't visible to others. They are not like a physical wall or a "no trespassing" sign we construct around ourselves. Nevertheless, you must set them, as well as let others know about them. That's essential for your health, mental wellbeing, and even safety.

You must set boundaries for:

- Personal space
- Sexuality
- Thoughts and feelings
- Possessions
- Time and energy
- Culture, religion, and ethics

Setting your boundaries and respecting those of others isn't rocket science, but still, you need to learn how to set them. Whether you want to set boundaries with your family or with strangers, here's how you can start.

Understanding and determining your boundaries

People usually misunderstand the word "boundary." They perceive them as a way to keep oneself separate from others. However, setting clear boundaries provides healthy rules for what you accept in relationships, personal or professional.

The benefits of setting your boundaries are:

Healthy relationships and enhanced self-esteem

Melissa Coats, a licensed professional counselor says that *"Boundaries protect relationships from becoming unsafe. They actually bring us closer together than take farther apart, and are therefore necessary in every relationship."*

Having boundaries allows you to prioritize yourself, whether in self-care, career, or in relationships.

Boundaries should be flexible

Boundaries shouldn't be drawn in permanent ink. You must reassess them from time to time and make the necessary changes. Too rigid, or too inflexible of boundaries give rise to problems rather than benefits.

Boundaries help to conserve your emotional energy

When you can't advocate for yourself, you seem to lose your identity. Your self-esteem dwindles. You build bitterness towards others. However, when you set your boundaries, you are at peace and conserve your energy for self-care.

Boundaries provide you a space to grow

Our feelings are not always that simple. It sometimes feels complicated. Setting the boundaries and breaking them when required shows your vulnerability. Simply talking about your complex feelings openly with your friends displays your authenticity. And when you do so, you welcome others to open up to you when they need to.

However, vulnerability and oversharing are different. Vulnerability is genuine and brings people closer. On the contrary, oversharing blackmails emotionally and forces the relationship over another person.

Pointers to oversharing are:

- Attacking someone personally on social media
- Not using a filter to who views your daily dramas on social media
- Sharing personal details with new people in the hope of hurrying the friendship along
- Dominated, one-sided conversations
- Expecting friends and family to give you on-call emotional therapy

By oversharing, you could be trampling other people's boundaries.

How to set your boundaries

Setting your boundaries is not a tutorial you can search on Google. Each one of us has their own set of boundaries that vary from one person to another.

What shapes our boundaries?

- Our heritage or culture
- Where we live in or come from
- Whether we are introverts, extroverts, or somewhere in between
- Our life experiences
- Our family dynamics

We all have a different family dynamic. Each of us understands situations differently. And we all change our boundaries as we grow older and shift our perspective. One size doesn't fit all.

Self-reflection helps in setting your own boundaries. It includes the knowledge of:

1. What are your rights?

Identify your basic human rights when setting your boundaries. These include:

- Right to say no without feeling guilty.
- Right to be treated with respect.
- Right to give equal importance to yours and others needs.

- Right to accept your mistakes and failures.
- Right to deny others' unreasonable expectations.

Once you are aware of your rights and believe in them, it gets easier to honor them. When you honor them, you'll stop spending energy pleasing others who don't respect your rights.

2. What do your instincts tell you?

You can clearly make out when someone violates your boundaries or when you need to set one based on your gut feelings. Signs like an increased heart rate, sweating, chest tightness, and stomach uneasiness tell you that you aren't comfortable in a situation and must draw a boundary. For example, do you clench your fists when you find your roommate reading your journal? Does someone asking about your married life make you tighten your jaw?

3. What values do you have?

Your boundaries and your morals are closely related. Identify your ten important values and pick out the three most significant ones. What challenges do these values face that make you feel uncomfortable? This tells you if you have set strong and healthy boundaries for yourself.

Setting your boundaries – taking action

Tips to confidently establish your boundaries:

1. Use assertiveness

Assertively setting boundaries exhibits your firm stance and, is actually being kind to others. With assertive language, you are not harsh, but non-negotiable, without criticizing the recipient. Aggressive language, on the other hand, seems harsh and pushy.

Using "I statements" reflect assertiveness. It shows confidence and sets a good boundary by expressing your thoughts and feelings without fear.

For example, consider these two sentences:

First: *Keep your hands off my diary!*

Second: *I feel encroached upon when you see my diary because it's my private space where I pen down my thoughts.*

Which one do you think allows others to respect your privacy? The second one, of course. Because it's clear, non-negotiable, and expresses what you want and why.

2. Develop the habit of saying no

As discussed earlier, by saying "no," you bless yourself. You don't need to explain yourself to the person you are refusing.

3. Protect your spaces

Set boundaries for your personal stuff, physical and emotional spaces, as well as your time and energy. Take the help of your tech gadgets for this.

- Lock your private items in a drawer or box.
- Instead of a paper journal, use a password-protected digital journal.

- Schedule non-negotiable alone time or time when you do things you love.
- Use passwords or other security features on devices and tech accounts.
- Set aside a specific time for answering emails or texts.
- Use the "out of office" responder on email accounts when on a vacation.
- Send verification of your time off days in advance.
- Temporarily delete email and messaging apps when you don't want to be contacted.
- Use the "Do Not Disturb" feature on your phone and other devices.
- Promise yourself not to respond to messages or calls sent to personal accounts.

Others may expect us to reply to work emails during non-work hours. However, this can take a toll on your wellbeing and relationships. So, strive to create a balance between your work and personal life each time you can.

As an adult, you also have the right to secure the privacy of your mail accounts and messages. Communicate your boundaries to others about your digital devices as well.

4. Ask for assistance

If you are mentally ill, depressed, anxious, or have experienced any trauma, it may be hard for you to define and assert your boundaries. In such cases, reach out for help from a mental health professional.

How to recognize and honor other people's boundaries

As important as it is to honor our own boundaries, it is equally important to recognize and honor others, lest we might overstep them.

But, how do we do this? Just follow these three rules:

1. Check the clues

Taking note of social cues helps you identify others' boundaries. If someone is uncomfortable with closeness, they'll step back when you step forward while talking to them.

These are some clues that others want more space:

- No eye contact
- Turning away or sideways
- Taking a step back
- Short response to conversation
- Excessive nodding
- Sudden high-pitched voice

- Gestures that reflect nervousness like talking with hands or talking fast
- Folding arms or stiffening the posture
- Cringing

2. Watch out for neurodiverse behaviors

Neurodiversity or neurodiverse behaviors are shown by people with autism, dyslexia, ADHD, and other developmental disabilities. Such people use certain gestures all the time or have poor eye contact or difficulty starting a conversation. Look out for such behaviors when talking with someone who has developmental disabilities.

3. Seek permission

Never underestimate the power of questioning. Always enquire before engaging in physical touch, like a hug, or if you can ask a personal question to the person.

Boundaries are there to help us

Setting boundaries should be thought of as bracing our relationships with others rather than building walls to keep people out. And boundaries help us much beyond that. They can give us a clue about damaging behaviors. We often neglect our instincts thinking them to be unreasonable, but if something constantly feels uncomfortable or unsafe, it's a sign of trouble.

If anyone pushes or violates your boundaries again and again, pay attention. Also ask people in your life to honestly tell you if you push their boundaries accidentally.

Sometimes boundaries don't work

Setting boundaries is an advanced form of assertiveness. It involves taking a position about who you are, what you're willing to do or not do, and how you want to be treated in your relationships.

However, even if you have set your limits, sometimes they don't work! Despite your efforts, your boundaries are often ignored or crossed! It frustrates you, but it's not always the other person's fault. Here's why your boundaries don't work despite communicating them assertively:

- You set the boundary in anger or by nagging, for example, "I've told you a hundred times..."
- Your tone is blaming or critical rather than firm.
- You didn't set consequences for violating your boundary.
- You withdraw assertion when challenged with reason, anger, threats, name-calling, or silent treatment.
- Your consequences are too frightening or unrealistic to carry out.
- You don't appreciate the importance of your needs and values sufficiently.

- You don't exercise consequences on a consistent basis, i.e., each time your boundary is violated.
- You give in to sympathize with the other person's pain and place his or her feelings and needs above your own.
- Your consequences insist others must change. Consequences aren't meant to punish someone or change their behavior, but rather require you to *change your behavior.*
- You lack a support system to reinforce *your new behavior.*
- Your words and actions contradict each other. Remember, actions speak louder than words. Actions that reward someone for violating your boundary prove that you aren't serious. For example:
    - You tell your neighbor to always call first before coming to your apartment, and then you allow her to come into your house uninvited.
    - Telling someone not to call after nine in the evening, but answer the phone.
    - Telling your colleagues not to send mails on Sunday, but answering them on Sunday.
    - Nagging or complaining about the unwanted behavior, but not taking any action.

What you can do?

While setting boundaries, it's critical that you identify your feelings, needs, and values (e.g., honesty, fidelity, privacy, and mutual respect). Do you honor or override them? Once you know your comfort zone, you can determine your boundaries easily. Assess your current boundaries in all areas by thinking about:

- What specific behaviors have you allowed that violate your values or compromise your needs and wants?
- How does it affect you and your relationships?
- Can you put in the risk and effort to maintain your boundaries?
- What are the rights you believe you have?
- Have you said or done something that didn't work? Why?
- What are the consequences you can live with if someone violates your boundaries? Always keep your word and follow through with consequences. Don't give empty threats.
- How will you handle the other person's reaction?

To maintain your limits and make them work, you need to have the conviction that the limit is necessary and appropriate. This conviction comes by realizing how much you have to pay in relationships and health by not having the limits in place.

Areas you need to set boundaries

There are several areas where boundaries apply:

- Material boundaries to determine giving things such as your money, cars, clothes, books, food, etc.
- Physical boundaries to safeguard your personal space, privacy, and body. Do you give a handshake or a hug – to whom and when? How do you react to loud music, nudity, or locked doors?
- Mental boundaries apply to your thoughts, values, and opinions. Do you know what you believe? Can you hold on to your opinions? Can you open-mindedly listen to someone else without becoming rigid?
- Emotional boundaries distinguish separating your emotions and their responsibility from others. Healthy boundaries prevent you from blaming others or accepting blame. You don't shoulder your negative feelings over someone else. They also protect you from feeling guilty for others' negative feelings and taking their comments personally. If you react with strong emotions, arguments, or defensive mode, you may have weak emotional boundaries.
- Sexual boundaries protect your comfort level with sexual touch and activity.
- Spiritual boundaries relate to your beliefs and experiences in connection with a supreme power.

Internal boundaries

Internal boundaries regulate your relationship with yourself. Consider them self-discipline and healthy management of time, thoughts, emotions, behavior, and impulses.

If you procrastinate or do things you neither have to nor want to do, or overwork without getting enough rest, you are neglecting your internal physical boundaries. If you can't manage your negative thoughts and feelings and stay in balance, you have weak internal emotional boundaries.

Healthy physical and emotional internal boundaries help you to not obsess about other people's feelings and problems. You think and prioritize yourself, rather than agreeing with others' criticism or advice. Since you're accountable for your feelings and actions, you don't blame others. If you're blamed and you don't feel responsible, instead of defending yourself or apologizing, you can say, "I don't take responsibility for that."

Guilt and resentment

If you feel resentful or victimized and blame people or situations in your life, it means you haven't set your boundaries. If you feel anxious or guilty about setting them, remember your relationships may suffer when you do. Setting boundaries makes you feel empowered, less anxious, and without resentment or guilt. In addition, you receive more respect from others and your relationships improve.

How to set healthy boundaries

Take the following steps:

Remember, no boundaries = little self-esteem

Self-awareness and being assertive are the first steps to setting your boundaries. Your boundaries are your values. Boundaries show others how much or how little you respect yourself. Boundaries are your best friend.

Decide what your core values are.

Who are you? What are your values? What's your comfort zone and what exactly makes you feel uncomfortable? For example, I don't like to be disturbed when I'm working on my laptop. So, I set my phone to "do not disturb" while I'm working. In my relationships, I value and expect honesty, quality time, and one hundred percent transparency. Once you are clear on what matters most to you, you can take the next step of communicating this to others.

Pro tip: Instead of creating your boundaries around a difficult relationship, make your boundaries about you. For example, my boundary with my phone time is about honoring the fact that I tend to lose focus if I am distracted during my busy writing schedule. This boundary is to decrease my stress and frustration, and not about avoiding phone calls.

You can't change others, but you can change yourself

We all want others to change. We get into arguments with our partners, parents, or peers, hoping and expecting them to change. Though we know we can't change others, we still sometimes try. So always remind yourself that you are not responsible for what comes out of someone else's mouth, the choices they make, or their reactions.

Bottom line?

Since you can't change other people, change the way you deal with them. When we change our ways, the world around us will change, too.

Brahma Kumaris, a spiritual organization, always recommends to first change *your* thoughts about the other person and to think positively about them no matter how they behave. This changes your behavior towards them, and they are motivated to change themselves. Doesn't this chain reaction sound good?

Decide the consequences ahead of time

So what do you do if someone pushes your boundaries (because they will)? Decide the consequences beforehand and communicate it clearly. However, don't make empty threats or give in if others violate your boundaries.

For example, if my friend calls me repeatedly during my work time, I simply do not answer the phone. The best way to figure out your own boundaries and consequences of violating them is to sit quietly with yourself and make this all about you. Remember, boundaries are about honoring *your* needs, not about judging other people's choices.

Let your behavior speak for you

Present your boundaries clearly to people and then let your behavior do the talking. People *will* test, push, and disrespect your limits. But you need to stick to it and follow through with the consequences you've set forth each and every time someone violates the boundaries you've set for yourself.

When you don't react in anger for violating your boundaries, it indicates a healthier you, emotionally and physically.

Say what you mean, and mean what you say

You may have set the healthiest of boundaries for yourself, but if you do not communicate them clearly, you are going to make them easy to manipulate. Moreover, it will create confusing relationships, for you and everyone involved.

When you say one thing and do another, people get an opportunity to question your character or authenticity. Why take such a chance?

Sometimes, we're afraid to confront our loved ones and tell them the truth about our feelings. We're scared to admit that we hate going to certain restaurants, or have trouble spending time with a friend's toxic cousin, or hate when a boss dumps deadline on us at six o'clock on a Friday.

But, keep in mind: the more you ground yourself with your boundaries and values, the more clearly you'll be able to communicate them to others.

How to talk about your boundaries: ASSA Technique

Ding dong!

Yes, that's your doorbell! But what if it rings at an unreasonable hour? What if it's also from the same person every time?

My mother, a passionate housewife, really gets disturbed by this. Do you know why? Blame it on our neighbor. Every other day, at 2:30 p.m., her kids ring the doorbell to enquire about where their mother is, or if she has left the house key with us. And that's my mom's nap time. She gets up early in the morning at 4:30 a.m. and finishes all her chores. Post-lunch she feels the need to relax and take a little nap.

Thanks to the neighbor and her kids, she can't make it to an undisturbed nap most of the time. She has informed her neighbor several times about her nap, but to no avail.

"Can't she give the extra key of the house to her kids? They are mature enough. Or why is she not at home by the time her kids come from the school? They disturb my sleep every day." That's what my Mom mutters to herself frequently. Of course she would, because she has reacted passively to such behavior from our neighbor. She doesn't want to yell at them, but telling them not to disturb hasn't worked either.

So, should she continue to accept their behavior? Or should she shout and make them follow through?

Well, none of these options seem to be the right choice! Being passive and accepting the boundary-crossing behavior makes her furious; it's only that she doesn't express it. But she won't be able to hold it in for long. And yelling won't help. It will only spoil the relationship.

Does this sound familiar to you? Or do you face a similar situation? How do you tackle it? How should you handle people when they take you for granted?

Follow these 5 steps:

Step 1: Define your boundaries

Decide your limits and stick to them. What behaviors are you willing to accept from other people and what are you not? This doesn't mean rigidity, but have a limit and stick to it.

Step 2: Forgiveness doesn't mean not taking action

Most of us have a forgiving nature. That's what has been taught to us. Forgiveness is a quality of courageousness and helps people change. But, if you continually forgive someone for their bad behavior, they get much worse. This, of course, doesn't do them any good. Constantly forgiving and allowing bad behavior ceases to *be* a "bad behavior" in the eyes of the person doing it.

Research shows that people who insult their spouses, throw items, or exhibit any type of violence get more aggressive if their partners repeatedly forgive them for it.

Though forgiveness can compel others to change, it has to be accompanied by an appropriate action. By appropriate, I don't mean acting aggressively, but setting a limit on your tolerance.

So how do you set this limit to their bad behavior?

Step 3: Practice the ASSA technique

Practicing assertiveness needs a strategy, whether it's with your colleague, a disrespectful partner, or a cranky neighbor. Assertiveness is a calm, clear communication, and not a verbal onslaught.

Often when we are upset with someone's behavior, we shout or scream, but they genuinely might not know the reason for our bad mood. Don't expect people to read your mind and just *know* that you are upset. Tell them about your bad mood, and the reason for it.

Follow the "ASSA" technique, which stands for:

Alert the person that you wish to speak to them. For example: "I want to talk to you about the backtalk you do in front of my friends." You don't blame or use any emotional language to make your point.

State your problem. What and why it's a problem: "I don't like it when you shout back at me. It makes me feel insulted and I think it makes you look rude in front of my friends."

Sell the benefits of better behavior. Say "In the future, if you disagree with me, it'd be better for you to have a private conversation with me. This will make you appear more mature and resolve our conflict."

Agree to behave differently in the future. "Shall we agree that from now on, you won't backtalk me? If you wish to have a word with me, you'll do it privately in our room?"

In the future, if ever they repeat the bad behavior, remind them what you had agreed upon.

Notice the clarity of this type of communication. You've neither passively accepted their bad behavior nor lost your cool and insulted them.

This type of assertive communication is a powerful method to correct someone's bad behavior. Though they might not change their ways (not immediately at least), you have given them an opportunity to behave better and openly communicated your boundaries.

Step 4: Stay calm

That's super important. When people overstep your limits, it's natural to lose your cool. But you can handle the situation with a little presence of mind. And for that, you need to be *calm*. The moment you start criticizing or yelling or sobbing, you invite defensiveness from the opposite side. Staying calm in such a situation takes practice. That's why it's important you rehearse what you're going to say.

Step 5: Practice honesty

We've all received an appalling gift from a relative or friend, and even if we didn't like it, we pretend that it's awesome. Because we think that being honest may hurt their feelings. But, by being honest, you'll gain more respect for yourself and others. Ultimately, it will help the other person to seriously look at their behavior and assess it. People won't be forced to live under the illusion that their behavior is okay when it really isn't.

Sometimes you need to use a clear, concise, and direct language.

How about you?

1. Have you set your boundaries at work and in relationships? If not, what stops you from doing it?
2. What are the situations where you feel people overstep your boundaries?
3. How do you react to people who do so? Do you forgive them and let them cross your boundaries again, or take concrete action?

Chapter Summary

- You can set boundaries for your personal space, possessions, sexuality, thoughts and feelings, time and energy, culture, religion, and ethics.
- Setting your healthy boundaries and respecting those of others improve your self-esteem, conserve your emotional

energy, gives you a space to grow, and build healthy relationships.

- However, your boundaries won't work if you set them in anger, make them too rigid, get critical about others, or don't set a consequence for overriding them.
- Convey and assert your boundaries using the ASSA technique.

In the next chapter you will learn:

- Why it's difficult to express your feelings
- Tips for opening up about your feelings
- Techniques for expressing yourself
- Assertive communication formula

CHAPTER SEVEN

Assertive Self-expression

Expressing what and how you feel is the second category of assertive behavior. However, openly expressing feelings easily doesn't come naturally to everyone. Men typically have a more difficult time expressing their emotions, but almost everyone at one time or another in their life finds it difficult to say how they feel.

When it's difficult to express how you feel

When you learn why you have trouble expressing your feelings, it goes a long way into changing that behavior. You can learn how to express your feelings, just as readily as you can learn how to fix a faucet or mend a button on a shirt.

Here are the nine common reasons people find it difficult to express their emotions to others:

You don't know exactly what you feel

A person might be experiencing feelings such as sadness, rejection, disrespect, hurt or shame, but it's better to be precise. Knowing exactly what you feel helps you connect with yourself, the values you have, and those you wish to live by. It also increases the likelihood of being understood by others.

Fear of conflict

We are afraid of angry feelings or conflicts with people. You believe that people with good relationships should not engage in verbal "fights" or intense arguments. Plus, you fear disclosing your thoughts and feelings to those you care about would result in their rejection of you.

This is sometimes referred to as the "ostrich phenomenon" — burying your head in the sand instead of addressing relationship problems.

Emotional perfectionism

Some people believe that they should not have feelings such as anger, jealousy, depression, or anxiety. They think they should always be rational and in control of their emotions. Expressing these emotions will present them as weak and vulnerable. You fear that people will criticize or reject you if they know how you really feel.

Fear of disapproval and rejection

People are so terrified by rejection and ending up alone that they would rather swallow their feelings, and put up with some abuse rather than expressing them. They feel an excessive need to please others and to meet their expectations. Such people are afraid that others won't like if they expressed their thoughts and feelings.

Passive-aggressive behavior

Passive-aggressive behavior makes you pout and hold your hurt or angry feelings inside instead of disclosing them. You give others the silent treatment, which is inappropriate, and a common strategy to elicit the feelings of guilt on their part.

Hopelessness

When you are convinced that your relationship cannot improve no matter what you do, you stop expressing yourself. You feel that you have already tried everything, and nothing works. You blame your spouse (or partner) for being too stubborn and insensitive to be able to change.

These beliefs represent a self-fulfilling prophecy–once you give up, an established position of hopelessness supports your predicted outcome.

Low Self-Esteem

Due to low self-esteem, people feel they are not entitled to express their feelings or to ask others for what they want. You always try to please other people and meet their expectations in such a case.

Spontaneity

Only when you are upset, you have the right to say what you think and feel. If that's what you believe, you express feelings only at that time, and none other. However, during a calm and structured or semi-structured exchange, if you express your feelings, it does not result in a perception that you are "faking" or attempting to inappropriately manipulate others.

Mind Reading

You expect others to know how you feel and what you need (although you have not disclosed it to them yet). This expectation provides an excuse to engage in non-disclosure, and thereafter, feel resentful because people do not appear to care about your needs.

Martyrdom

You are afraid to admit that you are angry, hurt, or resentful because you don't want to give anyone the satisfaction of knowing that their behavior affects you. You take pride in controlling your emotions and experiencing hurt or resentment, which obviously does not support clear and functional communication.

Tips for Opening Up

Once you've explored why you have such a hard time expressing yourself, you can work on doing so more effectively and confidently. Here are a few tips which will help you feel more comfortable about opening up about your feelings:

1) Be clear about your desire to share your feelings

Ask yourself why you want to share your feelings in the first place. Do you expect the other person to change? Do you share to vent? Or do you want advice? Or are you sharing for self-exploration?

Be clear regarding your reasons and expectations whether sharing feelings with a therapist, friend, or a loved one.

2) Acknowledge the intimacy of sharing feelings

Before going into the actual conversation about your feelings, it's important you acknowledge that sharing is intimate. Your history of trust in others and yourself influences your openness to share your feelings.

3) Start small

If you don't feel comfortable discussing your feelings, don't dive in headfirst. Instead, first experiment by sharing those things that are least uncomfortable to share.

4) Begin with the people you trust most

Begin expressing your feelings with the people you trust most: a best friend, a sibling, or a parent.

5) Be mindful of the experience

Notice the experience you get by sharing your feelings so that you can make the next one even better. What part felt comfortable? Does it make you more likely to share the next time? If not, what do you need to feel more comfortable in sharing your feelings?

6) Remember the harmful effects of suppressed feelings

Lastly, remember that keeping your feelings bottled up inside doesn't do any good. Suppressing, minimizing, or denying your feelings make you less available to recognize them in others. In contrast, acknowledging your feelings increases your empathy. Recognizing and acknowledging your pain is a form of empathy. This awareness heightens your capacity for empathy with others.

Techniques for expressing yourself

Often people associate expressive assertiveness with standing up for your rights when you feel that someone has taken advantage of you in a negative way. However, being more assertive can also help you to move ahead in a positive way, toward your goals.

Assertiveness can help you:

- Speak up in meetings when you want to
- Say "no" when you don't want to do something, or
- Express positive goals and request the required resources to make them happen

Will you get what you want by communicating assertively? Well, there's no guarantee, but you will have the satisfaction of expressing yourself in a positive, self-advocating way. You'll feel better about yourself and your communication with others. This will increase the probability of getting what you need or want, if you can express exactly what it is.

Techniques for assertive expression:

Plan in advance what you are going to say. Visualize the scene and be positive.

Use "I statements" to express yourself. "I statements" help you focus on your own thoughts, feelings, and needs as well as acknowledge those of others. The real focus in I statements is on the "I feel," "I want," or "I think" part of the statement. Identifying your thoughts, feelings, and wants related to a situation keeps you from blaming someone else or getting caught up in the emotion of the moment. Avoid words that weaken the power of your messages like *could*, *sorry*, *not usually*, *maybe*, *suppose*, *possible*, *perhaps*, *er…* or *um…*

For example, "When you shout at me, I feel upset and put down, which negatively affects how I work. I would like you to speak to me properly, and with a normal tone so that I can do my job better."

Stick to it like a broken record.

Repeat your request several times so that your message is considered to be important. Don't give up if it was rejected at first.

For example, after you have requested your file to be reviewed and have not had a response, "I understand that you are very busy with… I value your input on my project file so that I can move ahead to finish my assignment."

Be empathetic and acknowledge others' feelings

For example, "I know you want the assignment to be delivered tomorrow, but I seriously can't, as I have other important issues to attend to."

State the consequence of not changing behavior

For example, "If you do not allow sufficient time to write the content, it will be less effective than you need it to be, and I'll have to write it again. I'd prefer not to do that."

Respond to criticism in a non-defensive way.

When someone criticizes you, they expect you to disagree or resist what they say, and to respond in a defensive way. However, you can put critical comments in perspective and still respect your point of view. You can agree with some part of what was said without being defensive.

For example: If someone says "That was a poor presentation you gave at the meeting." You might respond by saying, "Yes, I can see that I have some areas that could be improved."

If you can agree with some areas of criticism, you can respond by seeking to understand what is leading to the criticism. Continuing with the above example, you could ask about what could be improved and say, "Actually, I could have been better. What do you think could be improved?"

Acknowledge your weaknesses or mistakes

That's called "negative assertion." We all have areas where we can improve. However, we can acknowledge our mistakes and weaknesses without being self-demeaning.

Assertive communication formula: Sending the message clearly

Confidence and assertiveness are often thought to mean the same thing. However, they are different in many ways.

Assertiveness is conducting yourself with confidence and not hesitating to express your desires and beliefs. Confidence is defined as the trait of being certain of yourself and your abilities.

The main difference between the two is communication. You can be assertive only if there is someone or something for you to be assertive towards, whereas confidence can exist inwardly and in isolation.

Assertiveness cannot exist without underlying confidence and can only exist in a situation where there is communication. Assertiveness can be portrayed through strong body language, tone of voice, and expressions. Confidence, on the other hand, needs nothing to aid in its existence. Put simply, you can be confident without being assertive, but you can't be assertive without being confident.

Thus, speaking up and expressing yourself can be difficult, sometimes overwhelming if you are shy, lack confidence, or come from a culture where it is inappropriate to speak up. It can also feel awkward and unnatural if you're more inclined to voice your frustrations and discontent in an indirect or passive manner.

But, remember, while fears about speaking up are hard, they are not impossible to overcome. Using an "assertiveness formula" can help.

This assertiveness formula can be applied to any situation at your home or the workplace. Let's learn the three parts of the assertive communication formula.

Start with a short, simple, objective statement about the other person's behavior. For example: "When you interrupt me during my work..." Here your goal is to get the other person's attention without triggering their defensiveness. The statement should be short, to the point, and unemotional enough to let them hear your message and not immediately disagree or disengage.

Describe the negative effects of their behavior. Explain why the person's behavior is causing you a problem. For example, if the first part of the formula is "When you interrupt me during my work," you can add, "I lose the flow of my ideas." The goal here is to build a cause-and-effect logic. Link an objective statement of their behavior to the impact that behavior has on you.

End with a feelings statement. Here, you must indicate how their offending behavior has not only negatively impacted your actions but also hurt your feelings. An example of a feelings statement might be "I feel anxious" or "I feel distracted."

Putting it all together, you'll have something like this: "When you continually interrupt me during my work, I lose the flow of my ideas, and I feel anxious."

Of course, even with a formula in hand, assertiveness isn't always easy. It's quite possible that the recipient of your message may react negatively, so you must meet any response with a calm, steady, and confident presence.

What you can do is to accumulate as much evidence as possible to support your statement about the other person's offending behavior. You might keep track of instances when you felt hurt, undermined, or offended by the person's actions. Don't use this record to nag at the other person. Only use it as backup material if your counterpart refutes you and needs convincing. This evidence will increase the likelihood that your message will be heard and ultimately have the intended effect on the recipient.

One thing to remember is that there's no one-size-fits-all version of the message. You can, and should, tweak it to your own style to make the message feel as authentic as possible.

Speaking up is genuinely hard for many of us. And the results are far from guaranteed. The other person may respond in a positive way immediately; or respond positively and productively but with a significant delay; or might not respond at all. But for you, getting the courage to voice your opinions and frustrations in the first place is a significant win.

Homework for you

Answer the following questions before proceeding to the next chapter.

1. What stops you from speaking up about your feelings to others?
2. If ever you expressed your feelings, what was the response from the other person?
3. How likely are you to express your feelings to the same person (or others) in the future?

Chapter Summary

- People find it difficult to express their emotions because they can't figure out exactly what they feel. Plus, the fear of conflict, disapproval, and rejection, or emotional perfectionism, passive aggressive behavior, or low self-esteem also stop them from expressing themselves.
- Once you are clear on your feelings to share, begin by sharing things that are least uncomfortable to share. Share with people you trust the most: a best friend, a sibling or a parent.
- To express yourself assertively, first plan what you are going to say. Start with a small, objective statement about the undesirable behavior, describe how it affects you, and ultimately, how you feel. Remember to stay calm and empathetic throughout the discussion.

In the next chapter you will learn:

- How to ask for what you want
- ERPG/Assertive request formula
- How to ask for a raise
- Tips for assertive questioning

CHAPTER EIGHT

Ask and Receive What You Want

Asking for what you want

Many of us find it incredibly difficult to ask for things, especially at work, even though the request is completely fair. You may wonder what your colleagues will think of you. Will you sound greedy? Presumptuous? Will it irritate them? The list is endless!

If you have a lot of trouble asking for things, here are seven tips on how to ask for what you want:

Let go of the guilt

Let go of your guilt when making a request. Guilt usually surrounds those that are people-pleasers and dislike causing inconvenience to anyone. Always remind yourself that asking for things is not greedy. It's not wrong, rather it is healthy self-care.

Start small

Start small, like asking for a different table at a restaurant. This way you'll get used to how it feels to make a small, simple request. You'll also begin to realize that nothing bad will happen when you voice your needs.

Don't assume others to be mind-readers

We often assume our spouse, boss, work colleagues, or even our friends can read our minds. So when they don't act our way, we end up being hurt and upset. For any relationship to thrive, both parties have to take responsibility for clearly communicating their needs.

Be aware of the person you're asking

Psychologist Susan Krauss Whitbourne wrote that we must, "be conscious of the person we are asking and their needs, as opposed to solely focusing on what you want out of a situation." Put yourself in the other person's shoes, and you'll be able to frame your request in a way that is also beneficial to the other person, thus, increasing the likelihood of getting a positive answer.

However, if you put off the request because the timing never seems right, perhaps it's your own feelings of inadequacy or insecurity that prevent you from stepping forward.

Be honest

Honesty is always the best policy. Honestly express what you need and why you need it, and assure the other person that there won't be any rule changes down the road.

Ask and you shall receive... but you have to ask

It's said that "if you want something, you have to ask for it and risk not getting it, otherwise the chance of not getting it is definitely one hundred percent." Just imagine the things you might not have in life if you don't stick your neck out; from jobs, to pay raises, to simply getting someone's autograph.

Imagine the worst possible outcome

When you're afraid to ask for something, take a deep breath and imagine the worst possible outcome. Usually, it will be a simple "no" from the other side, which is not exactly life-threatening. I used this tactic when asking for my pay raise and it definitely helped. At worst, my recruiters would politely tell me no, but I'd still have a job that I was pretty happy to go to every day. Struggling with the simple task of vocalizing what you want can be incredibly frustrating, but the good news is it's a skill you can improve and finesse over time.

Assertive request formula

If you wish to make an assertive request to someone to change their behavior or get what you want, there's a simple "ERPG" formula to use. ERPG stands for Empathy, Respect, Problem, and Goal.

Before you apply the formula, it's ideal to have a clear understanding of our goals. Be clear in your mind as to how you want others to behave, what action to take, what their reaction could be, and how you'll respond. If possible, place an assertive request at the place and time convenient to you.

ERPG formula

Establish Empathy and Respect and state positive feelings

Before making the request, try to understand the other person's feelings, and communicate that you do.

For example, "I know you won't be able to hire another freelance writer for this assignment at a short notice, but I hope you'll understand that I am currently overworked."

Show your respect and care for the person, and acknowledge the parts of their behavior that are likely to keep your conversations positive and out of blaming territory.

For example, "I appreciate your support to ensure timely payments for all my assignments."

State the problem and negative feelings

Speak in a manner that convinces them to solve your problem and not turn against you. Ask for their help, but don't blame your negative feelings on them. If you're upset with their behavior, remember that it's your own feelings, your own way of reacting to their behavior that you can control. However, that said, you can still express your problem, negative feelings, and ask for their help.

For example, "When you continually blame me for my past mistakes, it hurts me and I start defending myself instead of addressing the real issue."

State the goal and request new behavior

Sometimes just expressing the problem is not enough. You may have to speak about the problem, as well as the goal you wish to achieve.

State the kind of new behavior you want and how it would affect you. But, let others choose their new behavior as much as possible. When things are in their hands, they are more likely to help and suggest solutions to the problem. The other person may even think of a better solution than you. This approach gets them to be considerate of your problem and help solve it rather than turning defensive.

For example, "Instead of blaming me for my past mistakes, you could describe what I did and how I can improve in the future. Then, I would feel less defensive and more accommodating of your suggestions."

Follow-up after making the request

If the person avoids your request, attacks you, gets manipulative, makes you feel guilty or angry, makes excuses, or simply refuses to do it, use other assertive techniques such as the broken record, disarming anger, or making a contract.

While making a contract, clearly jot down the points of agreement (and possibly the points of disagreement). The agreement should be written and signed by both parties.

While following the above steps of ERPG formula, make sure you use an assertive style of communication. Don't put yourself or others in a defensive mode. Try to stay calm, rational, and helpful as much as possible.

- Use words like "keep doing what you're doing" or "didn't do it the way I wanted it to be" or "you waited for me to make the decision" or "give me negative feedback."
- Avoid using critical words like poor job, dependent, unworthy, or profanity
- Pay attention to non-verbal responses like good eye contact
- Use "I statements"
- Be direct
- Reduce hesitation words
- Stick to the issues
- Maintain an understanding, caring, yet firm stance

The above steps of the formula can be summarized into a sentence like:

I understand/like..............; however, when you.................., I feel.......... I would appreciate it if you would.................

Asking for a raise

Besides asking for a new behavior, asking for a pay raise is yet another struggle. You know that you've added a lot of value to your company or organization, and you feel entitled to a raise.

So, how do you request a raise confidently and in a manner that is likely to succeed?

Research your worth to your employer

Before requesting a raise, research your company. Assess your worth to your company. Look at the profits you made or even the losses you might have incurred. Look at your department and calculate your present productivity against that of a predecessor, if possible. For example, if you work in customer service, have you been able to increase customer satisfaction?

Compare your worth with your competition

Research online what is your market value or what you would be worth to the competition. If you're not earning what you would in comparable companies or organizations, this will give you an advantage in negotiating a raise.

Arrange a meeting with your boss

Schedule a date and time to discuss your raise with your boss. Don't say you're going to request a raise; rather, say that you have something important to talk about and you'd like to set up a meeting to discuss it.

Before going into the meeting, write down the concrete reasons you deserve a raise and rehearse them to ensure a confident and convincing delivery. During the meeting, first state the facts you have researched before requesting a raise.

If your boss takes calls during the meeting or acts as though you need to rush through, ask to reschedule to a time when you can have their uninterrupted attention.

Don't beg, make demands, or threaten to quit

Don't beg your boss for a raise or threaten to quit. These may backfire because your boss may begin to have negative feelings against you.

State what you want

Specify a particular amount you would like to receive. Be reasonable but not conservative. Then raise it by at least fifty percent so you have some room to negotiate.

Negotiate your raise

If your boss consents to a raise but offers a smaller amount than what you requested, counteroffer with an amount higher than in the middle. Continue to negotiate until both you and your boss agree upon a suitable amount.

What if your boss says no?

Your boss may simply reject your request for a raise. One response is to complain about all the problems the company or organization is having and how it's not possible to squeeze out another dime because of it.

Or, you understand the problems at the company, but you have personal financial responsibilities too. Say it's not fair to penalize you for the company's problems, that you give the company your best effort, and expect to be fairly compensated.

Your boss may use the company's policies to bar you from getting a raise. Work with your boss to find ways around the policy or consider the reasons why you should be an exception to the rule.

Don't accept a symbolic raise

In lieu of a pay raise, your boss may offer a small token raise or perks such as the use of the company car or a corner office with windows. Don't accept it. This will start a pattern where you are willing to accept anything instead of the larger raise you want. Rather, tell your boss that it is insufficient and reiterate the amount you are looking for.

Take a promotion

One of the best ways to get a raise is to get a promotion. You can do this in three different ways.

First, you can move up in the organization to the next level. Secondly, you can take on more responsibility. You may need to eliminate lower function work to do this. And third, you can create a new job for yourself with a new title.

If you think your best bet is the third option, write out a job description before you go into the meeting. Detail what is lacking and provide a plan for solving the problem. Include things such as what your job would entail, time frames for accomplishing assignments, costs, and what you estimate the profits would be. Talk with your boss about supporting you, and then go up the chain of command to have your plan approved.

Do not take a promotion without a title or a raise

If your boss offers a promotion without a new title or a raise, turn it down immediately. Because you'll probably be expected to take on further responsibilities in addition to the work you're already doing. And this is not acceptable.

Tell your boss that a promotion is really not a promotion without a raise. If you're offered a new position, make sure it's with responsibilities that you accept and with a raise that is appropriate to the new title.

Points to remember when asking for a raise:

- Choose the right time for your request
- Ask after a big win
- Don't give an ultimatum
- Avoid giving too much personal information

Assertive questioning to get information

When attempting to get information out of your customers, friends or family, the question's length and the format determine its assertiveness quotient.

Longer questions asked with intent or context can make the prospects feel pressured to respond a certain way. Getting right to the point, on the other hand, sounds more assertive.

Tips for asking assertive questions

Leave yourself out of it

Remove pronouns, including "me" and "I" around things you want. The assertive person asks for what they want and waits for the answer.

Don't indicate your dislike of prospective answers

Accept their answer and ask if there's anything you can collectively accomplish.

Choose your verb carefully

Telling your prospect, "I'd really like to meet your boss" is not a question and is aggressive. If you want to meet their manager, say "I'd love the chance to explain the benefits of our product to your boss. Would it be possible for us to meet?"

It's always best to stick to single-sentence questions and skip the upfront explanation.

Homework for you

1. What stops you from asking others what you want?
2. Do you really feel you deserve a pay raise? Then, why haven't you asked for it yet?
3. Are you asking your customers the right questions, and in the right way?

Chapter Summary

- Overthinking about what others will think prevents us from asking them for what we want.
- Before requesting others to change their behavior, establish empathy and respect for them. State your positive feelings followed by the problem and in the end, the goal or the request for the new behavior.
- When asking your boss for a pay raise or a promotion, first research and note down the facts that make you eligible for it. Schedule a direct meeting with your boss and state those facts before requesting a raise. Never beg for a raise or threaten to quit. State what you want clearly.
- Never ask lengthy questions from your prospects or questions that pressure them to answer in a certain way. Ask what you want and wait for the answer. Never give upfront explanations.

In the next chapter you will learn:

- How to exercise assertiveness in daily life
- How to be assertive at work
- How to practice assertiveness with family and in relationships
- How to stand up and speak for yourself

CHAPTER NINE

Assertiveness Everyday

Assertiveness in daily life

Everyone wants to be more confident, but not everyone knows how to be assertive. If you learn to be assertive, you can express yourself easily and have a better chance of getting what you want.

Here are seven simple ways to become more assertive:

1. Understand that assertiveness is a skill
2. Be respectful of those with whom you communicate. Pay attention to your body language as well as the words you say, and make sure they are congruent.
3. Understand and accept the differences between your point of view and the others' points of view.
4. Speak in a way that doesn't accuse or make the other person feel guilty. Be simple, direct, and concise, and state what you know to be true for you.
5. Use "I statements" to be assertive without coming across hostile.

6. Stay calm when expressing yourself.
7. Set boundaries for yourself that help you decide what you will and will not allow.

When faced with a demand, consider the following:

Everyone, including you, has the right not to accept demand. You have the right to say “no” without justifying yourself.

When rejecting a demand, explain that it is the demand that is being rejected and not the person.

After rejecting the demand, stick to that decision. If you crumble under pressure, others will learn that you can be swayed. However, you have the right to change your mind if circumstances change.

When receiving criticism:

- Take time to decide if it’s genuine or is there some other reason for it.
- Acknowledge any truthful elements of criticism, even if they are hard to accept.
- Don’t respond by lashing back with counter-criticism.
- Avoid criticizing others. Instead, give constructive, albeit negative, feedback to change their behavior.
- When giving feedback, focus on the problem or situation rather than the person.

Complimenting is a positive way of giving support, showing approval and increasing the other person's self-confidence. However, some people find the giving and receiving of compliments difficult or embarrassing.

When you are complimented, thank the person giving the compliment, and accept it, whether or not you actually agree with it. When giving a compliment, ensure it is genuine.

Assertiveness at work

To exercise assertiveness at work, follow these steps:

Recognize your value. Nurture a realistic and respectful perspective on your value as a person.

Know your rights at the workplace. The notices, employee policy manual, your job description, etc.

Know your boundaries to avoid stress and frustration.

Prepare and practice

Practice being assertive with your close relationships. Imagine what it might be like to communicate something difficult to your co-worker or your boss. Ask yourself:

What is my goal, what and how would I like to say it?

Act it out in your mind, playing out both the ideal scenario and the scenario that scares you the most. If you don’t, when the moment comes, your nerves might get you tongue-tied and it can feel easier to give up.

Avoid using words like "hmm," "uh," "you know..." "well...," etc., that can make your speech sound unsophisticated, hesitant, or indecisive.

Control the volume of your voice.

Avoid degrading language

Now, let's apply these steps to a few situations in the workplace.

Situation #1: Getting the team behind your plan

Your team is in charge of launching a new advertising campaign, and you have a killer idea. You call a meeting to discuss how to get started and are excited to propose your idea.

- **Passive Approach:** You wait for your boss to make the first suggestion. Then, you passively nod your head to all his suggestions rather than putting up your idea or even suggesting ways to improve upon his strategy.
- **Aggressive Approach:** You immediately pitch your "perfect" idea to all your teammates, and without taking a breath, start assigning tasks. If anyone suggests an alternative, you outwardly reject it.
- **Assertive Approach:** You present your idea and welcome suggestions from all the team members. As you listen to the various suggestions, you acknowledge their strong points and also assume a role in solving potential challenges.

With an assertive approach, you state your case in a way that acknowledges others' perspectives and backs up your ideas with factual reasoning, rather than emotions. You successfully contribute value to the conversation, but not at the cost of degrading other team members.

Situation #2: You've asked for a raise, but your boss isn't making any moves

After asking for a raise during a meeting with your boss, she says that you'll have to wait for another six months as the company is just not able to give raises right now. She assures that you'll be considered for a salary bump when the time is right.

- δ **Passive Approach:** You swallow your disappointment and agree with your boss in the office. But later, when you go home, you complain about it for hours because you feel it's completely unjust.
- δ **Aggressive Approach:** You inform your boss that you'll begin to look for opportunities at other companies where someone will treat you like you deserve to be treated.
- δ **Assertive Approach:** You respect yourself and your need to be compensated fairly, and also understand your boss' reasoning. So you ask for more information on the company's future and define concrete goals and targets that you can review when you revisit your salary request again in the future.

Assertiveness in family and relationships

Establishing assertive communication with your family is far easier. It gives you the following benefits:

- Better emotional and mental health
- Improves your social and personal skills
- Better understanding and control over your emotions
- Improves your self-esteem and decision-making skills
- Leads to self-respect and earned respect from others

Here are some ways to foster assertive communication with your family:

Avoid comparisons

Parents should dissuade from comparing their children with others. For example, “John, you didn’t complete your homework. You should be more like Harry, who completes all his homework before going to the playground.”

Comparison generates insecurity and feelings of inferiority, resentment, and unhealthy competitiveness.

Be empathetic

Assertive communication starts with respect towards others. When all the family members understand how they all think and feel, it’ll be easier to engage in a healthy dialogue.

Ask for an opinion

Let your children participate and have a voice in making decisions that affect them and the family. This boosts their self-confidence and they feel their opinions matter.

Express yourself

For children to express their feelings and thoughts to you, you must follow suit. Tell them about your day, your concerns, and your interests. Similarly, listen attentively when children have something to share with you. Give them advice, if required, rather than judging and scolding them. Never punish them for telling you the truth.

Stand up and speak up!

Every day you make dozens of little choices. Sometimes, it's easy to assert your ideas, while at other times, it seems better to go with the flow to avoid potential conflict.

However, if you let people walk all over you; it can increase your feelings of stress and anxiety, and eventually lessen your feelings of self-worth.

Learning to speak up for yourself will help you take charge of your life, believe in your power, and embolden you to reach for your dreams.

So use these ten simple, yet powerful, steps to stand up for yourself in any situation.

Practice being transparent and authentic

It takes practice, but if you learn to express yourself openly and honestly, you'll get into the habit of making yourself heard by others.

Take small but powerful steps

Start by taking small steps to stand up for yourself. Even learning to walk with confidence – head held high and shoulders back – will help you feel and appear more confident. Channel this confidence in day-to-day interactions. Did someone push you out of the line at the Metro? Politely ask them to move back.

When someone attacks, wait them out

You'll sometimes come across people who will try to walk all over you. Stay calm but assertive if someone tries to bully you. Don't cater to them, but also don't react with aggression.

Figure out what bothers you

It requires a ton of courage to face something or someone that's bothering you. But, if you face it, it empowers you to make it better and diminishes its control over you. People can't read your mind; you have to vocalize your concerns.

Clarify before attacking

It's tempting to take a self-righteous stand, especially when the other person seems to be entirely in the wrong. But, resist your urge to react with emotion. Instead, take a breath and calmly explain your perspective to them. Avoid combative tones or accusatory words.

Practice, practice, and practice

Once you start getting the hang of it, practice assertiveness in situations where you need to stand up for yourself.

Be deliberate in voicing your concerns

Stand up for your time. Push back when appropriate or respectfully disengage with people or situations that submerge your schedule.

Remember, no one can invalidate your feelings, thoughts, and opinions. Learning to stand up for yourself won't happen overnight. It takes time to get comfortable with assertiveness. While you are in the learning stage, imagine that you are an actor learning to play a new role. Imagine that you are the most assertive person you know. So how will you handle yourself in a difficult situation?

So what about you?

1. Do you understand "assertiveness" now?
2. Do you feel confident in saying no? In expressing yourself? In asking for what you want?
3. Are you better equipped to stand up and speak for yourself now?

Chapter Summary

- Assertiveness is a skill that can be practiced and learned.
- Be respectful of those with whom you communicate. Understand and accept the differences between your and

other's point of view. Stay calm when expressing yourself. Use "I statements" to be assertive without being hostile.

- Set boundaries for yourself.
- Recognize your value, know your rights at the workplace, speak in a clear, direct language and avoid degrading words to sound assertive.
- Express yourself, ask for other's opinions, and be empathetic to exercise assertiveness in family and relationships.
- Take small but powerful steps to stand up and speak for yourself.

FINAL WORDS

Success at work and in relationships depends on your communication. Your style of communication should be such that it allows you to express, ask, and receive what you want in life.

There are three styles of communication – passive, aggressive, and assertive. But, it's only the assertive style that empowers you to be a winner in life. Passive communication makes you weak, submissive, and allows others to take advantage of yours. An aggressive style, on the other hand, makes you come across as domineering, haughty, and indifferent to others' feelings, thoughts, and opinions.

Assertiveness is the only way of communication that keeps your interests and those of others in perfect balance. You neither consider your own thoughts and feelings to be superior to others, nor give in to other's perspective and demands unnecessarily. Both hold equal value for you.

By using an assertive style of communication in your day-to-day life, you improve your self-esteem, feel more confident, make better decisions, feel respectful about yourself, and gain others' respect, too. You can establish healthy and long-lasting relationships at work and with friends and family.

However, our own fears and assumptions pose a hindrance to learn and practice the skill of assertive communication. We believe that assertiveness will land us in conflict with our loved ones, colleagues, and peers, and we'll lose their love and appreciation. But the opposite is actually true. You'll gain more respect from others when you respect yourself and stand up for yourself, your rights, thoughts, feelings, and opinions.

Be curious to learn new things and be open to new experiences in life. Take care of how you present yourself to others. How you talk, your tone, clothes, and even your body language. Your body language speaks volumes about your self-confidence. It's an important aspect of assertive communication to be aware of.

Learning the skill of assertive communication starts with building a positive self-image. Have a rational and positive perspective of your abilities, skills, and strengths. This makes you feel empowered; the power to set meaningful goals in life and lay out the path to achieving them. You are unique and so is your contribution to this world. No one else can contribute the way you can. But, to realize this power of yours, you need to think positively about yourself.

By learning the assertive style of communication, you'll create in yourself the following qualities:

- Expressing your needs and ideas clearly, directly, and without guilt
- Standing up for your own rights and those of others

- Conveying your feelings to others with confidence
- Self-reliance and independence
- Persistence in complex situations
- Great analytical skills
- Positive attitude at all times
- Taking pride in your accomplishments
- Having the courage to dream and develop the skills needed to turn them into reality

To practice the assertive style of communication, you must know what you want, ask for it, and finally, get it. It's as simple as that.

Assertive communication involves three components:

1. Saying "no" at the right time and in the right way. It's a part of setting healthy boundaries for yourself and lets others know what you'll accept and what you won't; be it their behavior or their demands. Setting boundaries is crucial for you to conserve your emotional energy, give yourself a space to grow, improve your self-esteem and relationships, and avoid letting others manipulate you; in business, work, or personal relationships. You not only set yours but also honor others' limits, if they've set them.
2. Clearly and confidently expressing how you feel about yourself and others' behavior towards you. You take

complete responsibility for your feelings without blaming or accusing the other person. You make a direct eye contact, use “I statements,” quiet voice, and a firm tone to deliver your message to others.

3. Asking others for what you want without losing your dignity and being empathetic and respectful towards others' needs, feelings, and opinions.

And the best part?

Assertive communication can be used in everyday life; at work, with family, and in your relationships. If you wish to succeed in life, or create healthy relationships, or gain more respect from others, learn how to be assertive. This is one skill that can transform you into a winner.

I have outlined the exact steps you need to take to learn the skill of assertive communication, and how to apply it to your life. So, practice these steps and design the life you want.

RESOURCES

Assertiveness | Psychology Today. (n.d.). Retrieved November 20, 2019, from https://www.psychologytoday.com/us/basics/assertiveness

Thackray, V. (2016, November 11). 7 revealing facts about the psychology of assertiveness - PostiveChangeGuru.com. Retrieved November 20, 2019, from https://positivechangeguru.com/psychologists-assertive-you/

Choosing Your Communication Style | UMatter. (n.d.). Retrieved November 20, 2019, from https://umatter.princeton.edu/respect/tools/communication-styles

The 4-Types of Communication Styles. (n.d.). Retrieved November 20, 2019, from https://www.linkedin.com/pulse/20140626185020-15628411-the-4-types-of-communication-styles

Liyanage, S. (2015, July 21). Assertive Communication. Retrieved November 20, 2019, from https://www.slideshare.net/SamithaLiyanage1/assertive-communication-50744208

10 Benefits of Being More Assertive. (n.d.). Retrieved November 20, 2019, from http://www.magforliving.com/10-benefits-of-being-more-assertive/

9 Advantages of Assertiveness. (n.d.). Retrieved November 20, 2019, from https://threeinsights.net/book/9-advantages-of-assertiveness/

Kumar, D. (2014, July 18). The Importance of Being Assertive in the Workplace. Retrieved November 20, 2019, from https://www.careeraddict.com/the-importance-of-being-assertive-in-the-workplace

The Importance of Assertive Leadership. (n.d.). Retrieved November 20, 2019, from http://www.leadershipexpert.co.uk/importance-assertive-leadership.html

2011-2019, C. Skillsyouneed. C. (n.d.). Why People Are Not Assertive | SkillsYouNeed. Retrieved November 20, 2019, from https://www.skillsyouneed.com/ps/assertiveness2.html

Three Barriers that Would Stop You from Being Assertive. (2018, November

16). Retrieved November 20, 2019, from http://compasscenterforleadership.com/three-barriers-that-would-stop-you-from-being-assertive/

Metaperceptions: How Do You See Yourself? (n.d.). Retrieved November 20, 2019, from https://www.psychologytoday.com/us/articles/200505/metaperceptions-how-do-you-see-yourself

Chan, D. (2016, April 16). Learning to see things from another's perspective, Opinion News & Top. Retrieved November 20, 2019, from https://www.straitstimes.com/opinion/learning-to-see-things-from-anothers-perspective

How to Be Yourself and Cultivate a Positive Self-Image. (n.d.). Retrieved November 20, 2019, from https://www.developgoodhabits.com/positive-self-image/

Self-Image - how you see yourself positive or negative. (n.d.). Retrieved November 20, 2019, from http://destinysodyssey.com/personal-development/self-development-2/self-concepts-self-constructs/self-image/

2011-2019, C. Skillsyouneed. C. (n.d.-a). Personal Empowerment | SkillsYouNeed. Retrieved November 20, 2019, from https://www.skillsyouneed.com/ps/personal-empowerment.html

Campbell, S. (2017, January 31). 8 Steps to Personal Empowerment. Retrieved November 20, 2019, from https://www.entrepreneur.com/article/288340

What Is Personal Empowerment?: Taking Charge of Your Life and Career. (n.d.). Retrieved November 20, 2019, from https://www.mindtools.com/pages/article/personal-empowerment.htm

Assertiveness Training: Empowerment - Empowered Life Solutions. (n.d.). Retrieved November 20, 2019, from http://empoweredlifesolutions.com/healthy-living/assertiveness-training-empowerment/

Marsden, L. (2014, May 13). 4 Tips to be Assertive and Empower Your Life - Laurie Marsden. Retrieved November 20, 2019, from https://lauriemarsden.com/4-tips-assertive-empower-life/

how to be a lion: 7 steps for asserting yourself positively. (n.d.). Retrieved November 20, 2019, from https://www.positivelypresent.com/2010/05/how-to-be-a-lion.html

Tartakovsky, M. M. S. (2018, July 8). Assertiveness: The Art of Respecting

Your Needs While Also Respecting Others' Needs. Retrieved November 20, 2019, from https://psychcentral.com/blog/assertiveness-the-art-of-respecting-your-needs-while-also-respecting-others-needs/

https://www.pennstatehershey.org/documents/1803194/10660403/OAW+Assertiveness+Training+1.pdf/9f8788f4-219d-4fc1-a034-24551034d840

Kass, A. (n.d.). Three Keys to Assertive Behavior. Retrieved November 20, 2019, from https://www.gosmartlife.com/marriage-intelligence-blog/bid/148841/three-keys-to-assertive-behavior

Leinwand, L. (2016, November 10). Why Is Saying 'No' So Important? Retrieved November 20, 2019, from https://www.goodtherapy.org/blog/why-is-saying-no-so-important-1110165

Doherty, Y. (2014, November 7). 10 Reasons You Should Speak Up And Never Regret Saying How You Feel. Retrieved November 20, 2019, from https://www.elitedaily.com/life/culture/speak-dont-regret-saying-feel/823735

Ramey, S. (2016, September 22). Assertive Communication: Express What You Feel Without... Retrieved November 20, 2019, from https://exploringyourmind.com/assertive-communication-express-feel-without-guilt/

How to be less emotional reactive. (2019, October 2). Retrieved November 20, 2019, from https://cassdunn.com/how-to-be-assertive/

Louise, E. (2019, February 19). Here's How to Ask For Help Courageously and Assertively! [2 Step Process] | The Launchpad - The Coaching Tools Company Blog. Retrieved November 20, 2019, from https://www.thecoachingtoolscompany.com/how-to-be-more-assertive-ask-for-help/

Why Is It Hard to Say "No" and How Can You Get Better at It? (n.d.). Retrieved November 20, 2019, from https://www.psychologytoday.com/us/blog/the-couch/201601/why-is-it-hard-say-no-and-how-can-you-get-better-it

Be More Effective - 12 Reasons Why It's So Hard to Say, "No." (n.d.). Retrieved November 20, 2019, from https://www.bemoreeffective.com/blog/12-reasons-why-its-so-hard-to-say-no/

https://www.cci.health.wa.gov.au/~/media/CCI/Consumer%20Modules/Assert

%20Yourself/Assert%20Yourself%20-%2006%20-%20How%20to%20Say%20No%20Assertively.pdf

Dondas, C. (2019, June 16). 7 Tips on How to Say NO in an Assertive Way ... Retrieved November 20, 2019, from https://lifestyle.allwomenstalk.com/tips-on-how-to-say-no-in-an-assertive-way/

Wilding, M. L. (2018, July 8). 3 Ways to Say No and Be More Assertive in Business. Retrieved November 20, 2019, from https://psychcentral.com/blog/3-ways-to-say-no-and-be-more-assertive-in-business/

Chesak, J. (2018, December 11). The No BS Guide to Protecting Your Emotional Space. Retrieved November 20, 2019, from https://www.healthline.com/health/mental-health/set-boundaries#how-to-define-your-boundaries

Lancer, D. L. (2019, May 11). 10 Reasons Why Boundaries Don't Work. Retrieved November 20, 2019, from https://www.whatiscodependency.com/setting-boundaries-limits-codependency/

Lancer, D. L. (2019b, September 9). The Power of Personal Boundaries. Retrieved November 20, 2019, from https://www.whatiscodependency.com/the-power-of-personal-boundaries/

mindbodygreen. (2019, September 4). 6 Steps To Setting Good Boundaries. Retrieved November 20, 2019, from https://www.mindbodygreen.com/0-13176/6-steps-to-set-good-boundaries.html

5 Golden Keys to Assertiveness and Setting Boundaries | Hypnosis Downloads. (2019, August 1). Retrieved November 20, 2019, from https://www.hypnosisdownloads.com/blog/5-golden-keys-to-assertiveness-and-setting-boundaries

Grohol, J. Psy. D. M. (2018, October 8). 10 Reasons You Can't Say How You Feel. Retrieved November 20, 2019, from https://psychcentral.com/lib/10-reasons-you-cant-say-how-you-feel/

Bennett, T. (2018, March 13). Why Is It So Hard to Express My Emotions? - Thriveworks. Retrieved November 20, 2019, from https://thriveworks.com/blog/hard-express-emotions/

» Assertiveness. (n.d.). Retrieved November 20, 2019, from https://www.emotionalintelligenceatwork.com/resources/assertiveness/

admin. (2019, November 20). The difference between confidence and assertiveness. Retrieved November 20, 2019, from http://buildyp.blogspot.com/2012/05/difference-between-confidence-and.html?m=1

A Simple Way to Be More Assertive (Without Being Pushy). (2018, January 31). Retrieved November 20, 2019, from https://hbr.org/2017/08/a-simple-way-to-be-more-assertive-without-being-pushy

Sheffield, T. (2015, November 6). How To Ask For What You Want & Be More Assertive. Retrieved November 20, 2019, from https://www.bustle.com/articles/122147-how-to-ask-for-what-you-want-be-more-assertive

Assertive Requests: Be more persuasive and diplomatic. (n.d.). Retrieved November 20, 2019, from http://web.csulb.edu/%7Etstevens/assert%20req.html

Foolproof Ways to Use Assertiveness to Request a Raise. (n.d.). Retrieved November 20, 2019, from https://www.selfgrowth.com/articles/foolproof-ways-to-use-assertiveness-to-request-a-raise

Hoffman, J. (n.d.). The Secret to Asking Sales Questions Assertively, Not Aggressively. Retrieved November 20, 2019, from https://blog.hubspot.com/sales/asking-sales-questions-assertively-not-aggressively

Daskal, L. (2018, June 20). 7 Powerful Habits That Make You More Assertive. Retrieved November 20, 2019, from https://www.inc.com/lolly-daskal/7-powerful-habits-that-make-you-more-assertive.html

2011-2019, C. Skillsyouneed. C. (n.d.-a). Assertiveness in Specific Situations | SkillsYouNeed. Retrieved November 20, 2019, from https://www.skillsyouneed.com/ps/assertiveness-demands-criticism-compliments.html

Sese, C. (2018, April 19). 6 Tips for Being More Assertive at Work. Retrieved November 20, 2019, from https://www.goodtherapy.org/blog/6-tips-for-being-more-assertive-at-work-0113155

How to Be Assertive and Get What You Want at Work. (2013, June 20). Retrieved November 20, 2019, from https://money.usnews.com/money/blogs/outside-voices-careers/2013/06/20/how-to-be-assertive-and-get-what-you-want-at-work

Wilding, M. (2019, June 5). How to Be More Assertive at Work (Without

Being a Jerk). Retrieved November 20, 2019, from https://www.themuse.com/advice/how-to-be-more-assertive-at-work-without-being-a-jerk

Lica, A. (2019, August 18). Assertive Communication with Your... Retrieved November 20, 2019, from https://exploringyourmind.com/assertive-communication-with-your-family/

Becoming Assertive? 4 Reasons Your Family Won't Like It. (n.d.). Retrieved November 20, 2019, from https://www.arenewedlife.com/becoming-assertive-4-reasons-family-wont-like/

Are You Too Nice? 7 Ways to Gain Appreciation & Respect. (n.d.). Retrieved November 20, 2019, from https://www.psychologytoday.com/us/blog/communication-success/201309/are-you-too-nice-7-ways-gain-appreciation-respect

Hutchison, M. (2015, August 6). 6 Assertive Ways To Get The Respect You DESERVE. Retrieved November 20, 2019, from https://www.yourtango.com/experts/moira-hutchison/how-gain-respect-others

Patel, D. (2018, November 9). 10 Powerful Ways to Stand Up for Yourself in Any Situation. Retrieved November 20, 2019, from https://www.success.com/10-powerful-ways-to-stand-up-for-yourself-in-any-situation/

Steber, C. (2019, June 12). 11 Little Ways To Stand Up For Yourself Every Day, No Matter What. Retrieved November 20, 2019, from https://www.bustle.com/articles/169607-11-little-ways-to-stand-up-for-yourself-every-day-no-matter-what

How to Speak Up for Yourself with Wisdom and Courage. (n.d.). Retrieved November 20, 2019, from https://www.psychologytoday.com/us/blog/prescriptions-life/201809/how-speak-yourself-wisdom-and-courage

Galinsky, A. (2017, February 17). How to speak up for yourself. Retrieved November 20, 2019, from https://ideas.ted.com/how-to-speak-up-for-yourself/

Winning Conflict Resolution Techniques

MASTER NONVIOLENT AND EFFECTIVE COMMUNICATION SKILLS TO RESOLVE EVERYDAY CONFLICTS IN THE WORKPLACE, RELATIONSHIPS, MARRIAGE, AND CRUCIAL CONVERSATIONS

GERARD SHAW

Table of Contents

INTRODUCTION

Why is conflict resolution so important? In this book, you will learn that conflict and conflict resolution skills are crucial to your success and personal growth. Everybody experiences conflict throughout their life. Conflict happens because everyone is unique. We all interpret and communicate ideas differently, and we don't always have the same priority or point of view. Conflict can be looked at as unhealthy and harmful, and it can often stress us out and lower our happiness and productivity. However, when we use conflict to develop better understandings with those around us, it can be a positive experience. This is because conflict can teach you a lot about yourself and give you tools to use in your daily life.

This book was written to help people like you who are unsure of how to address conflict. Do you avoid conflict and confrontation? Have you always struggled with communicating your ideas to others? Do your conflicts always escalate out of control? Do you wish you experienced more positive outcomes from the conflicts in your life? In the first two chapters of this book, you will learn about what conflict is, what causes it, and how we each deal with it in our own way. The remainder of the book provides you with seven techniques that are explained in detail so you can approach and resolve any conflict with confidence.

These seven techniques are:

1. Mastering the power of conversation through verbal communication tools.
2. Mastering the power of conversation through non-verbal communication tools.
3. Managing emotions.
4. Changing minds through persuasion and negotiation.
5. Developing emotional intelligence so you can resolve conflict like a leader.
6. The strategy of peace.
7. The power of keeping an open mind.

The seven techniques in this book are presented in a general and well-rounded way so you can customize our techniques to your situation. Examples are used to illustrate concepts so you are able to put the information in context. Part of the reason why conflict can be difficult to resolve is that we are stuck in our own minds and insist on getting our point across. There are many more points of view to consider than just your own. By using empathy and effective listening, we can engage with others in a more positive way. Dedication, self-reflection, and the techniques presented in this book will give you the knowledge to better understand conflict and what causes it. You will be able to identify your own triggers and how you contribute to dispute. Often, we don't realize that we are contributing to the problem. This book was designed to help you take a step back, manage your emotions, motivate you towards success, and resolve conflicts with confidence. Our methods are easy to follow so that you can learn quickly and practice them whenever you need them.

This book will help you to understand conflict within yourself, how to recognize pending conflicts, how you contribute to conflict with others, and what environmental factors play a role in helping resolution. By the time you are finished reading this book, you will have a different perspective about conflict and conflict resolution than you do now. If you are tired of conflicts in your relationships and within yourself, why wait longer to resolve them? Rather than procrastinating, you can start fixing the problem by reading more right now. All the tools you need are provided in this book so that in any situation you face you will know what to say, how to say it, and how to achieve a more positive outcome. By reading this book and using our seven techniques, you will be better equipped to solve problems and resolve conflict in your own life.

This book bundle comes with a FREE booklet on masterminding a winning routine to improve calmness and your level of confidence daily. Head to the bottom of this book bundle for instructions on how you can secure your copy today.

CHAPTER ONE

Understanding the World of Conflict

What is conflict? Conflict usually occurs when two or more individuals disagree on a subject and the disagreement leads to anger, hostility, or animosity. A difference of perception, beliefs or opinions is often at the forefront of conflict. However, you can also be in conflict with yourself. You may be questioning your perceptions or beliefs, or you might be unsure about the decisions you need to make. You may be in conflict with yourself as a result of a conflict with someone else. Three of the main discussion topics that most often lead to conflict are: money, religion, and politics. These topics can be described in terms of economics, values, and power.

Economic Conflict: There are a limited amount of resources available to the groups or individuals involved. Each individual has their own opinion about how to ration the limited resources. The individuals discuss or debate about the allocation of wealth or assets. When they cannot agree, the issue escalates into a conflict between the parties.

Value Conflict: These conflicts typically occur when someone's beliefs and morals are in conflict with someone else's. The argument often centers around behavior, religion, culture, or social issues. One party wants the other party or parties to believe or behave in a way that conforms to a social norm that they believe is superior. The refusal of either party to change can escalate into conflict.

Power Conflict: Power conflicts arise mainly in the political and organizational arenas, with authoritative public figures or groups. However, power conflicts can also exist between individuals on a personal level. When political values differ, or one person or group tries to dominate decision making on behalf of other parties, that can lead to conflict.

Whether the conflict is based on economics, values, or power, getting to the root of what caused the conflict is the first step towards finding resolution. When you understand what the conflict is about and why it escalated, you are more likely to succeed in resolving or diffusing the problematic situation. Whether conflict happens within us or with others, when we take a step back and evaluate the root causes of the conflict, we learn about the boundaries of others and ourselves.

Many people look at conflict as a bad thing, but it can be a positive thing. Conflict is negative and unhealthy when the people in the conflict feel attacked, violated, unheard, misled or misunderstood. What makes conflict healthy is the willingness to resolve it. Conflict is positive when it leads to both parties deciding to agree to disagree or to compromise to diffuse the situation.

There are very unhealthy ways to address conflict, and this is what most people resort to when handling stressful affairs. Some people have underlying characteristics such as anger issues, a superiority complex, narcissistic or sociopathic tendencies. This drives them to act and behave impulsively, or react with hostility and resentment when confronted. Other people may have grown up in an environment where conflict was resolved in a negative or hurtful way, so they emulate this behavior. Some people avoid conflict altogether. Some of the unhealthy ways people deal with conflict are listed below.

Avoidance and Denial: Avoidance or denial is used when people remove themselves from the situation and refuse to discuss or resolve it. They will often pretend there is no issue, and say things like "everything is fine" or "there's no problem" when asked about the topic. This rarely leads to resolution. The problem doesn't go away. Instead, it lingers in the background and festers, turning into a larger argument later.

Blaming: This occurs when one party accuses the other party of being at fault for the situation Blaming stems from anger and personal insecurities, and it only escalates the conflict further. The person who is blaming thinks that they are diffusing the situation by making the other take responsibility for their actions. This can be perceived as an attack and cause the other person to be defensive, refuse to accept blame and blame the other party in return. This can escalate quickly and lead to heated fights.

Power and Influence: Trying to resolve conflict in this way means that parties compete to "win" at the other's expense. The primary purpose is to win the argument rather than see the other's perspective. Negative behaviors may be used to convince the other party to give up or cause them to lose. Tactics include threats to job security, using things against one another, making complaints, sabotage, etc. When someone "wins," they may think the fight is over; however, the "loser" will likely be resentful, fearful, or sad.

Manipulation: Manipulation comes in many forms, such as brainwashing, gaslighting, control of assets, passive-aggressiveness, guilt-trips, and inequitable compromise. Manipulators are just trying to resolve a situation to their benefit and their perceived efforts at resolution are usually self-serving. Examples of manipulative behavior include the following scenarios: An individual proposes an idea but makes it seem like it was the other person's idea in order to increase the chance of it being accepted; A compromise may be proposed that is not fair to one party, but if that party refuses they look like they are not being cooperative; Someone might say, “If you were truly loyal, you would do X for me.”

Stages of Conflict

Conflict can be both positive and negative, and it can have both positive and negative outcomes. A positive way to approach conflict is by learning from the situation. From a positive perspective, we need conflict to help us develop our problem-solving skills and for our personal growth. The outcome can be positive when parties come to an amicable agreement. The conflict can be negative if we choose to deal with it in an aggressive way. The outcome is negative if the conflict results in the destruction of a relationship. Whether or not the conflict is positive or negative, there are common stages to all conflicts.

The five stages of conflict are:

1. The latent stage.
2. The perceived stage.
3. The felt stage.
4. The manifest stage.
5. The aftermath stage.

The **latent phase** of conflict means that something is happening that will lead to an adverse situation later, but no one realizes it. For example, your roommate asks you to pick up some shampoo and conditioner from the store for them since you are going to the store anyway. When you get to the store, you select and buy some shampoo and conditioner, not knowing that they wouldn't ever use that brand. This is the latent stage in the conflict. Neither of you knew there would be a problem stemming from this transaction.

The **perceived stage** of conflict is when both parties or the group of individuals know and understand that there is a conflict happening. When you come home with the hair products, an argument happens because she does not like the brand you bought her and she doesn't want to keep it. You think she should be happy with what you selected since she did not specify what she wanted. Similarly, if two employees are working on a project together, they might have different ideas about what needs to be done. No one is willing to compromise and they start to argue about which plan to support.

In the **felt stage**, emotions like anxiety, nervousness or anger are felt by one or all of the individuals in the conflict. In the example with the roommates, the felt stage happens when both individuals are heated due to the miscommunication and subsequent accusation about the shampoo and conditioner. Your roommate is annoyed because she assumed you knew which type to buy because you share the same shower. You are upset that she's ungrateful about the favor you did her.

In the **manifest stage**, the conflict is now in progress and it is either escalating or attempts to resolve it are being made. In the example of the two roommates, after arguing for a while, they agree to either do their own shopping, or to be more specific about what they want. In the workplace, if the conflict escalates between two employees, they might ask a manager which approach best suits the client's needs.

The last stage is the **aftermath**. This happens after the previous stages take their course, and the problem becomes resolved one way or another. With the examples of the roommates and the workplace, both conflicts had a positive aftermath. A negative aftermath would have been if the roommates' fight escalated to the point they could no longer cohabitate, or one of the employees quit because they could not tolerate not getting their way.

In addition to understanding the stages of conflict, it's important to understand the different types of conflict. There are five basic types of conflict.

1. Conflict within yourself.
2. Interpersonal conflict.
3. The conflict between a person and a group.
4. Inter-group conflict.
5. Inter-organizational conflict.

The first type of conflict is **conflict within yourself**. This usually means that you are considering violating a value, boundary, or moral that you hold dear, or that you have a difficult decision to make. Perhaps you are considering another person's opinion and you don't know how to react. Perhaps you are both honest and loyal, and a friend asks you to lie for them. That would compromise your values and you might be conflicted by your desire to be both honest and loyal to your friend. You might be wondering if they are truly your friend if they would ask you to be dishonest on their behalf. These are significant inner conflicts.

The next type of conflict is **interpersonal**. This type of conflict is probably the most common type of conflict, and it happens between two or more people. An example of this would be that two people share the same love interest, and both are competing for that person's attention. Another example can be found in the workplace. Three people may be up for a promotion, and all are equally deserving of the position but only one person can get it. This causes conflict between coworkers as they compete and when one "wins". It may also cause conflict between the employees and the employer who is responsible for making the decision.

The third type of conflict arises when there is a **conflict between one person and a group**. The conflict between a group and an individual happens when one person doesn't agree with the rest of the group's position but wants to get along due to the benefits of being in the group. For example, if you are at a book club and you get constructive criticism about your ideas, you may not agree with the group. You can only stay if you can get along, so you must decide if the disagreement is important enough to impact your overall participation. Another example is being part of a group that is arguing because some people want to create a petition for something, but you don’t think it’s a good use of the group’s time.

Inter-group conflict arises mostly in the workplace and with businesses and companies. For example, there may be conflict within a company if a new CEO and management team are hired to reorganize. When they come in with ideas on how to create a new division of the company, the people who have been at the company long term may not welcome the newcomers' ideas. This can cause conflict between groups of personnel.

Inter-organizational conflict mainly happens between two organizations such as buyers and suppliers, unions and companies, government agencies and advocacy groups. These organizations may run differently from each other or have different priorities about what should happen or how things should operate.

Conflict can be personal or professional. It can be between two people or two conglomerates. It can be small scale or large scale. No matter what, we are likely to encounter conflict in our lives. Identifying and understanding the underlying reasons for conflict is an important aspect of conflict resolution.

Causes of Conflict

There are many causes of conflict. Understanding the root causes of conflict is essential to having positive outcomes and avoiding mistakes. We know that the big picture causes of conflict are typically related to economics, values, and power. Regardless of what people argue about, there are many actions and behaviors that commonly lead to the initiation or escalation of conflict. These common causes of conflict are:

- Miscommunication.
- Lack of information.
- Misinterpretation.
- Different perspectives.

- Destructive thought patterns.
- The inability to regulate our emotions.

These things can influence the development of a conflict whether it is at work, in your relationships or within yourself. The most common way of preventing a conflict before it begins is to be aware of yourself and your surroundings. We can control our reactions and behaviors. When problems arise, it's usually because emotions have been allowed to run high without pausing and taking a step back from the whole situation. Many people struggle with this because they aren't aware of how they are feeling, they are emotionally impulsive or they fail to recognize the signs around them. Here are more examples of the causes of conflict in the various areas of our lives:

Professional Conflict

- Manipulation tactics used to climb the company ladder.
- Competition for recognition, promotion or raises.
- Not enough growth within a company or organization.
- Different beliefs about how management should act.
- Deadline constraints.
- Lack of information between different groups.
- Difference in opinions and thought process.

Relationship and Interpersonal Relationship Conflict

- Heightened emotions.
- Judgment or labeling.
- Defensive or offensive ways of communicating.
- Poor communication skills.
- Mixed signals.
- Pessimistic behavior.

Personal Conflict

- When an action doesn't match a moral or personal value.
- Different opinions or beliefs from someone else.
- Being in a compromised situation.
- Identity crisis - or not knowing oneself fully.

Once we recognize the stages and causes of a conflict, we are more fully equipped to address it and influence its outcome.

Chapter Summary

As you have learned, conflict and its resolution are more complicated than most think. In this chapter, we were able to identify what conflict is and how it starts. More of what was covered in this chapter includes:

- Unhealthy ways of dealing with conflict.
- The stages of conflict.

- The causes of conflict.
- The types of conflict.

In the subsequent chapters, you will first learn about the foundations of conflict resolution, and then we will dive into the seven techniques of conflict resolution and learn how to put them into practice.

CHAPTER TWO

Foundations of Conflict Resolution

Before we dive into the seven techniques for resolving conflict, we must first learn about the foundations of conflict resolution. Conflict resolution isn't just about being aware and staying patient with yourself and with the person you are in conflict with. It's about learning to read someone's behavior, tap into your emotions, and figuring out the best problem-solving skills to use at the right moment. The foundations of conflict resolution include knowing the signs of conflict before it happens, what to do during the conflict, and how to respond to the aftermath of an argument.

Everyone has their own way of dealing with conflict and coming up with solutions, and no two conflicts are the same because no two people or situations are identical. Conflict resolution is an important life skill because it can help you to maneuver more easily through life, to become more successful and to be more graceful and professional in difficult situations. You might think that conflict resolution requires that you never lose your temper. Wrong. We are all human, and we all make mistakes, say things we don't mean, and forget what we have been practicing from time to time. To be able to resolve conflict doesn't mean that you can never speak out or lose your temper. Sometimes, we must be assertive about our opinion to get our point across. However, conflict resolution teaches us how to avoid losing our cool in a way that hurts others or compromises the resolution of the difficult situation.

People who struggle with fighting and violence may have an underlying problem with handling challenging environments or confrontation because they cannot separate their own beliefs and opinions from those of others. When someone can identify their conflict triggers, they can learn how to cope with or prepare for any confrontation. When you understand what the root cause of the problem is, you can easily take a step back and work toward creative problem-solving, team building and long-term relationships. This requires you to figure out what your typical response to conflict is, and when it usually kicks in. Learning how to resolve confrontation quickly has many benefits, some of which are discussed below.

Stronger Relationships

Most strong, positive relationships are built on trust, loyalty, reliability, boundaries, and respect. When you learn how to resolve conflict and understand where it comes from, you can build healthier relationships. Honesty, healthy boundaries, and personal assertiveness are at the root of strong relationships. Not all conflict is wrong or unhealthy, and it can be okay to argue or have healthy disagreements. This is because to build relationships you need to understand the other person's perspective.

For example, one person might need to find a roommate, so they post an ad online. You see it, and everything they offer sounds incredible so you respond to it, and after a couple of weeks you are all moved in. After some time has passed, a conflict arises because they brought home a dog. You are allergic and have told them before that you are allergic to pet hair. They defied your wishes because they didn't think you would be home at the time and that it wouldn't be a big deal. As a result, an argument breaks out. After arguing for a while, your roommate takes the dog for a walk until the owner can come to pick it up. When they come home, you have a healthy and calm talk. The roommate says that they didn't realize you were so allergic and that in the future they will never bring an animal home. You believe that they are sincere and that they can be trusted. Hence the relationship grows, and you build a closer and stronger friendship.

Goal Achievement and Success

Conflict resolution skills can have a real impact on your ability to succeed and achieve your goals. When you switch your mindset, learn new ways to view things, learn body language cues and effective listening strategies, you are better equipped to face all challenges. Conflict resolution involves being aware of how you speak, how your message is perceived, and how to present the right message. This takes self-awareness. You cannot just see confrontation coming and immediately know how to handle it. You need to know what the other party is thinking or feeling. These skills take time, dedication, and motivation to master. This perseverance and self-discipline are key to successfully setting and achieving goals.

Showing Excellent Leadership and Team Management Skills

Conflict resolution skills help you to look at situations in a way that views every confrontation as "us" instead of "me." A leader thinks of others and how decisions will affect the team. A good leader shows empathy for others and tries to understand how decisions will impact those around them. Leading others effectively requires commitment and dedication to follow through with actions once they say they will do something. Conflict resolution skills set you up for leadership and for being a stronger part of a team.

Embracing New Perspectives

Our perspectives greatly influence our actions. Some people are stubborn, and others are flexible. Some people are short-tempered while others are patient. Some people are closed-minded while others are open-minded. Conflict resolution skills help you define who you are and how you perceive and respond to dispute. It's about learning how others feel and think and about being open to learning new points of view. Conflict resolution gives you further insight into how to combine your perspective with the views of others so that an equitable outcome can be achieved.

It's true that we cannot avoid conflict, and that it is likely to come into our lives at some point. Most times conflict is seen as a bad thing because it triggers strong emotions. However, conflict can be positive since it is an opportunity to grow as an individual. Embrace change and be open to the perspectives of others.

Conflict Resolution Theories

Throughout history, there have been many theories about conflict resolution. Four of the major theories are discussed below.

Conflict Theory One: Morton Deutsch - Cooperative Model

The first theory is the Cooperative Model by Morton Deutsch. His theory is based on interpersonal relationships being motivated by either cooperation or competition. The cooperative process allows us to resolve disputes by being willing and open to another person's ideas and views. This has a positive effect. Competition however, means that two parties cannot cooperate because of the inner motive to compete and win. Deutch's theory says that almost always, competition in a conflict will have a negative consequence with one person coming out as the "winner" and the other as a "loser". His research suggests that constructive conflict resolution results from a cooperative nature and a desire to resolve problems. Deutch concluded that if both parties are cooperative, they can more easily come to an understanding of each other's views. He believed this could be achieved by learning the norms of cooperation. These norms are honesty, respect, acknowledgment, empathy, forgiveness, and a mutual understanding of the situation and the conflict.

Conflict Theory Two: Roger Fisher and William Ury - Principled Negotiation

In the Principled Negotiation Theory, Fisher and Ury were brought together at Harvard University to work on a project called "The Negotiation Project". In 1943, Fisher studied Law at the University and took on the interest of solving people's disputes. He was impressed by Ury's research paper on Middle East peace negotiations and invited Ury to work with him after he became a professor at Harvard in 1960. Together, they wrote the book "Getting to Yes" which quickly became a best-seller. Working with Fisher and his teachings, Ury became a mediator and negotiation advisor.

The Principled Negotiation Theory discussed in "Getting to Yes" discusses how to achieve a good negotiation outcome. They believed that people are problem-solvers and that a good agreement is wise and efficient. This means that it satisfies the interests of both parties. In their findings, Fisher and Ury set out four essential principles for how to make negotiation effective. They were to separate the person (or people) from the problem (or conflict); to focus on agendas, not situations; to create ideas for mutual understanding; and to use objective guidelines. The focus of this theory was to have each conflicted party (person) achieve agreement and compromise by negotiating on those terms.

Conflict Theory Three: John Burton - Human Needs Model

Burton's Human Needs Model is based on the belief that conflict is a social matter or a personal problem related to human needs. Burton says if social inequity is the root cause of conflict, then it is irrelevant to try to solve it until social norms are corrected. Burton suggests that social norms would have to be adjusted to suit the needs of every individual. He believes that aggression and antisocial behavior stems from social circumstances and the denial of human needs. He concludes that in order to stop future conflicts and damaging behavior social changes must be achieved, for example, employees must be given recognition, and teenagers must be given a role in society. Burton suggests that it isn't the people who need to change for society, but the society that needs to change for people.

Conflict Theory Four: Bush, Folger and Lederach - Conflict Transformation

The Conflict Transformation Theory suggests that instead of trying to resolve or manage conflict, we should transform it. Transformation requires a solution that satisfies the interests of all groups. Bush, Folger, and Lederach's idea of conflict transformation requires changing an individual's attitude and behavior and the relationship between two or more conflicting parties. Lederach suggested that by focusing on mutual needs and understanding, instead of the differences between the parties, we are more likely to transform conflict into dialogue and be empowered to resolve issues cooperatively.

Now that we understand some major theories of conflict resolution, let's look at how to identify our own behaviors and responses to conflict.

Problem-Solving Behaviors

When we look at people's behaviors, we observe how they act in various situations, their values, personality, and characteristics. So, what exactly are problem-solving or conflict resolving behaviors? These are behaviors that people have when they try to diffuse an awkward encounter or solve an issue. Assertiveness is one of the most common behaviors people use when they are in conflict. Other common types of behaviors people exhibit when dealing with confrontation or dispute are:

- Accommodating roles.
- Avoidance.
- Compromising.
- Collaborating.
- Competition.

The **accommodating** response is when people put aside all their needs and wants for those of others. While this may seem like a good approach, it can actually be hurtful as the accommodating individual may feel as though they are unable to get what they want from the situation. This can lead to or stem from a lack of confidence or self-esteem. Although this might be good behavior to diffuse a situation or prevent an issue from escalating in the short term, it can be used as a form of avoidance or in order to push the root problem aside. The only times where this method may be useful is when the issue is not that important to you, or if you have been manipulated or pushed to agree and you don't want to fight anymore. Sometimes, it can be used in order to gracefully exit a situation.

The **avoidance** behavior signifies fear or lack of responsibility in most cases. The avoidance technique is to either pretend there is no conflict, ignore the issue, or procrastinate until the problem “fixes itself.” This type of conflict resolving behavior is perhaps the most inefficient way of handling conflict. It can stem from fear of confrontation, or if the person feels as though they are too superior to handle such “petty” issues. This approach may be used if someone believes they can’t “win” the argument anyway, or if they are waiting for more information to bolster their case.

A **compromise** can be efficient and effective when both parties come out equally on top. It’s a positive behavior based on finding a middle ground or something that each party is willing to lose in order to gain something else. This is best when the dispute is between two people rather than a large group. A compromise can be effective if the goal is to reach a mutually agreeable solution. A compromise can be difficult to attain if both parties refuse to adjust their position.

Collaboration behaviors include the expectation that everyone wins. If this isn't possible, the conflict resolution may result in compromise and negotiation strategies. This type of behavior is perhaps the most rewarding method to resolve conflict as it helps everyone to work together and see eye-to-eye. Everyone wins and everyone benefits. This will often result in both parties getting everything they need, since each party helps the other with their goals.

Competition is only positive behavior when it's fun and friendly, such as minor gambling, friendly bets, games, sports, or races. Other means of competing, such as with your partner for an interest that only one individual can gain is negative behavior. The competition behavior is common in an argumentative person that always has to get the last word in. Even though you address their issues, prove your point, and define your concerns, you still lose in their eyes due to their competitiveness. They want to "one-up" someone else or prove their point without hearing anyone else's.

Everyone has their own ways of managing an awkward situation. Some people are more aggressive than others, while some people give up trying to win. Effective conflict resolution sometimes requires you to "pick your battles". Sometimes, we are not in a position to win, or we don't have time to argue. We need to learn when to speak and when not to speak, as well as when to listen. In all cases, we need to approach problem solving and conflict resolution with positive intent, using principles such as openness, empathy, equality, and positivity.

Openness

To be open means to have an "open mind". This requires us to listen effectively before responding out of emotional impulse and to take the time to truly consider the viewpoint of the other person. Your main goal is to recognize their viewpoint, state your true feelings and then work together to identify the root problem and an effective solution. Using "I feel" and "How do you feel about...?" statements and questions can help you to be more open in conflict situations.

Empathy

Empathy means truly trying to understand the experience, perspective, and feelings of the other party. It requires that you listen intently with the objective of understanding their point of view. You must put aside all judgments or previous notions about the party that you are in conflict with. You must truly try to be compassionate about their experience or viewpoint. An empathetic statement such as, "I didn't realize I made you feel that way" can help, or "I didn't realize this decision would have that outcome for you." If you are empathetic without being ingenuine, use positive language without using condescending tones, then it can show the person that you understand their needs and really do want to solve the issue.

Equality

Treat people as if they are equal to you. Many people say they know what equality means, yet they look down on the homeless, or resent their bosses or people that are different from them. The truth is that there will always be someone tougher, stronger, smarter, or wealthier than you, but you will also be tougher, stronger, smarter, or wealthier than someone else. Equality means that all judgments are put to rest, and you see others as having the same value as you regardless of their economic or social status. To practice this, consider everyone's ideas on the basis of merit only.

Positivity

If you approach issues with a negative mindset, and bring negativity with you everywhere, you will be inherently pessimistic. When you opt for positivity and optimism, you bring everyone's spirits up and motivate yourself and each other to find solutions, instead of focusing on problems. To practice positivity, express your enthusiasm for finding a solution, and help others see that their opinions are not being dismissed.

If we behave in these positive ways, we can be sure to find a solution, build healthier relationships, and succeed at a faster rate than those who are destructive and negative. When you are known for finding solutions in a positive, painless, and efficient way, you will be more highly regarded by others, feel better about yourself, and obtain further opportunities in your career and life.

Chapter Summary

As you have learned by now, there are different approaches to conflict resolution. To have a successful outcome, conflict resolution requires a positive mindset and behavior. If your typical response to dispute is aggressive, or someone has ulterior motives, the conflict will escalate and end negatively for everyone involved. Each person is different, thinks their own way, has their own views, and acts according to what they think is right. By using positive strategies that consider the needs of all parties, we are more likely to find an equitable solution to our conflict.

In this chapter, you learned about the foundations of conflict management. Specifically, we covered:

- The benefits of conflict resolution.
- Four well-known conflict theories.
- Typical problem-solving behaviors and responses.
- How to approach and de-escalate conflict.

The next chapter is the first of seven techniques for how to master conflict resolution. You will learn how to send the right message using effective verbal communication. You will gain a deep understanding of the power of dialog and why some people are harder to talk to than others.

CHAPTER THREE

Conflict Resolution Technique 01 - Mastering the Power of Conversation Through Verbal Communication

There are four main forms of communication: verbal, non-verbal, written, and visual. Verbal is often argued to be the most essential way of communicating. When we think about verbal communication, what comes to our minds? It's talking to each other about interests or issues. There are endless potential topics of discussion. But, are we talking to each other or at each other? In today's day and age, people communicate through texts, emails, social media, or other written forms of communication. When we are with someone face-to-face, we are often also on our phones or digital devices. This stops us from listening effectively and we completely miss dialogue. Many people think dialogue is when two or more people have a discussion, each taking turns to speak. However, dialogue is not just about talking to each other. It's about understanding what is being communicated, and determining what the message behind the words used are. Verbal communication has many more components than just speaking aloud. It's about learning to listen, gaining insight, thinking before responding, and ultimately preventing conflict as efficiently as possible. When you combine verbal with non-verbal communication (which you will learn about in the next chapter), you can become a master at communication.

Verbal communication is the practice of listening to what is said, interpreting it in the way that the speaker is meaning to convey their message, and responding appropriately to their statement. Many people hear what is being said but don't listen to what they are hearing. Poor listening skills result in misinterpretation of the facts, which can lead to conflict. The problem is that most people aren't really listening to understand. They listen to respond, and they are too focused on the things they want to say rather than what was just said by the other person. The solution to this problem is to learn effective listening techniques and then focus on conveying your message in the terms they are speaking about.

The basic skills that you need for effective verbal communication are:

- Effective speaking
    - Choose the right words to convey your message. Who is your audience?
    - Use the correct tone and don't be condescending, dismissive or aggressive.
    - Respond specifically to what the other person said.

  - Make sure there are no mixed signals from contradictory statements.
- Context
  - Know who you are speaking with and what is important to them.
  - Understand the topic you are discussing. Collect more information if needed.
  - Ensure the location and time is appropriate for the conversation.
- Active listening
  - Be open-minded.
  - Stay non-judgmental.
  - Avoid thinking of a response until you've listened fully to the other person's statement.
  - Be patient and take the time to listen. Ask questions if you need something clarified.
  - Stay focused on the speaker. Don't watch the TV over their shoulder, check your phone or change the subject.
  - Listen to the full sentence, not just single words you heard throughout the conversation. You could misunderstand the overall message.

Learning to converse effectively takes practice and patience. You can both speak and listen by asking questions based on things you don't understand. Asking questions also tells the speaker that you want to know more, that you are enthusiastic about understanding the message they are trying to convey, and that you respect their right to be heard. It also shows that you are willing to engage without redirecting the conversation to yourself, which also builds rapport and trust. The last step to mastering effective verbal communication is ending the conversation in a respectful matter. Once there is an opening for the conversation to end, such as a pause of some length, you can close the discussion with the appropriate closing words. This may include respectfully summarizing what's been said, or saying, "That was really interesting. I'm glad we had the chance to talk."

Effective Speaking

Part of verbal communication is learning how to speak effectively. Effective speaking is as much about patience and listening as it is about the words you use. One of the problems with today's society is that no one wants to take the time to listen to each other speak. We are all too busy listening to our own thoughts and trying to get them out quickly. We often don't take the time to think carefully about what we are about to say. With social media, networking, and promotion building, we may be conversing with each other, but we aren't talking, and our focus is not on the conversation. It is with ourselves. For example, when you go to a social outing you may have the intention of promoting yourself and your ideas. How many people go to a gathering just to learn about other people and listen to their perspective? Effective speaking starts with effective listening.

Part of speaking effectively requires "saying what you mean and meaning what you say". In other words, you have to be genuine and truthful, and follow up on the things you promised to do. Speaking effectively requires you to convey your message according to how you want your message to be acted on. If you want a positive reaction you will use encouraging tones and words. If you want help from others, you would use a questioning tone or word the question based on what type of feedback you are looking for. Effective speaking requires the proper word choice and tone of voice. Also important are your breathing, the pitch of your voice and the clarity of your message. Pacing of delivery and diversity of word choice also plays a significant role in speaking competently.

Word Choice

The words you use are the most important aspect of effective speaking, and they must be chosen carefully to ensure they have the desired effect. You must take into consideration the context of the situation and who you are talking to. You wouldn't choose the same hard to read, complicated words with a child or a foreigner as you would with an authoritative academic person or native language speaker. Consider your audience and use words you know they will understand. If you aren't sure, use smaller sentences and simple language to ensure everyone knows what you are saying. When using examples, describe situations they can relate to. Words should always be positive and empowering, rather than negative or condescending.

Tone of Voice

There is so much you can tell about a person's mood, motive, and attitude just by listening to the tone of their voice. For example, a reserved person might talk quietly and hesitantly. The pitch and tone used by the speaker suggest they are shy, lack confidence, and are looking for leadership. For a shy person, you would approach them with an empathetic and reassuring nature and use a calm, quiet voice to encourage them to listen to you.

On the other hand, someone who is more confident will have a firm and commanding tone of voice. This implies that they know what they are talking about and that they can take a leadership role. Consider how you speak to others. Do you seem shy, confident, or somewhere in between? The tone of your voice matters since it influences the impression you give to others and their willingness to listen to your point of view.

The Effect of Breathing

Emotions come out in our voices. If we are nervous or anxious, our breath will be short and we might hyperventilate, or our voice might come out cracked and hesitant. If we are comfortable, our breathing will remain steady and be even and calm, which will help our voice come out smoothly. Our breath influences our body language, as well. For example, if our breathing is sporadic, our posture is stiff, and our muscles feel tense, these body language cues send signals to our brain that make us anxious, disturbing the calm flow of our voices. Imagine if singers couldn't get over being shy and reserved when they got on stage in front of large crowds. They wouldn't sound as confident or as competent as they do in the studio when only a few individuals are present. Singers and public speakers practice their breathing and record themselves, so they can identify the voice mistakes they make and can fix them. Make sure you are taking deep, regular breaths to convey confidence when you speak. Breathing deep and steadily has a calming effect, which will help you be more relaxed, focused and able to moderate your speech. Breathing influences tone, pitch and volume. The topic of breathing will come up again later in the book, so remember what you have learned here, as it will be reinforced later. That's how important breathing is to effective speaking.

Volume

Choosing the volume of your voice determines how effectively you are heard. Breathing plays a significant role in how loudly or quietly you speak. When we breathe deeply, we are able to project our voices loudly, which is sometimes necessary. For example, when trying to be heard in a group or a large room, speaking quietly is ineffective. You want to project your voice to the back of the room. However, if you are talking to someone that is directly in front of you, you do not want to yell at them. Instead, you will bring your volume down to where only they can hear you, or to a volume that is not overly loud. It is easier to speak in a calm, low voice when we are breathing at a calm and steady rate.

Transparency and Clarity

Transparency and clarity often determine the level to which you are understood and trusted. It is essentially about sending mixed messages. We may mean one thing but imply something different, or we may explain something in such a complicated manner that the point is misunderstood. Are you pretending to be okay when you are actually upset? Are you "beating around the bush?" This leads to mixed messages. This makes it hard to resolve conflicts because no one is focused on the actual issues.

Silence and Pauses

To send the message you want to convey in an appropriate matter, you must combine strong speech and appropriate pauses. If you are constantly speaking, the other party does not have a chance to listen, process the information and then respond. Once you are finished with one idea or sentence, take a quick pause before continuing to your next point. This gives the other person time to think about what you have said. Look at the other person to see if they are about to respond. Give them a chance to speak if they want to.

Difficult Conversations

Most conflicts arise because of, or during difficult conversations. A difficult conversation is a discussion about a topic that is uncomfortable for an individual. Most people do not like to engage in difficult conversations for fear of the consequences and the unpredictability of the outcome. Usually, tough conversations stem from wondering what happened, heightened emotions, differences of opinion about beliefs or behaviors, or personal identity questions. Effective speaking and listening strategies can turn an escalated argument into a learning opportunity. One thing to always keep in mind when you are entering or enduring a tough discussion is that you cannot control anyone but yourself in a heated moment. This ultimately means that if you must take a moment to collect yourself, you should do so. Let's review three difficult situations and how to manage them for the benefit of all parties.

"What Happened?"

Usually, in the "what happened" conflict, one individual thinks they know everything about an event, the motives of the opposing party, and how they felt. A situation may escalate quickly due to a misunderstanding or hastily said words. For example, if you unintentionally said something out of anger to your friend, they might assume that you said it to hurt them, and might conclude that you are a spiteful person. Another "what happened" moment can occur when one person thinks it's all the other person's fault, or they think it's all their own fault. This can result in blame, rejection and upset. The "it's all my/your fault" method of thinking is hurtful because it makes someone feel bad and reinforces the belief that only one person is to blame.

A better way to look at the conflict is to admit that all parties played a part in the events that led to the disagreement. Figure out who is responsible for what stages of the event, without pointing out blame. In the heat of the moment, you may assume that you know all sides of the story. This approach is closed-minded, which gets you nowhere. Instead, you must hear each other out by using your active listening skills and trying to see from the other person's side. More than likely, they have perceived the situation differently than you. One thing to remember when beginning a difficult conversation is that you are entitled to your own feelings and thoughts but you can never predict or assume you know what's going on in someone else's head.

Heightened Emotions

Heightened emotions may include rage, upset, sadness or confusion. When emotions are heightened, it can be challenging to get past them and focus on listening to someone else. Irrational emotions are something that we need to work through before we can go into a complicated discussion. Otherwise, they will blind us from seeing the truth and understanding the other's point of view. The challenge of heightened emotions type conversations is that they are hard to de-escalate and we may ultimately blame the other party for making us feel the way we do. In these moments we are vulnerable and because we believe they are the reason for our problem, we feel as though it's their responsibility to fix it and make us feel better. Our mistake in this way of thinking is that we actually have total control over how we feel at all times. Rather than looking for sympathy or for someone else to calm us down, the power is in our own hands to self-soothe. When intense feelings are causing a difficult conversation to escalate, we may lash out with harsh words or avoid talking calmly with the individual that made us upset. Analyze your own feelings, identify the trigger for the heightened emotion, and discuss what made you upset without judgment or blame. This will help to diffuse the conflict.

Personal Identity

This type of conversation exists within ourselves. It's all about what we say to ourselves and how much we listen to our inner critic. It's about who we are and how we present ourselves to others. Personal identity affects how we view others and ourselves, and how we assume others see us. As a defense to the outside world, we may throw up defensive walls around ourselves or become reclusive, or we may be unpredictable as a way to protect an all-or-nothing self-image. If someone makes us question our identity or second-guess our opinions or actions, it can cause conflict within ourselves and with others. It is important to understand that having a difference of opinion with someone does not mean they are questioning your personal identity. We all want to be heard, seen, and appreciated.

Managing Difficult Conversations

Engaging in difficult conversations feels uncomfortable, and sometimes we avoid these types of discussions so that we don't have to face the consequences. However, the more we avoid things, the more we are going to have conflict in our lives because we don't learn how to solve problems effectively. During a dispute, we tend to say and do things before we have had time to think about it. This causes conflicts to escalate. If we continue to do things this way, we end up with a history of broken friendships, and the loss of partners and jobs. We teach our brains that it's better to defend ourselves so that we don't get hurt rather than train our minds on how to resolve an issue to the benefit of all parties.

The first step to managing a difficult conversation is to prepare yourself mentally. Commit to being calm and non-adversarial. Be willing to look within yourself to see how you contributed to the conflict. Ask yourself why you are having the debate and what you want out of it. Start the discussion at a good time and in an appropriate place. Start by introducing the conversation and stating what your intent is. Make sure you are calm and focused. Observe the other person for clear signs that they are ready for the discussion. Once you are both ready to commit to the conversation and to resolving the problem, you can continue with the tough discussion. Make sure that your thoughts are clear and write them down if necessary. One of the first mistakes people make when starting a difficult conversation is that they describe the conflict only from their perspective. Talking in a third-person point of view helps things run more smoothly because it puts a neutral tone on the conversation. Ask the other person what their perspective is and then pay full attention to the speaker when they respond. In any conflict, the goal is to discuss things in a mature and calm manner and focus on solving the problem. Once all thoughts are shared you can begin to figure out how to resolve the issue. Expect that there may be disagreements and understand that there might still be tension afterward. If no resolution is reached at the end of the discussion, you may want to consider leaving things alone for a while. Some time and distance can give both parties the chance to evaluate their positions.

Here are some positive ways to approach conflict and work through challenging conversations:

Stick to Having a Fact-based Discussion

When you stick to the facts it is easier to focus on the objective of the conversation which is to solve a problem or conflict. During the discussion, your intent should be focused both on listening to the other's point of view and to getting your point across. Each person should get the opportunity to state the facts as they understand them. Decide what you agree on, and agree to find out the true facts about the items that you don't agree on. The conversation should be strictly fact-based until it is resolved. After the problem is solved you can decide whether or not you want to discuss other topics.

Be Assertive Yet Empathetic

Sometimes we need to recognize that what we say may seem offensive or hurtful if it is misunderstood. When it is your turn to speak, and you know something may be interpreted as offensive or upsetting, start by introducing the potential conflict. For example, "What I am about to say might offend or upset you, and I don't mean to, so I apologize in advance. I feel xxx". Always be objective by stating how you feel while avoiding "you" statements which can be interpreted as blaming. The goal is to assert your opinions while also keeping in mind how others feel. Remember that what you say may lead to a greater conflict.

Stay Confident While Being Transparent

We seem more confident when we effectively use our voice at the correct volume and tone. When we are clear about our point of view and have anticipated the point of view of others, it is easier to confidently get our point across. Going into the discussion with openness and transparency is practical because it causes us to get the point and be honest. Offer information freely and ask for the other person's opinion.

Don't Take Anything Personally

When involved in conflict we often take everything that is said to heart, which hurts our feelings and can cause us to respond irrationally. Listen objectively and try not to take what the other person is saying too personally. Try staying focused on the issue, and not on how it makes you feel to be in conflict. When resolving a conflict by having a difficult conversation, be truthful, listen effectively and leave sensitivity at the door. Chances are, if they are willing to talk with you, their intent is not to hurt you further, but to be open and honest with you.

Get Curious and Stay Interested

Cut out all distractions so that you can be fully present with the other individual. Show curiosity and interest, and let the opposing party know that you genuinely want their perspective. This reinforces the idea that you want to solve the problem, not just that you are doing it because of your own selfish needs. Set all expectations aside, throw judgment out the window, and make sure that you're willing to listen to their feelings and opinions.

End With a Solution or Purpose

Once you have engaged in the conversation and listened to each other's perspectives, summarize where the issue currently stands. Summarize the main points of view and any areas of disagreement and common ground. If there has been a resolution to the argument, confirm what it is. If there has not been a resolution, commit to discussing it again when you have had a chance to consider what you talked about.

Chapter Summary

Verbal communication is the foundation for resolving conflict. Verbal communication requires skill and practice. In this chapter, you learned:

- What verbal communication is.
- How dialogue is used.
- What effective speaking is.
- The different skills you need to send the right message.
- What active listening skills are.
- What a difficult conversation is.
- How to manage challenging conversations.

In the next chapter, you will learn about non-verbal communication and why it's vital to successful conflict resolution. You will learn about body language, how to read someone else's body language and how to diffuse situations using non-verbal communication.

CHAPTER FOUR

Conflict Resolution Technique 02 - Mastering the Power of Conversation Through Non-Verbal Communication

Non-verbal communication is a way to express yourself that does not involve words. The truth is that we use non-verbal communication every time we talk, and every time we walk into a room. We use non-verbal communication as a way to communicate with others. There are many components to non-verbal communication. It's the way you move, listen, look, stand, present yourself and react. When you become aware of your body language you can learn how to emphasize the right message. What your body language says can influence the outcome of your conversations and disputes. For example, did you know that the space you put between you and other people is a non-verbal communication tactic? Or that your emotions play a role in the movements you make and the expressions on your face? Did you know that to improve non-verbal communication, you must become very aware of yourself and others?

Conflict can arise when you use negative body language or when verbal and non-verbal cues are sending opposite signals. For example, if your voice is calm and quiet, but your arms are crossed and you don't make eye contact, this can seem condescending or rude. However, when you use open, non-threatening body language and face someone while making eye contact, it shows that you are treating them as an equal and are willing to listen to what is being said. A few examples of non-verbal communication are discussed below.

Facial Expressions

Most of us are familiar with the use of facial expressions to express ourselves. A wink is a sign of flirtation or a shared secret, a smile is a sign of friendliness or approval, a raised eyebrow is a sign of sarcasm or lack of understanding, a scrunched forehead represents a person deep in thought or concerned about something, etc. You can generally tell how a person feels or what their mood is simply by looking at their faces. Did you know that facial expressions are a universal language? When you are sad, tears may form, or a frown may be present. A smile is a facial expression that represents happiness. Anger is displayed with furrowed brows, intense stares, clenched teeth, and pursed lips. These facial expressions are the same in every country across the planet.

Movement and Posture

Mirroring someone's posture or gestures is usually a sign that there is a connection forming. It is a way to make the other person more comfortable with you. What our movements and posture say about our moods and the way we carry ourselves says a lot. For example, if you're walking with a straight posture and your head and eyes are looking straight ahead, it implies that you are a confident person on a mission. If you were walking with a slouch, eyes to the ground and your pace is slow, you may not seem confident or you may seem upset. That being said, everyone has their own style of movement, so it's unfair to say that body language is always consistent with a certain mood. Some people move around a lot, which can be a sign of anxiety for you. However, just because these ways of acting may indicate anxiety or low confidence to you, it doesn't necessarily mean that that individual lacks self-esteem or is anxious.

Gestures

Facial expressions are universal, but gestures, such as hand signals are not. What thumbs up means in one part of the world may not mean the same thing somewhere else in the world. Gestures include waving, pointing, shaking your fists, talking with your hands (waving them in the air, or using your fingers as a form of sign language to get your verbal point across). People from similar cultural backgrounds or regions usually share common gestures and are able to communicate partially using them.

Eye Contact

Looking directly into the eyes of someone else is a prominent characteristic of friendly communication. You will make eye contact with your boss if you are having a serious discussion. You would look at your friend in the eyes if you are trying to resolve a dispute or debate. There are different ways to look at people that can make you seem friendly, serious, angry, or sad. The way you look at someone can send different types of messages. For example, you wouldn't look at your boss the same way you would look at your husband or wife. Eye contact can represent interest, hostility or affection depending on how it is used.

Touch

A light touch on the cheek represents interest or affection. A nudge after a joke suggests a shared experience and closer bonds. A firm grip on the arm, leg, or other parts of the body suggest hostility, control or fear. As you can see, communication through touch can send many messages. How would you interpret a weak or overly strong handshake? How does a close and tight hug make you feel? Touch isn't just about the physical contact you get from someone; it is also about the emotion it creates for you. For example, if you receive a hug from a family member, you are going to feel happy and warm, whereas if you received a hug from someone you are in conflict with, you might not be comfortable.

Personal Space

Personal space, otherwise known as proximity, is the distance between individuals or groups. The space between people can influence our sense of comfort or safety. For example, if you are standing in line at a grocery store and you can feel the person behind you literally breathing down your neck, what would you do? How would you feel, and why? In a similar scenario, would it be okay if the person standing that close to you was a spouse or a best friend?

The spaces between people create the boundary of our comfort zone. For example, if you are the type of person that likes your own space around you, then you will have a limit on how close even your friends can be to you. You may not like hugging people to say hello. If you are more of a physical, touchy person, then less space is no concern to you. You may hug or shake hands with everyone. People feel different about the proximity they have to other people. Misunderstanding how much space people need between them can lead to conflict or make conflict resolution more difficult.

Non-verbal communication can go wrong very quickly. The way you carry yourself, the way others see you, your sense of presence, your actions, and your expressions all speak to others without using words. If you are good at poker, you would be good at hiding your body language. If you are poor at non-verbal communication skills or are unable to control them, someone playing poker with you might be able to call your bluff quickly, resulting in a loss for you. When non-verbal communication goes wrong, it's often because there are mixed signals. The individual is unaware of the messages they are sending, which makes the opposing party's attempt to interpret body language unsuccessful. Here's an example: Person A and person B just met a week ago and they are on a coffee date. Person A has a nervous twitch and finds it difficult to keep eye contact. Person B sits up straight and holds a confident pose which they expect person A to have as well. During the whole date, person A isn't nervous, and the conversation flows nicely, but their body language is not attentive. Person B interprets this non-verbal communication as disrespectful and points it out to person A. This results in a dispute over the fact that person B doesn't feel like person A was interested or listening. Person A tries to apologize but is still unaware of their body language and doesn't look at person B while apologizing so person B doesn't feel the apology was genuine and becomes offended. The coffee date ends in a disagreement.

The problem here was that person A was unaware of how their behavior was perceived, and person B interpreted the body language of person A incorrectly. Person A has always behaved that way so they felt no wrongdoing on their part. However, because person B doesn't know person A very well, they received mixed signals which upset them. Non-verbal communication can go very wrong so it is important we understand it, and how it can contribute to conflict. Learn appropriate and effective ways of communicating non-verbally. This will help to send the message you want to convey.

Signs That Conflict is on the Rise

Conflict can happen in any situation and it can happen when you are least expecting it. The goal is to figure out ways to resolve it or diffuse it before it begins. Most people are unaware of the signs that dispute is about to happen. You must know what to look for. Read your own body language and that of others. Most of the time you can read the signs of negative feelings just by watching for specific non-verbal cues. Some symptoms include finger or foot tapping, squeezing the temples, rubbing the forehead or back of the neck, furrowed brows, or tense postures. If you catch yourself feeling heated or recognize that your patience is thinning, it might be time to take a personal break to collect yourself before an argument happens. Some people might not even know that you are bothered so this a good time to calm down. If you notice the person you are with is using those non-verbal cues, you can use that knowledge to diffuse the situation.

Be sure to interpret non-verbal cues correctly. For example, tapping of the foot or fingers is often a sign of anxiety, not just irritation. The same goes for irregular breathing. Often, we find ourselves puffing out a hot breath when we become heated or frustrated, so it may seem like someone is angry if they are doing the same. Really, it could just be that they are short of breath or anxious. Look at various expressions of their body language and derive a conclusion. If brows are furrowed, the forehead is wrinkled, and their facial expression resembles disgust or disappointment, it is a sign that an argument may be about to break out. Along with anxiety or other emotional signals, you can tell if a person is angry by their sudden movements. If someone is pacing, they might be deep in thought, or they might be mad. So, if there are many signals communicated with body language, and they may not all have the same meanings to different people, how do you tell if someone is angry or not? If you aren't sure, ask them.

Imagine you are watching your neighbors argue in their front yard. In this example, we will use the woman as the one who is angry with the man. You cannot hear what's going on, but you see her arms flail up in the air, her head is shaking from side to side, her face is flushed, and she keeps moving her feet as if ants are biting at them. The man is standing very still and then tries to leave by turning his back on her. This is when you notice her grab his arm firmly and appear to shout something. You clearly see that her eyes are like daggers, and her teeth are firmly clenched. The man then turns to face her and tries to give her a hug, but she turns away by whipping her whole body around and marching to the front door of their house. The man leaves. In this example, you recognize the body language used by the woman as frustration and anger, but why? How did you know they were having a fight? Throughout the entire episode, her facial expressions and body movements were angry and agitated. She was scowling, her arms flailed, she was yelling, she would not accept his hug. These are all clear signs of anger or frustration.

In this specific example, the couple is unable to resolve the conflict at that time. Both parties walk away, which is a very clear body language. Before a conflict escalates to that point, minimize negative body language to keep a conversation on track. Some things that can cause conflict to happen or escalate are as follows:

- **Being distracted:** During the conversation, distractions can turn another person off and will send the message that you don't care to hear what they need to say.
- **Not making eye contact:** Lack of eye-contact shows that you are not focused on the speaker. If eye-contact is a problem for you, state this, and use other forms of communicating to show that you are there to listen.
- **Playing on your phone or digital device:** Even if you think you are listening with your full attention, you are not. When you use devices and phones during a conversation you are only partially listening to the speaker since your eyes are looking at your phone. You can't fully understand how the person is feeling or what their message conveys if you aren't listening fully and observing their body language.
- **Seeming off in space or not responding:** This body language shows a lack of respect and the individual will feel there is no point in having a conversation since you don't seem to be really listening. Responding to the other person shows you are listening and thinking about what they have said.
- **Talking too fast or too quiet:** Whether we realize it or not, talking too fast or too quiet can upset people because they have to try too hard to understand, and it can be a sign of being untrustworthy. It can be hard to follow and lead to misunderstandings or frustration.

- **Invading personal space:** Personal space defines our level of comfort around others. It may be in place due to our morals, boundaries and values or because of our personal experiences. Once our space has been invaded, it feels as though the opposing party isn't respecting us, and we may feel cornered or attacked. We may be so distracted by the lack of personal space that we can't concentrate on the dialogue. We may act defensively, guard ourselves or act impulsively.
- **Closed body language:** In times of conflict, you may use closed-body language posture if you are defending yourself because there is a safety issue. However, when you are just conversing, a closed way of presenting yourself implies that you are unapproachable, grumpy or disinterested.

Displaying positive body language shows that you care and are paying attention. Next time you are talking with someone, think about your body language and then try to picture them using the same body language. How would you feel? What would you think? Use body language to help convey your message, to understand the signals you put out when you act in certain ways, and to evaluate the moods of others. If you want to send the message that you are angry and frustrated, then use the body language that sends that message. If you want to portray that you are happy, then you must use open, positive non-verbal tools that communicate that message.

Conflict Diffusion Techniques

Effective conflict resolution using non-verbal communication involves seeing others, being seen, and/or interacting face-to-face with others. Using non-verbal skills can stop conflict from escalating further. Most conflicts happen in the workplace or the home. This can impact our most important professional or intimate relationships. For the examples in this section, let's consider work-related and relationship scenarios. Here are ways to use non-verbal tools to diffuse conflict before it escalates:

- Take a personal moment.
    - Count to ten, twenty, thirty, etc. until you have calmed down.
    - Inhale deeply through your nose and exhale through your mouth letting all the air escape your lungs.
    - Clear your head, then return to the conversation or point of conflict.
- Be aware. Observe and notice everything.
    - What are you feeling?
    - What kind of body language are you using?
    - How is the other person acting?
    - What is the speaker expressing with their body language?
    - How much space is between you and them?

- Keep a calm composure.
    - Maintain eye-contact but try not to glare at the other person.
    - Breathe at a steady, easy pace.
    - Keep your facial expressions open, welcoming, or expressionless.
    - Appear willing to listen and stay empathetic.
    - Stand or sit straight.
    - Try not to fidget or become distracted by your surroundings.
- Listen.
    - Listen attentively.
    - Lean forward a little so they know you are paying attention.
    - Nod your head periodically to show that you heard and understand.
    - If you are unsure, use a questioning look to convey your confusion.

Most of the time, when we keep a calm composure and listen effectively, we can diffuse a conflict before it begins. In doing this, you must be completely aware of your own emotions, thoughts, and behaviors so that you can display positive responses. Show empathy throughout the conversation and make sure that you also feel safe. Remain calm and open even when the opposing party seems frustrated or hostile. Your positive non-verbal communication will have a calming, reassuring effect on others. If their body language continues to escalate in a negative direction, sometimes it is best to end the conversation and walk away. This is especially true if you are unsure about your safety.

Learning the POP Method

POP is an acronym for Person, Object and Place. This method is used mainly in the workplace or when a conflict has the potential for violence. Sometimes, resolving conflict is not an option, so that is why we must learn about POP to protect ourselves from danger. Have you ever felt heightened nervousness or anxiety? You may shake, can't think or feel like running. You may have difficulty breathing or feel nauseous. It's almost as if you forget everything, and all you know is the desire to survive. In a state of anxiousness or overwhelming emotions, your body may have a fight-or-flight response.

Person relates to the party you are in conflict with. The first part of the POP model requires you to take into account the details about who you are in conflict with. Notice their height, weight, ethnicity, age, gender, body type, etc. Observe the facts objectively without judgment. Just because someone may look intense, intimidating, and dangerous, doesn't mean that they will act threatening. Similarly, someone who is small or diminutive may be more dangerous than they look. Try to take note of the deeper aspects of their personality and behavior. What is their temperament, characteristics, mental or emotional state, etc.? Are they displaying aggressive tendencies? How vulnerable are they?

Object refers to what items are in the room and accessible to you and the person you are in conflict with. Are there weapons present? Are there pointy or heavy objects close to you or the individual that can be used as a weapon or in defense? If you are unsure and there are no visible signs of a weapon present, do not assume that there isn't one. For your safety, it's best to believe the person is equipped to harm you if the conflict escalates physically. Keep in mind that anything can be used as a weapon, including a phone book, a bottle, a fork, etc.

Place is where you are located. What environment are you in? This includes places like bars, outside, in your own home, at a friend's house, in the workplace, etc. Observing your environment plays a significant role in guessing what could happen in the heat of the moment. For example, if you are at work, it's less likely someone will make a scene, whereas if you are alone with them things could turn heated or violent. Are you somewhere you are familiar with? Do you know all the exit routes? Notice whether it's night or day, rain, or shine, cold or warm because this might impact why the person is in a moody or angry state.

When in doubt, trust your gut feeling. If someone is using body language that you find threatening find a way to get out quickly. The most important rule in being safe is always to be aware of yourself, the other person, and what is around you.

Learning the SAFER Method

The acronym for **SAFER** means - Step back, assess threat, Find help, Evaluate options, Respond. This method can be used anywhere, including the workplace, at home or in public places. When someone's body language is threatening to you, these tools can help you respond to danger.

Step back: This means to stop, look, listen, and remain calm. Acting impulsively may escalate the danger and prevent us from observing crucial facts. When we act irrationally, we don't think clearly and cannot make wise decisions based on the facts of the situation.

Assess threat: From your lesson about POP, you know how to assess the situation for danger. Look at the person, read their body language, assume there are weapons present, and evaluate your environment for weapons or defensive tools.

Find help: Look for an escape route or means of rescue. It may be a door or window, a means of transportation or communication, or another person. Know who is around you and how far. If you are at home, is your neighbor home? How far away is your phone? If you are at work, where is the next available person located? If it seems that there is no help, remain calm and keep thinking and observing.

Evaluate options: After you have gone through the options available for finding help, decide which is your best route to safety. Is conversation an option for settling the angry party, or do you need to enlist the help of someone else? Do you need to find a way out?

Respond: After you have considered all your options, the final step is to follow through with what you have decided. Be prepared for things to change and make sure that you have a plan B and even a plan C if necessary.

Chapter Summary

It may take time, patience, and practice to fully understand how non-verbal communication can help us diffuse conflict. Mastering non-verbal communication will make it easier for you to read people's behaviors before, during, and after conflict. It will also help you to manage your own body language to ensure you portray the right message and do not contribute to misunderstandings.

In this chapter, you learned:

- What non-verbal communication is and why it's important.
- How to recognize signs of conflict before it happens.
- How to diffuse a situation before it escalates.
- The POP safety measure.
- The SAFER safety measures.

In the next chapter, you will learn about emotions, how they contribute to conflict, and how to manage yours during a conflict situation.

CHAPTER FIVE

Conflict Resolution Technique 03 - Managing Emotions

When it comes to emotions and conflict, the fact is that we become so engaged in conversation that we may become unaware of how we are feeling in the moment. This happens because when we are in a friendly and approachable environment, we don't need to be in tune with our emotions as much. We get so comfortable that we may not notice a conflict arising. Perhaps a trigger word might have been said, a disruptive statement might have been made, or a certain vibe or body language might suddenly catch you or the other person off guard. As conflict starts to build, the heart rate quickens, breathing becomes short, thoughts go a mile a minute, etc. All of this heightened emotion increases, and before you know it, you say things you don't mean, you do things out of emotional impulse, and you become angry, depressed, anxious, etc.

So, how do you stop your emotions from spiraling out of control? How do you begin to notice the signs that you or those around you are becoming emotional? You have to be aware of your emotional state before and during the conflict. You must commit to observing the behaviors of yourself and others. You must learn self-awareness strategies and be mindful in almost every moment so that you can manage your emotions.

Developing Self-Awareness

Self-awareness is the ability to recognize and notice your own thoughts, feelings, character, motives, and desires as they happen. A person who has the keen ability to be self-aware means that they notice when their heart quickens or when their body language or tone changes. The self-aware take the time to evaluate themselves in every situation. Self-awareness requires you to be in tune with yourself and your personality and to understand your typical behaviors. You must know your strengths, weaknesses, beliefs and what makes you who you are. Self-awareness isn't just about yourself, though. It's also about seeing and understanding how others perceive you and how to tell when you have done something to upset someone else. It's about knowing what triggers you and being aware enough to understand other people and how they are feeling. It may be you or the environment, or they might be triggering themselves. Developing self-awareness is crucial to understanding and noticing things before they happen. This plays a significant role in resolving or diffusing conflict. Here are things you can do to start working on your self-awareness right now:

Take a Step Back and Observe Yourself

Sometimes we get so caught up in our own lives that we forget to take a step back to re-evaluate ourselves periodically. If you take the time to look at yourself objectively, you can define which aspects of yourself you don't like and work on changing them. Getting to know yourself in this way is incredibly rewarding. It might include the following actions:

- Think of things you are proud of yourself for.
- Identify your strengths and weaknesses.
- Capitalize on your strengths.
- Work on your weaknesses.
- Reward yourself often.
- Practice self-discipline often.
- Think about what makes you truly happy.
- Be honest with yourself.

Keeping a Journal

Journaling is proven to benefit our lives in many ways. You can write about anything in your journal. A few examples are:

- Your life.
- Your fears and concerns.
- Your goals and aspirations.
- Your strengths and weaknesses.

- Your thoughts.
- Your dreams.
- Notes about other people.
- Your meditation techniques (what works, what doesn't).
- Your fitness goals and accomplishments.
- A dietary record.

The possibilities are endless. Journaling is about writing what's on your mind so that you can vent, look at it from a different perspective, and gain insight into yourself. Sometimes it's used as a way to let go of thoughts by writing them down so that you can move on to other thoughts. It's a self-reflection technique and it has been proven to boost moods and motivate you to figure out what you want in your life.

Practice Self-Reflection

At the start of every day, wake up and ask yourself what you want from the day. What do you want to accomplish? How do you want to live today? At the end of every day, ask yourself if you accomplished what you set out to do today. Ask yourself if there is anything you would do differently. Reflect on the highs and lows of the day and define how you can do better tomorrow. These questions are not about self-judgment but about opening your mind to notice and understand your thoughts and behaviors. Self-awareness and self-reflection help you know yourself which leads to knowing where you want to go in life, and makes it more likely for you to get there.

Practice Mindfulness

Mindfulness is the practice of being one with yourself in this present moment. Put aside your thoughts, feelings, beliefs, and just be here with yourself. For example, when you are drinking a nice warm cup of tea, look at it as if you have never seen it before. You are tasting the tea for the first time. You are holding a hot cup for the first time. You are noticing the different colors on your mug for the first time. Mindfulness is practicing feeling and experiencing the moment you are in right now to its fullest. Right now, you are reading a section on self-awareness because you want to learn how to resolve conflict quickly and efficiently. So, at this very moment, nothing else matters. Don't think about what's happening outside or what someone else is doing. All that matters is right now, and the rest of the world can wait. Tada! You just completed a short moment of being completely mindful. Being mindful is not:

- Judging yourself.
- Questioning yourself or anything around you.
- Thinking about one thing then letting your mind drift to another thing.

Your first few times at practicing mindfulness might be challenging, and you will get distracted. When that happens, bring yourself back to the moment and focus again on what you are experiencing at that time.

Ask for Feedback

Knowing what others think of you but not taking it personally can help you identify what you need to work on. You can ask your most trusted friend about how you really are or how you appear to others, and if you don't like the answer you can work on changing it. If you do like the answer, then congratulate yourself for being perceived exactly how you want to be. Use self-awareness when you want to fix a behavior and you are trying to figure out when that side of you comes out. Learning to identify a trigger, emotion or setback in the moment it happens can sometimes only be achieved by getting feedback from others you trust.

Self-awareness happens when we are open to constructive criticism but do not judge ourselves and others. It is okay if you lack confidence or if you question yourself daily. Using strategies for learning self-awareness can also help to develop self-esteem.

Dealing With Anger During Conflict

A situation often results in conflict when someone feels that something is unfair and they get angry. We all have different personalities, different beliefs, and different ways of doing things. No two people are the same and though you can never be sure how someone will react, anger is a common emotion that people express during conflict. Many relationships end because individuals cannot manage anger during conflict. In extreme cases, this can lead to aggression and violence.

Some people have an angrier temperament than others or are more prone to angry outbursts or reactions. This temperament may be due to past experiences, learned behavior or inner conflict. Overcoming anger requires acceptance that there is a problem. Do you become heated out of nowhere? Does one person make you angrier than anyone else? Do certain situations regularly trigger intense emotion? Find out what your triggers are and then work at managing your anger before it contributes to conflict.

Here are a few ways you can manage anger or other intense emotions when you are in a conflict situation.

Patience

Managing anger and other emotions takes patience not just with another person, but also with yourself. Using patience as a self-awareness tool requires you to pause when you feel an intense emotion and suppress it before it contributes to a conflict. Patience is all about time; time to consider perspectives, time to allow your anger to calm down, time to stop crying, time to breathe, time to listen. Patience works with others as well. When you take the time to calmly approach a situation in an unhurried manner, others are less likely to escalate the situation, as our patient behavior has a calming effect on those around us.

Breathing

Using breathing techniques to manage intense emotions during a conflict requires that you work on staying mindful of your body. Breathe slowly and deeply and focus on the moment. The breathing strategy works to soothe almost all intense emotions. When you become irate, hysterical, or have a panic attack, you will notice your breath shortens, or you may hyperventilate or hold your breath. This is the time to take a moment to yourself to just breathe. The best way to breathe out your frustration is by deep breathing. There are a few ways to do deep breathing. Here is one method of deep breathing:

1. If you are able to, go somewhere quiet where you can be alone.
2. You can do this exercise sitting, standing, or lying down.
3. Some people find it helpful to put one hand on the stomach and one hand on the chest to help you focus.
4. This exercise is most commonly done with the eyes closed, but it can also be done with the eyes focused on something calming or pretty.
5. Breathe in through your nose for a count of 3-5 seconds, allowing your belly to rise, then your chest to rise.
6. Hold your breath for 3 seconds.
7. Release your breath slowly through your mouth for a count of 3-5 seconds.
8. Repeat the breathing pattern, concentrating on filling your belly, then your chest, then exhaling fully but slowly.

9. Repeat the breathing exercise until you feel your body and mind settle and calm. Some people do up to 10 repetitions several times a day as part of their regular health routine!

10. End your breathing session by opening your eyes and slowly returning your breath back to normal.

11. Get up carefully and slowly.

Some people also do a variation where they only allow their bellies to rise and fall or just their chest. Try all of them, and find out what works best for you.

If you are trying to breathe discreetly during a conflict, simply put your hands in a comfortable position and breathe deeply, quietly, and slowly. Even doing it once or twice can be enough to have a calming effect.

Walk Away

Sometimes, a dispute can get out of hand, and that's when hurtful words and actions can occur. Before this happens, walk away from whatever is upsetting or angering you. If it's a person, let them know you cannot engage any further and that you need a break. Tell them that you are walking away to clear your head, not because you are unwilling to resolve the conflict. Sometimes, they might call after you as you walk away, but in some situations, this is your only option. Upon walking away, distract your mind from what is bothering you. Some things you can do are:

- Go for a light jog.

- Take a walk in the park or around the block.
- Work on a project you have in progress.
- Pick up a hobby.
- Watch a show, listen to music or an audiobook.
- Read a book, eBook, magazine or blog.
- Call a friend or family member to see how they are.
- Deep breathing.

This might seem like an obvious technique, or you might think that it isn't really a technique at all. When our emotions are heightened, we often don't think before we act or we say things to escalate the conflict further. Have you ever been in a disagreement where you get interrupted, or nothing you say seems to be working? Now voices are raised, body language is negative, facial expressions are hostile or sad, and whatever pops into your head flies out of your mouth before you can take it back. Patience and breathing should be used before a dispute escalates, but if you need to, let the opposing party know that you need to walk away and take some time to think before responding so that you don't say the wrong thing.

Laugh a Little

Okay, so you are probably wondering if humor should be used but you are concerned about using it at the right time and place, right? Sometimes conflicts escalate because we are taking things too seriously, or don't take the time to laugh at ourselves and try to make light of a situation. Humor can be effective to redirect anger and move toward resolution. Make sure the humor is not an insult to either party. For example, if you and your partner are in the middle of a huge argument, instead of having things escalate even further, you could make a humorous statement such as, "geez, if this gets any more heated, we might just have to get someone to hose us down." This should result in both of you laughing with each other. Make sure you are laughing *with* one another, not *at* one another. Hopefully, it will lighten the situation. As long as you are genuine, and make sure there is no sarcasm or condescending attitude, humor may get you to a more positive place.

Positive Self-Talk

Often we listen too much to our inner critic or the opinions of others, and this makes us question our identity or point of view. When in a difficult conversation, if someone has insulted you or insists you are wrong, instead of reacting negatively and escalating the conflict, use positive self-talk to manage your emotions. You can say to yourself:

- I believe in myself.
- Breathe (your name) it's okay, this isn't going to last forever.
- I am okay, I am fully capable of handling myself appropriately.
- They are mad, and they don't mean what they are saying.

- I am confident about my point of view.
- I will not let their words hurt me or impact my self-esteem.
- I am not going to react in anger.

Positive self-talk is about calming yourself down, supporting yourself and believing in your position. Do not accept the negativity directed at you.

Forgiveness

Forgiveness can be hard. It requires you to let go of your anger and no longer harbor resentment. You may be upset with another person, or even with yourself. It could be because someone did something bad to you or someone you love. It could be because you disagree about something that was done without asking your permission or opinion. Some things are easier to forgive than others. Forgiveness isn't always about forgiving another person, but about forgiving yourself for contributing to the conflicts in your life, or for something bad that you did. Holding onto anger, frustration or hatred means that you have less space in your mind and heart for the happy and positive things in life.

Be More Accommodating and Less Prideful

Often, pride clouds our vision. We feel superior, or we compete to win an argument because it's in our nature. If your pride doesn't allow you to back down and accommodate the needs of others, then you will likely have a lot of conflict in your life. You may have been taught to do unto others as they have done to you. But why must you conform to these beliefs and aim to hurt someone else? Just because someone insults you or disagrees with you doesn't mean you have to be angry or retaliate. When you have been in a heated disagreement, have you walked away regretting something that you said or did? If you answered yes, it's because pride has gotten in the way. Let go of your inflated ego, and stay accommodating while practicing assertiveness and boundary control.

These techniques are presented to give you options when you are in a conflict situation. No one strategy or method works for every person. You can try different tactics, examine the outcomes, and decide which tools work best for you in various situations. Only you know what works best for you, so try something for a little while, and if it doesn't work, try something else. You may have to use a combination of strategies to manage your own heightened emotions when in a conflict.

Chapter Summary

Perhaps the most important lesson that you have learned during this chapter is that by managing our emotions we have a better chance of resolving conflict. Managing our emotions by developing self-awareness and dealing with emotions such as anger can help us diffuse a conflict before it escalates.

In this chapter, you learned:

- How to build self-awareness.

- Techniques to manage heightened emotions before they escalate.
- How to let go of anger during conflict.
- In the next chapter, you will learn about how to use persuasion and negotiation to change the minds of those around you.

CHAPTER SIX

Conflict Resolution Technique 04 - Changing Minds through Persuasion and Negotiation

Technique number four in conflict resolution is about how to change people's minds, including your own, through perspective, persuasion, and negotiation. We often try to solve a dispute the same way we settled our previous conflict, yet the current situation may be different from the previous experience. What most people don't realize is that there is no "one size fits all" solution to resolving conflict.

The reason it is important to understand the perspective of yourself and others is so you can empathize with how a conflict appears to someone besides you. Once you understand what is happening, you can become better at persuading others to see your side of things. As you have learned in the previous chapters, reacting emotionally or being verbally and non-verbally aggressive limits the options for resolving conflict. Understanding someone else's perspective tells you how the person thinks and why they respond the way they do. During a conflict, some people don't consider another's perspectives because they are prideful or want to win an argument rather than resolving the conflict to the mutual benefit of both parties. If the goal is to come to an agreement or compromise, then sacrifices can be made to find middle ground and resolution. If you respond to a conflict in a competitive or prideful way because you want to "win" the argument, the outcome may be that you lose your job, your friend, or your spouse as a result.

Adopting the perspective of someone else for the purpose of understanding their position can increase our chance to persuade others and negotiate a resolution. The benefits of understanding and adopting the perspectives of others are:

- Gaining more information about the situation.
- Learning more about yourself and another individual.
- Enabling you to choose effective verbal and non-verbal strategies.
- Promoting listening skills.
- Increasing the chances for healthy relationships.
- Helping us define who we are.
- Creating empathy.

According to Michael Carroll, an expert in neuro-linguistic programming (NLP), using what's called the triple position means that you use a combination of three different ways of looking at things in order to fully engage and understand the perspectives of a situation. The first position is to look at yourself, which you also learned about in the previous chapter about self-awareness. The second position is viewing things from the other side and using empathy and emotional intelligence to increase the chances for resolution. The third position is to look at the situation from the neutral overview perspective. Lastly, when you achieve the triple position, you are able to look at each party's perspective, as well as the whole picture to create a greater understanding of the overall situation.

First Position: Self

Think of the first position in the same way that you would think of the first-person point of view in writing. It's your perspective and personal opinion on what's happening in any type of event or situation. First position means that you are only looking at things from your own point of view and no one else's. First person perspective can be both negative and/or positive. Often, the first position is adopted by the people who are competitive, narrow-minded, and self-absorbed. You can use the first position to be in tune with yourself completely, or you can consider your own perspective while being selfishly obsessed. It can be positive when you feel your own emotions fully and can go after what you want with a clear picture of the goal in mind.

Second Position: Others

An example of someone who uses the second position is a therapist, sales associate, mediator, or judge. These people must clearly understand the perspective of others in order to do their job. These types of people have significant negotiation skills and can understand another person's way of thinking. Second position is much like explaining or viewing something from the second-person point of view in a story. For example, in storytelling, the writer is using "you/he/she/they/them" statements and telling the story in a way that speaks directly to the audience. Second person point of view is a general way of speaking rather than being about an individual's personal perspective of their experience. Adopting the second position in conflict resolution requires you to be empathetic and understanding when it comes to another's thoughts and feelings.

Third Position: Observer

Telling a story from the third person point of view explains every aspect of the story. This is also called narrative style. You aren't writing from the perspective of one of the characters. Instead, you are describing the whole picture, such as he felt XXX, she said XXX. It's the explanation of what's happening to every character in a story. Third position is the last position in the triple perception experience where you, as an individual, can take a step back and view the scene as a whole. Think of it as if you have taken a step outside of yourself. You are no longer looking at your own emotions or feeling empathy for someone else's perspective or thoughts. Instead, you have taken a complete step out of the situation and are now looking at it as an outsider - the third person. This position is helpful when you want to reflect on everyone's behavior or when you want to evaluate a situation objectively, non-judgmentally and non-emotionally.

The Combination: Triple Position

In a triple position perspective, you successfully combine all these positions and use them to deal with conflict effectively. Typically, a dispute will arise if each party in the conflict is stuck in first position. Ultimately it is not our fault if we view things from the first position because we are all unique and individualistic and often focused on our own needs, so it only makes sense that we view things from the first position. When you actively build upon your empathy skills, you are practicing the second position. As you practice observation of the overall situation, you are mastering the third position. Now you can move into the triple position by using the positions at the same time, which is ultimately the most helpful in resolving conflicts. These skills can be used before, during, and after a dispute has taken place.

Perspective is about using your self-awareness, social skills, leadership abilities, and observation abilities to fully understand a situation and redefine it altogether. Using the triple position tool promotes success in resolving conflict. When reading the rest of this chapter, keep in mind the power of perspective using the triple position method.

What is Persuasion? What is Negotiation?

Conflict resolution requires that we learn how to change the minds of others through persuasion and negotiation. As much as persuasion and negotiation may seem alike, they have very distinct differences. Basically, the fundamental difference between persuasion and negotiation is that persuasion is the art of informing someone such that they change their mind and take your side, and negotiation is more like bargaining or trading concessions until both people agree on what will be the final agreed position. Fundamental to both persuasion and negotiation is understanding what is the primary interest of all parties involved.

Persuasion

Persuasion is the ability to get someone to do something by asking, proving your point, or conversing with the intent that they adopt a different way of thinking. Persuasion is a form of communication which may include informing, convincing, entertaining, and narrating. It is well known that persuasion can be a manipulative tactic, but if used correctly with the right motive, persuasive techniques don't have to have devious intent. To be persuasive, you must first explain your situation or reasoning, then explain all the benefits of your position. Persuasive tactics include:

- Debating.
- Informing.
- Convincing.
- Influencing.
- Finding commonality.

Negotiation

Negotiation means to reach an agreement among all parties, and it is well known as a conflict resolution strategy. The outcome of a negotiation is usually that neither party gets exactly what they asked for, but both will get aspects of what they want. This is done by mutually agreeing about what concessions are possible for either side. During a negotiation, fairness, mutual understanding, and benefit, and maintaining trust and closeness are essential factors to consider. Negotiation uses tools such as:

- **Questioning:** Ask the other party questions to obtain an understanding of the facts or the perspective and needs of others.
- **Exploring:** Find out the needs of all parties and explain them to each other. Use the answers to the questions to inspire conversation.
- **Motivation:** Understand what motivates the parties to argue or insist on their position. Are they driven by morality, finances, or other specific issues?
- **Priorities:** What are the things that each party wants the most, and what will each party give up to resolve the conflict?

How Do You Choose?

In deciding which tactic or technique to use when trying to change someone's mind or perspective, you must decide if the primary goal is an outcome that will benefit all parties in the conflict. Most people will choose persuasion over negotiation because their primary purpose is to convince someone to take on their point of view. They may not really understand or even care about the needs of the other person. Other people will choose negotiation when their goal is to find common ground. Most people resort to persuasion tactics because we primarily take the first position perspective, and it is hard to negotiate with someone if we only consider our own needs. Negotiation can only become possible when we use the second position. However, it is not a rule that you only use one or the other. When persuasion is combined with negotiation, you may find that the end result is a better outcome than if you were to choose just one approach to changing someone's mind.

How to Resolve Conflict Through Persuasion and Negotiation

This section of the chapter will help you identify persuasion strategies and negotiation strategies so that you can use both of them to resolve conflict. When you are focusing on being persuasive, you must take emotions into consideration and adopt emotional intelligence to gain insight on how to influence your audience. When you focus on negotiation, you must take empathy and reading someone's body language into account before proposing your compromise.

Using Positive Persuasion Techniques to Resolve Conflict

Approaching conflict with a positive attitude increases the chance of an amicable resolution. There are many positive persuasion techniques you can use. We will discuss five of them below: positive reinforcement, respect, opportunism, acknowledgment, and success.

1. Positive reinforcement

Positive reinforcement strategy is used in child development. It's where you ignore bad or challenging behaviors and enforce positive behaviors. Rather than paying attention to temper tantrums and aggressiveness, you would instead make every good thing a child does a big deal. For example, if a child paints a pretty picture or counts to ten on their own, you would clap and say, "Wow, good job." If they have an angry outburst, you might ignore them instead of yelling.

Positive reinforcement as a persuasive tactic requires you to praise the actions of the other person in order to encourage them to act in a manner that is favorable to you. If you foresee a potential conflict, you might thank them for previous consideration they have given you. For example, if you are trying to persuade a friend to help you with your truck, you might start by thanking them again for the last time they helped you.

2. Respect

This strategy involves showing genuine consideration of the assets or accomplishments of the other person. You can remind them of their best qualities in order to help them imagine themselves again doing something generous or helpful. When you want to show that you respect and believe in someone, provide proof by explaining why. Then paint a picture about how they are the only ones who can truly help you. This will encourage them to consider doing it.

3. Opportunism

Seek opportunities to get what you need or want by understanding the habits and preferences of the other person. For example, if you need to borrow money and know that a generous colleague likes to go for coffee, you would arrange to run into them at their preferred coffee shop, have coffee with them, and then persuade them to lend you money.

4. Acknowledgment

Much like the two previous strategies, using acknowledgment in persuasion means to use someone's accomplishments to help you get what want. In a conflict scenario such as a dispute with a coworker who involves themselves in your personal business too much, you may need to create a positive situation before you are comfortable talking to them about the issue. You might tell them how much their skills contributed to the success of a recent project. Then you might tell them you really enjoyed working with them but that you're very private about your personal life, so you would rather just talk about work.

5. Success

If you come across someone who has a competitive nature, then you can use this in a positive way to resolve conflict with them. For most competitive people, success is their main goal in life. You can explain ways in which you are successful, and how aligning with you would be a benefit to them. This will help to persuade this individual that it would be better to stay friends with you than to stay in a dispute with you.

These strategies might seem manipulative, but consider your intentions behind the persuasion. If your motive is to get the help that benefits you both, this will lead to a positive outcome. On the other hand, if your intentions are selfish, you will seem ingenuine and likely have little success resolving the conflict. Always think of the other person's needs before you start using persuasion and negotiation tactics.

Using Negotiation Techniques to Resolve Conflict

Negotiation techniques are easier than persuasion techniques because it's easier to compromise than to sway someone completely to your side. The art of finding a middle ground, compromise and gaining mutual benefit is at the heart of negotiation. Persuasion can be used in conversation before resorting to negotiation, or you can dive straight into negotiating. If you dive right in, it might seem as if you are being aggressive and only bringing up the conversation to get something out of it. On the other hand, when you explain what you see as the conflict and ask if you can discuss a resolution in the form of compromise, you are more likely to succeed in your negotiation. Three effective negotiation tactics are:

1. **Take the interests and values of each party into account.**

When resolving conflict using this tactic, make sure that you are separating your own beliefs from those of the other party. Identify what their values are so that you can problem-solve around them. The opposing party will trust you more if you first let them know you were listening to their point of view and taking their values into account. Make it clear that just because you are in conflict doesn't mean that you are trying to take away what's important to them. Put everything else aside and focus on the problem at hand.

2. **Develop your verbal and non-verbal communication strategy before approaching the other party.**

Practicing what you want to say and how you present yourself before engaging with the other party contributes substantially to resolving a conflict. This will help you to confidently deliver your message, and make you more resilient to the reactions of the other person. You don't have to memorize every word and posture that you will use. Make a list of your main points, and practice different ways of saying them, taking the time to consider how each sound, and how it might be interpreted by the other person. While you are practicing also try out different ways to stand or sit while delivering the information. Make sure that your posture and hand gestures are calm and non-threatening.

3. **Consider the common ground you have. Share this information.**

Negotiation is like bargaining. It is about trading and building on what interests both parties in the conflict. Both parties should get some of what they want, and give something up to the other person. For example, if you and your sibling accidentally bought the same outfit, and you both like the piece of clothing equally, you may have a conflict if your sibling wants you to return yours. They argue that they don't want to be seen wearing the same thing as you, especially at the same time. You could start to resolve this conflict by telling your sibling that you both have great taste. Then you might propose that you will never wear it on the days that you are going to see them, and that on special holidays where both of you will be present, you will both choose a different outfit. In doing so, you both get to keep the outfit, and neither of you is seen wearing it at the same time. Point out ways you can both enjoy the outfit, and focus on the issue of being seen at the same time, rather than insisting that only one person can keep the outfit.

During a conflict or dispute, there are differences in personality, values, and opinions that can impact the outcome. Boundaries might have been crossed because of something that was said. When you address these concerns with the other party you will gain insight into the differences in your opinions, allowing you to negotiate ways around them. For example, you and your boss think that management should be handled in different ways. You think there should be more employee support but your boss feels there should be more customer support. The conflict is that there are personal differences in opinion about what should take priority. Resolving this conflict could involve identifying why you feel differently and gaining insight into both aspects of the business. Perhaps you could negotiate some improvements to both. Successful negotiating is about working together to resolve disputes so that both people win and the conflict ends. Sometimes you need to really understand your differences so that you can find common ground.

Chapter Summary

Changing the minds of others and yourself is about seeing the whole situation, coming up with a game plan, and resolving it using persuasion and negotiation strategies. This chapter was written to help you gain perspective about the triple position approach, and to assist you when using negotiation and persuasion as a conflict resolution technique. Let's recap what we've learned in this chapter. In this chapter you learned:

- The triple position.
- What persuasion is.
- What negotiation is.
- How to persuade.

- How to negotiate.
- How to resolve conflict by combining persuasion and negotiation.

In the next chapter, you will learn how to develop your emotional intelligence skills. This will help you succeed and resolve conflict as a great leader does.

CHAPTER SEVEN

Conflict Resolution Technique 05 - Developing Emotional Intelligence So You Can Resolve Conflict Like a Leader

Many great leaders attain success because they are great at managing and resolving conflict. How do they accomplish this? They have developed their emotional and social intelligence skills to enable them to resolve any problems that arise. You can learn how to resolve conflict like a great leader does. What else makes a great and successful leader? How does emotional intelligence contribute to success? Here are a few characteristics of great leaders:

- Leaders work on the needs of the group, and usually put others before themselves.
- Leaders are assertive, but not aggressive.
- Leaders are great conversationalists and speakers.
- Leaders learn about the people around them.
- Leaders are honest but tactful.

- Leaders know how to influence the people around them.

You don't have to be a great leader to succeed at being emotionally intelligent. Anyone can learn and use this skill. So, what is emotional intelligence exactly? It's the ability to control and regulate your own emotions while being understanding and empathetic of someone else's emotions. Everyone can learn the skills it takes to be emotionally intelligent. However, not everyone can put their skills into use when intense emotions are involved. Great leaders have this ability because they trained their minds to be emotionally stable even during conflicts. This allows them to lead large crowds and groups of people with confidence and poise. One of the main skills required for emotional intelligence is self-motivation. Sometimes that means that you aren't motivated because wealth or power is involved, but because your personal growth is. It can also mean that you are able to accomplish things without pressure from others. Let's discuss four major skills that have to do with emotional intelligence. When you use them together effectively, you can confidently state that your emotional intelligence is high. The four skills are:

1. Self-motivation.
2. Self-regulation.
3. Self-awareness.
4. Empathy.

Some people have developed these skills to a higher degree than the others. Other people have only a few or maybe none of these skills. However, if you don't have all of these skills, or are working on them still, this chapter will help you get there. Every leader is different in their own way, but what they all have in common is that they all know that conflict management requires teamwork, self-reflection, negotiation, and respect. The most effective leaders also have high emotional intelligence. By learning the different skills that lead to high emotional intelligence, you learn leadership skills that give you the ability to resolve conflict. Since we learned about self-awareness in chapter five, we will now focus on self-motivation, self-regulation, and empathy.

How to be Self-Motivating

Self-motivation is the ability to take the initiative and strive to do something without being asked or pressured by anyone else. It's the ability to see something and go after it, to fulfill your purpose, and to only be driven and motivated by yourself or the dream of the successful outcome. Some people may interpret this as thinking they are driven to make money and be successful, but this is not what self-motivation is really about. A truly emotionally intelligent person motivates themselves without thinking about money, power, praise, or acknowledgment because they don't need that to fuel their desire to go after what they want. When it comes to conflict resolution and self-motivation, you have to truly want to solve a conflict and not be afraid to bring up the difficult topic. Be proactive rather than procrastinating. Use your drive and ambition to help you persevere during the conflict. Here are some ways to help you build your emotional intelligence:

Surround Yourself with Positive People and Environments

Everyone knows that being negative only attracts more negativity into your life. When you surround yourself with positive people or highly motivated like-minded individuals, your self-motivation will increase significantly and your perspective will be more positive and hopeful. The biggest difference between a negative individual and a positive individual is that a positive person will come up with solutions not just point out the problems, while a negative person will come up with excuses not to solve problems and focus on the negative aspects of the issue. A positive person will see the good in every bad situation while a pessimistic person will always view the negative.

Do Not Overthink

Most overthinkers are people who listen too much to their inner critic or are perfectionists. When you are working on something that you need to think about, it is instinctive to analyze every aspect of it if we set our expectations too high. Not everything needs to be perfect. Ask for feedback, but don't obsess about it. It is a proven fact that perfectionists often fail because they try too hard at excellence instead of just getting something done to an acceptable level of quality. For example, a project result may be perfect, but it took too much time and went beyond the scope and was over-budget.

Track Your Success

Throughout our lives, we achieve great things but rarely get noticed or reward ourselves due to the lack of acknowledgment by others. However, a self-motivator recognizes these achievements and rewards themselves once they complete a task they have been working on. Over time, these rewards and successes will build up, so add these to your track record. A year later, you can look back at what you have accomplished, and this will continue to motivate you to keep going forward.

Be Helpful

Science says that the most empowering thing you can do to lift your spirits is to help others. Regardless of whether they are richer or poorer than you, when you help someone, it sends happy hormones to your brain, which makes you more motivated. For example, if someone comes to you and they are sad or need to vent, naturally you are going to want to cheer them up. By cheering them up through motivational and positive speech, you will feel better as well. This positive energy results in more self-motivation to continue your path towards success.

To gain emotional intelligence you need to be self-motivated and strive to achieve positive outcomes. You need the motivation to stay on track and build healthy habits such that emotional intelligence tools such as self-regulation and empathy come easier to you.

How Self-Regulation Decreases Conflict and How to Develop it

Think of self-regulation like self-control. It's the ability to process your emotions and calm them in conflict situations. It is another aspect of managing your emotions. Self-regulation first requires self-awareness. Self-awareness allows you to notice when you are angry or disappointed. Self-regulation gives you the functionality to calm yourself down before you escalate a conflict. Building your self-regulation skills increases your emotional intelligence and helps you make rational decisions, which is essential in conflict management.

In chapter five, you learned about self-awareness and what triggers your emotions. With self-regulation, once you know what triggers or upsets you, you can more effectively manage your emotions and their contribution to a conflict. When you learn self-regulation, you can:

- Delay your emotional responses.
- Develop efficient ways to calm yourself.
- Reflect on your thoughts.
- Understand the emotions of others.
- Regain composure.

Some self-regulating strategies are:

Become Open to Change

Narrow-minded people are so lost in their own world that they are unwilling to see the value in another person's opinion. When you are open-minded, you can manage change and variety in your life more easily than if you are closed-minded. For example, someone who self-regulates well is open to spontaneity and resilient to change if they need to be. For example, if you got demoted in your job, your heightened emotions might make you confrontational with your boss. This lack of self-regulation could escalate the situation even further, possibly resulting in you losing your job entirely.

Practice Self-Discipline

Self-discipline is when you can avoid temptations and get a job or task done on your own without anyone else pushing you to complete it. It's being able to define your weaknesses and work towards improving them but not seeing them as a barrier or roadblock in your success. Persistence and control are the foundations of self-regulating your emotions and conquering internal weaknesses. Self-disciplined people have higher emotional intelligence and are more focused on how they can accomplish what they need to in life. This promotes the chances of resolving conflict because self-discipline helps to keep attention on what really matters.

Talk Back to Your Inner Critic

Part of self-regulating is being able to talk back to your inner critic and reframe your negative thoughts. For example, if someone says you are not good at being creative or have poor communication skills, you may start to believe what they say about you. However, if you practice talking back to these thoughts, you can regulate how you feel about yourself and others. Eventually, the negative things people say, and the negative things you say to yourself won't bother you anymore, and you will be able to counter these thoughts with positive arguments. You can practice this by stating positive mantras to yourself every morning and visualizing success.

Breathe Under Pressure

Self-regulation requires being able to stay calm in a high pressure environment. For example, if you work in a fast-paced business, you will feel under pressure to do your best and move quickly. Self-regulation is about managing your self-awareness skills so that you can keep your composure in front of other people. Effective breathing allows us to address every situation with calm and composure. We talked about breathing in previous chapters, and learned that deep, regular breathing has a calming effect and helps us to focus. Practice this by using breathing techniques and other relaxation methods such as meditation whenever you feel pressured.

Identify the Outcome

When you can think rationally about what the outcome of your actions will be during a time of conflict, you further develop the skill of self-regulating your emotions and behaviors. Since self-regulation relies on knowing yourself, your triggers and what upsets you, only you can choose the right approach to resolving conflict. Think before you act and consider the consequences of your actions. Self-regulation requires taking responsibility for your contribution to a problem and finding ways to resolve it efficiently. This requires an awareness of what the optimal outcome of the situation is.

How Empathy Can Resolve Conflict

Empathy is the foundation of emotional intelligence. Emotional intelligence is about understanding your own emotions while recognizing the feelings of others. Empathy is the ability to put yourself in other people's shoes and see their side of things. Highly empathetic people feel the pain of others around them. For example, if your friend is sad, you might feel sad too. If your family member is angry, you might feel some of their anger "rub off on you". So, what does empathy have to do with conflict resolution?

While some people are aware of the emotions of others, some individuals cannot be empathetic. Conflict resolution requires you to see someone's point of view in order to help resolve the problem effectively. So, how do we learn to be more empathetic?

Push Your Limits

Doing uncomfortable or unfamiliar things teaches us to evolve personally, adapt to change and handle whatever conflict comes at us. By learning something new, such as playing a musical instrument or painting, or doing something hard like exercising or meeting new people, you will be more relaxed, humble, and skilled. Humility is a critical factor in developing empathy. Push your limits so that you can grow as a person.

Ask for Constructive Criticism

Part of learning to be empathetic is understanding how others view you and your weaknesses so that you can work on them for the benefit of others. Check in with your closest friends or people who know the real you and ask them how you respond to conflict or relationship issues. If someone tells you that you are great at helping out but bad at listening, then you know that you need to work on your listening skills.

Check in Often

The opposite of empathy is caring only for your own benefit, which shows that you are selfish or self-centered. To break this habit of always wanting to talk about yourself or do things that only help you, make a conscious effort to check in with the people you care about. Instead of calling someone for help, call someone to see if they could use an extra hand. Rather than asking someone to hang out for the intention of wanting something in return, call and see if you can take them for lunch or coffee just because you want to hear what is new in their life.

See Someone Else's Point of View

Although seeing someone else's perspective might be challenging for some people, making a conscious decision to really listen to someone else's point of view increases your empathy skills. When engaging in conversation, really listen to what the other person is telling you and think about how you would feel, what you would think, and what you would do if you were in their situation.

Keep Your Judgment at Bay

Say no to judgment. Just because you wouldn't do something that someone else is telling you that they did doesn't mean you are smarter than them. Everyone has their own reasons for why they do what they do. Judgment is the opposite of empathy and should be left at the door when practicing how to be more empathetic, and when trying to resolve conflict.

Ask Empathetic Questions

When engaging in conversation, show that you want to know more and that you are enthusiastic to hear their side by asking questions related to the topic. For example, if you don't know anything about dog training, but someone else is venting about their career, they might say that they had to train a misbehaved dog. If you cannot relate to them because of your dislike for dogs, disinterest in the career, or other personal views, you can start asking questions. Some empathetic questions might include, "How did you feel when the dog jumped on you? Why did you choose this career if it's so difficult? What is the worst day you have had, and how did you deal with it? What are the parts of the job you most enjoy?" By learning more about what another person feels and experiences, you can start to relate more to their situation.

You will develop empathy by putting these skills into practice and by being dedicated to the experience of personal growth. Empathy is not just a sign of high emotional intelligence but also a top sign of leadership and influential capabilities. Empathy can help you progress in many aspects of your life because it helps you relate to others on a higher level, and when we truly relate to others, we are less likely to have conflict with them.

Chapter Summary

Developing the four aspects of emotional intelligence we have discussed can dramatically affect your chances of resolving a conflict. Having a high emotional intelligence means that you can address the situation, see from another's point of view, be empathetic to others and regulate your own emotions so that conflict does not escalate any further than it needs to.

In this chapter, you learned:

- What emotional intelligence is.
- How to increase your emotional intelligence.
- What self-motivation is and why it's important.

- What self-regulation is and how to develop it to resolve conflict.
- What empathy is and how to use it to resolve a dispute.

In the next chapter, you will learn how to make peace with conflict, even if the conflict cannot be resolved. You will understand constructive confrontation and how it relates to the many aspects of making peace with argumentative and narrow-minded people.

CHAPTER EIGHT

Conflict Resolution Technique 06 - The Strategy of Peace

In this chapter, you will learn the strategy of making peace. The ultimate goal of conflict resolution is a peaceful conclusion. A resolution where all parties receive an equitable outcome and have a deeper understanding of each other is what we strive to achieve. Regardless of what strategies are used, or how successful it is, in the end, the goal is to end the conflict. Making peace during or after a conflict requires that you effectively use positive solutions that are based on mutual understanding. As you strive towards a peaceful outcome to your conflicts, there are many tools you can use to create opportunities for resolution. The tools are based on constructive confrontation, the realization that you don't always have to be right, and how to know when to walk away gracefully.

Constructive Confrontation

Approach the conflict situation by creating a constructive confrontation opportunity. Constructive confrontation happens when you can communicate with the other party that you realize there is a conflict and you want to resolve it. Approach the other party with sincerity in your words and your heart. Use non-threatening body language. Start with taking responsibility for your contribution to the conflict. Be clear that you want to understand their perspective, come to a mutual agreement and make peace. Here are some tools you can use before and during a constructive confrontation event:

Observe the Situation

As you learned in chapter six, triple position is taking a step back and looking at the conflict as a whole while still considering the needs of each party. Take a step back and consider each aspect of the conflict. What is the root of the conflict? What is contributing to its escalation? What is the position of each party? Is there a common ground? Is this a safe appropriate space to have this constructive confrontation? Is there enough time to have a good talk? Is the other party argumentative, upset, or hostile? What kind of body language is being expressed by the parties? Are they mirroring your body language? Are they expressing body language that is closed off or angry? What does the vibe in the room feel like?

Use your emotional intelligence and observation skills to gather information that will assist you in developing a strategy for the situation. Regulate your emotions and be objective so that you can proceed calmly. When dealing with conflict, it is always best to talk face-to-face so that you can observe the situation fully.

Identify All Your Options

In order to identify all of your options, use the information you collected while observing the situation. Objectively consider different approaches to the constructive confrontation. Go over various scenarios in your head. Use what you know about the situation, the issues, and the other party to imagine what would happen if you used one approach, then imagine what would happen if you used a different approach. What words are they most likely to listen to? Do you need to make adjustments or accommodations to increase the chance of a successful outcome? Should you be sitting or standing? Should you be alone or in a public place? Think about what the potential outcomes are for every potential scenario you can think of. For example, consider these scenarios. If you are standing and they are sitting, and you say, "I think you're wrong about something and I want to talk about it," it is unlikely to go well. There is a chance the person will feel intimidated and say okay, allowing you to start with the conversation focused on you. There is a greater chance that the person will feel that you are overbearing, blaming them for something, and get upset or angry. However, if you were to start with both of you sitting, and you said, "I think we had a misunderstanding about something, and I'd like to talk about it," there is a good chance that the person will be receptive to the conversation and interested in resolving the misunderstanding. Identifying your options gives you the opportunity to choose the best potential solution. Consider the various options you have. Rank them as plan A, B and C just in case the person does not respond in the way you anticipated and you need to try another approach.

Confirm Understanding

Sometimes, to resolve conflict, it is best to confirm your understanding of everyone's point of view, and how they are similar or different. The most important thing about making peace is developing mutual understanding. Let the other party know that you realize there is a problem, and that you want to understand their point of view. Ask them to explain their perspective on the conflict, and listen carefully to what they say. Confirm what you believe they have said, and ask them if it is correct. Ask questions if you are unsure about anything. Validate their answer rather than immediately comparing it to your point of view. Thank them for helping you understand. It is then okay to say something like, "I think I understand your point of view better now. Is it okay if I explain my point of view and then maybe we can talk about the similarities and differences in our opinions?" Once you have exchanged points of view, you will both have an opportunity to recognize that the opinion of the other person is valid even though it is different from yours. If they are open to discussion, compare both of your points of view and talk about your common ground if there is any. Give feedback about their opinions, and ask for feedback about yours. Try to stick to facts rather than stating personal views, or at least be clear about what is fact and what is opinion. Talk openly about what exactly is the root of the conflict.

Reminisce on Past Success (NOT Past Mistakes)

All too often, we resort to bringing up past mistakes, which can make someone automatically defensive. Instead, you can point out the positive things that have been said and done before. Relate these to the situation you are in now or state how a conflict was solved amicably between you in the past. Talking about past successes may assist you to diffuse the conflict in a healthy, peaceful way. For example, if someone says, "I am mad because you don't understand, and you never have." You can make them feel more comfortable and redirect the conversation by responding in a calm tone and saying, "I understand that those are your feelings right now. I want to remind you that it worked really well when we agreed to XXX and we followed through. That helped us to understand each other. Working this out is important to me." Discuss how you were able to successfully understand each other when certain words, phrases, body language, time of day, location, etc. were used. Discuss how it feels when you use language that is blaming or hurtful. Choose to have a positive conversation. Agree to exchange points of view and have a constructive conversation about the successful resolution of your current conflict. Talk about what has worked for you in the past, so that you can apply any lessons learned from those situations.

Allow Time for Thought Processing and Effective Responses

Many times, during a conflict, we are impatient to hear a response to what we have said, so we pressure the individual to respond right away. All that does is cause more conflict because it heightens anxiety or hostility. This can also often result in saying things we don't really mean. Things may escalate quickly, and violence may even occur if someone is pushed too far. We are so anxious to get to the end that we push too hard, and don’t take time to really consider what is being said. Instead, you should both take your time to calmly present your points, listen to the other person, think carefully about what was said, and discuss a clear path forward. Do not let your haste to be out of the uncomfortable situation compromise your need to take the time for clear composed thought and reflection.

Take Breaks

If you feel yourself getting flustered, or notice that the opposing party is agitated, suggest that you both take a break from the conversation. Ask to grab a coffee for you both, or suggest to change the subject to something lighter for now, with an intent to return to it later. However, do not forget to come back to it when you are both feeling better because avoiding or ignoring conflict will likely make it worse when the dispute resumes at a later date.

Constructive confrontation is about letting go of all judgment and making sure that you get involved entirely and personally in the conversation. Making peace requires you to be open to working out your conflict to the benefit of both parties, even if the only benefit is both parties walking away from the dispute. If you are in a conflict, take the initiative and actively seek out the opportunity to resolve it. Sometimes constructive confrontation is hard because you are too close to the person you are in conflict with. To be constructive in your approach, you have to look at situations from every perspective, including objectively like a therapist or a mentor would. Identify how you feel, what this person means to you, and decide if you can look at it from a triple position. Not all conflicts are resolved, but all conversations must come to an end eventually. When trying to end a heated discussion, try suggesting the last tool, taking a break, until you are both calm and can think rationally.

You Don't Always Need to Be Right

Competitive people are the ones who are the most argumentative because they need to get their point across and will not settle until others agree they are right. Does this sound like you or someone you know? If it's someone you know, sometimes just not saying anything argumentative can make all the difference. You might say, "You seem to be convinced it's true, so I will think about it." All you can control is yourself and your response, so why risk an argument if you already know that this person has to be right and will never back down?

If you are the competitive one, it may be best to consider the questions below so that you don't become your own worst enemy.

Some of the most important lessons you can learn are: you don't always have to be right, some arguments aren't worth winning, the fault may actually be yours, you may have misunderstood, or maybe you are being mean or prideful. Always be willing to take responsibility for your own role in a conflict.

Am I Right or Am I Being Prideful?

The truth of the matter is, you may think you are right, but in reality, maybe you are just being overly opinionated, prideful and self-centered. Having opinions is not bad; however, when you mix it with a competitive nature and bad conflict resolution skills, you may not be able to get along with people. What if it matters more how you handle conflict with others than whether you are more correct than they are? Maybe you have the drive and confidence to speak out, and you believe you know what you are talking about. What if you are actually wrong? Try considering how many times you have been right. Is it all the time, or do you only think you are right all the time? Maybe people are just tired of arguing with you. Constantly trying to prove to others that you are right is prideful.

Sometimes having to be right stems from a competitive nature. It may result from not being heard by others or from feeling neglected when we were young. Competitiveness makes us feel better about ourselves because when we win arguments we feel successful and like a winner. Being competitive does not contribute to effective conflict resolution. Don't be so competitive. Be cooperative. Next time you are confronted with a conflict, don't focus on winning or being right. Consider letting someone else be right and see how you feel. If you feel emotionally crushed, or unreasonably angry when you don't win an argument, it might be best to look into the underlying causes of this. Go talk to a counselor to identify your core patterns so that you don’t miss out on future opportunities to build closer bonds with others.

Is it Worth Winning the Argument?

Determine if an argument is worth winning, and if it is, understand what the cost will be to your relationship, circumstance, or safety. Maybe it’s not worth winning. It’s okay to let someone else have their way. Look at your environment and analyze the situation. Where are you? Who are you talking to? What is the argument about? Do you really need to win? If you win do you risk losing a friend or loved one because they are so hurt by your approach to winning? Do you risk offending or angering someone who is in a position of power over you? There is a big difference between arguing with your boss about their reaction to your finished project as opposed to arguing with your friends about a local political issue. During a debate with your friends, it’s okay to try to vigorously win a friendly argument; however, even a minor disagreement with your boss might cost you your job. A dispute with your wife over how to parent may not be the right fight to try to win; however, a disagreement over a guys' night out might be okay. If someone suggests you do something unsafe together and you don’t want to, it is very important that you win the argument.

If they suggest you do something boring and you don't want to, it doesn't really have a large consequence who wins.

What Caused the Conflict?

Instead of arguing with your friends, your spouse, your boss, or a family member, think back to what caused this current argument or others in the past. Is this a recurring argument or a new disagreement? Is it a difference of opinion on something intangible, or is there an opportunity to resolve the conflict based on facts? Is there something to be gained or lost that is fueling the conflict? Identify the underlying cause of this confrontation so you can find a constructive way to deal with it. If you are working together to resolve the conflict, make sure you both agree on what the root cause of the conflict is.

Are You Being Spiteful or Hurtful?

When we are wrapped up in the moment, we can become spiteful by bringing up past events or saying deliberately hurtful things. We don't usually intentionally try to hurt the other party; however, because we know them, we also know what buttons to press to get a reaction. Ask yourself if you are deliberately provoking the other person. Are you saying things that are mean or upsetting to them? Being hurtful towards the other party will escalate a dispute and possibly end your relationship.

When Conflict Cannot Be Resolved

Sometimes people just can't agree and the discussion has to end. Making peace doesn't always have to mean that the conflict has been resolved to the satisfaction of all parties. Sometimes making peace can mean just agreeing to disagree and parting company with no hard feelings. In these circumstances, you need to understand when it's appropriate to just let things go. For example, if the other party will not let go of their point, and no matter what you say, it will only lead to an escalation of the dispute, you might choose not to say anything more.

Depending on what type of conflict you are in, and who you are speaking to, it's best to know when you should talk things out, when to be silent for a while, and when to let it go completely. So, how are we to be sure when to talk things out or not? When should you just make peace with the situation and move on? Consider the following:

- Is the conflict big or small?
- Will it matter in a weeks' time or change anything if it isn't settled?
- What are the consequences of winning, losing, or walking away?
- Is it worth losing the person you are speaking with?
- Is it worth losing yourself in the moment?

- Are you hungry, tired, emotional, or is something else contributing to the dispute?

Sometimes it's easy to make peace. If the battle is something small and silly, make some humor out of it and say, "Gee, this is quite silly and has gotten out of hand don't you think?" However, when you make this bold statement, make sure it is something small like an argument over cutting potatoes or which movie to watch. Sometimes, we don't notice that small things may be contributing to our behavior. If we are hungry, tired, prideful, or selfish in the moment we can escalate a minor issue into a hostile conflict. When an issue is minor, be quick to say, "This issue isn't worth arguing about." Observe the situation objectively and then decide if you should just stop arguing and make peace.

Ending A Conflict Gracefully

Ending a conflict gracefully requires you to end on a positive or neutral note. It also means accepting the outcome without holding a grudge or hard feelings. Many people view conflict as a problem but rarely see it as an opportunity for positive change and inner growth. Although the conflict may seem to be something negative, conflict is actually a positive thing because it helps us define who we are and who someone else is on a deeper level. You have not ended the conflict gracefully if you haven't really ended the argument. If you are just holding on to the hostility with a plan to argue later, or you are planning to avoid the person in the future, or one of you ends up leaving disappointed and unheard, then you haven't resolved anything. Resolving conflict gracefully means knowing what to say, when to stop talking and when to walk away. Here's a recap of some of the essential skills for making peace and ending a conflict gracefully:

- Keep negative thoughts to yourself. Don't say them out loud.
- Focus on positive common ground.
- Practice effective listening skills.
- Validate the other person's feelings.
- Stay on topic.
- Bring up what has worked in the past
- Don't say hurtful things.
- Focus on the solution, not on being right.
- Remember why you value having this person in your life.
- Stay away from making it a competition.

This chapter is about what to do when you can't resolve a conflict but you want to make peace. It's about how to end the conflict and walk away peacefully. This may take both actions and words. Sometimes the conflict escalates because of the words you are using. Let's look at some examples of how you can say positive, constructive things and work towards making peace.

"I needed to hear that, thank you. I will keep that in mind."

Stating this validates the person you are talking to. Even if you don't agree or relate to their opinion or view, it shows that you are trying to understand, and that you will put more thought into it. It helps them know that they are being heard and that you are open to their point of view.

"I have something to say. Is now a good time to tell you about it?"

This statement can be said in the middle of an argument or before you start a potentially difficult conversation. It lets the other person know that you have an opinion and need to be heard, but that you need their full attention. At times, it can also make someone aware that they might be getting off-topic or venting too much, and that it's your turn to speak.

"What do you think about us searching for some facts?"

As mentioned previously, some arguments are all about being right. In some cases, it is possible to find or provide proof of which position is actually correct. In this situation, both parties must agree to respect the outcome of the fact finding.

"I am interpreting what you said like XXX. Is this correct? Please help me understand if I am wrong."

Effective verbal communication includes re-phrasing what the speaker has said to you so that you are sure you understand it. If you aren't clear about what they mean, you can ask them to explain themselves or provide examples. This shows that you are trying to get the full story without jumping to conclusions.

"I am not very comfortable with that idea, can we come up with something else?"

Stating this shows that even though you heard what they are saying, you aren't on board with it but still want to work together to solve the problem. This is an effective way to open the door for using negotiation and persuasion techniques which you learned about previously.

Thinking before you speak and saying constructive positive things can significantly increase your chances of walking away from the conflict with a solution or at least with the peace of mind that you tried your best.

How to Apologize

You must be thinking, "I know how to apologize, why is this even a heading?" It's because apologies can come off as aggressive or ingenuine if you just apologize because that's what the other party wants in order to settle the conflict. The number one rule of apologizing is that you must mean it. It must be sincere.

The only way to show that you are sincere is to genuinely think about the conflict and be truly sorry you hurt then. You must also be willing to not do what you said sorry for in the future. For example, maybe your spouse gets upset with you because you don't fold the laundry or help around the house. You might have your own opinion that you do help out and that it goes unnoticed. However, to end the argument before it begins, you might just automatically say sorry. Then you do it again because your first apology wasn't genuine. You never intended to actually change your behavior. You said sorry in order to end the conflict at that moment in time. With this type of apology, sorry soon starts to mean nothing, and the other person is likely to lose trust in you and your sincerity.

Here is what a genuine apology sounds like:

"I can see that I hurt you. I am sorry."

Make sure that when you apologize, it comes from within, and that you genuinely mean it. Be prepared to explain how they were hurt and what you are sorry for. Otherwise, an apology will seem ingenuine, offhand and dishonest. The opposing party may not be able to trust you when you actually are sorry in the future. Here are some examples of what an insincere or ingenuine apology sounds like:

- "Whatever, I am sorry."
- "If you want an apology from me, here it is, I am sorry."
- "I am sorry that you are so XXX."
- "You are right, I guess I will never learn to please you."
- "It's all my fault. I am such a horrible person."

So, what exactly makes an apology genuine? The best apologies happen when you:

- Do not rush it and explain why you are sorry for what you have done.
- Take responsibility for the part you played in the dispute and don't expect or ask for an apology back.
- Do not justify what you have done, explain why you did what you did and acknowledge that it was the wrong approach.
- Promise to make the changes necessary to ensure it doesn't happen again.
- Ask for forgiveness.
- Follow through with any promises made.

Acknowledgment

A proper and respectful apology is interpreted and received better if you acknowledge that there is a dispute and that you are not happy about being in conflict with the person. Summarize the dispute from the third position perspective. When you are being sincere, acknowledge the dispute, your role in the dispute, and have thought about the entire situation, you can quickly clarify what is wrong and what you will do differently next time.

Responsibility

Some people are too wrapped up in the heat of the moment to consider their own actions or how they contributed to escalating the conflict. Taking responsibility means admitting what you did to contribute to the conflict, and letting the other person know. To practice taking responsibility you can:

- Examine the scenario without putting blame on the other person or parties.
- Consider everyone's contribution including your own.
- Apologize for what you have done.
- Learn from your mistakes.
- Choose a peaceful approach.

Taking responsibility for your actions doesn't have to result in an apology. Just the fact that you have realized what you have done wrong means that you are one step closer to resolving conflict peacefully.

Understanding and Empathy

After you have acknowledged the dispute and taken responsibility for how your own thoughts and actions contributed to the argument, show empathy and compassion by thinking and stating how you believe the other person feels. True understanding may not happen until after the conflict ends, and you've had a chance to think about it.

When apologizing, make sure you have put thought into your apology and remember to listen to what the other person has said. Give them a chance to respond to the apology. Your intention may be to be forgiven, but this doesn't always happen right away. Sometimes accepting that someone needs more time is the only way to resolve an issue for the time being. Don't forget to forgive yourself. Look at yourself in the mirror, apologize to yourself and forgive yourself for the way you handled things. Holding onto anger and hate or betrayal can cause anxiety and deepened stress. Forgiveness is not always possible, but if you walk away from an unresolved conflict satisfied with your own approach, you can continue to learn and develop conflict resolution skills in the future.

Chapter Summary

Whether you are constructively criticizing, confronting, or resolving, peaceful conflict resolution is about learning positive ways to end conflict gracefully. When conflict cannot be resolved, it's best to be quiet and listen, identify your contribution, and let go of wanting to be right. When saying sorry is about ending a conflict just to end it, you are ingenuine. When you say sorry because you actually are, you are more likely to have a peaceful end to the difficult situation, even if you don't fully resolve the conflict. Now you know techniques to effectively and peacefully end a conflict even if there is no true resolution, or you are not forgiven.

In this chapter, you learned:

- What constructive confrontation is.
- When to end conflict and when not to.
- When to let unresolved conflict go.
- How to speak in a way that will lead to a graceful end to a difficult conversation.

- How to apologize authentically.

In the next chapter, you will learn how to open your mind and rethink problems and conflict. By reframing your point of view and using conflict to positively change your life, you can master yet another tool available to you as you strive to resolve conflict in your life.

CHAPTER NINE

Conflict Resolution Technique 07 - The Power of Keeping an Open Mind

Keeping an open mind is all about perspective, alternate interpretations and reframing your way of thinking. The reason this technique is so beneficial is that often our minds are so set in our own thinking patterns that we can forget that someone else sees it differently. As you have learned throughout this book, having a competitive nature or a closed-off attitude can heighten conflict. Keeping an open mind influences our behavior and sets up how we approach conflict and discussion. The reason most people are comfortable with keeping thoughts to themselves or having a closed mind is that during the conflict, they feel uncomfortable or defensive and a closed-off attitude makes them feel secure. Without realizing it, this type of behavior contributes to an escalation of the dispute or argument. You might ask, "Why would I allow myself to be vulnerable if I feel threatened? If the other party in the conflict continues to put me down and doesn't make me feel comfortable, then why should I try?"

In this state of a closed-off mind, we might wait for an apology or think that the other party has to make the first move before we are willing to consider resolving the conflict. In some cases, this approach is healthy if you feel the other party has truly wronged you and you need space and time to consider the situation. However, before thinking they need to make the first move, consider your relationship and the overall perspective of the conflict. Take a step back and evaluate the whole scenario before making a sudden and permanent decision. Would having an open mind make it easier to understand the problem? Are you ready to consider other perspectives? Is there something you can do to understand the situation better? What can you control, and what can you not control regarding this matter? Perhaps you wonder why you should open up when you don't feel like it? Perhaps you are scared of getting hurt. That's natural. There are many benefits to opening your mind to the perspectives of others and to the potential of a positive outcome.

Here are some of the benefits:

- You may learn that you are not the only one who might be feeling threatened.
- You might discover that their behavior is stemming from fear.
- They might not realize they can't control themselves during a conflict.
- You stay non-judgmental by keeping an open mind.

- You may be able to decrease the level of hostility which will improve the chance of resolving the conflict.

In chapter seven, you learned the power of emotional intelligence and how it can help you resolve conflicts. Using empathy can help you understand that being closed-off will only escalate things further because you are closed-off to what the other person is thinking and feeling. That's not to say that your feelings and opinions don't matter. However, the ultimate cause of the rising conflict could be that you both feel the same way but don't know how to express it. So, how do you fix this? Consciously keep an open mind and reframe your thinking. Remember the importance of effective listening strategies. Keeping an open mind requires active listening skills.

Reframing Your Mind for Effective Conflict Resolution

The concept of reframing one's mind is to view things differently than you have been. In the previous chapters, you have learned the concept of empathy, which is to understand another's opinion and how they feel and think. Reframing your mind doesn't mean to look outside the box or think of the bigger picture. Reframing your mindset is the act of reshaping the way you see or view your own point of view to be receptive to the opinions of others. This allows us to expand and evolve our perspectives to include new information based on the perspectives of others.

Usually, when you go into a conflict you already have an interpretation of what the problem is, how to solve it, and where it came from. Only you can know your own thoughts and what you want to do about it. However, you don't truly understand what another feels and thinks. It could be completely different from what you have assumed. With emotional intelligence tools such as empathy you can try your best to relate to the person or people you are in conflict with. Reframing your mind is not about looking at things from your own side differently, nor is it looking at things only from another's perspective. It's about understanding that you can look at the conflict in many ways and that there may be many valid and invalid components to everyone's point of view. One way of practicing reframing your mind is to get advice from different people who are not involved in the conflict.

One of the barriers to reframing your mind when it comes to a dispute is that during an argument, we revert back to first person perspective and get caught up in the desire to win. However, when you remain calm and keep your composure you can reframe your mindset and get a healthy view of the situation. You can reframe more than just your own thoughts. You can reframe the terms of the whole conflict by helping others to see the bigger perspective and the positive side of the situation. However, reframing and thus altering the outcome of a conflict requires you to first reframe your own state of mind. Strive to understand all aspects of the issue and then address the concern in a calm manner. Here are ways to reframe your mindset:

Underline the Root of the Issue

The first step to reframing your mind about the conflict is to identify what the underlying cause is. Many disputes escalate because we get caught up in the heat of the argument and focus on what's being said in that specific moment. However, we sometimes don't realize that the things that are being said and done right now have nothing to do with the actual root of the crisis. For example, if your boss accuses you of not working as hard as everyone else and recommends that you pick up the slack, it may not be because you aren't working hard enough. The underlying cause may be that your boss is having a rough day or a rough patch in their own lives, and that they are taking it out on you. Alternatively, it may be true that you aren't working hard enough because you are tired from being up all night with the baby.

Reframe the Negative

Once you have figured out what the underlying cause of the dispute is, you can restate the negative and think more positively about the scenario. Some ways to do this are:

- Change the intensity of the conversation by speaking calmly and using non-threatening body language.
- Use empathy and compassion.
- Find out what might work for both parties.
- Find a positive thing that you can both agree on.
- Restate the problem to make sure you both understand.

- Redirect the discussion back to the underlying issue.
- Focus on a solution.

In order to effectively reframe the conflict with your boss you can apologize genuinely and explain that you are having a rough patch at home but will try your best to focus. Or, if your boss is having a rough day, you might politely say something like, "I'm sorry it seems that way to you. I've actually accomplished XXX today." Let your boss know that you are doing your best.

The main focus behind reframing is to shift your view or the other party's perspective about how the dispute feels to you or them and say something positive that will lead to a solution.

Viewing Conflict as a Positive

Almost all people who have been in conflict with another individual think of it as a bad thing. However, disputes and quarrels between you and someone else should not be looked at as a bad thing. As we talk about the root causes of conflict, part of reframing your mindset requires you to look at conflict as something healthy. Once your mind is in the right place, you can approach the dispute in the right way. Regardless of if conflict makes you feel angry, sad or disappointed, there are many reasons why conflict can be a positive thing in your life. As the saying goes, it always rains before you see a rainbow. Think of the conflict as the rain, and the resolution the rainbow.

Three types of growth can come from conflict and conflict resolution. Those are:

Personal Growth

Conflict helps you define your own deeper emotions and thoughts. This helps you to achieve enlightenment, accept change, and have a deeper understanding of yourself. We grow and evolve when we challenge ourselves and face conflict with an open mind.

Relational Growth

Conflict may exist with other people; however, the process of resolving conflict helps you grow both individually, and in relation to others by gaining a deeper understanding of how someone else thinks. When you work with others to build positive outcomes, your relationships will also develop in positive ways.

Structural Growth

Structural growth comes from your work environment. Conflict can sometimes happen at work. If we didn't have conflict at work, we might never really understand the extent of our responsibilities, what people around us think about our work, or what others need from us. We would not learn how to speak professionally, swallow our pride, and resolve conflicts with grace. These qualities might lead to getting recognized as a leader, or as someone who is resilient to change in a challenging workplace. We gain structural growth by learning how to succeed despite conflict.

Aside from these three types of growth and the opportunities we gain from experiencing conflict, there are many other reasons why conflict can be a good thing. Some of the reasons why conflict can be positive are that it:

- Provides us insight.
- Gives us the opportunity to express ourselves.
- Helps us evaluate our core needs.
- Teaches us responsibility and empathy.
- Makes us listen to understand.
- Shows us our own behaviors and unhealthy patterns.
- Turns something negative like a conflict into positive solutions by addressing needs.
- Allows us to work on our communication skills.
- Helps us identify our values and set clear boundaries.
- Promotes emotional balance and control.
- Allows us to view problems from the point of view of others.

When you look at it, conflict is a great thing, especially when your goal is to solve a problem and build positive relationships with others.

FINAL WORDS

The problem with conflict is that it's always around us. No matter where we go, what we do or how we think, conflict inevitably finds us. You may not be in conflict right now, but you have probably experienced it in the past. You are likely to experience conflict in the future. It is essential to have techniques and tools to recognize, defuse and resolve conflict.

Is conflict itself really the problem, or is it how we deal with it? As you have learned in this book, conflict resolution is about how you deal with conflict and change the ultimate outcome of the situation. There are healthy ways to deal with conflict, and there are negative ways to manage conflict. This book has shown you the ins and outs, the ups and downs, the negatives and positives of conflict and conflict resolution so that the next time you are confronted, you can handle it effectively.

Ask yourself what you can take away from reading this book. Think back to what your state of mind was like before reading this book and compare it to what you feel and believe now. Ask yourself what you know now that you didn't before. What is your contribution to the conflicts you have been involved in? How are you going to handle things differently? How can you learn about yourself and others? How can you find solutions that are mutually beneficial? These questions are good to ask and will lead to positive behaviors. Conflict cannot be avoided or ignored.

In the introduction, I assured you that you would gain a greater understanding of how to resolve conflict better and figure out what roles you play in escalating issues. Do you now have a deeper understanding of yourself as well as of others? Are there things you learned about yourself that you didn’t know before? By now, you should have a different perspective on the disputes you have been a part of. You should also have a variety of techniques at your disposal that can assist with resolving the conflicts in your life.

In this book, you have learned seven different techniques to help you resolve conflict. By practicing and mastering these techniques you will achieve personal and professional growth and experience the benefits that conflict resolution skills bring to your life. Remember these techniques and use them the next time you are in a situation that requires conflict resolution skills.

Let's review the seven techniques again to ensure this book ends with our best advice to you.

1. Mastering the power of conversation through verbal communication tools.

2. Mastering the power of conversation through non-verbal communication tools.

3. Managing emotions.

4. Changing minds using persuasion and negotiation.
5. Developing emotional intelligence so that you can resolve conflict like a leader.
6. The strategy of peace.
7. The power of keeping an open mind.

My wish for you from this point forward is that you approach every challenge and conflict with grace and gratitude. Continue to practice our seven techniques, keep learning, and move towards growth in all aspects of your life. Now that you have effective tools to resolve conflict in your life, the possibilities are endless. Don't stop now, reach for your goals and dreams with confidence.

All the best,

Gerard Shaw

RESOURCES

B. Spangler (2003) Reframing. Retrieved from https://www.beyondintractability.org/essay/joint_reframing

Brenda (2016) The Awesome Communication Tool: Reframing. Retrieved from http://brendahooper.com/the-awesome-communication-tool-reframing/

C. Childs (2019) 8 Steps to Continuous Self Motivation Even During the Difficult Times. Retrieved from, https://www.lifehack.org/articles/featured/8-steps-to-continuous-self-motivation.html

D, Bellafiore (n.d.) Interpersonal Conflict and Effective Communication. Retrieved from http://www.drbalternatives.com/articles/cc2.html

D, Prothrow-Stith (n.d.) Conflict Resolution: The Human Dimension. Retrieved from https://www.gmu.edu/programs/icar/ijps/vol3_1/burton.htm

D, Stone, B Patton, and S. Heen (n.d.) Difficult Conversations: How To Discuss What Matters Most Handout. Retrieved from https://www.mdmunicipal.org/DocumentCenter/View/3656/Difficult-Conversations-Handout?bidId

D.W Johnson (2019) The Importance of Taking the Perspective of Others. Retrieved from https://www.psychologytoday.com/ca/blog/constructive-controversy/201906/the-importance-taking-the-perspective-others

Dr. T, Alessandra (May 2018) Conflict Resolution Behaviors. Retrieved from https://assessments24x7.com/blog/conflict-resolution-behaviors/

E. Katrina (2014) 7 Tips to Follow to End Any Argument Peacefully. Retrieved from https://www.realsimple.com/work-life/work-life-etiquette/sticky-situations/things-say-keep-peace

H. Shorey (2017) Managing Relationship Conflict: Letting Go of Being Right. Retrieved from https://www.psychologytoday.com/ca/blog/the-freedom-change/201710/managing-relationship-conflict-letting-go-being-right

J. Denny (2006) Constructive Confrontation. Retrieved from https://cmoe.com/blog/the-power-of-constructive-confrontation/

J. Segal, M. Smith, L. Robinson, and G. Boose (2019) Nonverbal Communication. Retrieved from https://www.helpguide.org/articles/relationships-communication/nonverbal-communication.htm

J.C. Williamson (2017) Effective Apologies Turn Conflict Aftermath into Healing Afterglow. Retrieved from https://www.huffpost.com/entry/effective-apologies-turn-_b_11950994

L Puhn (2017) 10 Things to Say to Keep the Peace. Retrieved from https://www.realsimple.com/work-life/work-life-etiquette/sticky-situations/things-say-keep-peace

M, Clayton (2017) Roger Fisher, and William Ury: Principled Negotiation. Retrieved from https://www.pocketbook.co.uk/blog/2017/06/27/roger-fisher-william-ury-principled-negotiation/

M, Dixit (2004) Theories of Conflict Resolution. Retrieved from http://www.ipcs.org/comm_select.php?articleNo=1531

M. Carroll (2012) The Application of NLP Perceptual Positions. Retrieved from, https://www.nlpacademy.co.uk/articles/view/resolving_conflict_by_exploring_different_perspectives/

Melissa (2018) The 5 Aspects of Emotional Intelligence and Why They Matter. Retrieved from https://awato.org/5-aspects-emotional-intelligence-matter/

Nick (2016) POP for Safety. Retrieved from https://nicholas-davies.com/pop-for-safety/

P. Scott (2016) The Power of Constructive Confrontation. Retrieved from https://cmoe.com/blog/the-power-of-constructive-confrontation/

PON Staff (2019) Four Conflict Negotiation Strategies for Resolving Value-Based Disputes. Retrieved from https://www.pon.harvard.edu/daily/dispute-resolution/four-negotiation-strategies-for-resolving-values-based-disputes/

R. Reece (n.d.) Emotional Intelligence and Conflict Management. Retrieved from http://emotionalintelligenceworkshops.com/emotional-intelligence-conflict-management.htm

Rob (June 2014) 5 Stages of Conflict and Workplace Conflict Resolution. Retrieved from https://blog.udemy.com/stages-of-conflict/

S, Amaresan (March 2019) 5 Conflict Management Styles for Every Personality Type. Retrieved from https://blog.hubspot.com/service/conflict-management-styles

S, Kukreja (n.d.) Types of Conflict Situations. Available at: https://www.managementstudyhq.com/types-of-conflict-situations.html

S, London (n.d.) The Power of Dialogue. Retrieved from http://scott.london/articles/ondialogue.html

S. Campbell (2016) The Benefits of Conflict. Retrieved from https://www.entrepreneur.com/article/279778

S. Kline (n.d.) 8 Ways to Improve Self- Regulation. Retrieved from http://preventchildabuse.org/wp-content/uploads/2016/10/8-Ways-to-Improve-Self-Regulation.pdf

S.J. Scott (2019) What is Self-Awareness and How to Develop it. Retrieved from https://www.developgoodhabits.com/what-is-self-awareness/

Stefan Jacobson (March 2017) The Benefits of Conflict Resolution. Retrieved from https://www.conovercompany.com/the-benefits-of-conflict-resolution/

T. Coke (2015) The Power of an Open Mind. Retrieved from https://www.hrmagazine.co.uk/article-details/the-power-of-an-open-mind

Unknown (2012) What Makes an Apology Authentic and Effective as a Resolution of Conflict? Retrieved from https://www.choiceconflictresolution.com/2012/10/31/what-makes-an-apology-authentic-and-effective-as-a-resolution-of-conflict/

Unknown (2014) What is the Difference Between Negotiation and Persuasion? Retrieved from https://www.scotwork.com.au/negotiation-blog/2014/what-is-the-difference-between-negotiation-and-persuasion/

Unknown (2015). Signs of Frustration. Retrieved from https://flowpsychology.com/signs-of-frustration/

Unknown (2016) 8 Ways to Improve Your Empathy. Retrieved from https://andrewsobel.com/eight-ways-to-improve-your-empathy/

Unknown (2017) 14 Ways to Approach a Conflict and Difficult Conversations at Work. Retrieved from https://www.forbes.com/sites/forbescoachescouncil/2017/07/17/14-ways-to-approach-conflict-and-difficult-conversations-at-work/#237397023cfd

Unknown (2018) Why Conflict is Good. Retrieved from https://www.christianmuntean.com/why-conflict-is-good/

Unknown (2019) Summary of Cooperation and Competition. Retrieved from: https://www.beyondintractability.org/artsum/deutsch-cooperation

Unknown (August 2013) What is Conflict? - Understanding Conflict. Retrieved from http://www.typesofconflict.org/what-is-conflict/

Unknown (n.d.) Conflict De-Escalation Techniques. Retrieved from https://vividlearningsystems.com/safety-toolbox/conflict-de-escalation-techniques

Unknown (n.d.) Dynamic Risk Assessment - SAFER. Retrieved from http://www.conflictresolutionmanchester.com/risk-assessment.htm

Unknown (n.d.) Life Skills Development Module Three: Conflict Management. Retrieved from https://wikieducator.org/Life_Skills_Development/Module_Three/Unit_3:_Conflict_Management/Elements_of_conflict

Unknown (n.d.) Skills You Need - Effective Speaking. Retrieved from https://www.skillsyouneed.com/ips/effective-speaking.html

Unknown (n.d.) Skills You Need - Verbal Communication Skills. Retrieved from https://www.skillsyouneed.com/ips/verbal-communication.html

Unknown (n.d.) Summary of Difficult Conversations: How To Discuss What Matters Most. Retrieved from https://www.beyondintractability.org/bksum/stone-difficult

Unknown (n.d.) Ten Persuasion Techniques. Retrieved from http://www.how-to-negotiate.com/ten-persuasion-techniques.html

V. Greene (n.d.) Persuasive Tactics to Close Your Next Deal. Retrieved from https://www.neurosciencemarketing.com/blog/articles/persuasive-tactics.htm#

VC. Nuance (n.d.) Deal with Anger in a Conflict Situation. Retrieved from https://visihow.com/Deal_with_Anger_in_a_Conflict_Situation

Young Entrepreneur Council (2018). 14 Negative Body Language Signals and Speech Habits to Avoid. Retrieved from https://www.forbes.com/sites/theyec/2018/05/04/14-negative-body-language-signals-and-speech-habits-to-avoid/#1a6da62622f5

BOLD BODY LANGUAGE

Win Everyday With Nonverbal Communication Secrets.

A Beginner's Guide On How To Read, Analyze And Influence Other People.

Master Social Cues, Detect Lies And Impress With Confidence.

Gerard Shaw

Table of Contents

INTRODUCTION

Would you like to influence others and forge deeper connections with them? Maybe you have a friend who always seems to accurately read the room or know what someone is thinking. Interested in public speaking or presenting, but worried that your nervousness would be too obvious?

Do you have great ideas but can't seem to get them across? Maybe it's because your body language is giving them the wrong message. Or perhaps theirs is telling you something that you can't quite figure it out. Did you notice what they were trying to "say" to you without actually speaking?

If you find yourself struggling with any of the issues above, then this book will help you solve these problems. You'll learn what body language is and how it's used. More importantly, you'll find information that you can actually use in your own life: how to read what another person is conveying to you with their body and how to use your own body to convey information. Get the results you want, just by practicing nonverbal communication.

Have you ever looked in the mirror and thought, *Boy, I have got it going on today!* Maybe you were dressed up for an event. I remember going to a party just out of college. I had just bought a motorcycle at the time, and I arrived in my biking gear. I looked cool. And I remember people turning to look at me all night—noticing me, paying attention to me. It wasn't that I'd suddenly transformed into a James Dean-esque character with my leather jacket. But I felt confident, and that's what everyone was responding to. I walked into the room with my head held high.

The best part is, you don't have to put on new clothes. You don't even necessarily have to feel confident. You just have to project confidence for people to notice and pay attention to you. Maybe you're not a big partygoer, but you want your boss to notice you more at work. Or maybe you're giving a presentation, and you want people to pay attention.

Want to know these secrets? I wrote this book because I have learned how to work my own body language with great results. I've combined my own experience with science and proven data, and I share all this with you in the book as well. I've increased my ability to develop deep relationships with others. These connections have provided me with an amazing network of people in both my personal and business life. My effective communication has also brought in a steady flow of opportunities.

The knowledge of body language and how to use it is backed up by scientific studies. I don't go into the theoretical aspects in depth because that doesn't bring the success people want. (I leave all the theorizing to the PhDs.) Instead, I have a book full of practical advice. Once you absorb the knowledge, you can apply it using the techniques I provide in this book.

I'm passionate about the advantages of nonverbal communication and strongly believe that knowing how to skillfully utilize and interpret nonverbal cues can change your life for the better. And it's not just me! I've heard the testimonies of others and seen the transformation that takes place when people learn to "speak" nonverbally. People who used the knowledge in this book acquired a whole new vocabulary they didn't have before. They project confidence and success not just professionally, but in all aspects of life. Everyone benefits when our messages are delivered correctly and with fewer misunderstandings.

By reading this book and putting the actionable steps in place, you too can become more successful day by day. I have collected a wealth of valuable information that will help you improve your communication skills as well as your style and people skills. Presenting yourself to others, even those whom you don't know, doesn't have to be a difficult ordeal!

This book is for anyone who wants to be successful in any aspect of their lives, whether it's their relationships, professional career, or just to achieve the goal or purpose they've set for themselves. Many young adults rely on email and social media to stay in touch. But real life requires you to show up in person too. Survival in today's world isn't just about the words you use. It's how you convey your message when you're talking to other people.

Words are only part of what you're saying. The rest of your body contributes too. In fact, most face-to-face communication takes place through your visual senses, not your auditory ones. The techniques in this book show you how to move (or not move!) depending on what you want to say. When you choose to sit closer to someone, you'll know exactly what you're telling them. When you cross your arms, the message you're sending will be deliberate.

You'll learn how to read other people since reading body language is a skill that can be learned just like reading a book or riding a bicycle. And, just like riding a bicycle, the more you practice, the better you'll be. If someone you're talking to crosses their arms, you'll know what they are actually trying to tell you!

Once you start taking action, you'll see an improvement in your ability to communicate not just with others but with yourself as well. Some nonverbal cues actually produce positive feedback loops for you when you use them. You'll discover how to fake it 'til you make it. For example, the more you use your body to convey confidence, the more self-assured you feel. Others notice this behavior and respond positively to you, which makes you more confident! When you use body language even just to improve your outlook, you'll be amazed at the results.

How do you become more charismatic or stand out in a room? Develop meaningful connections? Speak in public so your audience wants more from you? First, I discuss the science behind body language—how information travels from what you see, hear, smell, taste, and touch to your brain and how this triggers the release of chemicals, both neurotransmitters and hormones, which have varying effects on your body.

Once you learn how the body links to the brain and vice versa, I explain the body language "giveaways" to certain moods and emotions. You'll uncover the secrets to controlling your own reactions. Then, you'll be able to read the reactions of other people. Which parts of the body are the most communicative, and where should you start "reading"? What should you look for in others so you can clarify their message?

At that point, you'll have a pretty solid background on body language in general. Then the book goes into the specifics of how to create engaging presentations, spot deceit in others, become charismatic, and build meaningful relationships.

Finally, there are tips and tricks for everyday usage. Body language is a "use-it-or-lose-it" type of skill. Your ability to communicate without words improves the more you work on it, but once you stop, you'll gradually start losing this ability. This isn't a skill to be briefly dabbled with and then forgotten. Fortunately, these steps don't require a lot of intellectual thought, deep meditation, or any other time-consuming process. Communicating nonverbally is a habit you'll use for the rest of your life, and it isn't a lesson that works better when you delay it.

If you could apply everything you'll learn about nonverbal communication right now, you would be opening up opportunities this very instant. You would be connecting with other people, even an entire audience in an honest and deep way…right now.

Interested in changing your life for the better? Then you need to take action. If you do what you've always done, you'll get what you've always gotten. As Einstein said, "The definition of insanity is doing the same thing over and over again but expecting a different result."

You don't have to completely change your life or schedule, or overhaul everything you do from morning until night. However, you'll likely need to make some adjustments to the movements you make and practice observing others for the messages they're sending without words. But to find those opportunities and to have that growth, action must be taken.

Words are important. The right words are key. But let your body get in on the action, too, by expressing your message nonverbally.

So keep reading. Find out which steps to take…and then take them.

This book bundle comes with a FREE booklet on masterminding a winning routine to improve calmness and your level of confidence daily. Head to the bottom of this book bundle for instructions on how you can secure your copy today.

CHAPTER ONE

The Science of Body Language

You've probably heard of it, but you might be wondering exactly what body language is. Body language is a conversation without speech using facial expressions and physical gestures. The components of body language also include tone of voice, posture, volume, rate of speech, eye contact, and other characteristics. Nonverbal communication is often more important than the words you actually say in terms of getting your message across.

You might not have been paying a lot of attention to body language before, which is okay. But you probably have noticed some extreme examples.

Imagine that you're looking at a person whose head is hanging down. They're slouched, shoulders slumped, and not looking you in the eye. Would you believe them if they said in a monotone, "I'm so happy right now"? Of course not. The way in which they're expressing themselves physically is not that of a happy person.

By contrast, imagine someone standing tall and straight, looking you in the eye, and shaking your hand firmly with a smile on their face. Would you believe them if they said, “I’m so happy right now”? Probably so, because their body language is positive.

Both body language and speech are necessary to communicate. We learn how to speak in school, from our parents, or perhaps from movies and TV as well. But we don’t often learn how to use our bodies to help us say what we mean.

Using body language isn’t about changing your personality or becoming a different person! It’s about enhancing your ability to communicate and expanding your social skills. Body language is not an exact science because it’s based on human behavior, and not all individuals will react the same way in every situation.

It’s both nature and nurture. We’ve evolved with some aspects of body language that may be almost reflexive in nature. These are the behaviors that you might not even be aware you’re demonstrating. Other behaviors are taught by culture, so they may differ from country to country.

Nonverbal communication came before speech, so some of it will always be with us. Consider animals and how they express some things to each other without speaking. Charles Darwin began the scientific study of how humans and other animals communicate nonverbally, and much of the later science rests on these foundations.

Neuroscience behind body language

The brain controls body movements, both voluntary and involuntary. Humans have a central nervous system which consists of nerves in the spinal cord along with the brain itself. We also have peripheral nerves located everywhere else in the body that take inputs and pass them on. For example, when your nose smells a flower, the peripheral nerves involved send signals to the spinal cord. These signals will be electrical and/or chemical in nature. The spinal cord then passes the signals to the brain's sensory processing centers and to other functional areas when needed.

Part of the central nervous system is the autonomous nervous system, which is not under conscious control. This system regulates things like breathing, the heart's pumping, and releasing the muscles' energy reserves. It has two parts that work in opposition to each other and keep each other in check.

The sympathetic system increases stimulation and activation. It releases chemicals to accelerate breathing and widen the blood vessels, minimizing blood flow to parts of the body that don't need it in a state of increased alertness, such as the digestive system. Its opposite, the parasympathetic system, comes into play during rest and relaxation: breathing slows, the digestive system is stimulated, etc.

The human brain also contains the prefrontal cortex, which controls decision making, reasoning, and other complex behaviors. When action must be taken, the brain relays this intent back to the motor neurons of the peripheral system. These nerves then signal the appropriate muscles to perform the action.

Obviously, this process takes less time to do than it does to describe! Some actions don't even have to travel up to the brain first. When a reflex nerve is stimulated (hot stove!), the requisite motor neurons are activated (yank your hand back).

The prefrontal cortex is restricted to humans. Other animals don't have one. We do, however, have some parts of the brain in common with other animals. You might have seen these parts referred to as the "lizard" or "reptilian" brain. The older part of the brain is responsible for the "fight-or-flight" reflex, and when this part is active, the prefrontal cortex is inactive.

That's because we evolved in the African savannah alongside wild animals that could kill us. The people who survived are the ones who ran when they saw lions because their fight-or-flight reflexes activated, not the ones whose prefrontal cortex slowed them down to ask which action to take! But how does that fight-or-flight reflex happen?

This reflex is all chemicals and electricity in the brain, believe it or not. When nerves connect to each other through electrical signals, they release chemicals known as neurotransmitters. These neurotransmitters can either excite the next nerve ("go") or inhibit it ("no-go"). This system determines which messages continue through the system.

Neurotransmitters come in several forms. In addition to the "go/no-go" switches, they can also affect mood and behavior. Readying the body for action comes in two flavors: norepinephrine (called noradrenaline in the U.K.) and adrenaline (epinephrine). Norepinephrine increases alertness and is at its lowest level in the body during sleep. It focuses attention and speeds up your heart. It's also responsible for anxiety and nervousness. Adrenaline also increases heart rate and speeds up blood flow to your muscles. Anxiety, sweatiness, and shakiness are associated with it as well.

Pleasure transmitters include dopamine and serotonin. Neurons release dopamine when you experience pleasure and excitement. Dopamine tells your body to go do more of whatever caused the pleasure. As seen with addictions, this isn't always a good thing! Serotonin is used in the body for mood and sleep and to fight depression.

Hormones are similar to neurotransmitters. But instead of relaying information between nerves, they work in the bloodstream. Some chemicals, such as adrenaline, can be both hormones and neurotransmitters. It and the hormone cortisol are released when the brain wants to be in a state of awareness. Other hormones include oxytocin, which promotes bonding in humans; androgens, including testosterone, which drive male maturation; and estrogens such as estradiol, which control female maturation.

The neurotransmitters are important in regulating emotions and feelings. Serotonin, for example, can mitigate anger and violence. You'll need to be able to restrain yourself from acting on your emotions if you want to make sure you're sending the right signals for your nonverbal communication. Also, ensure that your emotions aren't getting in the way of the message someone else is trying to send you!

All these systems and chemicals affect your body language. Your brain senses a threat and sends out signals to put your body on alert. However, the part of your brain responsible for the fight-or-flight reflex can't tell the difference between the threat of a tiger and the threat of speaking in public. In both situations, you'll have the same chemical release of adrenaline and cortisol, which speed up your heart and make you nervous, among other things. Later in the book, I'll discuss what you can do to reduce the threat level so you'll be able to be charismatic and confident instead of shaky.

Learning about body language

There are some things about humans that cannot be changed. When you're anxious, certain chemical reactions occur. However, humans (and other animals) can be conditioned or trained to associate a stimulus with a reaction.

For example, you've probably heard of Pavlov's dog. In his experiments, Pavlov conditioned dogs to associate food with the ringing of a bell. Over time, whenever the dogs heard a bell, they would start salivating.

There is a biological basis for this behavior. Dogs salivate when it's time for food. Classical conditioning requires a biological basis, whether you're working with dogs or people. Throughout life, people are conditioned, often without knowing it. We're biologically trained to be alert when there are potential threats. For example, the color red is used to signal danger in various ways. When we see red, we often become alert, even unknowingly.

However, people can also learn without a biological basis. This process is known as operant conditioning or learning from experience. It doesn't even have to be your own experience, though that certainly tends to be the best teacher! You can learn from something someone else did or something you read. Human brains use shortcuts to make the work easier. These different types of learning and conditioning affect body language.

They can also help to change habits. Want to have better body language? You'll need to learn them. The best way to do that is for your brain to see that the new behaviors come with positive reinforcements. But first, you need to understand where the habit comes from. Then, you can take control of it. Reprogramming your body language has to be done consistently for it to stick.

The body parts of body language

There are four main communicators in our bodies that can let other people know what we're feeling, no matter what we're actually saying. In order to make sure your message is getting across, you need to control these aspects of the body and ensure that they are "saying" what you want them to. Being aware of your body is the first step to improving your nonverbal communication. What is it saying now, and what do you want it to say?

1. Your head—it's not just about your face!

Even your scalp will provide clues to your state of mind. Didn't have time to brush your hair? You'll look frazzled. Those who are bald need to be careful of their eyebrows, which are more prominent when there's no distracting hairline. Brows can be used to express yourself, but you want to do that consciously.

Tiny movements around the eyes and mouth, known as microexpressions, can give you away. Whether you're afraid or deceitful, these little areas can let others know. You'll need to learn how to control them, and fortunately, you can.

Neither staring at someone nor avoiding eye contact is polite or sends the message that you're interested in them in a friendly way. Making the right amount of eye contact is important.

Your chin and neck provide clues too. Jutting your chin out makes you look stubborn. Most people want to improve their body language so they can be more likable, leading to new opportunities and friends. Appearing stubborn won't get you there!

A poised person stands with their neck straight, neither slumping towards the floor nor lifting their face to the ceiling. Either one of those postures sends a message of disinterest or lack of confidence.

2. **Torso—including hands and arms**

Some body language messages mean different things in different contexts. You'll need to be aware of them when you're "speaking," but also when you're reading others. If you want some sympathy, sag a little around your shoulders. But if you're always slumped, this will be read as unconfidence. Standing straight with your shoulders back is the posture of a happy, confident person.

Arms can be very expressive! Fidgeting makes you look nervous or bored. Arms crossed tightly across your torso? Angry and defensive. Hands on hips make you seem arrogant. But they can also make you feel more confident, so you can stand in this pose in private when you need a little ego boost.

When you're sitting, the easiest way to adopt a neutral expression with your hands is to fold them gently in your lap. Palms up is a supplicating position.

3. **Legs—you know how to use them**

While you're sitting, if your legs are tightly crossed, you look closed off. An open stance can be welcoming, but don't open so wide as to be sloppy! And if you're male, avoid "manspreading" and taking up too much space in public.

Women wearing skirts have to be careful about how they're sitting. If you're nervous about whether your skirt is too short, pretty soon everyone around you will be as well. Solution: Don't wear skirts that are too short when you're trying to make a good impression. Wearing a longer skirt is easier than constantly worrying if something is exposed. Clothes shouldn't make you fidget.

Are you nervous or anxious in general? This is often expressed by shaking your legs (whether you mean to or not!). Crossing your legs at the ankles is neutral, just like the hands in lap suggestion (assuming appropriate clothing length).

4. **Feet**

Need to be somewhere? You're probably tapping your feet, but that can come across as rude. A steady stride makes you look confident. Even if you're not feeling very self-assured, you can still move like you are. Plant and pick up your feet as you go.

If you're stumbling, shuffling, or otherwise not moving with good posture, you may seem scared or even shady.

Chapter Summary

- Body language adds or detracts from your speech, depending on how you use it.

- Movements are controlled by the brain through nerves, neurons, neurotransmitters, and hormones.
- While some of our movements are unconscious, others are conscious, and we can learn to control them.
- New habits, like that of body language, can be learned through experience.
- There are four areas of the body that are key for nonverbal communication: head, torso, legs, and feet.

In the next chapter, you will learn about the basic process of communication, the barriers to it, and the ways that body language contributes to it.

CHAPTER TWO

Conveying and Receiving the Message

The communication process isn't quite as simple as one person talking to another. About three-fourths of any employee's time is spent in interpersonal situations while at the workplace, and there's often miscommunication on one side or misinterpretation on the other. Imagine how much of the message gets lost in each conversation! And if 75% of work life is being conducted this way, how much time and productivity is lost?

One person has to decide the message they want to convey. Then, they choose the words, the tone, and the way they express it. This may be done clearly, or it may not.

Some of these choices aren't always entirely conscious, either. Have you ever opened your mouth to convey one thing but said something else instead?

Messages are also usually laden with the speaker's emotions, mood, and feelings about the conversation and the people in it, or even those tangential to it. The speaker may still be angry about something that happened earlier and have it affect an entirely different conversation.

The receiver, meanwhile, must decode the message—not just the words but the context, tone of voice, gestures, and expressions. As a result, the interpretation is sometimes quite different from what the speaker intended! The listener may infer contradictory emotions and feelings or might view the words from a different perspective. They're also influenced by their own mood and emotions, which may or may not be related to the conversation at hand.

Sending and receiving aren't only between individuals, either. We communicate with a group of people or an audience as well. Those in the audience or group may also come back with different interpretations of what the speaker said.

There's a mayor of an American city who often says very quickly, "Got it," in response to constituents explaining their issues. The phrase can mean different things, so her intent is sometimes unclear. And depending on her normal rate of speech, this could read as dismissive or simply how she talks. (She is a fast talker, as it turns out.)

Does she mean, "Got it, I'm not an idiot, you peasant, now stop talking"? Or "Got it, I understand what you're saying, I'll take it back to my office and work on it"? Or "Got it, no more explanation needed, stop talking"? Or "Got it, this is an issue that has been raised several times, but we haven't been able to find a solution yet"?

If you're feeling annoyed and unheard, you might think she's saying the first one. If you respect her and know that she's working hard for the people of your city, you'll likely interpret her message as the last one. Once you know the basics of body language (which is coming up in Chapter Three), you'll be able to connect her nonverbal communication to what she's saying.

In other words, it's pretty easy for things to go wrong. The message might not be received in the way it was intended, or even not at all. For example, the mayor may have said, "Got it," because she now has an awareness of the issue and will have her staff work on it. But you might have interpreted her as saying, "Shut up, peasant!"

Nonverbal cues can help the receiver decode the message or lead them to a completely different conclusion. That's why it's important to be aware of what you're saying, both verbally and nonverbally, to give your intended message. Also, be aware of the meaning behind signals you receive, so you can more accurately understand what they want to tell you.

Barriers to communication

When people are talking to each other, there are several obstacles a successful message has to overcome, especially when the individuals don't know each other very well. Many of these difficulties can occur within a culture. Meaning, someone with a

South London background can completely misunderstand another person from South London, even though they share the same culture. Therefore, you can't assume that the person listening to you will understand what you're saying just because you have similar upbringings.

1. **Language**

   No two people experience words in the same way. For example, if someone talks about "the color red," people listening to that person will have unique images in mind for "red." For some people, it may be a warm-toned red. For others, a blue-red. The color might be lighter or darker from person to person.

   With speech, there is plenty of room for interpretation, and no guarantee that the receiver will interpret the words how the sender intended them. A speaker might try to be as descriptive as possible, for example, "fire-engine red." Then, everyone whose firefighters drive red trucks will probably have a color close to the speaker's intended one. But those who come from places where the engines are yellow, white, or another color, won't get it.

2. **"Perceptual" bias**

   We're busy! We constantly have a lot of information coming at us that we need to filter through and assess. So, our brains use shortcuts or rules of thumb for a lot of the information, just to reduce the amount of work they have to do.

This is where we find stereotypes, self-fulfilling prophecies, and projections. For example, you might stereotype women as being uninterested in the sciences. When you're talking to a woman about a scientific topic, you would assume they know nothing about it. You might end up explaining something they already know, especially if the woman in question works in the field.

3. **Relationships**

A past experience with someone will influence how you interpret them. If they came off as arrogant the first time you met, you'll interpret them as being arrogant the next time, even if they're not overbearing in the moment. If you consider them to be dishonest or untrustworthy, you probably won't receive their message as they intended. We're more willing to give the benefit of the doubt to someone who we feel has treated us well in the past.

At work, differences in hierarchy create barriers as well. An employee may interpret their boss saying, "Got it," very differently to a colleague saying the same thing. The person speaking assumes their listeners have the same assumptions they do, which is unlikely to be the case in a large, diverse workforce.

4. Cultural differences

When speaking to someone from a different cultural background, it's very easy to get the message mixed up, especially if the other culture is an unfamiliar one. There are numerous gestures that are polite in one culture and not in another. Or vice versa.

These differences encompass perceptions around privacy, time, and personal space. Some cultures tend to see punctuality as a virtue and see tardiness as a sign of disrespect. Other cultures may place more value on relationships, accepting tardiness to one function because people were enjoying time at another.

Some cultures, particularly those of European heritage, require a larger distance between two people who are interacting (personal space). In other cultures, they may stand much closer, not to infringe upon privacy, but because they're used to being closer when they speak to one another.

Nonverbal communication

Up to 90% of communication between people is nonverbal. Unfortunately, many times, the verbal and nonverbal messages are different. The listener has to figure out which is more likely to be the true one in addition to interpreting the actual words being used. Most people will assume that the body language is the true language and reflects what the speaker is feeling, rather than the verbal language.

It's hard for anyone to trust or give the benefit of the doubt to someone who sends mixed messages. The difference between what they say with words and what they say with their body suggests that they have something to hide. It also muddles the message itself. Even if the speaker has nothing to hide, the audience still doesn't know what they mean. Delivering a clear message, the one you want to send, depends on the body language backing up the speech.

Nonverbal communication has four components: visual, tactile, vocal, and spatial.

Visual cues include facial expressions, posture, and gestures. These are very important to humans for communication. We evolved to be drawn to other people's faces. Emotions are less likely to be expressed verbally, and more likely to be demonstrated with facial expressions or other body language signals. Humans have had emotions longer than we have had language!

Posture indicates mood and emotion. Unlike some of the other nonverbal signals, high-level posture cues are pretty similar across cultures and ethnicities. A strong stance, with shoulders back and head high, demonstrates self-assurance. Slouching, looking down, covering your crotch with your hands ("fig-leaf" position): this is not a happy or confident person. The actual mood might range from defensive to nervous to deceitful.

Gestures (at a high level) are key for communication. You might use your hands to emphasize a point you're making or turn your palms up to show that you're not sure of something. Specific gestures can be very easy to misinterpret because so many of them have different meanings across cultures.

Touching the other person is the tactile aspect: a hand on the arm, a hug. These are often used to indicate interest or caring for the person. It's something that charismatic people often do. (More detail about charismatic body language in Chapter Five.) A handshake is also tactile, and a firm one shows self-assurance as well as warmth toward the other person. Crushing handshakes or limp ones send negative signals.

The vocal aspect of body language isn't in the words or language used, but rather in the intonation and speed of your speech. Imagine saying "Got it" to your teammate when you're playing flag football. Then, "Got it" to your coworker who is droning on and on … and on … about the spreadsheet you're looking at. Or, "Got it" to your superior, who has just explained to you why you need to change a cell in that spreadsheet.

Do you think you'd say "Got it" with the same tone of voice to each of the three situations above? Of course not. If you used the same tone with your boss as you did your annoying coworker, you might get fired! You probably would have changed how fast you said the words as well. Quickly dismissive to your coworker, and more slowly to your boss, to show that you have taken in what they're saying.

The vocal aspect may still be misinterpreted since these also vary across cultures. What's supportive in one might be quite rude in another. Some languages are spoken much more quickly than others.

The spatial component of body language includes time, space, and image. Arriving early or late for a meeting often sends a specific message. Arriving late can signal dominance, dislike, or disinterest. On the other hand, someone who's interested, either in the topic being discussed or in moving up the career ladder, will usually arrive early to a meeting.

Crowding someone's personal space is also a nonverbal cue. It makes people feel uncomfortable, at the very least, possibly even threatened. However, this differs very much from culture to culture. Americans, for example, have a much bigger conception of personal space than many others do. People in the U.S. need about two feet of space from their closest friends and two to four feet for friends. They require even more distance from strangers. Possibly due to this large amount of personal space, Americans also do less interpersonal touching than others.

People also communicate with items, clothing, or other aspects of appearance. Often, "things" signal our values. Someone carrying a high-end designer handbag appears to value luxury. But these cues can also be misinterpreted, so remember to take context into account. If the person is driving a standard, non-luxury car and wearing clothes that aren't designer, they may have received the bag as a gift or bought it on sale because they thought it looked pretty.

Five roles of nonverbal language

You now know that much of someone's message is communicated by various expressions that aren't put into words. Body language can play different roles with verbal communication, either agreeing with it or detracting from it.

1. **Repetition**

   Body language may repeat the message from the words. Your friend says to you, "I'm so happy!" They're smiling, or maybe hugging you. They're standing straight and looking you in the eye.

2. **Contradiction**

   The nonverbal cues may mean the opposite of what's being said. This is where listeners get mixed messages. They have to figure out whether the words or the body is telling the truth. Your friend says to you, "I'm so happy!" But they're not smiling. They're slouching, with eyes on the ground and arms crossed over their chest.

   Your friend's words do not match up at all with their body in this case. Which would you believe, their words or their body? That they're happy or unhappy? Most people would choose unhappy, or in other words, the body's speech. And they would probably be right about that!

3. **Substitution**

Maybe the words don't need to be said at all. Picture someone rolling their eyes. Do you need words to go with that? This particular signal seems to be pretty similar across cultures, too.

Or you just got engaged, and you run up to your friend. You thrust your hand with the ring at them, smiling. There's no real reason to say the words, "I'm engaged!" unless you just really like how they sound.

4. **Complement**

Body language can complement the verbal language. You praise someone verbally in a meeting, then pat them on the back. It's not a repetition exactly, because a pat on the back isn't necessarily praising. But obviously, it's a positive movement. You're complementing the words with a gesture.

5. **Accent**

Nonverbal language can underline the point a speaker tries to make. Someone who's passionate about what they're saying might pound the table, for example. Or if you're angry at what the speaker is saying, you might throw a shoe while shouting at them.

When you're trying to demonstrate the huge increase in profits that your product made over the past few months, you could swoop your hand up.

As an exercise, watch the speaker at your next get-together, whether it's a meeting or lunch with friends. See if you can tell what the speaker's gestures mean. Are they accenting the words? Detracting from them? This will help you increase your awareness of body language and its use in communication.

Why are nonverbal cues so important?

If you want to influence other people, or develop better relationships and be more successful, people need to trust you. People do business with those whom they like and trust. And as I noted above, when the verbal message doesn't match the nonverbal cues, you come across as hiding something. No one trusts a person who seems to be concealing a part of themselves.

Most people, when faced with a conflict between the two messages, will assume that the nonverbal cue is the real one. Are you consciously sending mixed signals? Saying one thing but meaning another? If you're not paying attention to what your body is saying, you have no idea whether you're saying (with your body) what you think you're saying or intend to say. In addition, you might not be aware of how other people are reacting to you. Aligning what you say in words with the message of your body increases your effectiveness.

Have you ever started ordering something at the coffee shop and got completely tongue-tied? Did the order taker still know what you meant? Thanks, body language!

It's also important for you to understand what others are trying to communicate with you. If you tend to be a talker, people will start sending you signals when they want you to finish up: looking away, tapping their foot, yawning, etc. Being aware of these expressions and what they mean can help you be a better conversationalist! And, people will find you less boring when you recognize you're losing your audience and can adjust.

Even if the language is a bit muddled, you can read someone's body language to figure out what they're trying to say. If they're underlining what they say by throwing shoes or pounding the table, you'll know they're passionate about whatever it is they're discussing!

By contrast, you may also be warned when someone is potentially untrustworthy. They're saying one thing with their words and something totally different with their bodies. They may just be unaware of what they're saying, but you'll still have to try to sort out which is the true message. Or, they might be deceitful, in which case, you need to know ahead of time before you decide to do any business with them!

Chapter Summary

- Unfortunately, the communication process is not as simple as putting words together in a coherent framework, and having someone else hear and understand them!
- Language, both verbal and nonverbal, is subject to misinterpretation due to a variety of factors including culture, work hierarchy, shortcuts, and previous encounters with the listener(s).
- Nonverbal communication includes touch, visual cues like facial and body expressions, tone of voice, and time and space (comfort zone).
- Body language may enhance the verbal language by repeating, complementing, or accenting it. It can alternatively detract from verbal language if what's being said by the body isn't the same as what's being said with the words.

Now that you recognize the importance of body language, Chapter Three brings practical applications for your newfound knowledge.

CHAPTER THREE

When Body Talks and What It Means

There are plenty of signs that another person may nonverbally send you. Some are more obvious than others. When you're not confident in reading other people's body language, keep it simple and look at the big picture. You don't want to spend so much time trying to look for little signals that you miss what they're actually saying and the overall message they're sending! Read the big gestures, not the little ones. As long as you're paying attention, you'll know if they're bored or engaged.

Have you ever tried to do something, started overthinking it, and then completely lost your way? That's pretty common. Dancers, for example, have a lot of muscle memory. Beginning dancers often find that they get into their groove. However, as soon as they start thinking about the steps, their feet seem to get all tangled up. This is the Law of Reverse Effect, when you try to force your conscious mind to take over something that your subconscious usually handles.

The small signals from another person's body language are decoded by your subconscious. Once you start thinking about and looking for them, you'll start to see little signs everywhere and be more likely to mistake an innocuous twitch for a subtle signal.

Let your subconscious handle the small stuff. Some of the nerves discussed in the previous chapter are actually found in your digestive system. So yes, gut instinct is actually backed by science (sometimes)!

Preparing to read body language

Don't overthink it! Fortunately, to have a solid working knowledge of body language and how to interpret messages, you don't need to get too analytical. Consider the larger picture and look for the obvious signals: smiles (or a lack thereof), arm and leg placement, what the hands are doing. Just a quick scan can get you the information you're looking for. Speed-reading the big signs is often enough to get you to your goals.

It does help if you're relaxed when you're attempting to read other people. Even if the situation is tense, you need to be calm and in control. Be comfortable with discomfort, in other words. Mindful breathing and relaxation techniques can help you with this mindset, but long meditation sessions aren't necessary (which is a good thing because you won't always have time!).

When your brain senses that you're under threat or you feel anxious, the hormones and neurotransmitters mentioned in Chapter One spring into action. To reverse the heart-pounding and other effects of your fight-or-flight response, try a simple breathing exercise. Breathe in for three counts, hold for three, exhale for three. Do this three times. Another way to calm yourself to try "box breathing" a few times. Inhale for three or four counts, hold for three or four counts, exhale three or four, hold three or four counts, and repeat.

Breathing relaxation methods are especially helpful when you're in public. They probably won't even be noticed by anyone else. You might also do these exercises backstage or out of sight before you do your power poses to feel more confident. (I will talk about these in detail in future chapters. Appearing confident, whether you feel it or not, is important in a number of situations.)

Make sure that your emotions aren't affecting how you read others! Feeling particularly stressed, bored, or defensive might cloud your own thinking. You might not be able to express yourself in the way that you want, and you might not interpret what someone else is saying in the way that they intend. In addition, the other person might pick up on this too, and change their own language.

Context is important

When reading others, bear in mind that body language always has to be put in context. For example, I previously noted that tightly crossed arms over your torso show anger or defensiveness. However, this behavior is also something people do when they're cold. If you're in an igloo talking to someone, they may not be angry or defensive. They may simply have insufficiently warm clothing!

The other person's physique also should be taken into account. They might not be slumping as the result of an emotion but have back pain or naturally slumping shoulders. Maintaining eye contact isn't necessarily the sign of a liar, especially if the other person has a social anxiety disorder. They may simply find eye contact extremely uncomfortable, for reasons that have nothing to do with your conversation. People with arthritic hands may not squeeze your hand as firmly when they shake it.

By contrast, other people might need a gentle nudge to push themselves out of their comfort zone. If they're the poker-faced type, you need to catch them off guard for them to let the "mask" slip off. People who are feeling shy and defensive may hold an item like a notebook in front of them as a shield. You can offer them a drink, ask them to hold something, or suggest some other action that uncurls their body.

All this being said, there are more obvious signals that you can pick up on pretty quickly. You can look for them without being creepy and understand what they mean. They're pretty common across different cultures and areas of the world and will help you determine what the other person's actual message is.

Eight common body language codes you can decipher

1. **Eyes**

Did you know that people commonly look up and to the left when they're remembering something? And up and to the right when they're using their imaginations? If the other person is looking up to (their) right, they could be lying. Sometimes blinking too much indicates deceit too. And not looking at you in the eye, especially if they're looking to the side, might also indicate to you that they're not telling the truth.

Not looking you in the eye can also mean boredom. If they're looking down during your conversation, they could be nervous or submissive.

Think about the last time you spoke to someone who didn't make a lot of eye contact with you. What kind of impression did you get? Probably not that they were confident or excited to talk to you!

Someone who actually does want to speak to you might have dilated pupils as a result of the attention chemicals in the body. This one's a little harder to see than some of the other clues! Don't spend too much time staring into the other's eyes to determine if their pupils are getting bigger or not. Take a look at some of the other signals they're sending instead.

2. Face

The eyes may be the window to the soul, but the smile is a window to the mood. Are they smiling? Is it genuine? If so, a happy person who is engaging with you. A slight smile combined with slightly raised eyebrows means the person is feeling friendly and not anxious about it.

A tight smile or half-smile, however, is the opposite signal. They may be bored, irritated, unsure, or something else. Definitely not happy and engaged. Keep in mind, their expression or mood may have nothing to do with you, so don't take it personally if their smile is tight and fake.

Lips tight and pursed together? Also not a happy person. Relaxed lips and mouth shows a positive mood. In fact, relaxed facial features and muscles are generally positive signals. Think about what you do when you get stressed out. Clench your jaw? Grind your teeth? Tense your shoulders and hunch them around your ears? Most people don't react to stress by relaxing. They react by tensing and clenching.

If the other person is touching their mouth or covering it as they talk, they very well might be lying to you. It's their subconscious shining through and trying to prevent false words from slipping out. (Or, they might be in the middle of eating and don't want to spit food at you accidentally. Context!)

3. **How physically close they are**

This particular clue, as noted in Chapter One, is definitely affected by culture. Different cultures have different social guidelines.

However, subject to that caveat, people who want to engage with you or are feeling positive about you will be closer to you. When you're with your good friends, do you tend to sit closer to them than you would to someone you don't know? Or farther away?

If you approach another person and they pull away, that's a good indicator that they're not feeling great about chatting with you! Someone who's standing a good distance from you may be naturally shy or a bit reserved. Look for more clues to see if they really don't want to talk to you personally or if they're just a bit standoffish with people they don't know.

4. **Whether they're mirroring you**

It's natural for humans to reflect the gestures of someone they care about or want to get to know better. If you lean an elbow on the table and the other person does too within a few seconds, they're mirroring. Sip your drink. Did they pick up their drink too?

We'll get into this more in future chapters, but mirroring someone is a good way to get them to like and trust you.

5. Head and neck movement

Ever been in a class or meeting where the presenter droned on and on and on? Did you feel yourself nodding your head faster, desperate to get that person to wind it up or stop talking?

Right. A slower nod means more patience. The person is interested in what you have to say. They're not frantically trying to get you to shut up, but they're showing you that they get it. They might also tilt their head a bit to the side to show interest.

Not moving the head at all when speaking is a sign of being very serious, or having authority. When you're a bobblehead, people will take you about as seriously as they will a bobblehead figurine. Too much movement looks nervous, not confident.

You've probably been in a situation where you were talking with your colleagues while waiting for a meeting to start. What happened when the boss walked in? People stopped talking to pay attention. Those with less power are looked at less often. To determine the most important person in the room, find who everyone's looking at.

By contrast, if someone's leaning their head back, away from you, they're uncertain or suspicious.

Rapid swallowing is often a sign of fear or embarrassment. A hand to the throat is often someone trying to hide this. Very simply, people who make motions to conceal or cover up something are likely hiding something! That's the subconscious speaking.

6. **Legs and feet**

Looking at the position of a person's feet is a great way to see how they are really feeling! Many of us control our faces and gestures but don't pay as much attention to the feet.

Where are the other person's feet pointing? If it's toward you, then they likely do want to connect with you. Interested and engaged people are turned toward you with their feet and their faces. If their feet are pointing away from you, they want to head in some other direction, toward another person, the exit, or wherever they're aiming their feet. You don't have to spend too long looking down at the floor. A quick glance should tell you whether they're interested or not.

Maybe as you look down, you see the other person's feet angled inwards or curled around either themselves or a chair leg. Does that seem like confident body language to you? Probably not. These are signs the individual you're studying is feeling awkward or anxious.

Someone's posture or how they stand is also a good indicator of their true emotions. A relaxed stance with legs shoulder-width apart shows you a confident, relaxed person, or at least, someone who is trying to appear so!

Having legs and feet together signals anxiety. The person is trying to make themselves smaller. Similarly, having crossed legs or feet is another attempt to appear smaller. A confident person will take up space.

7. **Hands**

When making hand gestures, people tend to aim towards someone they feel they have a relationship with. These movements may also include elbows, depending on the position. Pointing fingers is considered rude, at least in the United States. But your hands are usually in the direction of the person you're interested in just as your feet are.

Hands are also used to make gestures when people are talking. Open, sweeping gestures are usually found in people who are confident in themselves and what they're saying.

When sitting down and resting their head or chin on one hand, a person is showing interest in what the other person is saying.

Negative or unfavorable gestures are likewise pretty clear. Keeping hands in pockets or on the head indicates nervousness or deceitfulness. Sitting with their head in both hands usually signals boredom.

Someone who holds an item like a folio or a purse in front of their chest as a shield while talking is defending themselves from the other person. This is a pretty clear gesture. Many times, it has nothing to do with the person they're defending themselves against! It's more of a sign that they're nervous or feeling defensive in general.

8. **Arms**

Crossed arms, as mentioned previously, can signal anger and defensiveness but also anxiety or being closed off. However, when the crossed arms are paired with a relaxed and confident body, they can actually signal a positive attitude.

Hands on hips is asserting dominance, at least when done in public. Standing with legs spread wide and hands on hips is also a power pose that makes many individuals feel more confident, especially when they're about to do something like give a presentation to a big audience.

Reading body language by mood

There are plenty of gestures and expressions that you can look for when trying to understand another person's nonverbal communication. As you saw above, different parts of the body can be involved in a conversation in varying ways.

This means that reading other people's body language is not an exact science. There are general clues to what someone is saying with their body, but these gestures and positions may be interpreted differently depending on whether they come from a different background or whether they have a disorder or physical issue that changes their body language.

Many times, the way to resolve apparent contradictions is to see if most of the cues are leading in one direction or the other. If most of the expressions are those of someone who's relaxed and happy, then an expression that normally indicates tension and anxiety is likely due to outside influences such as the weather.

This method works in the other direction as well. Imagine someone who's slumped, clenching their hands, and staring at the ground, but has their feet pointed in your direction. Are they likely to be enthusiastically engaging with you? No, the feet are probably just a coincidence.

Below are common body language signals for different types of moods and emotions.

1. **Happy/positive/engaged**

   When people are feeling positive, they tend to carry themselves with good posture. Arms, legs, and hands are relaxed. Their body is open to you, not crossed or blocked off. They may be smiling—a genuine smile, not a half-baked one. They will make regular eye contact with you, but not stare awkwardly.

   If they want to hear more from you and are engaged with you, they will likely stand closer. They may nod slowly as they take in what you're saying or tilt their heads a bit to the side. If they're sitting down, they may prop their head up on one elbow.

In general, their hands, elbows, and feet will be pointed towards you. They'll reflect back or mirror gestures that you make. If you can see their pupils, they will be dilated.

When you take a sip of water, they will too. People who want to engage with you will reflect your gestures.

2. **Deceitful**

Someone who's lying has difficulty looking you in the eye. They may be looking up and to the right or blinking too often.

When speaking, they may touch their lips or cover their mouths. Alternatively, they might put their hands in their pockets out of sight.

If their body language is about hiding or covering, it's very likely that they are not being truthful with you.

3. **Awkward/anxious/nervous**

These people are not looking you in the eye, either. They may curl their feet around themselves or a chair leg if they're sitting down. They also might be blinking a lot or swallowing too often. An anxious person stands with their legs squeezed together. Their arms may also be crossed in the interest of making themselves physically smaller.

You might also notice that they're slouched. Usually, their bodies aren't open towards you. They're holding something in front of them to ward you, and probably other people, off or away from them.

Someone who's feeling anxious is also likely to look pretty tense—clenched jaws, clenched hands, tight mouths. They might be looking around the room, scanning for threats. They're not particularly focused on you (unless they find you a threat in some way).

4. **Negative (or at least not favorable) towards you personally**

   If they're nodding their heads rapidly, you should probably take a break from talking! Take a look at their feet. If their feet are pointed away from you, they'd probably rather be somewhere else. And if they're seated with both hands supporting their head, they're bored.

   If they're smiling, it won't be a real smile, but a tight or fake one. Their lips may be pressed together. They're not mimicking your gestures. Regarding eye contact, they may not even look at you in the first place.

Step-by-step body scan

So far, I've taken all these indicators and clues piece by piece—first by body part, and then by mood. How do you put them all together? In order to "speed-read" someone else, recall that it's the larger movements and expressions that will give you a quick overview of what the other person is trying to tell you.

1. **Overall posture**

   When you take in another person as a whole, what is the impression you get? Are they standing tall and relaxed? Or are they hunched over and slouching? Can you see if their muscles are clenched? Do they seem to be making themselves smaller? Or are they taking up a reasonable amount of space? If they're making gestures of some kind, are the movements small and constrained, or are they more open?

2. **Face**

   The first thing you look for, because it's a major indicator, is a smile. If they have one, is it genuine? As you start talking to them, are they making eye contact with you? Are they nodding as you speak, taking in what you're saying? Or are they nodding vigorously, their eyes darting around the room? Is their face relaxed or their jaws clenched?

3. **Arms, legs, hands, feet**

   Are they open or relaxed? Facing in your direction?

   Or are they twisted, crossed, clenched, or squeezed? Are they hidden or aimed at someone or something else in the room?

Case study

Imagine you're in an office observing two people, Pat and Chris, who stand facing each other.

Pat is standing straight, with legs about shoulder-width apart, nodding slowly at what Chris is saying. Pat's feet are pointed at Chris. Her hands are relaxed and open. There's a faint but real smile on Pat's face as she looks directly at Chris.

Chris stands with his legs close together, and he is holding his folio close to his chest. His feet are pointed a little bit inwards at each other. He's mostly looking at Pat, but every so often, his gaze drifts off in a different direction. He's not smiling, and when he's not talking, he presses his lips together.

What do you conclude as a result of your observations?

Pat is confident in herself, and she's also interested in what Chris is saying. He's a bit defensive and feeling nervous.

What's the relationship between the two? Because Pat is not asserting dominance, she is either not his boss, or she is his superior but trying to put him at ease. He might be new, or he may just be a nervous person in general.

Speed-reading is an exercise you can do pretty much anywhere you see other people. Try it on your morning commute, the coffee shop, your company's cafeteria, or even a networking event. Study the way people hold themselves. How does their body language come across to you? If you see two people talking, try to figure out what their relationship is.

Chapter Summary

- Our subconscious, or gut instinct, does a lot of the work in reading body language for us, particularly with the small movements that most of us make unconsciously.
- We don't need to overthink someone else's nonverbal communication or spend too much time analyzing it.
- There are some larger gestures and obvious cues that we can read to understand how someone else is feeling or what they're trying to tell us.
- Different body parts have varying ways of expressing nonverbal messages.
- In general, open and relaxed postures, faces, and gestures indicate positive emotions and interest.
- By contrast, those squeezing themselves together to look small or showing obvious tension are not at ease and may need some special handling.

In the next chapter, you will learn how to develop winning body language for a great personality!

CHAPTER FOUR

How to Develop a Winning Personality With Your Body Language

You can project confidence and interest. (More details in the last chapter, if you haven't had a chance to get there yet!) By learning about how others communicate nonverbally, you now know some of the gestures and postures that you can use when you're in front of other people.

But you want to be successful! That requires more than just smiling when you're speaking to someone. In fact, smiling too much can have a negative effect, making you look nervous or less confident.

Think about people you admire and want to listen to. You don't have to know them. Maybe they're on TV, or you've seen them on the Internet. How do they come across? Do they seem insecure or nervous? When they're being interviewed, does the interviewer's gaze wander? If the person being interviewed is charismatic and appealing, you'll notice the interviewer stays locked on their guest unless they're turning to the audience to make a point.

Or maybe you've observed people at the office. When you're in a meeting and the people in charge aren't there yet, you and your colleagues probably chat among yourselves or play on your phones. But what happens when the CEO or manager walks into the room? Everyone looks at them, sets down the phone, and wraps the conversation they're having with their neighbor. Look at the person in charge. Does that person fidget, seem anxious, or appear defensive? Or do they walk in like they own the place?

Have you been to a comedy show lately? Do you laugh harder with a comic who knows they're funny or the one who looks relieved if someone chuckles during their set?

Human beings prefer to follow leaders who seem confident. Think about who you want to pay attention to, and who seems to draw your focus naturally. Do you want to listen to someone who seems unsure of themselves or avoids your eyes when they talk to you?

No matter how the leader is feeling at that moment in time, they need to be seen as secure in themselves. No defensive, anxious, or nervous body language will be displayed. If they do, they lose the audience. To have power, others must acknowledge that person's power. And if they display weakness in one way or another, they'll lose power.

Maybe you're feeling unsure of yourself right now. Body language may be new to you, and you recognized your body in the descriptions of those who are defensive, anxious, or negative.

That's okay. You don't actually have to be self-confident to act like you are! And as a bonus, the more self-assured you act, the more confident you'll actually be. It's a positive feedback loop. If you act confident and feel confident, others will respond to your confidence, making you feel more confident.

What else do you need to consider when you want to project confidence? You can condition yourself to act with more assurance. Fortunately, we're in the age of the internet, so there are plenty of videos of successful people like Richard Branson, Steve Jobs, and Mark Cuban. Want to be more confident? Study their body language and copy it. Practice these moves and bolster your own confidence.

Body language of the "Winner's Club"

How about the fist bump? Germaphobes prefer this to a handshake, as Richard Branson does. It says you're a little unconventional and not too stodgy. Or, consider a double thumbs-up, which is what Jack Ma of Alibaba (a Chinese company similar to Amazon in the US) likes to use. It has connotations with Buddha in China but also sends a positive message to Americans.

I mentioned mirroring in the last chapter, which is something you often see Mark Zuckerberg doing. Interestingly, if you mirror someone else, you become more empathetic and are more likely to understand the other person's message.

Sheryl Sandberg tends to lean towards her audience or whomever she's speaking to. She tilts and pushes her head forward in a controlled manner. This shows her listeners that she has lots of ideas and is interested in engaging with them.

There's more about public speaking in the next chapter, but what made Steve Jobs so effective was that he actually made eye contact with his audience. It's very powerful when audience members feel that you're speaking to them personally.

The go-to move for Mark Cuban is a genuine smile. It conveys warmth, but can also command respect when paired with authoritative body language such as big gestures.

Angela Merkel, the Chancellor of Germany, is known for "steepling" her fingers. You don't have to sit down to do this because it works while you're standing up too. Hold your hands in a triangle, with the fingertips just touching. This position is also great if you have trouble with what to do with your hands when you're not gesturing!

Notice that all these gestures are pretty natural. None of them are strange contortions that you have to practice in the mirror for weeks to get right. You might even be doing some of them already. In other words, using body language effectively and successfully doesn't have to be difficult or unnatural.

In addition, these motions all convey warmth. You're not coming off as stern or unapproachable, because that doesn't make you likable. You don't have to be a taskmaster or a robot to deliver an effective message. In fact, being a robot will make you less effective! Being confident and having a good personality mean that you're seen as trustworthy, open, and friendly. That is the kind of person that other people want to get to know, connect to, and be influenced by.

Nine ways to command (positive) attention

All of the people mentioned above are known for their physical presence. Others pay attention to them when they're speaking, partly because they're powerful people who have influence in their fields, but also due to the confident body language they use while in public. Here are six ways to bring attention to yourself so that people can engage with your message.

Many of these tips are based on being or appearing confident. People don't pay much attention to someone who isn't confident. They'd rather hear from a person who is, even if that person doesn't really know what they're talking about! As long as the person is faking it well enough, others will believe it.

1. **Meet in the other's space for a firm handshake**

   Don't wait for the other person to shake your hand. Step forward and offer yours first, as the sign of a person confident in themselves.

   When it comes to the handshake, no limp hands! Firmly grasp the other's hand, but not so firmly that it's painful or crushing. Shake up and down a few times with eye contact and then release. If you're concerned about whether your handshake is too delicate or too strong, ask friends and colleagues to give you some feedback.

2. Don't move too much

Animals under threat often duck their heads in small movements. Their eyes dart around, seeking escape. Well, we're animals too, and the same goes for us.

If you move your head a lot when speaking, you'll look powerless. Keeping your head still conveys seriousness and a sense of authority. This is especially true for women, who are often seen as less serious due to their gender.

Stop fidgeting. Yes, just like your mother told you! People fidget in various manners, but all of it needs to end. Twirling your hair, shaking your feet, playing with your hands and fingers, touching your face or neck as you speak—all of these make you look anxious. You may need to practice sitting and standing still!

Try poses and postures that don't allow you to fidget, especially those that are power signals in and of themselves. For example, steepling your fingers is a sign of authority and confidence. But it happens to keep your fingers from fidgeting around your face, neck, or hair as well.

As with many of the body language signals I discuss, there's a positive impact when you do something, but a negative impact if you do too much of it. For example, people who frequently use arm and hand gestures come across in a more positive way than people who do not. However, once the gestures get too frenetic, or they're happening in the air above your shoulders, it's no longer authoritative. These gestures make you look out of control, and therefore less powerful.

In short, some movements are beneficial and will make you more confident and likable, but they must be controlled to have a positive impact. You need to look like you're consciously making a choice to make the movement, whatever it is, not allowing yourself to flail or move too much.

3. **Fake it 'til you make it**

   Fakery doesn't work for everything. For example, if you're fearful, you won't easily be able to pretend that you're not. Your body language will leak clues that you're afraid.

   In contrast, taking on confident stances such as power poses, postures, and gestures often gets the point across. Not only does it send the message to others that you're confident, it helps you send that signal to yourself! Over time, as your confidence grows, these gestures will be more authentic.

   Power poses include standing with arms and legs apart. This makes you look bigger, instead of small and fearful. It's the Superman stance. Putting your feet up on the desk may not always be advisable, depending on who's on the other side of it, but it is a power pose as well.

Dressing for success is an actual concept, though not in the sense of whether you should or should not wear a suit. (That depends entirely on your field.) The more confident you feel in your clothes, the more self-assured you'll be.

Therefore, don't wear anything that pulls or tugs or needs constant adjustment. Fiddling with your clothes makes you look nervous. Wear something that you know you look good in and that you can stand or sit in while wearing. As they say, dress for the job you want, not the job you have. Let your clothes communicate confidently too.

And if you're going to fake it, fake it properly. (Who knew there was a right way and a wrong way to fake it?) In other words, make sure you're using gestures and power poses thoughtfully.

It's often a bad idea to point your finger. Some may think it expresses dominance, but most people read it either as annoying parental control, or bullying. Remember that the secret to a winning body language is likeability and confidence. No one likes a bully.

4. **Watch your palms**

There is meaning to whether your palms are facing up or facing down. Palms down is the more confident posture. Whether seated at a desk or standing to give a presentation, not showing your palms signals confidence and authority. In fact, if you're behind a desk, you may need to occasionally turn them upward, so you don't come off as overbearing!

Palms up indicates less power. You may notice when others are presenting their thoughts, their palms are up, asking for acceptance. Palms down is more control over the conversation.

However, in some instances, you may want to have your palms up, even though it is more supplicative. Depending on the circumstances, such a gesture helps convey that you're trustworthy.

Either way, when shaking someone else's hand, keep your palm dry. A sweaty palm is definitely not a friendly palm!

Maintaining relaxed hands and palms is important as well. Clenching your fists indicates anger. Gripping an object, such as a purse or notepad, too tightly, betrays nervousness. If you can't hold them loosely, set them down. Doing so will also help you avoid using the item as a shield between you and other people.

Hiding your hands, maybe behind your back or in your pockets, suggests to others that you're hiding something. You want to come across as open, so make sure that wherever you place your palms, it's in full view of whomever you're speaking to.

When sitting down, steepling your fingers together a la Angela Merkel is a welcoming yet confident gesture. Try it!

People trust those who “talk with their hands," so don’t be shy about using them. Before we had words, we had nonverbal communication, and hands are an important part of it. When you show your hands, you seem trustworthy

5. **Pinch your thumb and forefinger together**

   This gesture is especially effective when you want to emphasize a specific point that you’re making. Use it sparingly, and you’ll convey authority and confidence. If you use it too frequently, it just looks …weird.

6. **Raise those eyebrows**

   This gesture indicates you’re open. People feeling vulnerable are often closed off and defensive, so showing openness is a sign of confidence. Turning your head slowly and then raising your eyebrows as you look at someone is a command for attention. Think of Roger Moore’s James Bond character for inspiration.

7. **Stand (or sit) up straight**

   Yes, just like your mom told you. Hold your head high and shoulders back. Good posture is not just a pose of confidence and authority. It helps prevent unnecessary back and neck pain and allows for proper breathing. Believe it or not, that’s important for self-assurance too! If you’re not breathing properly, you'll probably be tense, and your voice will come out higher than normal. Relaxed breathing is confident breathing.

When sitting, your back should still be straight, with your feet flat on the floor. If you're shorter, there may be times when the available seats won't let you plant your feet. In that situation, you may choose to stand, especially if the alternative is letting your feet dangle like a child's. When you're in your own space, you may want a footrest to avoid the problem.

Take up space. Avoid making yourself look small, which reads as completely powerless and vulnerable. Arms and legs should not be crossed as that makes you smaller. Hunching over or pulling inward in any way is a powerless posture, as is holding your hands in the classic fig-leaf position in front of your crotch. Let your arms be at your sides, not your middle.

This is another important tip for women, who, in many cultures, are expected to be less powerful or to defer to men. Women leaders must display confidence just as their male counterparts do. You don't want to spread your legs so wide that you're sprawling, of course. But there's no reason to cross your legs or hold your arms close to your torso. If you are sitting behind a desk or table, spread the materials out.

If you're standing, legs should be at least shoulder-width, and possibly hip-width, apart. Plant feet firmly on the floor.

Although putting your hands on your hips takes up space, other people find it too aggressive. Avoid standing with your arms akimbo. Try steepling or using more gestures with your hands and arms.

8. **Facial expressions, including your smile**

Your mom probably told you to smile too, and for a good reason. Smiling helps you appear trustworthy, which means people will pay attention to and engage with you. Like power poses, smiles have a feedback loop; smiling makes you happier.

Smiling is the go-to power move for some powerful people. A genuine smile is open and displays your trustworthiness and likeability. It's warm and an indicator of interest in the other person.

Try not to yawn in someone else's face! You can't signify boredom any more clearly, even if your yawn is due to something else.

9. **Eye contact**

This doesn't mean staring into the other person's eyes like you're trying to suck their soul out of them. But you also need to avoid looking away or down for too long, which are fearful and avoidant gestures. Confident people look the other person directly in the eye. Don't let your eyes flit from person to person or around the room if you're in the middle of a conversation. You'll seem bored and uninterested.

Do you wear eyeglasses? If so, looking at other people over the rim of your specs conveys contempt, especially if doing so causes you to look down at them. Looking through your glasses instead of over them makes you appear friendly and open.

If you're indoors, don't wear your sunglasses. Because people can't see your eyes, you look like you're trying to hide something.

Having a likable personality is easy to develop through your body language. Before even opening your mouth, you can command the attention of other people. And best of all, even if you don't feel particularly confident right now, you can work on your self-assurance by using the techniques mentioned above.

Confidence is not the same as arrogance. Being self-assured does not mean being self-absorbed or feeling superior. Those things are not particularly likable! A winning personality is open, friendly, and trustworthy.

One more thing to be aware of is phone etiquette. It's helpful at all times, but especially when talking to someone who grew up before the era of the smartphone. If you're looking at or fidgeting with your phone while someone's talking, you come across as very disrespectful. Whether or not you mean to be, that is what your body language is saying.

If you want to be respected by others, you also need to show them respect. People don't look up to someone who calls themselves a leader but is rude and demeans or ignores others. Good phone etiquette is essential. If you're in the middle of a conversation, you don't need to look at or answer your phone (unless you're a first responder). Taking calls while you're surrounded by other people is also rude.

The best way to show your interest in someone else is to stay in the conversation with them—not looking around the room, looking at the floor, or checking the phone every time someone likes your Instagram post. It's not checking your email every two seconds, but engaging with the other person, being genuinely interested in them, smiling and making eye contact. When you do that, your audience will leave thinking you have a great personality!

Using the language of self-confidence is the language of successful, charismatic individuals. And you can learn this language by using the techniques mentioned above.

Chapter Summary

- Watching successful people interact is a good way to find how others project confidence.

- To improve your confidence, watch powerful and successful people on TV or online, and mimic what they do as much as you can.
- Confidence is a characteristic that you can learn, and faking confidence actually leads to having it.
- Certain gestures, such as a firm handshake and controlled arm movements, make you appear more confident, as will smiling and making more eye contact.
- Practice confident body language to command the attention of others.

In the next chapter, I will discuss using nonverbal communication for good public speaking. Assure yourself and your audience that you know what you're talking about, and listening to you will be worth their while.

CHAPTER FIVE

Public Speaking and Presentations

What's the most important aspect of nonverbal communication when you're speaking in public? Projecting confidence! Audiences want to hear experts, so you need to carry yourself like one, whether you're feeling self-assured or not. Fortunately, confidence is something that you can fake, and acting confident in itself will help you be confident! There's more detail in Chapter Four about the positive feedback loop of confidence if you haven't had a chance to get to it yet.

Many people get nervous about speaking in front of people, especially in their initial engagements. So in addition to the nonverbal communication, I will talk more about in this chapter, there are a few things you need to do to prepare a talk. First, know what your key points are. Trying to memorize or read a speech leads to bad body language, so avoid it. And make sure you rehearse your talk beforehand. How long did it take you? Make sure it fits into the time allotted to you.

Prepping will help you feel more confident. There are other ways you can use your body language to become an effective public speaker and presenter.

Entering the room

You've probably heard that you never get a second chance to make a first impression. It seems a bit cliché, but it's true. Your public presentation begins the minute you're in public! If anyone watches you enter, they need to see self-assurance right away.

Any time you're in front of an audience, it's important to stand tall and with good posture. Slouching won't win you any respect. While you're standing, plant your weight on both feet. This will help you stand still and avoid fidgeting, which makes you look nervous. Remember that excess movement gives off the impression of being weak and powerless, which is exactly what people listening to you don't want to see.

Avoid shuffling as you walk. It makes you look like you don't know where you're going! Pick up your feet as you go, with a deliberate stride. Here's another fake it 'til you make it tip: Look like you know where you're going. It doesn't matter whether you do or not; you just need to create that impression.

Just as it's better to avoid looking down when you're speaking to someone face to face, don't look down as you're entering a room either. Keep your head and eyes up, which is a good way to command respect. At the same time, swaggering is also a bad idea.

You'll seem cocky instead of confident. And don't be rude! Avoid stepping on toes and bumping into others.

Prepping and beginning the presentation

Use the same confident strides to walk toward the podium, or wherever you'll be speaking. Before you start talking, give yourself and the audience a moment to settle. Settle your weight equally on both feet. Make some eye contact with audience members. Take some deep breaths to soothe your system so your nerves don't get the better of you.

When you first start giving presentations, you might feel safer staying behind the podium. You can place your hands on it to avoid fidgeting, especially if you're the kind of person who moves around a lot when they're nervous. Standing solidly in one spot might help you feel grounded. Plus, every time you take even a quick glance down, you'll have your notes right there.

However, audiences like it when you remove the shield or barrier between you by moving around the stage, out from behind the podium. A quirk of human nature is that we tend to like people who are physically closer to us. So approach your audience, particularly if you've given your talk a few times, and you know it pretty well. You might emphasize a certain point by stepping towards the audience to deliver it, and then move back to where you started from.

When you're moving, don't deliver your key concepts. Save those for when you come to a stop close to the people listening.

Remember that stillness conveys authority, so being solidly planted in one spot will help the audience focus on your words. Complete the thought or idea before you (literally) move on.

Gestures also help you underline important parts in your talk. Using movements natural to any anecdotes you're telling makes you look more confident. Discussing something rising? Swoop your arm up, but not above your shoulders. If you're not sure what looks natural or fits with your talk, search online for someone who talks about your subject. Watch their presentations. Do the gestures look natural? Do they help clarify the topic? If so, practice them.

As with many body language communications, you need to strike a balance. Gesture, but not too much! Only do so enough to signify expertise. If you overdo it, you look nervous and unsure. Shifting your weight, touching your face/hair/neck, and repeatedly clicking your pen are all nervous gestures. While you don't want to be so still that the audience mistakes you for a robot or automation, you don't want to make so many gestures that you look erratic and untrustworthy either. Choose your movements with restraint.

Suppose you've watched some videos and know the main points you'd like to include. How do you add gestures into your speech? As you're writing out your talk, or the outline of it (since effective speeches are usually not scripted word-for-word), look for places where movement would add to the presentation.

Where did the person you watched use movement to improve their talk? Do you have any anecdotes or stories that could use some gestures? What are the important points you want the audience to take away from your talk? Reinforce those points with some body language.

Knowing which movements you want to keep will help your speech pack more of a punch. There's a bonus, too! It'll give you some idea of what to do with your hands as you're speaking. Clasping them like you're holding fig leaves in front of your crotch makes you look pretty much the opposite of confident! If you're using your hands and arms for movement, they don't have a chance to sneak down there.

Feel your presentation as you're developing it. When Brene Brown speaks, she often gestures toward her heart, which is a way to be earnest and suggest that's where she's speaking from.

People make decisions based on emotions and then justify them with facts afterward. If you can make your audience feel something, they'll be more engaged. It will also help you be more confident about your speech.

What emotions link you with the subject matter? What emotions do you want your audience to feel? How can you use body language to express it? You might want to go back and watch the speaker on your subject again, to give you some ideas. The more your audience is emotionally tied to the presentation, the more likely they are to respond the way you want.

You rehearse your words, right? Do the same for your movements. Practice your talk with the movements that you think will make your talk more powerful and engaging. You can rehearse in front of a mirror, or record it and play it back later. Do the visuals match the verbal language? Are there more places where you can use gestures? Effective speakers use more movement in their talks than less effective ones do. Add in more if they improve the clarity or impact of your words.

Essential body language to own the stage

Once you've rehearsed your speech and decided on your gestures, make sure that you're engaging with the audience when you deliver your talk. They've come to hear (and see) you. They're taking time out of their schedules, so make it worth their while. Keep them interested in what you're saying. Make sure their attention on you, not on their phones or the trees outside the window.

How can you do that? Once again, body language saves the day! When you're using it and maximizing its power, people will be drawn to you.

Have you ever had to sit through a presentation given by a really dull presenter? Did you listen to them the whole time, or tune them out at some point? Did you keep your eyes on them, or did you end up staring out the window, or doodling in your notebook, or playing games on your phone? Did you wish really hard that you were anywhere else but there? It probably felt like a complete waste of time, even if the material was interesting or relevant.

Don't be that dull presenter. It's likely they read off their notes the whole time. Maybe even in a droning monotone. They didn't look up at you at all. Maybe they even read their slides word-for-word.

It's possible they were so boring that you couldn't remember their name afterward. Or you made a note of it, so you knew never to attend one of their sessions again! Could you remember any of the points they made? Did you even hear any of the points they made or were you completely tuned out after a few minutes?

Right! Think about what they did…and do the opposite. Here are six ways to use your nonverbal communication skills to improve your public speaking. Whether you're giving a presentation or a talk, these suggestions will help you make the impact you're looking for.

1. **Find an appropriate level of nervous energy**

   You're probably not going to be perfectly calm. Even experienced speakers have some nervousness before they go on stage or deliver a presentation. Having some energy is actually good for your presentation. A little stress is good. Those neurotransmitters and hormones from Chapter One also help you focus and get clarity, in addition to increasing your heart rate and blood flow.

   Too much stress? You'll be jittering all over the place and displaying plenty of nervous body language. Balance!

Try taking deep breaths that reach all the way to your stomach. Let them out slowly as well. You can combine the breaths with tensing your muscles too. For example, clench your fists on the inhale, and allow your hands to relax and hang loosely on the exhale. When you relax clenched muscles, it makes your brain think you're relaxed. Then, the chemicals behind the anxiety signals will decrease as well.

Stress relievers are best done backstage, or at least out of sight of your audience. Remember, you're looking to appear calm, cool, collected, and likable. They don't need to see you struggling with your nervousness.

2. **Avoid showing the audience your back**

Humans are very attuned to faces. This is how we get information about people. In fact, our brains are so used to looking for faces that you might see them in inanimate objects like the moon, fruit, or toast. (This effect is known as *pareidolia.*)

Our fascination with faces is also why people who run or walk in the road should run facing traffic and not with traffic as cyclists do. People are more likely to see your face, recognize that you're a person, and try to avoid hitting you!

Faces and facial expressions are an important part of communication. People read emotions not from the words another person says, but from their body language. If someone can't read your expression, they may not understand or misinterpret the message you're trying to deliver. Your audience needs to be able to see your face when you talk, so they get what you're saying.

Turning away from the people you're speaking to breaks your connection with them as well. Have you ever felt engaged with someone's back? Of course not, you connect with people whose faces you can see. Why are webinars and online video chats so popular? So the people on the call can see each other.

For the audience to be engaged in your talk, you need to connect with them. And for that to happen, they can't be looking at your back or profile. They need to be seeing you full on.

3. Look up from your notes

Have you ever seen a presentation, either live or on video, with a terrific speaker? Someone who commanded your attention, who made sense? You couldn't look away from them. What did they do? They probably didn't spend much time, if any, looking down at their notes. They spoke to their audience. They made eye contact with people in the room and interacted with those gathered in front of them.

If you're staring down at your notes, by definition, you're not interacting with the people who are there to listen to you. How do you engage with people? Not by looking away from them. Not by looking down at the podium in front of you.

In addition, when you're not looking up, you don't look confident. If you keep your eyes on your notes the whole time, it'll seem like you have to do that because you don't know your material. By contrast, someone who barely looks at their notes, if at all, clearly knows what they're talking about!

Know the important points you want to make. Write keywords and phrases on your notes to remind you of these points. That way, you can simply glance down at them occasionally to make sure you haven't forgotten anything while looking at your audience, so they feel as if you're knowledgeably speaking directly to them.

4. **Look at audience members specifically, instead of letting your eyes roam over them**

Keeping your eyes on the air above people's heads while you're speaking disconnects you from the audience. They can tell you're looking over them, not at them. Do you think that reads as confident? Nope! They'll take it as nervousness, which it very likely is.

Recall that you're there to be an expert in whatever you're talking about. Even if you don't feel confident, you need to look confident. Make eye contact with specific people in the audience. This is the act of a self-assured speaker who has mastered their material. Even the listeners you're not looking at in that particular moment will respect your knowledge.

Eye contact also makes a direct connection between you and the person you're looking at. While you may be the only one talking, it feels more like a conversation than a monologue to that other person. It gives them the impression that you know the struggles they've been through, and the solution you're discussing was developed with that particular person in mind.

As with moving around the stage, maintain eye contact for an entire sentence or thought before moving on to the next person and idea. Otherwise, the connection breaks or the contact seems more accidental than deliberate.

5. **Keep your body open to the audience and use the gestures you practiced**

When you appear defensive or closed off, it makes you look like you don't want to be there, or that you don't agree with what you are saying. Either way, it's not a positive message. It suggests you are not confident in your message, and you don't want to engage with your audience.

Even if the above is true, you still don't want to communicate that to your listeners! Avoid crossing your arms or holding your notes as a barrier between you and the audience. It's another reason to step out from behind the podium as well. Now there's no shield between you and the audience. It's a vulnerable position, but when you do it on purpose, that shows confidence.

Move around. Watching someone stand perfectly still, whether they're behind a podium or not, is still boring! Approaching the audience will make you more likable, too. The closer you are to people, the more connected they feel to you and what you're saying. Obviously, you'll need to have a firm grip on your content, so you can leave your notes for a bit in order to engage.

When you step toward your listeners to deliver an important point, make sure you don't keep moving as you explain the point. Plant your feet firmly until you've made it. Then you can walk back to your starting position.

Using your gestures can make a strong impact, particularly if you're standing still. You've practiced these movements, so they are natural and occur appropriately during your talk. You're not raising your arm when talking about a decline in a statistical number, for example. If you naturally talk with your hands, as many people do, go for it. Your natural movements appear authentic.

The more appropriate movements you use during your talk, the better. Audiences rate speakers who use more gestures better than those who use fewer. As always, balance though! Waving your arms around for no apparent reason won't add to your speech but detract from it.

6. Avoid power poses *during* the presentation

I discussed the impact of these in the previous chapter. Adopting a powerful pose makes you feel more confident, so you perform more confidently. The more confident you are, the more people respond. Therefore, if you're feeling nervous or in need of a little confidence booster, you can pose and hold a few times backstage. Or somewhere else where you're out of sight of the audience.

Why not in front of the audience? As I mentioned above, people don't want to see you trying to be more confident. They want to see a confident person the minute they see you.

In addition, they mostly look aggressive. Standing in the Superman position with legs spread wide and hands on your hips comes off as intimidating. As a speaker, you want the audience to respect you and your confidence. You don't want them to feel that you're trying to dominate or intimidate them.

An engaging presenter isn't trying to force the audience to do anything even if your speech includes a call-to-action, as most of them should. You want them to feel confident that you have something to say that is valuable to them. That's why they should listen to you, not because you're intimidating them into taking action.

Charisma and body language

You've probably heard about charismatic people, and you might even have met someone with a lot of charisma. Former U.S. President Bill Clinton was known for his charisma. When he spoke to you, no matter who you were—a truck driver, a diner waitress, a political opponent—he made you feel that you were the only person in the room.

The public generally enjoys listening to and learning from charismatic people. Most find them easier to engage with than less charismatic people. Fortunately, even if you're not sure that you have this characteristic at the moment, you can learn and practice it just as you're doing with body language.

How is charisma defined? It's the confluence of three factors: presence, power, and warmth.

Presence is being in the moment. When you're talking to someone, focus on them. As Clinton demonstrated, the person you're talking to is the only person in the room at that moment. You're not looking at your phone, thinking about your shoes, or looking to see if a more interesting person has entered the room. Being present is a way to show respect as well as a way to connect. You can't engage with anyone, much less an audience, if your mind is elsewhere.

Power is the ability to influence others. Raw power is not engaging or likable. Raw power is the bully who can take your lunch money because they're bigger than you. Without leavening it with presence or warmth, power is domineering, aggressive, and confrontational. It's difficult to connect to. But the whole point of a presentation is to actually create a link with your audience and put them in a position where they want to follow your lead, accept your call to action, or whatever the point of your talk is. In other words, your presentation should put the audience in a position where you can influence them.

Warmth makes you appear friendly and approachable. On its own, it won't help you be successful. Just being amiable and warm to other people is a nice characteristic to have; however, it's not sufficient. When you marry it with power and presence, though, you find a balance. You're not overbearing, but neither are you a doormat. You become an approachable leader, using your influence to help others, not harm them.

Everyone can develop more charisma. You might not be a second Bill Clinton, but you can increase your presence by being mindful when you talk to people. Being more confident also brings you more ability to influence other people. And even if you're not naturally an enthusiastically cheerful type of person, you can use body language to appear a bit warmer. Developing charisma is about overcoming the obstacles in your way of improving these three characteristics. I've boiled it down into three steps.

1. **Get comfortable with discomfort.**

   It's normal, and everyone feels it at some time or another. You're no different, so don't let it get in your way.

Breathing exercises, meditation, surfing the urges all help you stay with the discomfort until you can get through it.

If you have been warm and not powerful, then increasing your ability to influence people may feel uncomfortable at first. That's okay. It doesn't mean you should stop working on it.

2. **Turn your negative thoughts into neutral ones.**

   A thought is just a product of some random brain signals, and it's not necessarily true. If you have an inner voice that's always critical, give it a name. It's not you thinking these negative thoughts or being overly critical, it's Negative Nat or Negative Nellie.

   When your negative voice appears, you'll know it's Negative Nat talking! Maybe Nat's saying something like, "I can't do this." Turning that into a neutral thought might sound something like the following. "I can't do this now, but I'm going to learn how to do it." "I can't do this now because I don't have the time to tackle it, and that's ok." "I can't do this, and I don't have to if I don't want to."

3. **Find the positive. After you've acknowledged the negative thought, what are the positives to the situation? Can you imagine a way in which things will turn out for the better?**

> When Negative Nellie chimes in with, “I can’t do this," the positive might be, “I can’t do this right this second, but I’m learning how to do it, and in a few months I’ll be able to do it.” Or, “I can’t do this, but I can do something else that makes my life better instead.”

None of these suggestions say to ignore the negative thoughts, because that actually doesn’t help. Your brain still knows they’re there. Acknowledging negative thoughts, and changing them to neutral and later, positive ones, allows you to move through the discomfort.

Breaking down the barriers, or hurdling the obstacles, if you prefer, is one way to help you develop the charisma you’re seeking. There are some body language moves that can help as well.

Some of them I’ve discussed in previous paragraphs or chapters. For example, maintain good posture without making yourself smaller. That’s a power move. Recall that people want to be influenced by someone who has confidence. Standing tall with an open body without defensive postures is a great way to project self-assurance.

Be like Bond, James Bond. Does he aim to please other people? Do you ever get the feeling he’s looking to others for approval? Of course not. He’s the movie definition of self-assurance! His posture is regal and confident, not fidgety or needing reassurance. He’s a great role model for those who want to be charismatic without veering into arrogance when they’re trying to increase power. As always, though, aim for balance. Don't overdo it and act aloof or above it all! Remember that power needs to be tempered with warmth and presence.

A great move to increase your charisma is to mirror the person you're talking to as long as they're in a positive frame of mind! If they're slouching and looking away, you don't want to mirror their body language. But you might still want to mimic a gesture, like a hand movement or taking a sip of water. You might not make the exact same gesture, but amplify it or make it smaller instead. Reflect the normal gestures that feel comfortable for you. If they're doing something unusual or something that doesn't work with your body, you don't have to mirror it.

Mirroring others helps you with presence. In order to mimic what they're doing, you actually have to be aware of it. Staring at your shoes or looking around for the exit means that you'll miss the movements they're making. Mirroring also increases your warmth, as far as the other person is concerned. We mimic those we like. If you're mirroring them, then you must like them. If you like them, they're more likely to find you warm and friendly.

What if they're angry? You don't want to be mimicking clenched fists or confrontational postures! Break their angry stance by having them hold something. Offer them a drink. They'll need to unclench their fist to take whatever it is you're offering. Then use your own positive body language. Smile, stand tall, and use positive hand motions. Once they've regained their calmness, you can mirror.

Or maybe you choose to walk away. In the next chapter, I'll go into detail about forging connections with the people you actually want to engage with. Opting not to engage, or develop a relationship with someone who's angry, is a perfectly valid choice for you to make. Rather than trying to shift someone else's mood, you might walk away. See if there's someone else you want to practice increasing your charisma with.

Chapter Summary

- Confidence is the key to public speaking. Fake it 'til you make it! You may need to pump yourself up before the presentation but do so in private.
- Enter the room and walk to the stage like you know where you're going and what you'll do when you get there.
- As you're preparing your speech, consider the body language that should accompany the words. Where can you use gestures or move around? Where can you show emotion? Watch a good speaker on your topic for inspiration.
- During the presentation, maintain your body language so that the audience feels engaged and connected with you. Stand tall, approach the listeners, and make eye contact.

- Charisma is a skill you can learn, and it is based on three factors: warmth, power, and presence. Body language can help you improve each of these.
- Learning to be more charismatic means that you'll need to overcome common obstacles like discomfort and negative thoughts.
- To increase your power, use your confident postures: standing tall and walking purposefully.
- To increase warmth and presence, mirror the other person's movements.

We've talked a lot about connecting and engaging with other people, especially in this chapter. In the next, we'll take these skills and apply them to developing deeper relationships with others.

CHAPTER SIX

Forging Meaningful Connections

Connecting with other people is an important survival skill for human beings. Even introverts need a community! Theirs might be smaller than that of extroverts, but either way, communication with others is key for a happy and meaningful life. Everyone needs some people with whom they have a deep and reliable connection.

Finding someone to have this kind of meaningful relationship with isn't always easy. Though this relationship can be romantic, it doesn't necessarily have to be. It may also be a strong friendship where you rely on each other when things are difficult.

Nonverbal communication is very important for finding people and getting to know them. Being able to read the message someone else is sending lets you know if they're interested in forging a connection with you. And the more likable your body language is, the more probable it is that you'll be able to connect with someone else.

When done right, body language adds clarity to communication. Tonal shifts, facial expressions, and gestures help to improve the message and make it more understandable to others. When you first meet people, being able to read their nonverbal signals means you're more likely to get what they're saying. It can also help you decide if you want to spend more time with this person! On the flip side, knowing what body language makes you more (or less) likable can help you attract the right people.

Common cues that other people are sending you

Some body language indicators are very clear in what they express. They're unambiguous, whether the other's emotion or mood is positive or negative. However, others are ambiguous and may take more practice for you to decode them. Here are a few of the tells sorted by clarity and mood.

1. **Clearly positive**

   A (genuine) smile signals that the person is interested in you and what you have to say. If the smile is tight or doesn't reach their eyes, that's a different message!

   People tend to move closer physically to those they like and/or feel comfortable around. Therefore, someone who's interested in what you have to say will probably be near you or move closer to you.

   A gentle (nonviolent) touch, like a pat on the shoulder, also lets you know the person you're talking to is comfortable with you. Depending on your relationship, the touch might be a hug or a pat on the shoulder or arm or back. Ever hugged someone you didn't enjoy being with? Me neither!

Touch also has some cultural connotations. Americans tend to prefer more personal space, and they're also less likely to use much touch in their conversations. Other cultures need less personal space. They use touching more often with the people they're comfortable with.

Strong, confident stride? Here's a confident person. As long as they're not swaggering, it's not a show of arrogance. Confident people normally look like they know where they're going, whether they do or not!

Moments of joy are expressed by looking upward. This isn't necessarily a signal that you've caused someone joy! However, you might take it as a sign to approach the person. It's much easier to get to know someone who's in a positive frame of mind.

A person who's making eye contact with you is interested in you and wants to know more. When you're talking, and they're looking right at you, take that as a sign you may have a connection waiting!

2. **Unambiguously negative**

By contrast, not looking you in the eye indicates the other person is not interested, especially when they're looking down or looking around, either for someone more interesting or the exit so they can escape. They might be looking at their phones or even closing their eyes. They won't be smiling a real smile either, though they may have plastered on a fake one.

They may be fidgeting too. Restless hands and feet usually are a sign of boredom. You'll see them drumming their hands on the table or their own legs. They might also be drumming or tapping their feet. If you see someone pacing, change tactics. They're trying to tell you something!

Instead of adjusting what you're doing, you may want to go elsewhere and find someone who's not so obviously bored by your presence!

If you catch someone rubbing their eyes, they may be tired. On the other hand, they may be sending a message of impatience, particularly if they take off their glasses and rub the bridge of their nose.

Rather than being bored with you, another individual may be uncomfortable or defensive instead. Arms crossed in front of them? They're trying to shield themselves from you. It's a defensive move that shows you they're not feeling very comfy with you around.

Another clear indicator of nervousness is throat-clearing. Sometimes people have colds or allergies that cause post-nasal drip. But if their voice is clear and they're showing other signs of nervousness or boredom, it's not a cold that's causing their throat-clearing.

When you see someone giving off an angry message, reconsider whether you really want to approach them. It'll be much harder for you to work your body language magic on someone who just isn't having it. Their anger may actually have nothing to do with you. It could be the person they were just talking to or a situation they just left. Regardless, it doesn't really matter in the moment whether you're the source of their anger or not. It's much easier to approach someone who's presenting positive signs, as discussed above.

Look out for a person standing with their hands on their hips. They are probably angry, and most likely have lost all patience.

Are their hands bunched into fists? You want to give them a lot of personal space because that's often a sign of incoming violence. If you don't need to interact with them, don't.

You're probably familiar with the idea that little kids stomp around when they're angry, frustrated, or didn't get something they wanted. As it turns out, this behavior is true for some adults as well! If you see one stomping around, they're probably angry or trying to intimidate you. You definitely don't want to try to connect with someone who's stomping at you to scare you away like they would a bear or a feral dog!

3. Ambiguous

a. Hands behind your back

When you see this posture, know you'll need to read some more body language to make sure you're getting the right message.

In the military, standing with hands behind the back is a sign of respect. If you're speaking to someone who is or was in the service, this might be what their body is telling you. Individuals who demonstrate their respect are interested in potentially forming a relationship.

As I mentioned in a previous chapter, showing one's hands is a sign of being open. It shows that you're not carrying a weapon, which is what it meant hundreds of years ago. It's a signal of vulnerability that shows you're confident enough to walk toward another person without being armed.

Therefore, if someone's hands are behind their back, what are they hiding? It may be an indicator that the person isn't trustworthy. They may be interested in forming a relationship with you, but you might not want to reciprocate.

On the other hand, not showing your hands can also be seen as a sign of power. In this case, hands behind the back signals a person who's trying to dominate the people they're speaking to. In other words, no thanks, they're not particularly interested in what you have to tell them.

b. Pushing or jutting the chest out

This particular gesture tends to be gender-specific, although both genders will push out their chests for both reasons.

Men are usually pushing out to intimidate others. Just like many of our animal kingdom cousins, they're trying to look bigger as a way of showing their power. They want to look strong. This is often an attempt to intimidate other males. But it can also be a nonverbal communication to attract women.

Women typically push out their chests to attract men, rather than for intimidation. But they sometimes use it as a power play, too.

c. Staring

The messages behind this specific body tell are pretty similar to those for jutting the chest out. It may not be gender-specific, but the reasons for dominance or attraction are the same.

The other person may be staring at you because they find you attractive. They want you to stare back in return or respond in some other positive way.

Or, they may be staring at you because they're having a power contest. The first one to break the stare loses. The dominant member of the pair doesn't break first.

Whether the stare signals dominance or attraction, it's usually pretty obvious to the receiver what the message is. If not, other body language cues will help you determine what the person staring at you is trying to say.

d. Cocking the head to one side

Often, a head tilt indicates confusion. Ever seen those pictures of dogs where a human is talking to them, and they're tilting their heads from side to side, trying to understand? The same goes for humans, though we noticeably look less lovable or goofy when we do it.

However, cocking your head slightly may signal interest. Someone who's tilting their head as you talk and not looking confused or lost may simply be telling you that they're interested in what you have to say.

Hopefully, most of the readers of this book won't need to worry about this last message that a head tilt might be sending! In locations where there's usually plenty of violence, like jail or a pro wrestling ring, cocking the head is a challenge.

People connect with people they like, so use your body to increase your likeability

Not sure that likeability is key for relationships? Well, let me ask you a question. Do you have a deep urge to forge a link with someone you actively dislike? Probably not! Just as you don't usually hug people you're not friends with, you don't connect to people you're not friends with either. And other people behave in the same way.

At a minimum, most individuals need to feel comfortable with another person to genuinely relate to them. If you're looking to make more connections or deepen the ones you already have, you'll need to ensure that people feel comfortable around you, which means that you're likable and open. If you seem defensive or nervous or closed off in some way, others can't feel comfortable around you. They won't feel they can get to know you.

Of course, meeting new people to develop those new relationships is not easy and may be even more challenging for introverts. Making others comfortable in your first meeting gives you a better chance to create a connection over time. As an introvert, you'll be satisfied with just a few close relationships. You prefer not to interact with people you don't know more than absolutely necessary. Therefore, if you can start relationships with like-minded individuals right away, you'll be able to build your network more quickly. As a bonus, this means you don't have to go meet new people as often!

If you're an extrovert, being likable on the first meeting just means you have the opportunity to cultivate more relationships. You won't have to spend as much time developing the relationship because you start off strong to begin with.

Whether you're an introvert, extrovert, or ambivert, you can use nonverbal communication to make people more comfortable with you from the very first meeting.

But before you can be likable, you need to be presentable. That doesn't mean you have to go to your networking event in your best ballgown or expensive tuxedo, unless that's how your industry dresses, of course!

What it does mean, however, is that you, your clothes, and your accessories need to be clean. This includes teeth, nails, and hair. Again, I'm not saying that your teeth must be blindingly white or that you need a salon appointment every time you go to an event! However, you don't want people waving their hands in front of their faces because your breath is so bad, or your nails look like you were digging up bodies right before you got there. A good haircut is helpful, but at the very least, your hair should be combed.

In some cases, it's alright to dress more casually. Flip-flops, shorts, or ripped jeans (as long as everything's clean!) may be acceptable. If you're not sure, wear nicer clothing like trousers with a button-down shirt. If appropriate, dresses are sometimes good for events, and they're easy to wear as well. Make sure that your shoes are not scuffed, dusty, or dirty before you go.

In addition, avoid having a strong smell, whether you think it's a good scent or a bad one. If your body odor is bad, take care of that before you go. But don't douse yourself in perfume or after-shave either! Many people are sensitive to fragrances, and they won't find you particularly likable if your cologne is giving them a migraine.

Now that you're presentable, follow up with positive body language for success. Warmth is essential for people to like and trust you, as I discussed in the last chapter about charisma. Make good use of body language that helps you demonstrate warmth and trust.

While this book is specifically about nonverbal communication, have you ever heard the advice to talk less about yourself and ask more about the other person? People like to talk about themselves. They like to feel that others are interested in what they have to say. When they're talking more about themselves, paradoxically, they'll feel friendlier toward you! They're doing something pleasurable, so their brains are rewarding them with pleasure chemicals. And you're there, now associated with these pleasant feelings.

As always, though, you do need a balance. If they've heard this advice too, they'll want to know about you. When you're asking questions, try not to fire them off like you're trying to interrogate them! That doesn't feel warm and friendly to them.

Being associated with the brain's pleasure chemicals is where you want to be when you're talking to someone you think you'd like to connect with. Whether or not the other person is aware that it's happening, or the exact mechanism that you know about from reading this book. Fortunately, you can create this effect with nonverbal communication too. Here are ten ways to make the individual you're talking to feel good about themselves and you.

1. **Genuine smile**

   Funny how this one comes up time after time when discussing body language! If you only have time to invest in a few ways to talk without words, then work on your smile. No blinding white, perfectly straight-toothed grin is necessary. Just a warm smile that says, "I am glad to be here with you right now."

   A genuine smile doesn't flash briefly. You hold it while approaching someone, so they know it's sincerely aimed at them. When you're having a conversation, smiling continues to convey warmth.

2. **Positive touch**

   Some people are not as open to physical touch, but this is a powerful method of communication. It signals that you're comfortable with the other person and feeling warm toward them, which makes them feel warm and comfortable toward you in return.

   In other words, when it comes to a lot of body language messages, do unto others as you would have them do unto you!

   Would you give your enemy a pat on the back? Or briefly touch the arm of someone you didn't really care for as you spoke to them? Of course not. This communication is reserved for people you actually like.

One of the hormones that also acts as a neurotransmitter is oxytocin. It encourages bonding between humans and is released when you touch or are touched by another person. It's also thought to encourage trust between people when circulating throughout the brain. In the body as a hormone, oxytocin tends to help individuals relax and reduce stress and anxiety.

Therefore, you can see why touching other people can be so powerful! It promotes the release of a chemical that helps others do pretty much exactly what you want! Be calm and stress-free, so they find you comfortable to be around. As always, don't overdo it, especially when you don't know the other person. Too much touching might be interpreted as creepy, not bonding.

Make sure your handshake game is on point as well. Shaking hands is another opportunity for you to project warmth and openness, as well as confidence. But don't offer a feeble handshake. A weak handshake makes you look weak, which is not what you're going for when meeting new people.

You don't want to crush the bones in their hands either. That's aggressive and dominating. Just as you don't want your audience to feel you're trying to dominate them when you're giving a presentation, you don't want people you're meeting for the first time to feel that way either. A firm, respectful shake is all you need.

3. **Good but not rigid posture**

Many of these body language signals are easy to remember when you think about your goal: make other people comfortable around you and see that you're open and warm.

When you see other people looking uncomfortable, does that make you feel better or worse? It's hard to feel comfortable when someone else is obviously uncomfortable!

Well, have you ever seen someone standing rigidly in position? Maybe in a military parade, or even in a movie? Does it look comfortable? No way. Did you feel like you wanted to approach them and get to know them better? Nope! They don't come across as warm and friendly or open and interested.

By contrast, when you see someone slouching, do they come across as likable? Or confident in themselves? Would you rather get to know someone who's not self-assured? Or is it easier to get to know someone who's confident (but not cocky)?

Right. Good posture that isn't rigid reads as friendly and approachable. You're not worried that you're going to have to keep shoring up a slouching person's self-esteem if you get to know them better. Nor do you think the person is too closed off by rigidity to want to get to know you.

Someone with good posture comes across as self-assured. Humans tend to prefer getting to know confident individuals because they seem like they know what they're doing, and we like that quality in our friends and romantic relationships. We certainly like competency at work. If you have a colleague or boss who's incompetent, it can be even worse than if they weren't there at all. People are drawn to leaders who are confident, not those who seem wishy-washy or unsure of themselves.

If you've got good posture and you read as confident, you'll attract more people. You might not want to build connections with or get to know all of them, but at least you'll have better opportunities to find those with whom you can have a meaningful relationship.

4. **Face the other person completely: face, torso, hands, legs, feet**

As I mentioned above, it's a quirk of human nature that we like people who visibly demonstrate an interest in us by asking questions about ourselves and not talking too much about themselves!

Therefore, when you're not showing your interest in someone, they will likewise not be interested in you. Make sure you're not giving off signs of boredom. Avoid giving the impression that you'd rather be anywhere else but here talking to this person.

In the last chapter, we discussed how important presence is for charisma. Being fully present is the only way to truly engage with another individual. They need that feeling that, at that moment, you would rather be talking to them than anything else. Your body language needs to show that.

Have you ever spoken to someone who seemed like they really wanted to be there talking to you? Where were they facing? You, of course. Would you think they'd lost interest by turning their face away from yours? Of course. But they also turned their bodies toward you.

Had you looked down (which you might not have at the time), you would have seen that their feet were pointed right at you. It's impolite to point fingers, but they were probably turning their hands toward you as well.

They weren't shielded from you, crossing their arms over their torso or holding an object between the two of you. Their bodies were open, showing they were comfortable with you. If they'd been feeling defensive, you'd have seen it. Removing the barriers shows that you're open and unafraid to trust them.

Crossing legs is a defensive posture, too, so the person happy to talk to you is standing straight with their weight evenly planted between their feet. Good posture! They're confident and open talking to you.

You can use these tools when you're trying to make others feel comfortable and interesting. Don't cross your arms or legs. (If you have to go to the bathroom, excuse yourself and then return!)

Avoid any other barriers between their body and yours. This isn't restricted to just arms and notepads, but could even be something like a desk or a table. If you want the other person to feel at ease, you might need to move out from behind furniture in order to give them the open body that represents trust.

Aim your feet at the other person and not, say, the exit or anyone else in the room. If it's a crowded room, you might need to lean in to hear them better.

5. Maintain good eye contact

Like smiling, making eye contact is a key signal that you're open and interested. It gets you pretty far in many social situations. Looking around, down, or side to side is a signal that you're not interested in them. It makes you seem like you're looking for someone better to talk to, or that you're not self-assured, or that you don't want to be there talking to them.

If the person you're talking to says something or asks a question that you need to think about, it's fine to break the eye contact so you can think. Many of us think better when we're looking up or at a point in the distance. Once you're ready with your answer, make eye contact again when you deliver it. If you're still staring off into space when you start talking, you'll be giving the impression that you're bored with them.

Staring creepily at the person you're speaking with is also a problem. Feel free to blink when you need to!

A lot of the body language tips, and situations where you need them, are designed for when you're standing, be it in front of an audience or socializing at a networking mixer. But there are times when you'll be seated, for one reason or another. If you need to take notes, make sure you're not writing so copiously that you lose eye contact.

Also, writing too much will make the other person wonder what it is, exactly, that you're writing! Taking too many notes appears sinister, not friendly. Jotting down notes is one thing, writing the Great American Novel when you're supposed to be talking to someone is another.

Avoid looking at your watch, your smartphone, the clock, or the rest of the room while you're having a conversation. You want them to feel that you're interested in them, which automatically makes you more interesting to them! But if you're looking away, you're signaling that you don't care about them.

People often ask what to do when they're expecting a call. Taking calls in the middle of an event is pretty rude. But if your conversation runs over, or you just met someone you'd really like to get to know, let them know in advance. This shouldn't be something that you do a lot. If you're constantly taking calls at a time when you're usually socializing, you need to work out a better schedule.

6. **Use gestures—appropriately**

Can you imagine being best friends with a robot? I can't, either. Gestures are a very human and non-robotic way to communicate with other people. Most people have gestures that come naturally to them as they speak, so they shouldn't hold back.

As with eye contact, you need a balance. Flailing or using exaggerated gestures makes you look weird or out of control. When you're out in public or social events, your movements should appear deliberate.

Researchers found that the most popular TED talks are the ones where the speaker used a lot of hand gestures. In fact, the most-watched speakers averaged nearly double the gestures per talk than the least-watched ones!

You may not be giving TED talks, but people clearly prefer those who use more gestures. And not just during presentations, but also in more casual conversations. We had hands before speech, so talking with our hands is a pretty universal human characteristic. Robots don't talk with their hands.

One thing to watch out for is whether your gestures are appropriate from the audience's point of view. For example, if you're discussing a rise in prices, your natural instinct is to swoop your hand up from left to right. But that's backward for your audience. Swooping up from right to left looks correct to the people facing you, even though it's backward for you.

Huge or exaggerated movements make it seem like you're stretching the truth. Keep your moves authentically small. If you're a person who naturally uses bigger gestures, you don't need to make them tiny if that's not how you typically use your hands to "talk."

Gestures clarify and add impact to what you're saying. They can make you seem interesting when you use them to punctuate your story or conversation. Don't be afraid to use them, within reason.

7. **Avoid restlessness**

Just as windmilling around like a crazy person doesn't engender trust and comfort in the people watching you, neither does fidgeting. At least you won't seem to be a lunatic, but you will come off as being nervous.

Nervousness is off-putting, or at least not very likable, for a lot of people. Many of us prefer to be friends with, or close to, people who demonstrate some confidence in themselves. It makes the other person wonder if it's their fault that you're so nervous. No one wants to feel like they're the ones doing something wrong!

Are you comfortable when the person you're talking to is fidgeting? They might be playing with their hair, rapidly clicking a pen, shifting their weight from foot to foot, tugging at their clothes, or otherwise demonstrating that they're not comfortable, in which case you become uncomfortable as well.

Stillness has a certain authority to it. It makes you look more confident. People who are bobbing their heads or wriggling around look nervous or ill at ease, which doesn't promote trust in the other person. So plant those feet. If you need something to do with your hands, try steepling them, which is also a pose of confidence and prevents you from fidgeting with them.

8. Mimic the other person

Ever heard the phrase, "Imitation is the sincerest form of flattery"? What better way to indicate your interest and trust in someone else than by copying their movements when you're with them?

You don't have to act like a human mirror. This isn't an acting lesson! You can (and should) reflect some of their positive or neutral gestures. Are they smiling? You probably should, too. Have they taken a sip of their drink? Go ahead and try yours.

You can make your gestures a bit smaller than theirs as you don't want to overdo it. Also, you don't want to mimic them if they're giving you angry postures: hands on hips, clenched fists, etc. You want them to feel good around you, which means you need to feel good around them. Imitating someone else's negative body language is going to make you feel more negative.

9. **Make sure you're on the same level**

If you're sitting on a chair that's higher than where they're sitting, for example, you'll appear to be domineering. Or if you're standing and they're sitting. At the same time, you don't want to be at their feet either. That makes you seem too needy.

If you're a short person, sitting down is often your best move. People won't tower over you quite as much when you're both seated. Standing on a nearby stool will also help, but looks like you're trying too hard! Sitting to talk also works well on the other end of the spectrum, if you're very tall. You don't want the people you're conversing with to feel like you're looming over them. When you're both sitting, the height difference is minimized.

In a situation where everyone's seated around a table? Try to sit on the side and not at the head or foot. This helps people let their guard down around you. You won't seem aggressive or dominating but like one of the others. If you're in a room full of mutual strangers, taking an end seat reads as if you want to take control of the group, which is normally not appreciated.

10. Think of everyone in the room as a friend

If you haven't introduced yourself to someone before, they're simply a friend you haven't met yet! Are you warm and approachable with your friends and people you know well? Go and be likewise with new people.

This is an especially good tip for introverts, who often feel dread at the prospect of so many new people. Opening yourself up to others as potential new buddies encourages them to reciprocate. Now you have become their friend they just haven't met yet! And it takes the edge off a roomful of people you don't already know.

Extroverts may be doing this already. After all, what better way to relax and project confidence, than by assuming everyone in the room is or will be your friend?

However, not everyone is going to like you. And that's OK.

You can master all these body language messages and use them every time you're at a social event. There will still likely be people who don't reciprocate. They won't smile back. They won't point their feet toward you, even as you've pivoted your whole body to them. If they shake your hand at all, it'll be brief and probably limp. Their eyes will dart around the room, seeking someone else to talk to.

Most of the time, this really has nothing to do with you personally. Maybe you look like the person who broke their heart ten years ago. Your facial features are just like those of the math teacher who made them miserable in eleventh grade. You sound just like their father, with whom they have a difficult relationship. Your name is Ben, and a boy named Ben bullied them all throughout middle school.

And so forth. You get the picture. What should you do about it? Maybe over time, you could help them feel better about their mathematical abilities! Get Ben to apologize!

No. Let them go. Your job is not to save or fix other people. (They might be proud to be estranged from their abusive father.)

Instead, form relationships with others who are interested in doing the same with you. Care about connecting with people who are willing to connect with you. The other person's issue is not a challenge for you to conquer. You don't get a medal for forcing someone to like you. Consider their inability to see you as the wonderful person you are as their loss. Move on.

You might be comfortable already with some or all of these helpful techniques. If not, practice with friends, family, and coworkers. It might help for family and friends to understand what it is you're trying to do. But you may not want to share with your coworkers.

For example, maybe you decide to try mirroring your boss. They take a drink; you take a drink. They're fond of steepling their fingers; you start steepling your fingers. Not only might this help you develop your body language skills, but your boss might start to like you if they don't already.

Reach out and touch someone!

How to tell if someone else is lying to you

No one wants to be taken in by someone who's not telling the truth. It's embarrassing and might cause others to question your judgment. Body language is very helpful when you're sizing someone up to see if you might want to develop a relationship with them. They might be saying all the right words, but you'll see some red flags waving.

Being deceitful is usually signaled by a change from the other person's baseline. This is their usual body language when they are truthful. When you're familiar with someone, you're familiar with their baseline as well.

But you can still judge when someone else is being deceitful, even when you don't know them well or even at all. If you've been practicing the suggestions in this book, you can observe how they behave when you ask them a good baseline question. You'll be maintaining eye contact and watching for their nonverbal communications.

A good question to determine baseline is something like, "Where are you from?" or "How did you hear about this event?" These types of questions usually don't result in a lie. Their answers and how their body responds should give you a pretty good idea of their language when not lying.

There are four major ways that shifts in the body language of liars that give them away. The movements are often bodily expressions of what they're doing when they're fibbing, such as hiding, distracting, and trying to prevent the truth from slipping out.

Remember, these movements all need to be taken into context. Someone who's fidgeting may just be nervous, not lying. The other signals they're sending you will let you know whether they're untruthful or simply anxious people.

1. **Body movements**

   Lying can actually be hard for our brains to do. When the brain is busy coming up with a story, there may not be enough bandwidth to gesture and talk at the same time. Therefore, one of the signals that someone is not truthful is that the hand gestures come *after* their speech, not during it.

They've had to manufacture the movement after they manufactured the story for you.

People fibbing tend to use both hands when they do the gesture. Truthful ones often use just one hand. Here's where you really need to understand the baseline, because some people (and cultures) talk with both hands, not just one. An individual using both hands may be of a different culture, not a liar.

The liar may keep their palms out of sight, in their pockets, or behind their backs. Are they hiding something from you? Yes! These are classic "hiding" movements.

They also may fidget, squirm, and play with their hair while they're talking. These actions are reflecting their need to distract you from the truth.

2. **Facial expressions**

People not telling the truth may stare or look away at a moment when you would otherwise expect them to be making eye contact. Lips may disappear or be pursed during a lie.

Pursing their lips often signal that the speaker doesn't want to say whatever it is they're saying. Or, at least, their brains don't. Fibbing requires more energy because the tale has to be constructed. Our brains would prefer to use less energy, so telling the truth is easier.

Disappearing lips often signal a lie by omission. The speaker is trying to hold back something like facts or emotions.

Turning pale is often a clue to a lie, as blood drains from the face. Excessive sweating or signals of dryness can indicate deceit, too, depending on the person. Liars may find that their nervous system provokes T-zone sweating.

For others, the lie might cause dryness in the lips and eyes instead. This results in too much lip-licking or blinking, which are pretty obvious signals to look out for. If someone goes from rarely licking their lips at baseline to suddenly licking every three seconds, that's a strong signal for you.

3. **Tone of voice**

Stress tightens the vocal cords. You might hear a liar's voice being higher than normal.

It could also be louder, as people tend to pump up the volume when they're feeling defensive. Liars are often feeling defensive about the tale they're telling, but someone who isn't lying might have a reason to be defensive. They're not feeling comfortable around you because you remind them of that math teacher, and so their volume goes up.

4. **What they say**

If words like "honestly," "frankly," or "let me tell you the truth" come out constantly ... methinks they doth protest too much! Liars are also likely to add more placeholders like "um," "ah," and "er." Listen for slips where they accidentally let the truth out!

Trust and your body language

In contrast, you can show people that you're trustworthy and honest with your nonverbal communication skills. There is a lot of overlap between body language that you use to increase your likeability and body language you use to convey your honesty. Trustworthy people are more likable than those who aren't, and vice versa.

1. **Open body**

   Just like making someone interested in you consists mainly of you showing interest in them, being trustworthy has a lot to do with showing your trust in the other person. You're not defensive, so your arms and legs aren't crossed. Nor are you shielding yourself from the other person with a table or item held between you.

   They can see your hands. Liars hide their hands, so you don't. As noted in an earlier chapter, palms up is a supplicating gesture. Palms down is a more confident way to hold your hands. You might choose steepling here too. You do want your hands to be open and relaxed, not clenched or tense.

You're looking at them, not away from them like you're bored or hiding something. Your expression is neutral or friendly. As always, a smile goes a long way too.

2. **Deliberate movement, including mirroring**

Eye contact! Steady, that is not a stare or frequently flicking away. No bobblehead figurines either. Trustworthy people are usually assumed to be strong and confident, so showing weakness or a lack of self-assurance makes you look less trustworthy.

Likewise, make sure you're not flailing or making sudden moves. Your gestures should be slow or moderately paced if you're a person who operates at a faster speed than others. Movements should be intentional. People also tend to read smooth movements as more trustworthy as opposed to herky-jerky ones.

Mirror their actions, though not so precisely as to be robotic. You want them to feel that you're aligned with them, not that you're simply a mirror in human shape.

3. **Demonstrate concern for the other person**

Tilt your head, or even your body, forward to show that you're listening and would like to hear more. Touching someone gently often expresses concern, particularly if they're emotional. In addition, as I discussed above, touch releases the body chemical that promotes bonding and trust in human beings.

Eyebrows are a great tool too. You can use them to show surprise by raising them. Furrowing them indicates concern.

4. **Show respect**

If you want respect, you have to show it to others! Being attentive to them is key, so you're listening to what they have to say, maybe slowly nodding along. (Nodding too fast suggests annoyance more than respect.)

Don't crowd the person you're talking to, especially when you don't know them. Bear in mind the cultural issues around personal space! Having said that, moving closer is a sign of interest in the other person.

Put your phone down! It's hard to be more disrespectful than to pull your phone out and disengage from the conversation right in that person's face.

Be an influencer in person

How do you become the most memorable person in the room? Hint: body language has a lot to do with it! Research shows that there are four nonverbal ways you can increase your influence. With verbal speech, there are three methods: ask open-ended questions, so they talk about themselves; tell stories, not fibs; and ask for a favor, known as the Ben Franklin effect.

But let's "talk" body language.

1. **Give your audience a dopamine hit**

In Chapter One, I talked about dopamine, which is a neurotransmitter released when the brain recognizes pleasure. Whatever it is, the brain wants you to do that again! If the other person's brain releases dopamine as you're talking to each other, you're now associated with pleasure. Their brain wants you to be around because you have a pleasurable effect on them.

It's similar to the effects of oxytocin, as described in this chapter. When they get the oxytocin release and feel calm and relaxed around you, they'll associate you with that calm and relaxed feeling. Most of us don't need any more stress in our lives! They'll find you likable because you appear to relieve their stress.

But how do you get that wonderful neurotransmitter release in someone's brain? Connect with them emotionally. You might want to have some questions prepared like, "What are you currently working on that you're passionate about?" "What was the best part of your day?" This stimulates the emotional connection between the two of you. Once they're talking, you can respond appropriately without even using your words. Smile, frown, or nod, and mirror their gestures.

2. **Display confident body language**

Just as you wouldn't slouch when you're walking into a room or giving a presentation, don't slouch in front of someone you'd like to influence. No one wants to be led by an individual who appears nervous or unsure of themselves.

Much of what you learned in Chapter Five about public presentations also applies to speaking to people you want to influence. Projecting confidence is important. You don't want to bobble your head, tug at your clothes, look away from them or around the room, cross your arms or legs, clench your fists, hide your hands or put them on your hips, arms akimbo.

Stand up straight and firm, without being rigid or shifting your weight from foot to foot. Smile. Offer a firm handshake. Keep your hands in an open position where the other person can see them. Face the person you want to influence with your torso and feet as well as your face and arms. Maintain eye contact. Use your hands to help clarify and emphasize the points you're making verbally.

Gestures and signals that demonstrate confidence are great to practice any time you're in a social situation. Even if you're speaking with someone you don't necessarily want to influence, try out all these confidence postures. Act as you would if you were trying to influence them. See what happens!

3. **Show vulnerability**

When you show other people that you trust them, by being vulnerable, they will find you more likable and trustworthy.

Never underestimate the value of being real! People can relate to you (and find you more likable) when you show you're just another human being with flaws. No one relates to a robot or someone who either seems perfect or seems to think they're perfect!

Displaying emotions is a way to show vulnerability. Think about James Bond again for a moment. Does he appear vulnerable? Not often. Does he show emotion? Not often. Anger, maybe. But he doesn't have much of an emotional range.

Which is fine if you're a superspy trying to destroy the evil villains before they destroy the planet. But if, as I suspect, that's not you (apologies to James Bond if he's reading this!), then showing your emotions allows people to connect with you.

This also may be something you need to practice, especially if you're not someone who already tends to wear their hearts on their sleeves. If you start feeling sad, let that show on your face. Feel the emotion in your body, and let your body reflect it. Yes, you might slump a bit temporarily or look down at your feet.

You might be thinking this sounds completely contradictory to what was said before, about being confident and standing up straight and smiling! That's certainly how you want to greet people and present yourself in front of a crowd. That should be the first impression that you make.

But when you're listening to someone's story, or even relating your own, it's OK to allow the emotions to surface and express themselves non-verbally. If you need to take a moment, take a moment.

4. Be more charismatic

Increasing your influence means that your effect on others is positive and important. You've probably assimilated the news by now: people like those who make them feel good about themselves. Fortunately, this is another skill that can be learned. Some people do seem to come into the world with an innate sense of how to make other people feel important. But the rest of us, well, we'll need to put in the work.

As Maya Angelou said, people may not remember the words you say or the actions you performed, but they will remember how you made them feel. Charismatic people make others feel good through both their verbal and nonverbal communication styles.

If that doesn't make sense to you, think about the people who influenced you—a parent, a religious leader, a coach, a teacher, someone you've never met but read or heard about. How did they make you feel? Inferior or less-than? Incompetent or incapable?

It's certainly possible that you were influenced negatively. An adult told you you'd never amount to anything, so you worked hard and achieved just to spite them! It happens. But more often, people are influenced by the people who made them feel good, the people who told them that they could do it, that they were capable and equal to anyone else on the planet.

To be charismatic (also discussed in the previous chapter), you need to be present with the person you're conversing with. Not looking away or paying attention to anything or anyone else. You're focused on what they're saying, leaning in a bit to hear them better and indicate interest. Your torso and feet are pointed toward your audience, signaling that you want to be there conversing with them and not somewhere else.

Charisma also includes power, in the sense of influencing others. Here's where self-assurance is your best ally. You project the impression that you know what you're doing, and you know where you're going. You avoid signs of nervousness and anxiety like fidgeting, shifting from one foot to another, or tugging at your clothes or hair. You've got some authority in keeping your head still as you speak, not bobbing up and down or side to side.

The third characteristic of charisma is warmth, which also increases your likeability. If you're displaying raw power, that might come off as aggressive: not pleasant and warm. Nodding and smiling as appropriate when you're listening to someone else brings out the warmth in your persona. Warm body language signs also include an open body, hands with the palms showing, and plenty of hand and arm gestures.

Once you've practiced your influencing skills, make sure you use your power for good, not for evil. Influencing others in a positive direction will not only make them feel better, but it'll make you feel better as well. We are social creatures after all, and assisting others in our group, however that may be defined for each of us, makes us feel better. We get our own dopamine and other neurotransmitter "hits" when we're helping other people.

Chapter Summary

Connecting with others on a deep level is an important tool for human survival. We evolved to have relationships with others whether we're more comfortable with just a few close connections as introverts or plenty of them as extroverts. Body language is key to developing these meaningful relationships with others. It clarifies our message and demonstrates our own trustworthiness as well as our likeability and interest in others. In turn, they'll want to forge better relationships with us.

- Some body language, both positive and negative, is clear. Other cues are more ambiguous. Context is often important in deciphering unclear gestures such as putting hands behind the back, staring, and jutting out the chest. It's also useful in situations where cultural differences may muddy the message.

- People want to connect with others whom they like and trust. Increasing your own likeability helps you to build relationships with others, even when meeting for the first time. There are ten ways to increase your likeability and demonstrate trustworthiness with nonverbal communication alone. These include a warm, genuine, smile; open and confident body language; and mentally accepting everyone as a friend you just haven't met yet.
- Not everyone will like you, and that's alright. It may have nothing to do with you as a person. It's not a challenge to overcome or an opportunity to "fix" someone else. You're better off using your time to find people who are interested in you and visibly want to get to know you better.
- You don't have to like everyone else, either, particularly if you think they might be deceitful. Fortunately, you can spot a fibber through their body language. You'll see unconscious differences compared to their usual baseline nonverbal behaviors. Liars tend to change in terms of body movements, facial expressions, tone of voice, and words they say. However, it's also possible that someone is displaying these behaviors because they're uncomfortable and nervous for some other reason, not because they're actually lying.

- By increasing your connection with others, you can increase your influence. There are seven methods to be more memorable, and four of them are nonverbal. These include showing vulnerability through emotion, connecting emotionally, and encouraging positive neurotransmitter release through your body language.

The next chapter brings you actionable steps to communicate nonverbally in your everyday life. Whether it's to improve the understanding that others have of your message or to build better relationships with others, if you practice consistently, your skills will improve.

CHAPTER SEVEN

Great Body Language Practices for Every Day

You don't have to wait for a presentation or a networking event to use your new nonverbal communication skills! Following good body language practices can also help you in your current relationships, as well as make you feel more confident on a daily basis.

Make your body language work for you every day. Practice the techniques described below, and you'll be communicating exactly the way you want to, without even using your words!

1. **Increase your confidence with power poses**

   As with smiling, when you change your body to a pose of confidence, you'll feel more confident. Stand with legs wide, taking up a lot of space. Park your hands on your hips. Hold each posture for about a minute, so your body can really internalize what you're doing.

Just don't power pose in front of other people! The moves read as aggressive to them. You can do your Superman imitation in your own room, before venturing out for the day. Give yourself a little extra boost.

2. **When presenting, supercharge your energy**

   What feels extremely energetic to us often looks bland or boring to your audience. You'll need to push past your normal energy boundaries when you're speaking in front of others.

   Balance, though! You don't need to be manic. Making people think you're on illegal substances is not the look you're going for here. You do, however, need to pump up your energy volume a little past what feels energetic to you.

3. **Smile**

   Smiling makes you feel better, for one thing. How does it work? Well, when you're scowling or frowning or otherwise, your body gets the message that you're doing something difficult. It raises your stress levels to help you deal with this ordeal. Your brain can't tell the difference between a situation that's difficult because it involves a hungry tiger, or because you're working a difficult math problem.

Try it the next time you realize you're scowling. Consciously turn your frown upside down and see how you feel.

Your smile also has a positive impact on the people around you who can see it. You smile, they smile. We often mirror others who we like and trust. Help your friends out by smiling so they can release some of their stress!

4. **Pose for the camera if someone is confrontational**

Supermodels rarely face the camera head-on. They're usually at an angle. Normally, face on and open to the other person is a way to be warm and trustworthy. But sometimes this can seem threatening or confrontational. Maintain eye contact, but shift slightly, so you're at an angle to the other person.

If you can manage it, standing side by side is a collaborative pose. This may be helpful if the other person's threat level doesn't decrease with your angle posture.

5. **Gesture, but no higher than your shoulders**

Instead of talking *to* the hand, talk *with* your hands! More gestures make you more energetic and add to your likeability. Also, the more you fall into the rhythm of moving your hands, the more easily your conversation happens.

Movements above your shoulders look odd, so avoid that. You can still do plenty of gesturing without flinging your hands up to the sky.

6. **Make *them* move**

A good way to engage others, especially if they're defensive or slouching, is to get them to move. For example, if someone is sitting with their arms crossed (a typical defensive posture), ask them if they want a drink, or if they can hold your pen while you're pulling out your business cards.

In front of a group? Maybe you can ask questions to get them to raise their hands. Pass items around the room. Maybe even get them up from their seats to do something. You might find they're initially resistant to standing for what seems a silly exercise. You'll also notice when they sit back down how much more relaxed and open they are!

7. **Look away to think before you speak**

Typically, when someone asks a question where you need to think about the answer, you'll look away while you're thinking, be it upwards, to the side, or studying your feet.

Make sure you return to your open, standing tall posture before you answer. Hold eye contact as you're answering, even if you had to break it while you were thinking. Not maintaining eye contact while you speak reads as being shifty or hiding something.

Using body language to improve your own life and character

Nonverbal communication isn't just between you and other people. There are feedback loops between your actions and your brain. For example, we discussed smiling above. Changing your body language to incorporate a smile also changes your body, soothing stress. There are other moods and characteristics that you can improve just by adjusting your communication with your own self!

1. **Increase sincerity**

   Using the power of touch more often, and more consciously, at least at first, shows the person being touched that you're sincere in what you say. In fact, you can convey emotions quite well using just the touch of a hand on another's arm!

2. **Supercharge your creativity**

   A lot of readers are going to LOVE this one! Need to be more creative and innovative? Lie down! I'm not sure your boss will approve you moving a bed into your office, though.

   This is thought to be caused by the neurotransmitter norepinephrine, further discussed in Chapter One. More of it is released when you're standing, and it tends to inhibit creativity.

3. **Build your (willpower) muscle**

   By flexing your physical muscles! Doing so not only helps you better handle negative information, but also helps you resist unhealthy foods and habits.

4. **Nevertheless, you persisted**

   The idea that crossing your arms is a defensive mood is pretty well-known. What you may not know, however, is that doing so actually helps people stay with difficult problems longer. So if you're feeling stuck on a project, cross your arms.

   This is one you might prefer to do in private, so it doesn't give the wrong impression. Crossing your arms can also decrease nervousness.

5. **It's a bird, it's a plane, it's…you**

   Power poses increase confidence. Like crossing your arms, these are best done out of sight of others. But stand like Superman, legs spread, hands on hips. Feel that confidence grow! It's good for any time you need a little boost.

6. **Relieve your stress**

   Activate positive feedback loop, go! Target: smile. It helps decrease the amount of cortisol in your blood, which makes you feel less stressed. Your audience will start feeling less stressed, too, as you smile, and they smile back. Instead of a negative downward spiral of stress, spiral upward with a smile.

7. **Get comfortable**

Is your friend someone that you're always a little uncomfortable with? Probably not. You're comfortable with your friends and vice versa. The more comfortable someone is with you, even if they've never met you before, the more likely they are to like you.

Best of all, there's a simple little trick to it. Tilt your head forward a bit when you're introduced to someone. It lets them know that you're happy to meet them, which makes them more inclined to like you. That's reflected in their body language to you, making you feel more comfortable.

It's that upward spiral you're looking for!

8. **Better understand someone else's emotions**

Sometimes, when you're trying to connect with someone, you might have difficulty empathizing. You'll find improvement just by mimicking them.

It's a slightly different feedback loop compared to the others. Mirroring another's body language is mirroring their emotions, which in turn generates those emotions for you.

People are also more likely to befriend someone whose facial expressions are reflecting theirs. So you'll actually help boost some positive emotions for them, even if the ones you were mirroring weren't so positive.

9. **Work it, supermodel**

   Ease the tension by standing at an angle to the person who is possibly challenged or threatened by what you have to say. Or if they're confrontational already.

   Shift your feet so you stand like a supermodel, not facing the camera (or the other person) head-on. It's a less adversarial pose than standing face to face, especially if the faces are way too close together!

10. **Retain what you learn**

    As it turns out, kids learn better when they use their hands. This works for adults too! It's an alternative way to cement new information into memory.

11. **Feel like a cheerleader**

    Not feeling happy and upbeat? Pom-poms won't help, but chewing gum will! (For the sake of your teeth, choose the sugarless stuff.) It can make you more alert, plus help you focus your attention. And put you in a better mood.

Naturally, you don't have to do all these things separately, although you can as well! Stuck on a tough problem? Lie down, cross your arms, and chew some gum. Feeling nervous before a networking mixer? Stand like Superman out of sight, then smile and tilt your head forward when meeting new people.

Improving your body language literacy

Nonverbal communication clues are complex. Someone may be demonstrating several cues at one time, all of which have different meanings! There are general rules that can be used in most cases, though context is always a concern. Most people who study nonverbal communication do so only briefly, and so they don't take the time to learn these messages and retain them.

However, the ability to read other people's nonverbal language is a skill that can be learned. It's definitely a use-it-or-lose-it type of knowledge, so daily practice is your friend here. Reading it and using it effectively boils down to a few key points.

1. **Awareness**

   The first thing is to understand some basic nonverbal messages and how they're sent. At the beginning, you may not even be aware of the signals that you're sending, much less what they mean. How do you express emotions?

   Learning about cues can help with your own body language development as well as helping you better read what others are "telling" you.

2. **Desire to learn**

   With no particular reason to care about nonverbal cues, it's easy to get away without learning very much. However, someone who really wants to make deep connections with others, be a superstar presenter and speaker, or ensure that they're sending clear and unmistakable messages will reap the benefits of studying this "language."

3. **Receive feedback**

   Sometimes, especially in the moment, it's hard to see what our bodies are actually doing, especially when we're earlier on in the awareness process. Are you really being energetic? Or are you closing off without realizing it?

   Feedback is important for you to understand the message that you're actually sending, not just the one you think you're sending. Also, it will help to ensure that you're reading someone else correctly.

   If you don't have a mentor or colleague that's willing to help, use your friends and family as a sounding board.

4. **Practice, practice, practice**

   It's not just how you get to Carnegie Hall! As noted above, nonverbal communication is a skill that needs to be maintained over time. It's not something where you can have an AHA! moment and suddenly stop slouching forever! (Your mom will agree with me.)

   Instead, try these techniques as much as you can. As you've read this book, or even this chapter, you've learned quite a few easy actions to take. You know by now that standing tall (not slouching) increases confidence. Go ahead and sit up straight right now, if you're seated.

You know that a (genuine) smile has a positive feedback loop effect. Smile. When the delivery guy comes to the door, tilt your head forward. When your uncle becomes belligerent over the Thanksgiving holiday, stand at an angle to him if you feel the need to tell him why he's wrong.

Nonverbal communication is like many other skills: the more often you work them, the better you get at them. Were you perfectly balanced the first time you got on a bike? What happened the first time you drove a car? The first time you got in the water, were you an instant champion? Even Olympic swimmers need to practice, practice, and practice some more.

You may never be the most memorable person in the room. You may never get to the point where you can tell what someone's going to say before they even open their mouth. But you can be more memorable. You can be better at understanding what someone else is saying. You can make your own messages clearer.

Improvement is better than nothing!

EQ: as important as IQ

Most people are familiar with IQ, or intelligence quotient, as a measure of your smarts. But are you familiar with EQ, or emotional quotient? There's no standard EQ test out there. Emotionally intelligent people understand their own emotions and can empathize with others too. EQ is an important skill to develop whenever you want to improve your relationships with others or even with yourself since, as with smiling, there's a feedback loop between your expressions and body language and how you feel.

There are four components of your EQ that relate directly to body language.

1. **Self-awareness**

   To be able to read and understand other people, you have to first do so for yourself. What are your triggers? What are your avoidance or defense mechanisms? What do you tend to do when you're tired/irritated/frustrated? It's the ability to view yourself almost as if you were a different person. Not-you can see what makes you tick.

   When you're self-aware, you can see if your nonverbal communication is sending the right message. Do you want to appear confident? See if you're standing tall, with your head held high.

2. **Self-management**

   This is your ability to regulate your actions. You may be tired, bored, and frustrated, but you don't always want to show that. Even if you feel like hitting out, either physically or verbally, you restrain yourself.

   Obviously, if you can't take control of your actions, you won't be able to communicate nonverbally in the way you want. Maybe if you're frustrated, you smile, knowing that it has a positive feedback loop.

3. **Other-awareness**

   Hopefully, after reading this book and practicing, you have improved your ability to read other people. You can be sensitive to the needs and feelings of others and react accordingly.

   Much of being able to read other people is found in body language. Emotions are most commonly expressed nonverbally, and you need to be able to pick up on these cues. You'll understand their message as well as where they're coming from.

4. **Relationship management**

   Are you able to interact well with other people? The better you are at relationship management, the better your relationships tend to be. Whether you're an introvert and run with a small crew, or an extrovert with plenty of phone numbers when you need to talk, having a social network is key to human happiness.

   In terms of body language, you'll need to change and adjust your posture and gestures as the situation demands.

Five emotions tend to come up in relationships, especially at work. There are common expressions of these five that you can learn to recognize.

5. Confidence

Do you have a confident colleague? Someone who always or almost always gives off an air of self-assurance? Think back to how you've seen them behave. They likely walk with a strong stride and offer a firm handshake. They're relaxed, with an open body and free gestures. They maintain eye contact in a way that suggests they want to hear what you have to say.

6. Nervousness

In contrast, do you know anyone who blinks or looks away a lot? That doesn't read as confidence, does it? They're more likely to offer you a flaccid handshake than a firm one.

Their stride is uncertain, and when they're standing (or sitting still), you probably see their arms crossed over their chest pretty frequently.

7. Defensive

These people also tend to cross their arms over their chests! Nor do they look you in the eye, though they are more likely to look down at the ground. If they move their hands at all, the gestures are muted and small. Their hands are clenched, and so are their faces! Both are tense and tight. They probably turn away from you too.

8. **Bored**

   This person has no interest in listening to you or what you have to say, so they're hardly making any eye contact, if at all. They may have a glazed or blank stare in their eyes, and their pencils are busy doodling, assuming they're not face down in their phone, that is.

   They won't sit up straight but instead slouch when seated.

9. **Thinking (prior to speaking)**

   Breaking eye contact isn't always a bad thing. It could just indicate that the person is thinking. If so, they're often looking far away into the distance where the answer is, or looking up.

   There are a lot of head and hand gestures that people use when thinking. In addition to looking away, their heads tilt at an angle. They might be stroking their chin, resting it on their hand, or resting a cheek on their hand.

   Once they've completed their thinking, their eyes will return to you.

Chapter Summary

The ability to read body language, and to match your verbal message with your nonverbal one, takes practice.

- Nonverbal communication is very much a use-it-or-lose-it type of skill.

- There are seven ways to practice communicating in your daily routine, including shifting your position if the situation becomes confrontational and looking away to think before you speak.
- You can use body language in eleven different ways to change or improve your own character and mood. Power pose to increase your confidence, cross your arms to get through a difficult problem, and chew some gum to increase your alertness.
- There are four ways to improve your ability to read body language on a daily basis, and these methods include receiving feedback and having a sincere desire to learn.
- Because body language often expresses emotions, the higher your emotional intelligence (EQ), the better you'll be at interpreting what others are "saying."

There are emotions and moods that often appear, such as boredom and defensiveness; they all have signals you can learn to recognize, such as lack of eye contact and what people are doing with their arms.

CONCLUSION

Body language is an important part of the communication between two human beings. Why do people find it so easy to misunderstand emails and text messages? Because the body language doesn't come through! Even talking on the phone is better, because the tone of voice is an important clue to the message of the person talking. In the absence of nonverbal communication, conversations are liable to misinterpretation.

Being able to read another individual's body language depends first on being aware of the messages that you're sending yourself. After reading this book, you might have realized that you often slouch, giving off the impression that you're not confident. Or maybe you cross your arms over your chest, which makes you seem defensive.

Fortunately, as you've discovered, nonverbal communication also allows you to communicate messages to yourself as well! If you want to feel more confident, you decide to stand in a power pose for a minute or two in private, legs spread wide and hands on your hips. You opt to smile when you're feeling grouchy, knowing that smiling tells your brain that you're happy.

Using your own body language supports you when you're trying to solve difficult problems. When you're stuck, you lie on your back and cross your arms over your chest, since these movements increase your determination and creativity. Just what you need to figure out the answer!

Many people find speaking or presenting in public a terrifying prospect. But in this book, I shared the secret with you: fake self-assurance. You now know how to use confident body language not only to boost your own confidence but also to be more appealing to your audience. You may need some power poses in secret backstage first, but you choose to stride firmly up to the podium or dais. You stand tall with your body open, making eye contact with audience members as you talk. Your weight is planted firmly on both feet, so you're not rocking or bobbling.

Any movements you make are done so consciously. You use your hands to emphasize and communicate. Once you're comfortable enough with your material, you also move out from behind the podium and approach the audience. You know to stand still to make your point, and only then move again. And you smile because you know people respond to warmth and friendliness.

Many of these same techniques are also handy when you're meeting people for the first time. Faking confidence is still perfectly fine because you will end up with more self-assurance over time. Faking it makes you feel more confident, so you're able to charm more people, which makes you feel more confident. Think upward spiral.

People want to get to know those individuals that make them feel comfortable and welcome. You provide a firm but not crushing handshake, and tilt your head forward, indicating interest when you meet someone. You're open to them, not using your arms or anything else to shield your body from the person you're talking to. Maintaining eye contact, you nod appreciatively, and get them talking about themselves, which is everyone's favorite subject and makes you instantly more likable!

Now that you're aware of your own nonverbal communications and have been practicing your own movements, you can use those same skills to read other people better as well. Understand what they're actually saying and even feel what they're feeling by mirroring their movements.

You can tell someone is closed off from you when they're not facing you with their whole body and their arms (and maybe their legs too!) are crossed. Or perhaps they're holding their purse or briefcase in front of them as a shield. If you do want to forge a connection with them, you'll need to get them to open up first. Hand them a drink so that they have to uncross themselves.

You can also opt to move on. You might have the friendliest, warmest, most charismatic body language out there, and still have someone dislike you. In the interest of saving time or finding someone who truly is interested in what you have to say, you can start with someone else entirely.

A person who wants to hear more from you will be smiling a genuine smile and facing you with their arms, feet, and body. They'll be looking you right in the eye and look relaxed as opposed to tense.

If you do find someone who's tense, angry, or frustrated, you'll see their fists clenched. You don't want to get too close because that will be read as confrontational or threatening. So, you choose to stand at an angle like you're a supermodel. You're still facing them, but not completely head-on, which diminishes the threat level. Assuming you don't avoid this person entirely, which is also a good option!

The number one takeaway

If nothing else, remember that nonverbal communication is a skill that can be learned. It's not something you're born with necessarily. With practice and feedback on a regular basis, you can improve your own body language and your ability to read that of others.

You can practice with friends and family. If you have friendly colleagues at work, bring them in as well. This way, you can receive feedback as to whether or not you're sending or interpreting messages as intended.

You can also practice reading people when you're out and about. You might not get the feedback, but you'll still reinforce what clues you're looking for. You should be far enough away that you can't hear what people are saying to one another. Study their body language. Defensive? Bored? Is it a couple who just had a huge fight or a couple that's enjoying their time together?

Practice makes perfect, and it can be fun too! Nonverbal communication is a skill that can deepen your relationships with others, make you a better speaker and communicator, and make you a better friend and colleague to others.

REFERENCES

An, S. (2019, March 27). "7 Body Language Tricks to Become Likeable in the First Meeting." Retrieved from: https://www.shoutmeloud.com/body-language-tricks-become-likeable.html

Bradberry, T. (n.d.) "15 Body Language Blunders That Make You Look Bad." Retrieved from: https://www.talentsmart.com/articles/15-Body-Language-Secrets-of-Successful-People-2147446605-p-1.html

"Body Language: Six non-verbal ways to command attention." (2019, February 20). Retrieved from: https://www.creativeboom.com/tips/body-language-six-non-verbal-ways-to-command-attention/

Bortnicker, C. (2011, March 4). "What Steve Jobs' Body Language Means for Apple Stock." Retrieved from: http://www.minyanville.com/mvpremium/what-steve-jobs-body-language/

Fletcher, J. (n.d.). "The Important Connection Between Body Language and EQ." Retrieved from: https://www.linkedin.com/pulse/important-connection-between-body-language-eq-joan-fletcher

Fremont College. (2018, March 8). "How to Read Body Language - Revealing Secrets Behind Nonverbal Cues." Retrieved from: https://fremont.edu/how-to-read-body-language-revealing-the-secrets-behind-common-nonverbal-cues/

Haden, J. (2018, May 17). "8 Powerful Ways to Improve Your Body Language." Retrieved from: https://www.inc.com/jeff-haden/8-powerful-ways-to-improve-your-body-language.html

Haden, J. (2018, May 17). "Science Says These 11 Body Language Secrets Will Make You More Successful." Retrieved from: https://www.inc.com/jeff-haden/science-says-these-11-body-language-secrets-will-make-you-more-successful.html

Haden, J. (2019, February 19). "A Body Language Expert Analyzed Popular TED Talks to Uncover the Top 5 Nonverbal Cues." Retrieved from:

https://www.inc.com/jeff-haden/a-body-language-expert-analyzed-popular-ted-talks-to-uncover-top-5-nonverbal-cues.html

"Harnessing the power of body language to deliver captivating speeches and presentations." (2015, May 27). Retrieved from: https://www.bytestart.co.uk/body-language-speech-presentation.html

Henry, Z. (2015, May 14). "5 body-language tricks of billionaire entrepreneurs." Retrieved from: https://www.businessinsider.com/body-language-of-successful-people-2015-5?international=true&r=US&IR=T

Hindy, J. (2018, January 3). "Top 20 Body Language Indicators." Retrieved from: https://www.lifehack.org/articles/communication/top-20-body-language-indicators.html

"How to engage your audience with the right body language." (2016, May 13). Retrieved from: https://wisembly.com/en/blog/2016/05/13/engage-audience-body-language

Jalili, C. (2019, January 25). "How to Tell if Someone is Lying to You, According to Body Language Experts." *Time.* Retrieved from: https://time.com/5443204/signs-lying-body-language-experts/

Kahnemann, D. (2011). *Thinking Fast and Slow*. New York: Farrar Strauss Giroux.

Kinsey Goman, C. (2012, February 13). "Seven Tips for Effective Body Language on Stage." *Forbes.* Retrieved from: https://www.forbes.com/sites/carolkinseygoman/2012/02/13/seven-tips-for-effective-body-language-on-stage/#41048061536d

Kinsey Goman, C. (2018, August 26). "5 Ways Body Language Impacts Leadership Results." *Forbes.* Retrieved from: https://www.forbes.com/sites/carolkinseygoman/2018/08/26/5-ways-body-language-impacts-leadership-results/

Krauss Whitbourne, S. (2012, June 30). "The Ultimate Guide to Body Language." *Psychology Today.* Retrieved from: https://www.psychologytoday.com/intl/blog/fulfillment-any-age/201206/the-ultimate-guide-body-language

Laliberte, M. (2017, September 29). "8 Ways to Use Body Language to Build Trust." *Reader's Digest.* Retrieved from: https://www.rd.com/advice/relationships/body-language-trust/

"Leadership 101: How to Command Respect Through Body Language." (2009, June 17). Retrieved from:

https://www.comparebusinessproducts.com/fyi/leadership-101-how-command-respect-through-body-language

Matthews, N. (2015, February 19). "How to Act Like the Most Powerful Girl in the Room." *Elle.* Retrieved from: https://www.elle.com/life-love/tips/g25706/how-to-fake-confidence-body-language

Mejia, Z. (2018, September 6). "What Sheryl Sandberg's and Jack Dorsey's Capitol Hill testimony can teach anyone about reacting under pressure." Retrieved from: https://www.cnbc.com/2018/09/06/sheryl-sandberg-jack-dorsey-body-language-tips-congressional-hearing.html

Misner, I. (2013, March 7). "4 Body Language Cues You Need to Know When Networking." *Entrepreneur.* Retrieved from https://www.entrepreneur.com/article/227257

Misner, I. (2018, July 11). "How to Display the Ideal Body Language When Networking." *Entrepreneur.* Retrieved from: https://www.entrepreneur.com/article/315358

"9 Powerful Body Language Tips To Instantly Boost Your Confidence." (2019, April 11). Retrieved from: https://liveboldandbloom.com/10/self-confidence/confident-body-language

Oakey, M. (2017, April 12). "How To Speed Read Body Language With Igor Ledochowski." Retrieved from: http://www.yourcharismacoach.com/blog/how-to-speed-read-people-master-hypnotist-igor-ledochowski-shares-his-secrets/

"Parts-of-the-body language." (n.d.). Retrieved from: http://changingminds.org/techniques/body/parts_body_language/parts_body_language.htm

Patton, M. (2014, December 19). "7 Scientifically Proven Steps to Increase Your Influence." *Entrepreneur.* Retrieved from: https://www.entrepreneur.com/article/240960

Riggio, R. (2011, June 15). "Reading Body Language: It's Not Easy, But You Can Improve." *Psychology Today.* Retrieved from: https://www.psychologytoday.com/intl/blog/cutting-edge-leadership/201106/reading-body-language-it-s-not-easy-you-can-improve

Roysam, V. (2016, November 8). "3 Things You Didn't Consider While Reading Body Language." Retrieved from: https://yourstory.com/2016/11/3-body-language-misconceptions

Sheffield, T. (2016, June 10). "9 Body Language Tips That Make People Want To Be Around You More." Retrieved from: https://www.bustle.com/articles/166064-9-body-language-tips-that-make-people-want-to-be-around-you-more

Study Body Language. (n.d.). Retrieved from: http://www.study-body-language.com/

"The Charisma Myth: Summary & Review." (n.d.). Retrieved from: https://thepowermoves.com/the-charisma-myth/#Charismatic_Body_Language

Thomas, J. (2018, July 28). "Unconfident Vs. Confident Body Language." Retrieved from: https://www.betterhelp.com/advice/body-language/unconfident-vs-confident-body-language/

"Trustworthy Body Language." (n.d.). Retrieved from: http://changingminds.org/techniques/body/trustworthy_body_language.htm

Wertheim, E. (n.d.). The Importance of Effective Communication. Retrieved from: https://docplayer.net/9673598-The-importance-of-effective-communication-edward-g-wertheim-ph-d-northeastern-university-college-of-business-administration.html

YOUR FREE GIFT IS HERE!

Thank you for purchasing this book. As a token and supplement to your new learnings and personal development journey, you will receive this booklet as a gift, and it's completely free.

This includes - as already announced in this book - a valuable resource of simple approach and actionable ideas to mastermind your own routine towards a more calm and confident way to tackle your everyday.

This booklet will provide you powerful insights on:

- How to formulate empowering habits that can change your life
- Masterminding your own Power of 3
- Just the 3 things you need to drastically change your life and how you feel about yourself
- How to boost your self-esteem and self-awareness
- Creating a positive feedback loop everyday

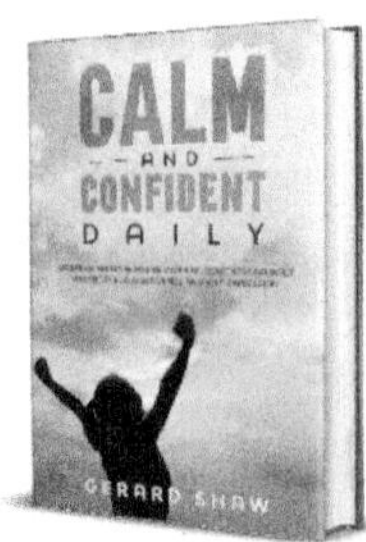

You can get the bonus booklet as follows:

To access the secret download page, open a browser window on your computer or smartphone and enter: bonus.gerardshaw.com

You will be automatically directed to the download page.

Please note that this bonus booklet may be available for download for a limited time only.

Printed in Great Britain
by Amazon

63700894R00444